EMPEROR SHAKA THE GREAT

D0165876

EMPEROR SHAKA THE GREAT

A Zulu Epic

Mazisi Kunene

Translated from Zulu by the author

HEINEMANN

Heinemann International
a division of Heinemann Educational Books Ltd
Halley Court, Jordan Hill, Oxford OX2 8EJ

Heinemann Educational Books Inc
361 Hanover Street, Portsmouth, New Hampshire, 03801, USA

Heinemann Educational Books (Nigeria) Ltd
PMB 5205, Ibadan
Heinemann Kenya Ltd
PO Box 45314, Nairobi, Kenya
Heinemann Educational Boleswa
PO Box 10103, Village Post Office, Gaborone, Botswana
Heinemann Publishers (Caribbean) Ltd
175 Mountain View Avenue, Kingston 6, Jamaica

LONDON   EDINBURGH   MELBOURNE   SYDNEY
AUCKLAND   SINGAPORE   MADRID
HARARE   ATHENS   BOLOGNA

UNESCO Collection of Representative Works
African Authors Series

This book has been accepted in the
African Authors Series of the Translations
Collection of the United Nations Educational,
Scientific and Cultural Organization (UNESCO)

ISBN 0-435-90211-3

Set in 10pt Baskerville by George Over Limited London and Rugby
Printed and bound in Great Britain by
Cox & Wyman Ltd, Reading, Berkshire

90 91 92 93 94 95 10 9 8 7 6 5

Dedicated to all the heroes and heroines
of the African continent
and all her children
who shall make her name great

Contents

Preface

It is regrettable in a way that this book should first appear in translation before it is published in the original. The reasons for this are many and complex. Suffice it to say here that its publication is in itself a tremendous achievement. It is only through the collective efforts of many of my relatives and friends that this has been possible. I was fortunate in having relatives both on my mother's side (Ngcobo family) and my father's side who took great pride in preserving and narrating our national history. As is well known, the peoples of the African continent developed, par excellence, the techniques of oral literature, its preservation and its performance.

Through these traditions and literary techniques I was able to learn much about the history of Southern Africa. The dramatization and enactment of the important historical episodes added great meaningfulness to the facts of the cultural life. Since I began travelling extensively in the African continent I have learned how greatly valued are the oral traditions of telling the story, of dramatizing the story and of making it socially relevant. This is true of much of the African literature from the northern part of the African continent to the southern part. I have, in translating my work from Zulu to English, cherished particularly the thought of sharing our history and literature with the many peoples of Africa and also of other parts of the world.

It is impossible to thank all the people who assisted me in this formidable task. I can only mention the few whom I think indicate the scale of involvement of people with different interests and skills. I thank particularly my brother and leader, Prince Gatsha Buthelezi, who greatly inspired and encouraged me. His glorious example of leadership is a true continuation of the tradition of his ancestor, Shaka the Great himself. Through such vision as he possesses, the actions of the forefathers became a living reality.

I thank, too, Rev. K. J. Msomi and E. Ngema who nurtured my talent. I thank my father who took direct interest in 'the thoughts and actions that reflect our traditions and histories'. I thank my friend Mathabo for her patience and encouragement. I thank Canon John Collins and Mrs Diana Collins who enabled us to live to tell the story. Collectively and with respect I thank all who contributed to the success of this effort. They include my friend and leader, Robert Resha, Professor Richard Hoggart, Basil Davidson, Serge Thion, John Rosenburg, Dan Sperber, JoDeen Urban and Melonee Moses (editors), my sister, Sthandwe Kunene, and my ever kind clansman and friend, Hon. Polycarp Dlamini.

I pay tribute to all the African martyrs from Algeria to South Africa who have shared the great dream of a great Africa for all her children.

I also thank UNESCO for its contribution towards the publication of this translation.

Finally, few authors have had so great and fulfilling an encouragement from their publishers as I have had from Mr James Currey of Heinemann.

If there are shortcomings in translation I hope they shall be compensated by other aspects that depict the vision of this incredible African genius.

Introduction

There have been many outstanding leaders and generals in the African continent, but none captures the imagination as Shaka of Senzangakhona. From a small volunteer army of approximately 200 and a territory that seemed, in comparison with other neighbouring states, no more than a small, local district, Shaka built in a period of ten years a formidable standing army of about 60,000 to 70,000 highly trained men. His rule extended over a large part of Southern Africa. Areas that were not under his direct rule were either under his protection or had fallen under the suzerainty of the generals who had adopted his military tactics. Many of these generals established their own powerful kingdoms.

Shaka was a consummate leader. Not only was he a great military genius, but his varied gifts demonstrated qualities of organization and innovation that were unique. The military machinery he initiated brought about, fifty years later, one of the most dramatic defeats the British army suffered in all its colonial history.

How did it happen? In order to reach a suitable answer it is necessary to cut through the thick forest of propaganda and misrepresentation that have been submitted by colonial reports and historians. The following epic poem is an attempt to present an honest view of the achievements of Shaka.

Political and economic background

The political development of the southernmost tip of Africa from the twelfth to the eighteenth centuries was characterized by elaborate population movements, as various clans and their regiments attempted to found family kingdoms and settlements. Because of various pressures in many of the

neighbouring regions and the constricted area of the southern end of the African continent, these family-states began to
compete with each other for land. At first the competition
was no more than a response to potential threats or con-
straints, but by the close of the eighteenth century the conflicts between states had become more and more acute,
resulting in a change in the methods and intentions of warfare. The late pre-Shakan period was marked by these conflicts.

The power of the original pioneering families eventually crys-
tallized in highly centralized governments. In most of
these states the ruling clan often combined with other
weaker clans to provide collective protection, and through
direct action and persuasion the larger clan attracted other
groups and nationalities to form bigger units, so that families
succeeded in strengthening their political authority and sub-
sequently extended their territorial claims.

Alongside these family-led states there existed the 'bandit
princes', who lived by raiding and by confiscating the wealth
of the settled communities. Often such princes commanded a
large following, comprising mainly the breakaway members
of the Junior House of the original ruling family but also
adventurers and admirers. In most cases they avoided
attacking the Senior House, or original family, since doing
so would have meant defiling the sacred graves of their forefathers. These wandering princes should be distinguished
from migrating groups like the Mkhizes, the Bheles and the
Hlubis, who went out in search of fertile lands and eventually settled. The bandit princes and their followers did not
and never intended to settle: they roamed wherever there
was opportunity for looting.

Emergence of powerful states

In this fluid situation there arose some powerful kingdoms,
among them the Nxumalos, the Mchunus, the Thembus, the
Ngcobos, the Mthethwas, the Buthelizis and the Qwabes.

On the second level were kingdoms that were independent or fell under the protection of more powerful kingdoms. Among these were the Zulus (who were allied to the powerful Mthethwa kingdom), the Mtshalis, the Khumalos and the Khozas, who constituted small, independent princedoms. These princedoms were scattered and much sought-after by rulers eager to augment their power.

The largest of the pre-Shakan states was the Mthethwa empire. This state owed much of its growth to the guidance of Dingiswayo. Dingiswayo was no ordinary ruler. He was an enlightened monarch who sought to build alliances with other states, with the Mthethwa state as the central power. His policy was to use persuasion where possible and force when necessary. States under the Mthethwa empire remained autonomous, each retaining its own armies until a general war was declared.

In his policies Dingiswayo differed from other neighbouring rulers, like King Zwide or King Macingwane, who ran their kingdoms as private estates. Their political strategy was based on strengthening their personal power and the power of their ruling families. They raided smaller nations not so much to augment their numbers as to accumulate their wealth. Their nations were neatly divided into the ruling clan *(abendlunkulu)* and the commoners *(abantukazana)*. Unlike his contemporaries, Dingiswayo introduced a system of political alliances which operated beyond the boundaries of his own family. Thus he created a sense of nationhood, a political unit in which power was based on communal involvement and not on membership of the Mthethwa royal family. The Mthethwa capital became a veritable centre for fugitives and refugees.

Warfare in the pre-Shakan period

The pre-Shakan period was also characterized by a type of reluctant warfare. At times a battle would involve only a single, chosen representative from each side. Conflicts were often solved too, by the initiation of national poetry contests and dances. In a full-scale battle the opponents would confront each other with throwing spears and would exploit tactical advantages until defeat was at hand. Dingiswayo's use of both force and gentle persuasion represented an advance on this type of warfare; yet he did not pursue his victories to their full and logical conclusion. He neither incorporated the conquered peoples into his realm nor did he remove the troublesome enemy leadership. Indeed, it was this magnanimity that eventually led to his assassination by the very man he had once released.

The emergence of Shaka

In 1795 Shaka, the great military genius, the great political organizer, the great visionary, was born. It is no exaggeration to say that he revolutionized African warfare on a scale few military strategists have equalled in history. Not only did he design a new weapon, a short spear, improve upon military concepts and tactics, but he also created and structured a society that survived long after his assassination. Although there have been generals and political leaders who have made larger territorial gains, few can claim the range of political influence and military organization which swept a great part of the African continent under Shaka's initiative.

The circumstances of Shaka's birth provided the driving force of his overpowering and charismatic personality. In fact, they were a significant influence on the qualities he would later display in his political leadership. Though conceived during a pre-marital relationship between two members of aristocratic families (an act considered a heinous crime in Zulu society but tolerated in the aristocracy), Shaka was not born illegitimately, as some have claimed. His father, King Senzangakhona, married his mother, Princess Nandi. It was not, therefore, the stigma of illegitimacy that caused the bitterness of Shaka's youth, but rather the violent conflict between his father and mother.

The flight of Princess Nandi

The discord between Senzangakhona and Nandi eventually forced her to embark on a long period of wandering from relative to relative. By all accounts, Princess Nandi possessed a strong will and sense of authority. She was far from being an obedient, domestic and subservient woman. She regarded herself as a representative of her family and entitled to respect and political authority as any male member of society. She not only attended the Zulu National Assembly, but the court historian tells us that she was in constant confrontation with the men of the Assembly (one would think with a sense of contempt for the often meaningless rhetoric of the Assembly). These qualities did not endear her to Senzangakhona.

It was inevitable that departure from the Zululand should affect both Nandi and her children, since it represented a failure of her marriage to Senzangakhona. Unable to tolerate the hostility among her own Abasema-Langeni people, Nandi took her children to live among the Qwabes, who were the relatives of the Zulus. There she met and married Prince Ngendeyana. Shaka, now a young man, found life intolerable among the Qwabes both because of his own restless mind and temperament and because of the jealousies of his relative, the arrogant Prince Phakathwayo.

Faced with continual frustration, Shaka decided to go to the Mthethwa court as a military recruit (probably with the active support of his parent, who was conscious of his destined role as a ruler). He was immediately recognized by the great King Dingiswayo as a highly intelligent young man. Shaka rose quickly from a raw recruit to the coveted position of a national hero and commander. As his popularity grew, his ideas caused greater and greater controversy. He argued not only with the generals but with Dingiswayo himself.

Military innovations

Shaka asserted that the policies of persuasion and forgiveness did not produce lasting peace in Nguniland, but rather provided an opportunity for the enemy to regroup and build up new alliances. He put forward the idea that the enemy must not only be totally defeated, but also incorporated into a common nationhood. In this way he would cease to be a source of constant danger. Dingiswayo never accepted these arguments He contended that such methods would only lead to fiercer and more costly conflicts. These arguments precipitated a debate about the type of weapons used in warfare and the strategies necessary to achieve lasting results. It was fortunate for Shaka that Dingiswayo, despite their differences on these issues, had absolute faith in him. He promptly gave him a position of command in which he could demonstrate the superiority of his tactics.

Shaka commissioned the making of the short spear and convinced his unit of the effectiveness of close-combat rather than spear throwing. Two heroes took immediately to his ideas, Mgobhozi of the Msane clan and Nqoboka of the Sokhulu clan. They were to be his life-long fighting comrades. Despite the success of Shaka's methods in battle, Dingiswayo felt they were too bloody and would only lead to bitterness that would never end.

It soon became clear that Shaka was concerned not only with the efficiency of military techniques but also with the consolidation of political authority. He saw the creation of a strong and efficient army as a means of establishing order and eliminating the rampant banditry of states and individual groups. It must be remembered that the political and economic upheavals in southern Africa, coupled with the Great Famine *(indlala kaMadlantuli)* of 1800, created an instability that resulted in the formation of many roaming groups such as the Ntulis, the Matiwanes and the Phephethas. The policy of establishing some type of order in the region had been pursued by Dingiswayo with limited success, but none saw the implications of this undertaking with the same visionary intensity as Shaka. He realized how deeply the habits of disorder had eaten into the body politic of the many Nguni states.

One of the most revolutionary concepts he put forward was the equal distribution of wealth and national affiliation. In the past the aristocracy, in alliance with the military, had appropriated all the loot; it was not uncommon for a ruler to grow fat while the rest of the population starved. This violated the traditional principle of responsible leadership. The national poet of Senzagakhona's times said of him:

> *His body was beautiful*
> *Even at the time of the great famine!*

A new king

During the course of a visit to the capital of Mthethwa, King Senzangakhona was finally confronted by his son after many years of separation. While watching a dance presented in his honour, Senzangakhona remarked on the exceptional skill of a young male dancer. Dingiswayo (who was keen on sponsoring Shaka as the next Zulu ruler) pointed out that this was, in fact, Shaka, his son.

By this time Senzangakhona had announced Prince Sigujana as his heir. Through psychological pressure and stratagem, Shaka asserted his claim to be heir. Filial loyalty and respect for his father restrained him from using any direct methods or making blatant claims. Not long after this encounter Senzangakhona died. Dingiswayo quickly reinforced Shaka's position by giving him his own crack regiment of izeChwe to stake his claim. In the conflict that followed, Prince Sigujana was killed. It was not many years after this episode that Dingiswayo himself paid with his life for the ideals of brotherhood and peace he had so fervently championed. He was killed by King Zwide in 1816 at the instigation of his fierce and powerful mother, Queen Ntombazi. Zwide had hoped that after eliminating Dingiswayo he would become the most powerful ruler over Nguniland and all the neighbouring territories. His plan was soon thwarted, however, by none other than the young King Shaka, who had become the ruler over the small Zulu kingdom.

No sooner had Shaka assumed leadership than he began to reorganize his army and simultaneously revolutionize society in Zululand. It is obviously impossible to enumerate and analyse all the military, political, economic and social reforms that Shaka initiated in a short introductory essay of this nature; suffice it to say that all the literature that has been written and shall be written is a testimony to his phenomenal genius.

The preparation of a devastating army

Shaka, now in a position to apply his ideas, set about training his new army in the techniques of fighting with the effective short stabbing spear. Each man was required to carry one spear into battle and to return with it. Realizing that the long period of training at the Adult School of Circumcision delayed the creation of an effective standing army, Shaka ordered the practice to be stopped. Believing as he did that speed is the decisive factor in all wars, he began training his troops to discard their cumbersome sandals and danced stoically with them on the hard ground and on thorns. He then expanded his espionage network and succeeded in making it so efficient and so extensive that he knew beforehand all the strategies and intentions of his adversaries.

At this point he proceeded to introduce one of his most significant reforms, concerned with the formation of the Zulu army; namely, the allocation of positions of command by merit rather than by family affiliation and/or national origins. Consequently to be a Zulu no longer signified merely clan membership or family position, but a political grouping whose composition was inter-family and international. It was this factor more than any other that demonstrated Shaka's outstanding political genius. Not only did he himself become part of the army; he also undermined the basis of privilege by making both commander and soldier, aristocrat and commoner, take similar risks in the front line. It was this approach which later prompted his assassination by his brothers, who resented their lack of aristocratic privilege. It must be mentioned here that despite Dingiswayo's benevolent rule, positions of leadership in the Mthethwa state remained firmly in the hands of the aristocracy. So important was Shaka's reform that many years later the Zulu generals who established kingdoms in various parts of east and central Africa commanded armies only about 10 per cent of whose warriors were 'true' Zulu. The rest were local recruits, who were able to rise to various positions of command and political authority.

For the new Zulu army to fight successfully, Shaka realized that it was necessary to impose on it strict military discipline. This involved establishing military towns for each of the regiments, under a military commander who took his orders directly from him. The army now became a disciplined and united force, organized in a crescent formation capable of encircling the enemy. No soldier could turn away from battle on pain of death, except in response to an order from the chief commander and as part of an organized retreat. The army was to fight not merely to prove a point, but ultimately to achieve the incorporation of all peoples in one single army and state. The defeated enemy was to be pursued relentlessly and his base of operation totally destroyed.

Perhaps one of the most significant of Shaka's reforms was the consideration he gave to the welfare of the fighting men. Shaka's approach meant that the Zulu army became a popular army, and many former mercenary heroes became incorporated into the new fraternity, which operated as a politically disciplined unit. They were infused with Shaka's vision of the unity of the Palm race and a sense of common national destiny. Confiscated cattle and food were distributed to the various military towns for the maintenance of the army. As part of his plan to guarantee the absolute freshness and battle-readiness of the fighting man, Shaka created units of young recruits who carried the weapons and food for the army. Hitherto each soldier had carried his own bundle of spears and had been forced to rely on getting food wherever he fought, which had meant that the choice of battleground had been greatly influenced by the availability of food. Needless to say, this had adversely affected considerations of military strategy. The confiscation of cattle and food had also caused a great deal of resentment of the raiding armies.

Shaka's reforms enabled the Zulu army to operate as a swift, effective military machine, conquering powerful rulers like King Phakathwayo, King Phungashe and King Zwide. In one of its most spectacular victories, Shaka's forces completely destroyed Zwide's army in 1818, despite the enemy's superior numbers. Having studied Zwide's tactics, Shaka ordered all the supplies in the area of conflict to be destroyed. No sooner had the two armies confronted each other than Shaka commanded his army to beat a strategic retreat. Zwide's generals, convinced that the Zulus had suddenly taken fright at the enormous numbers of the Zwide army, chased the Zulus for many days, until, tired and short of supplies, they realized that they had been led into a trap. The Zulus, still fresh and provided with all the food they needed, turned back to attack and defeat the Zwide army.

Strategic wars

Shaka's many military innovations ushered in an era of strategically planned wars, in which his enemies' numbers and courage were no guarantee of victory in battle. Shaka understood that for the army to fight efficiently, it must constitute a solid fraternity in which the commanders and the soldiers shared the experiences of everyday life. To meet this need he organized his regiments in accordance with age groups. These groups were then given their own individual sacred emblems, war songs and special colours. In addition, the regiments were separated from the rest of the community and formed a highly trained standing army.

Shaka quickly realized the potential of the gun as a fighting weapon. Yet he also understood its weaknesses, and he came to the conclusion that the time spent in the reloading of the muzzle gun would give the advantage to a faster attacker.

Political policies of the Zulu state

The cornerstone of Shaka's internal and external policies was the overriding concept of social order. This meant that a physical subordination of others was not enough: the state must guarantee equality to all of its citizens.

Early in his rule Shaka divided the regions of the state into political and military districts. The political divisions were as important as the military; indeed, the two roles were often interchangeable. The cohesion of the political structure was enhanced by non-sectarian representation at both local and national levels. Although the family played an important role as a basic democratic institution, it did not have the same decisive political authority that it had had in pre-Shakan politics. The military, as a specialist organ of the state, had its own councils. However, both the National Assembly and the Military Council complemented each other, and the king played a crucial role in linking the two. Indeed, one of the causes of the defeat of the Zulu army in the post-Shakan era was the gradual separation between the military and political structures.

It is clear from all this that the internal structure of the Zulu state was designed to promote the maximum participation of all members of society. The fact that Shaka overruled, at times, both the military and political councils attests more to his political acumen and the force of his personality than to flaws in procedure. As heroism was a central part of the Zulu national ethos, a recognized hero exercised greater political authority and influence than others. Shaka's egalitarian principles are nowhere better shown than in the fact Zulu princes, despite their aristocratic origins, never became national heroes or assumed significant military command. Many of the commanders and heroes exercised greater power in national affairs than members of the Zulu royal family. Extolling this political development, the poet of Princess Mkhabayi said:

> *She opened the gates to all peoples;*
> *Those of her family entered by the small gate.*

Shaka's internal reforms were matched by his external policies. In dealing with those rulers who endangered peace and order, Shaka was swift and unsparing. Among these rulers were King Macingwane, King Ngoza, Prince Matiwane and Prince Ranisi. One of the most outstanding testimonies to Shaka's prudent handling of foreign policy was the cordial relations he maintained with both the Lesotho and Ngwane kingdoms, both of which were ruled by kings who sought to amalgamate smaller states with their own.

King Moshoeshoe of Lesotho incorporated all the refugee groups from the neighbouring regions and created a truly composite nation. His kingdom was threatened constantly not only by the Hlubis and the Ntlokwas, but also by the powerful Prince Matiwane. As part of his policy of supporting the centres of order, Shaka sent General Mdlaka to rout the bandit army of Matiwane. Throughout Shaka's life he considered Moshoeshoe a close friend and a stabilizing force. The Zulu and the Ngwane royal houses also maintained close bonds; King Sobhuza of the Ngwanes visited Shaka's royal capital of Bulawayo and was fêted and entertained by him.

Zulu foreign relations

Shaka's relations with the whites (the English and the Portuguese) are well documented. From the evidence, however, it is clear the white chroniclers had very little understanding of the Zulu society and its motivations. There was a common belief, for example, that Shaka was unaware of the whites as a threat to southern Africa. On the contrary, his whole foreign policy was geared towards dealing with this danger. Indeed, on the verge of death in 1828, his last words concerned the inevitability of the white invasion: 'You kill me, my brothers, because you think you will rule after me? No, you will never rule; it is the swallows (whites) that shall take over the land.' Shaka's predictions were correct, as later history would demonstrate.

Among the Mthethwas Shaka had listened to many stories about the Portuguese, not only from Dingiswayo but from many others who had travelled as traders between the Mthethwa empire and Delagoa Bay. When he became ruler he received reports from his own agents about their activities in both the northern and south-western regions. It is true, however, that the whites were not at first considered a threat by the Zulus. When they began to arrive in sizeable numbers, Shaka gave them land on the coastal area and appointed Prince Mbikwane governor and co-ordinator of agencies studying their activities under Mhlophe. He hoped to settle them down to a normal family life and learn more about their life and military tactics. To achieve maximum co-ordination for this programme he moved his capital to a region nearer to their settlements. Out of the Mgumanqa regiment he created a special regiment to act as guards. This regiment he called 'The watchers over the monsters' *(u Khangela amankengane)*.

Shaka also sent two missions to King George IV, which were sabotaged by the white colonial administrators of the Cape. It was Shaka's intention that his delegation should learn the use of the gun and also establish friendly relations.

Shakan literature as a social and political vehicle

From a largely personal and romantic literature of the pre-Shakan period, Zulu literature changed to become a powerful vehicle of social and political ideas. The heroic epic was developed, the language-form changing in the process to express dramatic national events. Needless to say, this process of literary change had begun to be perceptible in the literature of the late pre-Shakan period. However, in the Shakan period, it reached the point of fullest expression. Nursery rhymes, satires and songs were all exploited for the social purpose of mobilizing the nation. The poet and the singer became central figures in Zulu society. They defined social values, celebrating what was historically significant and acting as democratic agents to reaffirm the approval or disapproval of the whole nation. It was through the poet and the singer that the criticism and evaluation of the heroes and rulers was fully and freely expressed. Needless to say, the great upsurge of nineteenth-century southern African nationalism stimulated a great deal of heroic literature.

In conclusion, I should acknowledge that this epic is only a limited statement about the achievements of Shaka, and it is hoped that it will stimulate more extensive scholarly interest in the varied ideas and innovations of this great African genius. Through the knowledge of his vision, many may understand the dreams and realities that have shaped the destinies of the peoples of Africa.

Notes

Translation

The translation of the epic does not claim to correspond word for word with the original Zulu epic. I have tried to give a faithful but free translation of the original. I have also cut out a great deal of material which would seem to be a digression from the story, a style unacceptable in English but characteristic of deep scholarship in Zulu. Throughout the epic I have attempted to give as accurate a historical account as possible. On rare occasions where I felt re-arrangement would make the central story more dramatic, without distorting the history, I have changed the sequence of events.

In translating, I have used words that correspond to similar concepts in English, although the meanings in the two societies may not be exactly the same. A royal city, for instance, may not have the same scale and architectural form in Nguniland as those of a royal city in Europe. However, the social and political attitudes towards such a centre would be the same. I have eliminated the colonial terminology like 'hut', 'chief', 'headman', etc., and, rather, based my terminology on corresponding terms in the two societies. I have projected the concept of power as defined by the society in question and as historically comparable with the concepts of another society under similar circumstances. For instance, in Britain (before unification) there were regions often referred to as kingdoms, even though some were no more than a third of what would amount to a princedom in the early Nguni and Sotho states of the pre-Shakan period. Equally, by Zulu empire I refer not only to the actual territory of Zululand, but also to those areas that acknowledged in one way or another the political authority of the Zulu state. Such states or regions kept peace either because they were backed by the Zulu armies or because they were bound by the same authority to keep the peace.

Oral Sources

Much of the material in this epic comes from oral sources. Highly trained national historians *(abalandi bezindaba zabadala)* have preserved not only details of each period but also incidents of each episode. Some national historians specialize in one episode, as for instance, the battle of Sandlwane. They are recognized throughout the land as specialists who know everything about that event. I consulted with many such historians in the course of my research into the Shakan period. My uncle, A. Ngcobo, particularly provided me with many intimate details and insights into the Shaka period.

Praise names

It is common in Zulu society to have both one's real name and a praise name or names. Praise names often describe one's heroic achievements or some outstanding quality of behaviour. Thus, Shaka is variously referred to as Nodumehlezi, one whose fame spreads while he sits unshaken, i.e. invincible; Mlilwana, a little restless fire, the name given to Shaka by his mother in his early youth to describe his aggressive temper; and Ndaba, a reference to one of the early famous ancestors.

'Bayede'

The royal salute 'Bayede' was originally 'Bayethe' meaning 'bring them (the enemies), we are ready to fight them.' The complete form is often used, 'Bayede wiZulu or UyiZulu' (Bring them, you who are as vast as the heavens).

uSo and uNo forms

The male and female qualities are depicted in Zulu by the

use of uSo- and uNo- forms which are the shortened forms of uyiso (father) and unina (mother). Though normally these indicate gender, they can be used descriptively to indicate male qualities in a woman or female qualities in a man, e.g. u Sonjalose means literally 'Mr Always' but is actually a reference to a male quality (such as defending the community) possessed by a woman (Mbulazikazi).

'Planet of dogs'

The 'Planet of dogs' is a mythical world which is supposed to be governed by the mothers-in-law of the canine family. It symbolizes the very limits of the solar system. On the sunniest days the powerful rays of the sun reach even these remote regions.

'Feast of Return'

It is customary in Zulu society to make a 'Feast of Return' after a year's period of mourning. In such a feast or ceremony the spirit of the deceased person is invited to join the ancestral guardians of the community. This is a moment of joy when the deceased reassumes his or her role in society. Various cleansing ceremonies are performed culminating in a huge feast.

Poems of excellence

Poems of excellence are so designated because of their social strategy — namely that of elevating highest desirable qualities in society. They have been wrongly described as praise poems. However they do more than praise and are more complex. Rather, they project an ethical system beyond the circumstances of the individual. Thus, individuals are heroes so long as they fulfil the roles defined for them by society. If they become arrogant and disrespectful of elders (guardians of social order) they are mercilessly lampooned and demoted. This is summarized in the Zulu saying: 'Never praise anyone when they still live'. The greatest exponents of this social doctrine are the poets whose freedom of speech is jealously guarded by society. The national poet is not a court poet who is hired by and speaks for the aristocracy, but a representative of society.

The heroic poems, or poems of excellence, included in this epic are fragments since their full meaning can only be realized through a performance in a social context. They may seem obscure to those readers unacquainted with Zulu history but they are so inherently a part of Zulu life that omitting them in a Zulu historical epic would reduce its quality. I have, however, included only abridged versions.

Some important names of the Shakan era

Bhuza:	General of the Mthethwa regiment of iziChwe, to which Shaka belonged.
Dingane:	The brother of Shaka and chief organizer of his assassination. He later became king.
Dingiswayo: *(alias Godongwana)*	King of the Mthethwas and founder of the Mthethwa empire.
Faku:	King of the Mpondo nation at the time of Shaka's reign.
Gendeyana: *(alias Ngendeyana)*	Shaka's stepfather on the Qwabe side of his family. Father of Ngwadi, Shaka's favourite brother.
Gambushe:	King of the Mpondos.
Hlambamanzi: *(alias Jacob* *Msimbithi)*	Shaka's interpreter and fugitive from white captivity.
Isaacs, N.:	One of the early white traders, who was kindly received and sheltered by Prince Myaka of the Mthethwas.
Jama:	Grandfather of Shaka, whose temperament Shaka's was said to resemble strongly.
Jobe:	Father of Dingiswayo and king of the Mthethwas.
King, J.S.:	The only white trader who could be 'trusted', but he, too, grabbed as much land as he could.
Macingwane:	King of the Chunus. A great and able fighter, but finally defeated by Shaka.
Magolwane:	A great national poet of the Shakan era and one of the greatest Zulu poets.
Mantantisi:	Queen of the baTlokwa, who led her own armies in battle.
Mashobana:	Zwide's son-in-law and father of Mzilikazi.
Matiwane:	Roving ruler of the Ngwanes, who was feared and hated by many nations on the western and southern regions.
Mbengi:	Ruler of abasemaLangeni and relative of Nandi.

Mbikwane:	Paternal uncle of King Dingiswayo. A highly respected political figure, he was made governor by Shaka over the white coastal settlement.
Mbiya:	A member of the Mthethwa royal family, who was Shaka's guardian at the Mthethwas.
Mdlaka:	Commander-in-chief of the Zulu army.
Mhlangana:	Shaka's brother, who collaborated in a plot to kill him.
Mkhabayi:	The most influential political figure in Zululand. She acted as regent when Senzangakhona was still a minor. She was Shaka's paternal aunt, who eventually collaborated in the plot to assassinate him.
Mkhabi:	Senzangakhona's main wife and his favourite.
Mshweshwe: (alias Moshoeshoe)	King of the Basothos. A great nation-builder and founder of the Sotho nation.
Mthaniya:	Shaka's paternal grandmother.
Mpande:	Shaka's brother, who later became king after the death of Dingane. The present Zulu royal house is composed mainly of his descendants.
Mudli:	Shaka's granduncle, who saved him from his father in his childhood.
Mzilikazi:	Leader of the Khumalos. A great general, who later broke away to form his own Ndebele kingdom in Zimbabwe.
Nandi:	Mother of Shaka and a great political force behind Shaka's achievements. In her own right she was recognized as a woman of sharp intelligence and iron will.
Ngomane:	Commander-in-chief of the Mthethwa armies and close adviser to Shaka.
Ngoza:	Famous king of the Thembus.
Ngqengelele:	Shaka's close companion. One of the most outstanding political thinkers of the Shakan period. His position was equivalent to that of prime minister, a position that was also ably fulfilled by Ngqengelele's son, the great Mnyamana.
Nomahlanjana:	Zwide's heir, who was killed at the battle of Qokli.
Nomchoba:	Shaka's sister.
Nomnxamama:	The great national poet of Shaka's era, who committed suicide at his death.

Ntombazi: One of the politically most influential women of the pre-Shakan and Shakan eras. Mother of Zwide and his great supporter.

Nxazonke: Shaka's maternal uncle and leader of the delegation that went to the north to look for iron.

Phakathwayo: King of the Qwabes and member of the senior branch of the House of Malandela.

Phungashe: King of the powerful Buthelezi nation, later defeated by Shaka.

Shemane: Zwide's heir after the death of Prince Nomahlanjana.

Senzangakhona: The father of Shaka and king of the Zulus.

Sigujana: Brother of Shaka and heir-apparent before the war of succession.

Sobhuza I: King of the Ngwanes (Swazis), with whom Shaka had strong marital and diplomatic bonds.

Sotobe: Leader of the mission that was sent to King George. He was a highly respected political figure even after the death of Shaka.

Zihlandlo: Head of the Mkhize clan and a close friend of Shaka. He was killed by King Dingane in his attempt to eliminate all opposition after murdering Shaka.

Zwangendaba: Member of the junior house of the Ndwandwe royal family and founder of the Angoni kingdom in central East Africa.

Zwide: The powerful king of the Ndwandwes (sometimes called the Nxumalos). He was defeated by Shaka in one of the most dramatic of the Shakan battles.

Some of the great Zulu heroes, heroines and commanders of the Shakan era

General Manyundela, son of Mabuya
Njikiza of the Ngcolosi clan
General Mdlaka, son of Mcidi
General Ndlela, son of Sompisi of the Ntuli clan
Zulu, son of Nogandaya of the Zunga clan
Mghobhozi of the Msane clan
Sotobe, son of Mpangalala
Nqoboka of the Sokhulu clan
Magaye, son of Dibandlela of the Cele clan
Zihlandlo of the Mkhize clan
Gala, son of Nondela
Nkayishana of the Khuzwayo clan
Manyosi, son of Dlekezeke of the Shandu clan
Princess Mkhabayi, daughter of Jama
Mzilikazi, son of Mashobana
Princess Nandi of Bhibhi
General Ngomane
General Nzobo of the Ntombela clan
Maphitha, son of Sojiyisa

Shaka's regiments

Male		Female
uFasimba		uMvuthwamini
uGibabanye		uNhlabathi
uFojisa	IziMpohlo Division	uCeyana
UMfolozi		
uNdabankulu		
uNomdayana		
amaPhela		
amaKhwenkwe	uMbelebele Division	
iziKwembu		
iziZamazana		
uMgumanqa		
isiPhezi		
uNteke	uMgumanqa Division	
uMbonambi	(uKhangela)	
uDlangezwa		
iziNyosi		
amaWombe		
uDlambedlu		
uJubinqwanga		

Genealogy of Zulu kings

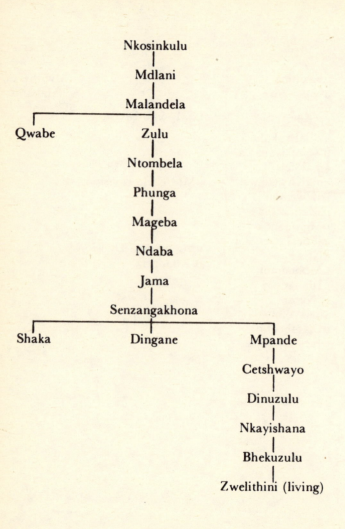

Nkosinkulu

Mdlani

Malandela

Qwabe — Zulu

Ntombela

Phunga

Mageba

Ndaba

Jama

Senzangakhona

Shaka — Dingane — Mpande

Cetshwayo

Dinuzulu

Nkayishana

Bhekuzulu

Zwelithini (living)

EMPEROR SHAKA THE GREAT

Book One: The prophecy

This book introduces the circumstances of Shaka's birth. It deals briefly with the Ancestors, whose deeds constituted the heroic history which was later to inspire him in building the Zulu empire. His outstandingly brave ancestor, Jama, is selected as the central figure, who transmits the dream of the great hero who is to be born. This vision runs into difficulties in the time of the playboy king, Senzangakhona. Not only does he find this idea offensive, but he tries physically to eliminate the infant Shaka. He is particularly unkind to his wife, the proud Princess Nandi of the Langeni clan. But the prophetic voice of the dream persists. The symbolism within the dream reveals the historical events and gradually the fantasy turns into reality. The second dreamer is no longer a prophet projecting remote events, but an interpreter of immediate reality. The recasting of the dreamer in this part is deliberate, to emphasize this point.

Great anthem, by your power break the boundaries of our
    horizons;
Fill the wide expanse of the earth with your legendary songs!
Say then: people have power, people tear the garments of the
5   night;
By their feet, they scar the grounds with new life.
All hail! The celebrants of the feast have come!
The Ancestors follow them,
Whispering: 'A great festival is to be repeated again and again!'
10 Generation after generation comes here to play.
Here they are: our Forefathers. They rise from the mist.
Striding across the earth to nowhere,
Calling the name that invokes the sacred ones of the festival.
All hail to the trembling rivers of the afternoon!

15 After the night has covered the earth
Rouse us from the nightmare of forgetfulness
So that we may narrate their tales.
You will see them, the Forefathers, by the brightness of the
    moon.

You will see their great processions as they enter the mountain!
Eternally their anthems emerge.
How then can we be silent before the rising sun?
How wonderful! We can sing the sacred songs of our
5   Forefathers!
By our ancient epics we are made beautiful.
The puffadders come and lick our feet.
Our pride shall be restored then,
And the wilderness shall echo with our songs!
10 We shall turn to the North, which is the source of our life,
Where the birthplace of our nation is overhung with trembling
      shadows.
From the womb of Nandi comes the language of their secrets,
Quivering on the forehead of him who shall be great.
15 It was because of these prophecies of our Forefathers; we
      listened;
They talked into the elephant-ears of future times.
Like Malandela, son of Mdlani of Nkosinkulu;
Like Phunga and Mageba of ancient times,
20 Who sat dreaming their greatness into our age.
Their progeny was their hand of sacrifice.
They vowed: 'Jama's fame shall radiate into the sun.'
The diviners prophesied the greatness of his house;
By their final word they said a nation of red spears shall be
25   born.

The diviner spoke at Jama's Royal House and said:
'Look! the fierce contest of the hurrying rivers;
One river swallows the other near the ocean,
Turning itself into a gigantic river
30 To enter the ocean triumphantly
Provoking a towering mountain of waves.
Turn your eyes to the turbulence of the winds.
Watch them as they skirt the central region like a hunting lion;
Watch them as they leap like the angered heads of the
35   whirlwinds.
Trees are torn by their roots —
They are flung into the hills
To give eternal fertility to the red earth.
On this ground shall grow the young plant of fire.

When it has reached maturity, birds will come,
Choosing the secrets of pleasure from under the leaves.'
Thus the diviner spoke, hurling her prophesies to the Assembly.
By these words she roused the anger of the House of Jama.
5   Jama himself intervened and said: 'Enough, my oracle!
Do not make us anxious about things we do not know!
No ruler is happy who is harassed by too much truth,
Or told of an era greater than his.'
But the diviner persisted as if nothing had been said:
10   'I see a vision of houses consumed by mountains of fire.
One day these little men shall rise
They shall invade the whole earth by the gate of the Cock.
I see crowds of the Ancestral spirits, exchanging words at dawn.
They pass each other, carrying glimmering spears.
15   When they arrive at the ruins they begin to talk to me:
'Speak of the thundering of the black shields!
Tell them the directions from which they came.'
A white hare is carried away by ibises.
They take it to build their own nests of summer.
20   It is from here the beautiful young shall be born.'
Once again, Jama tried to silence the oracle's horrid words,
Telling her she must not forget those who live
Who pride themselves in the glories of their own times,
Who only know the panorama of their own achievements.
25   It was as if he had spurred her on.
She threw herself on the ground,
Scorning with laughter those who listened to her,
Telling them how they deceived themselves
Claiming equality with the Eternal Cycles,
30   Unaware of the entangling fingers of decay.
'Those who do not know the softness of the earth are swallowed
      by her.
The middle yields, letting them sink into its eternity.
Those who resist, who seek their immortality, shall be consumed
35   whole!'
The oracle scattered a handful of earth and said:
'Here are your relations!
Here are those who feasted in ancient times!
We who are here tread on them.
40   They lived foolishly by the visions of their future times,

Yet only the stone remains to tell their tale;
The guardian of life, eternally waits to open the Mountain!'
No sooner had she finished than she took up her possessions
And vanished into the darkness of the mountains,
5   Disappearing with the spirits of the Ancestors
Who are always telling the winds to sing a new song.

Someone stood up to curse the whole clan of diviners,
Eager to make his voice stronger than that of the King.
Hysterical, like all who kowtow for praise,
10 Whose whole life is bent to please.
Jama himself remonstrated with him saying:
'Do not dismiss altogether the words of diviners
For, after all, each reign lays the foundation for another.
From our deeds our children shall build their monuments.
15 Besides, the ancestral utterances are never taken in vain,
Even if they come from the lips of fools.'
As Jama spoke he heard the disembodied voices of her
    prophecies:
'The generation to come shall rule the earth.'
20 The echoes of the wind troubled his mind.
For who ever hopes for the loyalty of his followers
Must contend with words from all sides
And attempt to remove doubts from his followers,
Implanting his own words of wisdom in their minds,
25 Making them see through his words their own future greatness.
It is unwise to let the subjects
Whisper the inadequacies of contemporary rule.
Such songs should be forbidden:
'The greatness that is to come should have been ours;
30 We should have been born a hundred years hence.'
Jama was tormented by all these thoughts.
He spoke to the wise councillor
'What do you think of these words that bury us alive?
They dig a grave for us at the feet of future times.'
35 The wise one was silent, reaping from within the wisdom of his
    mind.
Finally he spoke: 'Such are the cycles of life —
Time casts its shadows on the sand.
No era, no reign, shall remain unchanged.

Sometimes an era grows by its very tale of joyfulness
Or else offers only a memory to fertilize its ruins.
That generation is to be envied which bequeathes its greatness;
To it others shall say: "Because of them,
5   Those who put the stone on the cairn,
We inherit the secret songs of the mountain." '
As he spoke, King Jama nodded his head in consent,
Though he did not welcome these words.
He stared intently at Senzangakhona, his son,
10   Wondering if these prophecies would fall on his shoulders.
But he rebuked himself for despite Senzangakhona's skills,
He was not like the wild ones who open the paths of man.
He watched him as he turned to stare at his shadow.
He followed him as he admired his body
15   And thought: Such are never the favourites of the gods.
The Ancestors are careful; they begin at dawn to peer into
      the heart
And only by evening do they make their choice.
Only then do they decide: 'The guardians are still to be
20   born.'
As they speak, dogmas and fantasies disintegrate.
The substances of man's faith is fed by their judgement.

Senzangakhona, the son of Jama, 'the fierce bundle of spears',
Encountered the beautiful one, the Princess Nandi.
25   He said to himself: 'I shall exalt this woman with the angry
      ones.'
He spoke of her, Nandi, the daughter of Bhebhe.
As she walked she shook the earth.
She was the fear of the timid ones;
30   Of her the royal poets sang:
'Woman of many tongues, inhabiter of the high places of the
      Assembly.'
She feared no one.
She invaded the Assemblies of men and spoke defiantly:
35   'I am the daughter of the Prince of abasemaLangeni clan.'
Some thought she was possessed of an angry spirit;
Even on this day as she watched this arrogant lover
Her eyes bristled with anger.
She spat at his words, her eyes burning with pride.

But Senzangakhona, too, spoke angrily:
'The house of my father has never been shadowed by strangers.'
He forced his way through the gathering of his friends
Shouting: 'Give way! Let me see this woman with my own eyes!'
5   But no sooner had he broken through
Than he was halted by the fierce power of the daughter of
     Bhebhe.
His body quivered with desire; his words hung suspended on his
     lips.
10 Her presence was like a blaze of fire gone wild,
Like a hungry flame that consumes all other flames.
His heart fluttered like the throat of a frightened frog.
Softly he spoke to her: 'Stubborn woman,
I forbid you and your followers to proceed.
15 Let me fetch a large boulder to place it in the water
To enable you to cross safely to our grounds.
Hurry then! Bring all the gifts of your clan!
Let their beauty be like antelopes setting out at dawn,
Like droves of thirsty beasts drinking from pool to pool.
20 When we are sated with nourishment from your hands
We shall lie down, feasting on the long shades of the evening.
Grant this to our house, grant it to our royal clans, for us
     together.
When generations hereafter walk our path
25 Let it be to the echoes of our tales.'
Even Nandi said to herself: 'I have now met my soulmate.'
The words of lovers create their own illusions
In each generation they sparkle with freshness
As though no lovers in ancient times ever uttered them
30 Yet only the words of the wise are anchored in the heart of the
     earth,
Only they truly nourish each generation.
Nandi broke her pretence and began to laugh.
She laughed loudly until the mountains vanished from sight.
35 She said to Senzangakhona: 'You have been spoiled.
You have listened to those who know only one side of you.
They have not seen the hidden rottenness in your bones.'
The young man of Zululand was stabbed.
His mind was seared by the sharpness of her words.
40 Even Nandi was stricken with sadness.

Consoling him, she said: 'Forgive me, stranger.
Forgive my abrasive tongue.
With it I cut, and my heart bleeds for the victim.'
As she spoke she stretched out her kindly hand.
5   She scattered the seeds of her beautiful eyes.
Senzangakhona picked up the warm messages of her mind.
His wounds were cured.
They fell together behind the growth of bushes.
They loved as though to celebrate their final day on earth,
10   As though nothing ever again would disturb their minds.
Even those whom life has deprived of such joys
Let them share for now the richness of their fantasies.
There are many loves — some big, some small;
Some embodying the fullness of life; some plant their seeds of
15   pain.
How wonderful the spectacle of lovers
When they still sing their magic songs of Nomalumbo!
She, the nocturnal witch, ties up her children with invisible
           thread.
20   By her wisdom she leads them to the fields of fruitfulness;
Yet she does not manifest her joyfulness forever.
Such was the day when young women cursed Senzangakhona:
'You have disgraced our village;
Come out then and placate the anger
25   Brought on us by you and Nandi.
You have violated the ancient customs of our Forefathers.'
Such now were the loves that had once been the talk of all
           festivals,
Whose songs had been sung by all the men and women of
30   Nguniland.
Nandi and Senzangakhona had swallowed a poisonous herb.
The women shouted as if madness had seized their minds.
They took spears to gore the black bulls of Jama.
The cattle fell to the ground with monstrous bellows;
35   The whole valley was filled with their moaning.
It was as if by this act
Senzangakhona had brought down the wrath of the gods.
The bond of families is the sacred plant of generations to come;
From this the beautiful voices break the new earth,
40   Thrusting their echoes into myriad gates of future times.

It was this law Senzangakhona had defiled.
The women scolded Nandi, saying: 'You have betrayed us!'
They cursed and turned their backs on her
Leaving her there with her disgrace.
5   Nandi sat dejectedly amongst the strangers.
Such were the beginnings of Nandi's fate.
At first she was humbled, but then she rose to defy the winds.
Every day Nandi waited for Senzangakhona.
She hoped by their reunion life might set aflame their love
10   again;
Perchance he might recall
Their great moments of loving and dreaming.
But in the dark recesses of his father's royal villages,
She waited in vain.
15   Shadows flirted to and fro in the sepulchre that was now her
        home.
Hallucinations of horrendous snakes writhed around her.
They bound up her ribs; they put knots in her voice.
She began to lose her sanity, shouting the name of her lover.
20   She called his name; he did not answer —
Only the echoes came bounding from the distant cliffs.
In her madness she heard footsteps
As if echoing from passing crowds.
Sometimes they sounded like the familiar voices of friends.
25   Thus her imagination played tricks on her.
Many months of misery and waiting had passed
When she heard people wailing to announce someone's death.
Straining her ears to listen, she heard them shouting King
        Jama's name.
30   Over and over they shouted: 'The king is dead! The king is
        dead!'
The high mountains barked their grief to the sky.
Great anthems of clans and allied nations filled the horizon.
Royal cities and villages shook from the sounds of grief.
35   Nandi, the princess of abasemaLangeni, began to shout:
'Let my fate be finally sealed with tears!
Long ago it should have been fed with new hopes.
Yet when my day converges into the mists of tomorrow
I shall no longer be alone but with my own protector.
40   For him I shall compose a song; I shall dance for him.

8

Those who discarded me like a winter's weed shall swallow their
    words.
They shall crawl on their bellies in his name.'
She spoke words of bitterness against her enemies.
5   The mourners of the king did not understand her prophecies.
Only she alone understood the dawn that hung over the night.

Because of Nandi, the Langas and the Zulus stood on the verge
    of war.
The Langas had sent messengers to Jama of the Zulus,
10 But these messengers returned saying:
'They have denied responsibility for the child,
Claiming her pregnancy was only an illness of intestinal beetles,
A disease that invades the mind with madness.'
It was these insults that made Nandi withdraw in bitterness.
15 Nor did she care now for the grief caused by the king's death.
Her love for him was crushed by her own loneliness,
For it is hard to mourn with others when burdened by your
    sadness.
To her son she vowed she would tell of these cruel things.
20 Their bond was to be made eternal by their tears.
Nandi continued shouting her words:
'My mind devours the bitter leaf.
Tomorrow I shall sit beside the rulers.'
They ignored her, only commenting:
25 'Loneliness often breeds these fantasies,
Seizing with madness the willing root of the tongue.'
The great Assembly of the abasemaLangeni clan had gathered.
Princess Nandi gave birth to a boy.
Without delay they sent a message to Senzangakhona
30 Saying: 'Here, then, is the disease you had sought to discard!'
With these angry words they sent Nandi and her child to
    Senzangakhona.
It was Mudli, a clansman of the king,
Who on seeing them proclaimed the family's guilt.
35 Thus Nandi stayed in a place where there was neither love nor
    joy.
Whenever she heard crowds celebrating at the royal grounds
She would curl herself up withdrawing into the darkness of her
    house.

Through her messengers she sent these words to the king:
'Greet for me the king; tell him I still live.
I still harbour in my mind the memories of our love.
Tell him when he has feasted to his heart's content
5   He must remember: not alone does he inhabit this earth!
We wait for the rebirth of a better day, at his mercy.
We retain the memory of what was beautiful.
Someday the sun shall fulfil its promise with glittering spears.
From all regions the blade shall be fed with the living.
10 Our days shall be made complete by our readiness for battle.'
She directed these words to Senzangakhona,
Railing against him for his neglect of his beautiful son.
So long as the heart has life, it is open to barbs of grief;
It enfolds within itself swellings of throbbing pain.
15 By night it aches, envying those who sleep
In the nests of pleasant dreams.

One night Senzangakhona hurried to Mkhabayi, the princess
     royal,
And said: 'I bear a scar that refuses to heal.
20 Each time I try to lose myself in sleep
I hear Nandi's voice piercing through the darkness.
It is as if she has cast a spell over me.'
The great princess turned to look at Senzangakhona,
Staring at him with contemptuous eyes as if to denounce his
25   feeble generation,
Those who play with clay while disasters strike.
Finally she responded: 'Son of my father,
The royal staff which you see hanging on the wall
Once was carried by your Ancestors in ancient times.
30 It is the vow of our clan that it shall never be broken.
Should such a disaster befall our house,
The earth itself shall vanish.
So long as it is here, rule, son of Ndaba, rule without fear!
Do as you wish in the land of our Forefathers.
35 A ruler must rule, moulding at will the minds of people,
For they never follow for long a king who betrays fear.
Such must be your posture against all threats
Stand defiant against all winds.

Know that nothing terrorizes the mind unless so permitted by
    you.
It was you who created fantasies in her mind
When you said: "I shall give you all the joys of my family",
5 But these loves have brought only hatred amongst nations.
The abasemaLangeni clan bear us bitter grudges.
Gossiping tongues often comment:
"How disgraceful that our daughter lives like an orphan!
The king of the Zulus has discarded her like a rotten corpse.
10 To this very moment he does not know his newborn son;
He has not burnt the sacred herb in his son's name."
No great family abandons entirely its children;
Even if they be fools it stands firm in their defence.
Thus as long as they feel this pain,
15 The abasemaLangeni shall sleep bitterly on their weapons.
But through patience time shall come to wipe away their scars.'
She spoke these words as Senzangakhona listened intently.
He pretended he was eased of the heavy burden.
But it was only pride which made him rear back his shoulders.
20 From then on he set himself to sleep a defiant sleep,
Forcing his mind never again to succumb to guilt.
Indeed, to perfect his instruments of self-deceit
He summoned his trusted messenger, ordering him:
'Go to the people of the abasemaLangeni clan, ask them their
25   forgiveness,
Give them these beasts and say: "From the royal clan of the
    Zulus
To the royal clan of abasemaLangeni — may their loves be
    eternal!" '
30 He planned to make the troublemakers turn back in despair
As they see the two clans celebrate together their mutual
    bonds.
His ruse did not succeed.
The Langenis scolded and insulted his messenger and said:
35 'Go back, take back to him his despicable offer!
Tell him, with this, he must feed his own children!'

Once there was a man
Who seemed a curse to all the races of humankind.
His arms lumbered as if they were boneless;

Continuously he scratched at the back of his ears;
His face looked as though it had been danced on at a festival;
His eyes flickered as if searching for directions;
He fed on the ravenous hopes of humankind.
5 He searched the hidden chambers of their minds,
Reaping eagerly their fruits of love,
Supplanting them with his own visions of deceit.
When they failed utterly and became despondent
He generated terror in their minds
10 Making them drink from his mysterious powers of night.
All honour is due to him who brings the sun!
Thus did this witch approach Senzangakhona,
Humbling himself still more lowly to hoodwink the king,
Knowing too that restless souls are prone to facile belief.
15 Eagerly, in their confusion, they elevate simple truths,
Making them beautiful.
Such is the fate of all fanatics.
Knowing this, he presented himself before the weakened ruler,
Saying: 'I dreamed a fearful dream
20 As though the royal grounds were invaded with enemy armies
Who set on fire our royal city.
They were commanded by one who closely resembled my lord.
I regained my strength to shout:
"Why do you destroy your father's royal city?"
25 But he answered me with fierce eyes and said:
"My father's house is a wilderness of spears."
He pushed me aside
As I shouted and remonstrated with him in vain.
Finally I rushed to take up my own weapons,
30 Eager to protect with my life the ruler of our nation.
When I returned, seething with anger and ancient pride of
              battle,
I found only a collection of blood-spattered spears,
Pools of blood from our king spilt around the fireplace.
35 When the young man saw me, he rushed at me in anger,
Waving his glittering spear of destruction.
It was as though with one plunge he would spear me through.
Only by slipping behind a huge pillar did I escape.
As I stood there, panting with fear, I heard a voice calling.
40 It was this that woke me from my dream.

Even at this moment the dream haunts me.
It is for this I am telling it to my lord.
For such clear dreams often forebode what is to come.
Should the King fail to uproot the growing weed
5   The dwellings of nations may yet be left as empty shells.'
These words nourished the thoughts
Eating into Senzangakhona's mind.
He stared unblinkingly at this strange man,
Taking his words as if they lit the course of his future life.
10   He said: 'What you say issues directly from the Forefathers.
It devours the centres of my heart; it troubles my mind.
Too often I have ignored the gentle warnings of the gods.'
As he spoke he cast his eyes onto the ground,
His mind lost in terrors of things to come.
15   He thought to himself: 'I shall do as is necessary.
I shall send Nandi to her own people who have hurled insults at
     me.
When they receive my messages
They shall know: the bull elephant struts the earth fearlessly,
20   Tearing all things, opening the pathways to the lakes,
There to sit unconquered and overflowing with pride.'

Book Two: The unwanted heir

*Shaka is saved by his granduncle, Prince Mudli. The relations be-
tween the Zulus of Senzangakhona and the abasemaLangeni become so
strained that a war is inevitable. The Zulus win but Senzangakhona
decides not to take any loot nor to take back his wife and children.
This weakness becomes a source of quarrel between him and the powerful Princess Mkhabayi. Meanwhile Shaka's reputation grows, causing jealousy among Senzangakhona's favourites. His father grudgingly*

*stages his ceremony of manhood. The opposition to Shaka's growing
reputation, reinforced by the father's own guilt and jealousy, eventually provokes an expedition to kill him.*

Twelve months had passed.
The ceremony of bringing back Jama's spirit had been held.
Like his Forefathers, he towered over the rooftops of his nation,
Calmly watching the restless life of his son.
5   He saw Senzangakhona mourning his death in an alcove.
Here too Senzangakhona digested the words of his Queen
     Mkhabi.
At the great esiKlebheni royal city
She cast her shadow like a tall and awesome mountain.
10 To Senzangakhona she had said:
'How can I live in peace, pestered by scowling voices
And with Nandi hanging around my shoulders like a log?
Once I thought after giving birth to a second child
She would breathe peace and forgiveness towards all.
15 Her mind, I thought, would be carried away
By the birth of her daughter Nomchoba.
But at each and every feast tongues lash out at my feet.
I hear people talking of nothing but her revered son.
She is bringing him up to bewitch us all;
20 On him she has bestowed all her grudges.'
Senzangakhona had listened intently as she spoke
Hypnotized by her huge, round eyes.
She egged him on, stoking his fires of courage and recklessness.
Finally he said to her: 'I shall nip Nandi's boast in the bud;
25 I shall throw her troublesome son to the wild.
From then on eternal peace shall be restored to our house.'
Mkhabi did not comment but sat there savouring these words,
Thinking how they could serve her advantage.
By her insight she saw further than her husband.
30 She reflected on how other women would denounce this hideous
     act.
When Senzangakhona fell into a deep sleep
She stole into the fierce night of wolves
And rushed to the camp of Prince Mudli, the chief commander.
35 To him she called out: 'Father Mudli, open the door for me.

I come to reveal the secret intentions of the king.
Tomorrow at dawn the king shall punish Nandi.
He shall kill her little son.
The child shall die unless you intervene.

5   Only these few words I mean to say and then I must hurry
        back.
In the name of our Forefathers, I ask you to save him.'
Thereupon she ran back to the great house of the king.
Her heart was pounding and filled with guilt,

10 Mindful of the events she had set in motion with her tongue.
Knowing too that the loyalty of a man in love is fickle.
Prince Mudli remained troubled by her words.
He thought to himself: 'Why should this task fall on my hands?
Why did she not influence the king to her new way of thinking?'

15 Mudli himself answered his own questions:
'Should such a thing happen
It would destroy the very roots of our nation.
Yet I am reluctant to act.
How can I hesitate after she has braved the night

20 To tell me of these things?'
Thus did Prince Mudli debate within himself through the night,
Until infused with courage,
He saw how the fate of the nation lay in his hands.
He vowed in that dawn he would save Nandi's child.

25 The day opened in all its splendour in Nguniland;
Mists upon mists circled like clouds in turmoil.
In all the vast plains voices and songs echoed.
Happy were those who listened to the voices of their children,
Who were not like her, who was all misery,

30 She, Nandi of Bhebhe, who mumbled alone to her children
As though sensing the impending turbulence.
At this very moment the king's command penetrated the air.
He summoned Mzoneli, the official executioner
Who had accompanied many a criminal to his death.

35 To him he said: 'Mzoneli, son of Mpikane,
Today you shall spill royal blood.
You shall kill my son, who is born of Princess Nandi.
Only this can bring peace to the land of the Zulus.
Never let this be known to any living female,

For men, entrusted with secrets,
Whisper to their wives what they refuse to tell to other men.
Your failure to keep to yourself this secret
Shall bring a curse to your name from all generations.
5   Bitterly they shall mourn the bloodshed brought by your folly.'
The son of Mpikane saluted the words of his master,
Eager to do whatever he could to please his king.
But Senzangakhona himself grimaced in terror at this evil plot.
His eyes were turned away from Mzoneli's gaze,
10   Knowing that a ruler's weakness speaks through his eyes.
To relieve his mind he took a walk,
Following a path bypassing the big round cattle-fold.
Scarcely had he taken a few paces
Than he met his clansman, Prince Mudli.
15   Startled, he said: 'Mudli, what is it you carry in your bag?'
Mudli answered casually: 'It is only the young of a pig.'
Senzangakhona shot through with suspicion and disbelief,
Stared at him and said:
'Let me test on it my spear-throwing skill.'
20   He threw his long, glimmering spear,
Directing it at the centre of the immobile target.
Once, twice, thrice he tried, the bended-armed one,
Until, embarrassed by his ignominious failure, he said:
'Take your magic-powered beast and keep it away from us.
25   It seems jealously protected by the shoulder-blades of the
       Ancestors.'
Mudli deliberately hesitated, not daring to show eagerness.
He said: 'Try again, my lord. Perhaps this time you will
       succeed.'
30   But Senzangakhona dared not,
Lest his bizarre failure be known to all men in Nguniland.
Finally, Mudli took up his bag.
Proudly lifting it to his shoulders, he set out to give it to Nandi.
On the mountainside she had waited anxiously.
35   Nandi took her child, weeping uncontrollable tears of joy.
She said to Mudli: 'They shall pay for this one day.'
At the royal city of Senzangakhona there was great commotion.
Like ants they set out in all directions,
Searching for Nandi and her children.
40   Senzangakhona saw how he had been tricked by Mudli.

He said to himself: 'Oh, Mudli, you have outwitted me again.
But by your action you have brought me relief and peace of
    mind.
Such disgrace as shall befall Nandi is better than death.'
5 As he spoke these words he radiated forgiveness,
Knowing the blood of his son would not be on his hands.
He said: 'Perhaps by this act my fame shall rise again.
I shall be known for resolution and leopard-like ferocity.'
Those with him saw him suddenly explode with joy.
10 They, too, began to dance and celebrate with him,
Though unable to tell to what conquests they owed their feast.

Nandi and her children now set out on their journey,
Wandering like birds that had been robbed of their nest.
When she finally saw the familiar mountains of her homeland
15 She cried uncontrollably, her exile more painful than before,
For she knew she would be the gossip-joke of her own clan.
She consoled herself:
'How much better, still, this life than among strangers.'
Saying these words, she forged ahead,
20 Passing through familiar paths and climbing familiar hills.
Here she knew a certain man who had built an imposing
    settlement.
His reputation had spread throughout the land for his kindness.
In the shadows of the afternoon they reached his place.
25 Greeting them warmly he invited them to the vast roundhouse:
'I can sense you are born of a great ancestry.
For you I shall kill my favourite ox.
Though I have loved it, your day far surpasses my daily joys.'
Thus he killed for them the fattest beast,
30 Making them a feast and calling out the names of their
    Ancestors.
When the sun had gone to sleep, he said to Nandi:
'Not once did our family ever close its gates to strangers.
Why not honour us and rest your tired feet in our house?
35 Tomorrow I shall send my own fleet-footed messenger
To tell the king, your relative, to meet his own children.
For those who travel unaccompanied like you
Become the subject of gossip.'
They accepted his kindness, and praised his understanding.

Early at dawn the messenger began his journey.
With the fleetness of a pursued antelope he ran,
Until at last he arrived at the royal city of abasemaLangeni.
There he reported the fate of the king's relatives.

5   King Mbengi was startled at these foreboding words,
Knowing those in flight are often followed by armies in pursuit.
'Great evils threaten our house,' he said.
'From a messenger I hear of the news of my relative Nandi,
Who was driven into exile by the unkindness of the House of
10   Zulu.
She has suffered enough.
She comes now, bringing her two children.
This matter no longer concerns only those of the royal clan,
But all members of our heroic nation.

15 It is wiser to prepare for battle before the slogans of war are
         heard.
To await the unpredictable Senzangakhona would be foolish.
He might abandon his life of womanizing
And attack our nation in the name of his family honour,
20 Thus elevating its reputation and making the hurt more obvious
         than real.
This way he shall seem the injured party in the eyes of others.'
As the king concluded, the eyes of those in the Assembly
Flashed in all directions, showing the roused fears of war.

25 In their minds they saw the locust-like numbers of the Zulus
Precipitating their anger and pillage onto their peaceful lands.
Many concurred with the wise words of their king and
         commented:
'Indeed, whoever thinks of invasion is deterred by risks of defeat.
30 Preparedness for battle has vanquished many a potential
         enemy.'
Some rejected all these dark prophecies, arguing:
'We must return to him the lobola-beasts of friendship,
Enabling his councillors to restrain him from this reckless
35   course.
Perhaps he may yet listen and swallow his words;
For only by this recompense is custom appeased.
Mobilising for battle
Shall only make him tremble with suspicion.
40 In this state of anxiety he shall make our upraised shields

The sole reason for his precipitous onslaught.'
The Assembly argued until the midday cycle.
As the debate raged they heard from afar
Someone declaiming the great heroic poem of King Mbengi:
5 'All hail! You of the great clan of emaLangeni,
Puzzler who puzzled everyone
As he took the tortuous route to the Yeyeye ridge.
Patient one who waits till the sun sets.
How many times have you dared the forests of iron?
10 You told them to be silent
And when they refused, you silenced them all the same!
Here I come, the messenger of the descendent of Ndaba.
I come with his sacred word, he of our clan,
He who is known everywhere as:
15 "The sun which, as it rose, was mellow,
But when it reached the centre of the firmament it blazed.
The wild buffalo that overshadows many fords!
The branch of the gatepost of Nomgabi
Where only owls perched,
20 Where King Pungashe of the Buthelezi Nation sat,
Where Macingwane of Ngoyameni sat." '
As he spoke the ground of emaLangeni trembled.
He came closer and closer to the Assembly-place.
When he could be seen by all, he saluted.
25 The young men of the nation devoured him with their eyes;
They stood there guarding the royal city.
From there King Mbengi dispersed his bounty to all peoples.
In pursuance of these traditions, Mbengi invited him:
'Your journey has been long and tiring.
30 Come then, stranger, join us and quench your thirst.
When you put to us your king's words
You shall not be choking from the dust of the dry regions.'
The stranger bowed his head and said to the king:
'It is only to pay tribute to your famed generosity
35 That I consent to your invitation, you of the Mhlongo clan!
It was indeed in the nature of my mission
That I should not feel the steepness of mountains
And the endless stretch of plains.'
The stranger then took a big gulp of beer from a large beer pot.
40 After he had rested he addressed the king:

'You who are as huge as the shadows of mountains,
I am here carrying a tale of bitterness between families.
Says my lord, I must fetch the members of his royal house.
He says you know them by their names
5 Since they are on your lips day and night.
You, the lion that drinks from its own springs,
You shall not deter others from drinking from their own springs
Indeed by your kindness you shall send your own escort
To protect your children from all the creatures of the
10   wilderness.'
As he spoke those at the Assembly seethed with anger.
Their chests heaved and fell like the waves of the ocean.
Mbengi himself did not answer; only his aide spoke:
'Such important affairs demand a patient mind.
15 You must tone down the eagerness of your heart
And wait until you have met all the members of the royal clan;
Until the whole nation, indeed, has heard
And voiced opinions about so great a message.'
The messenger yielded, knowing he could not violate their
20   customs,
Nor could he return without a word for his master.
The king of abasemaLangeni gave orders:
'Take this stranger and give him a place to sleep.
Let him, when he tells the story of this journey,
25 Attest to his children and his children's children
The bounty that is in our house.'
The mountains and valleys resounded with songs.
The bright fires sparkled through the night-afternoon.
The great feasts of the joyful ones shook the earth.
30 A woman was heard ululating in a high-pitched voice;
The bride's singers followed an uphill path.
The whole earth was filled with themes of a thousand songs.
Young men threw up the dust from their feet into the moonlight.
Such were the magic dances from the famed clan of dancers.
35 Princess Nandi stood transfixed, listening from a distant hill.
She heard these festivities in a turmoil of yesterdays.
In her mind came back a vision of her youthful days.
Then, dawn was the brilliant eye of her morning.
Old Ngazana said, as he touched her on her shoulder:
40 'It is often wise to defy all pain and say: "Tomorrow is mine!"'

Nandi was startled by this unexpected voice.
Her heart was pounding at the sound of his friendliness.
She turned, her eyes overflowing with tears of joy,
And said: 'I thank you kindly, father Ngazana.
5   I thank you for bringing new life to a dying plant.
I am grateful for the warmth that is fresh in death.
Often a sad heart forgets the rich songs in the lips of others.
I ask you for a place where I can bring up my children.
I loathe to go to my father's house with its sea of eyes.
10   I have tasted the worst and the best.
I try to hold the bitterness that stabs me,
But my bowels are torn as if by the claws of a leopard.
From the very depths of my heart I am grateful for your
          kindness.
15   I entrust myself to you, knowing how little I can repay you;
For those who sit at the crossways beg constantly for affection,
Interrupting the passerby who carries gifts to the bridegroom's
          clan,
Who travels from regions of plentifulness to regions of
20   plentifulness.
Even I who am burdened on both shoulders with disgrace
Still appeal for a better life from the Spirits of our Forefathers —
Let them grant a home for my children.'
By these words she tried to build her strength for future
25   times.
Father Ngazana consoled the daughter of the king:
'My whole humble village is your dwelling place.
All its gates are open to receive you and all your relatives.
Be happy with us — the love-epics favour our clan.
30   Many are made happy by those who are chosen by the gods
Every season of sadness shoots forth its own flower.
Its seeds are often bitter to generations to come.
For this reason I condemned your long days of sorrow,
Knowing sadness lays the snake's eggs on the paths of our
35   children.
It restrains them, breaking their own paths of life.
The tears of a mother are unbearable;
They tangle the feet of the young and seize their freedom.'
Ngazana had observed how closely Nandi protected her
40   children;

How she was obsessed with fears of unseen shadows against
    them.
Nandi, stung by these remarks, said:
'You shall never know the violent pains I have suffered,
5   When I, still in love with Senzangakhona, was discarded by
    him.
He abandoned me, my husband, my lover, the father of my
    children;
Even the scum of the earth made fun of me.
10 Many laughed at me as I crawled and begged for his love.
I, the proud woman who was born of the sun!
Often I heard whispers crawling up the sides of walls.
I heard people giggling, singing and mocking me with their
    songs.
15 I groaned with pain at their violent tongues.
Then my sole comfort was only my children.
I knew one day my son would grow to overshadow the earth.
He shall tower high above all living beings.
The little mites that mocked us shall tremble before him.
20 They shall say: "Shaka is fearful. Shaka strikes
But no one dares to strike him back." '
She spoke as if each and every star
Stood out for her memorable grudge.
Her mind stolen away by her remembered pains,
25 She wandered lost in the very presence of Ngazana.
Remembering the present things, she turned to him
And with a sigh she said: 'I am grateful to you, Father
    Ngazana.'
Then in quick strides she left him and went back to her house.
30 There she buried herself with all her secrets.

Great commotions came from many lands because of Princess
    Nandi.
Nations sat restless in their little kingdoms.
Her relative, Mbengi, only half closed his eyes in sleep.
35 Whenever he heard distant voices singing
He would say: 'Sing, children of the great nation.
Dance until you spit your sweat to the east.
When the children of Zulu come
Let them find your bodies as sharp as the battle axe.

Stab them everywhere, even in their crooked feet.'
He spoke these words alone, tying up knots of revenge,
Having vowed that Nandi should not be expelled from her
    home.

5   At this very period Madlangezwe, who was reputed for his
        wisdom,
Requested the king's audience.
The king turned to him slowly, staring with piercing eyes.
He said: 'I am exhausted from struggling with many
10   thoughts.
Continuously they leap in every direction, giving me no rest.
There is no other way beside an honourable death;
For, indeed, should we send Nandi away with her children
We shall have condemned ourselves in the eyes of many.
15   But if we shelter her, only the dead of our nation shall judge us;
People shall curse her, recalling the bloodiness of her affairs.
Orphans and widows shall weep, cursing her name.
Indeed, because of this the nation itself might be split.
Future generations may yet comment:
20   "Was all this dying justified?
Or was it to please their king they indulged in these foolish
        acts?" '
Madlangezwe listened, his body taut with concentration.
Finally he said: 'My lord, I am frightened of these words.
25   My own mind cannot grasp what is right.
Its visions seem like hills covered with mists at dawn.
Despite all my uncertainties, I know we of Langa have no
        escape.
All traditions of our Forefathers demand that we die like men.
30   Besides, even if we retreat and seek peace
We would ultimately solicit only defeat.
For often those who sue for peace and friendship too obviously
Invite only the bandit nations of the earth against them.
Those nurtured in wars treat as cowards those who fight with
35   words.
As we lie on the battlefield as dead heroes
Enemy nations still shall fear our graves,
Avoiding even the ruins of our cities.
It is for this reason I applaud your far-seeing vision.

In these times our nation can only build itself with spears.
Perhaps when Senzangakhona hears of our preparations for war
He might retreat and begin to disarm his belligerent hordes.'
With these words Madlangezwe concluded the discussion.
5 A word from the king filled him with joy:
'Issue the great call to battle.
Summon all the regiments of the land.'
At these orders the face of Madlangezwe flowered with smiles
For he knew his moment of glory was near.
10 He lurched out of the door like a buck chased by a forest fire.
He ran shouting the words of war.
He set the fires of war in every home and mountain.
Those in the valley seemed glued perpetually
To their spear-sharpening stones.
15 The messenger of Senzangakhona disturbed from his sleep,
Awoke to the fierce calls of war.
The Langa king's deputy came to him and said:
'I bring with me the great wisdom of our lord. . . . '
But before he finished, the Zulu messenger cut him short:
20 'I have heard his words from the talking mountains.'
At that very moment he set out by the same route he had come.
Sometimes he stooped to stare at the rivers that would choke
        with bodies.
He was seized by the madness of war and, talking to himself,
25 He said: 'They have dared the children of the leopard!'
On his path were great processions of heroes;
The young and the old wore the paraphernalia of battle.
He heard the roar of war songs echoing in the mountains.
When he reached the borders of his own country
30 He let his anger rise and burn like a furnace.

Senzangakhona rocked with laughter at the messenger's report.
He said to those who sat with him at the Assembly:
'I hope you have heard these challenges.
We are ordered to fetch our own children!
35 The Mhlongos dare awake the lions in their peaceful sleep!
They disturb the locusts from their sanctuaries of the north!
They challenge the Forefathers in broad daylight.'
He repeated these words to mock the message of his enemy.
The poet who was there was seized by war-madness.

His voice quivered, bursting out over the mountains
And calling the sacred names of the Forefathers.
He shouted: 'My Lord of Mqekweni, scion of Mageba,
Turbulence of Jama, like a bundle of spears!
5 You, who are surrounded by the heads of men like an anthill,
You loomed high like the pyramid stone of Zihlalo.
It befriended those who came to sharpen their spears.
We of the warrior clan, we sit and wash our feet with a white
　　stone.
10 Wily one, who is the descendant of the wily ones,
You boasted with spears, you, the lion!
You hurried under the cover of the night of Mazolo
And returned by moonlight.
The heads of men were twisted in terror.
15 You will hear them say: "Close the gates, patient one."
They do not mean you; they mean your mother, Mbulazikazi —
She who barred the lion in this house.'
As he sung these epics the poet
Leapt to the sky as if to unhinge the sun.
20 The magic powers of war spread like wild fire.
Shields of the war-hungry warriors thundered from a distance.
The hills resounded with battle songs in the lands of Malandela.
In the lands of Langa battle songs echoed in response.
Women shouted their songs of anger;
25 They entered the dark lands of the Ancestors.
They touched their feet; and shook them from sleep.
The Ancestors walked on earth, hugging their children.
The two armies faced each other across the mountains.
People killed the black bulls for the Forefathers.
30 They burnt the aromatic fat for the Ancestors.
The sweet smell spread with lightness to the Forefathers.
The voices of war echoed all night through.
From the crimson flames shone clusters of weapons.
Old men and women and children sang the songs of past heroes.

35 The great processions of regiments climbed the hills of dawn.
Behind them followed the restless clouds of vultures,
Anticipating morsels for their feast.
Senzangakhona stood tall and fierce as he urged his generals.
The two armies halted facing each other in hatred and in fear.

Nogamfela of the Khuluse clan rushed forward, shouting
And leading them in the war songs of Ndaba and Jama's heroic
    epics.
He came close to the Langa army, boasting and challenging it.
5   Long spears flew through space, falling on targets of naked flesh.
One man held his jaw, hugging tight his pain.
Everywhere were cries of half-dead men drowned by shouting
    voices.

From a distance hordes of women egged on their heroes.
10   Sometimes they raised an alarm
As sinister shadows crept round their men.
Many a hero rushed off into the forest of spears,
While the lips of iron plunged into their hearts of flesh.
They cried out, bursting their voices into the skies.
15   Their shoulders were broken like little birds.
Their intestines tumbled on the ground.
The brave commander of the abasemaLangeni people shouted:
'Enough is enough! Our family has been destroyed!'
It was because of his words
20   They fled stampeding over mounds of anthills,
Like footsteps of runaways pounding louder than those of
    elephants.
Senzangakhona's army shouted its songs of triumph.
They hugged the spears of victory, praising them with battle
25   songs.
At that very moment an old man shouted:
'It is enough, son of Jama!
Where now can we raise our children?'
As he spoke he hurriedly crossed the river.
30   In the commotion Senzangakhona's voice restrained his soldiers.
They stopped suddenly like bulls subdued by their horns.
Senzangakhona abandoned booty;
He did not interfere with Nandi and her children.
The abasemaLangeni were baffled by this act.
35   Perchance, they thought, his heart had been conquered by love.
He spoke to his army and said:
'Since I have proved the worth of my father's house,
It is enough. No more innocent blood shall be spilt.'
Senzangakhona departed, leaving Nandi like a tree

That is tossed in all directions by the wind.

When Princess Mkhabayi heard of this ignominious return
She rushed out to meet Senzangakhona with a fusillade of angry
    words:
5   'You have disgraced my father's house!
You have left bones in the fields of unfinished battles!
You return from a battle like children, empty-handed.
It is as if your "Sweetness" does not fade from memory;
She seizes your senses and plays with the blood of our nation.
10 What ruler would leave his victories unfinished
Unless he, like you, is possessed of the iron feet of cowards;
Unless, he, like you, rules only to win the acclaim of women?'
Mkhabayi sought to disabuse him of his tenderness,
Knowing such rulers often impose their indecisions on their
15   subjects.
Mkhabayi knew too, with these words
She would strengthen him against the many poison tongues
That would denounce his rule.
She rubbed this pungent herb into his wound.
20 Princess Mkhabayi was reputed for bravery and wisdom in
     Zululand:
Of her the poet said: 'Father of the wily ones,
You destroy a man as you trap him with a tale.
Slippery one, who initiated the great paths of Zululand,
25 You said: "Let all people find ways through to the capital." '
She spoke vehemently to her brother:
'My brother, son of my Forefathers, you have failed!
You shall be the saliva wetting the tongues of many nations.
They shall say of you, you lost heart at the battle of the
30   Mhlongos.
You fought and returned empty-handed;
Followed only by widows and their children.
Yet you must know: true manhood must complete what it has
     begun!
35 Those like you earn only derision of friend and enemy alike.
People mock such rulers as you.
For in our times a true ruler boasts of the spoils of other lands.'
Princess Mkhabayi denounced him, too, for leaving Nandi:
'Such acts are seen by others only as acts of foolishness.'

After listening to her without comment, Senzangakhona spoke:
'I thank you for your words, my esteemed sister.
But your thoughts do not tally with mine.
For, in truth, from the start it was my plan not to take Nandi.
5   Still, I am grateful for the gift of words from your heart.
The memory of our home shall not give Nandi any peace.
She shall not forget the joys of Zululand.
Our land boasts of generosity to its children.
Besides, it is unwise to follow a snake to its hole.
10 These days, too many kings and kinglets lure fugitives;
And with them build their great cities and countries.
Only the future shall reveal the essence of my plans.'
Mkhabayi poured on his head peals of laughter:
'Let me leave you, O King of girls and of old women.
15 Tomorrow is not yours but for kings who wield flashing spears.'
As she said this she turned away and departed,
Passing through great columns of dancers who celebrated this
        victory.
A din of song rose to the sky.
20 Even the vultures of heaven flapped their wings in joy.

Such was not the lot of those of abasemaLangeni.
Their land was filled with songs that cursed the deeds of men.
Someone shouted, cracking the stillness of the afternoon:
'The country has been laid to waste by the king's daughter.
25 I weep for Njiza who lies on the ground in the old maize field.'
As she sang, her voice climbed the ridges of the hills.
She hid her grief in the Cliffs of Eternal Echoes;
Her songs spread like the voices of travellers;
The mourning was heard by the crickets of the evening.
30 Some sang: 'Nandi's tears are like a huge ocean;
They are harsh like the taste of an aloe plant.'
Villages sang poisonous lullabies against her.
Listen to the children's songs:
'What had people done?
35 They had been warned about a woman of many affairs.
What were people saying?
They said: "Alas! Many nations shall perish."
What could seize the people at peace in their harvest?
Illegitimate children populate our land.

On our land is a chasm that is filled with earthworms.'
Nandi heard these songs and vowed in anger:
'I shall tend to my child till he is old.
He shall grow in my hands
5 Until he stands between day and night, blazing his own sun.
I shall trouble him and give him no rest.
When he tries to sleep
I shall say to him: "Awake, my child, listen to the winds!
They are calling you; they are shouting the names of your
10   Forefathers."
He shall learn and follow their heroic paths.
He shall not turn back; he shall have no fear
He shall take his weapons and sharpen their points.
He shall survive the wilderness!'
15 She spoke, feeding her memory
So that she might not forget her sadness
But would awake one day with her daggers of yesterday,
Picking her enemies one by one from the eyes of the forest.

The beautiful nights are often crowded with stars,
20 Revealing sometimes the glittering of knives.
Their sanctuaries breed deep voices of anger.
Shaka, the son of Nandi, heard the long night talking to him.
Those who spoke cut his young spirit with violent tongues.
All eyes surrounded him like those of fire.
25 Even old women who were reputed for their kindness said of
       him:
'Is this the infamous son of Nandi?'
They stabbed him with their eyes.
They whispered their endless streams of hissing words:
30 'So this is Mlilwana, the fierce-tempered boy?'
But Shaka of the tiger never bowed his head.
All feared his anger.
Even those who claimed the authority of age retreated from him.
He sharpened the horns of his clay bull and said:
35 'My bull shall never be overcome by those of upstarts.'
He was born in the time of the stubborn mountain.
Among the crowds he sat grinding his teeth.
He was possessed by the spirit of a fighting bull.
It is of him the sacred words of the ancestral epic speak.

By the sharpness of his mind he challenged his seniors.
And his wise words made him a favourite and enemy to others.
His friends wandered the forbidden paths.
Listen to their whispers as they say:
5   'His heart is a home of young puff-adders;
It is a breeding place for stratagems against others.
Often he defies the peacemaker, listing to no one.
He withdraws to a lonely stone that is his companion.
There he sits brooding, his eyes red with diabolical thoughts.
10 From these nights he emerges with vows of anger against our
        clan.'
The tears of a beast pour out and are wasted,
But those of a human being have feet and hands and lips.
Those who sung of his parent
15 Rubbed the raw wound and kept the night from sleeping.
Nandi whispered to him in the tongues of the winter winds.
And said: 'One day, my son, the forest will tremble.'
He grew tall in size and reputation
Until the day came for the ceremonial gifts for manhood.
20 They said: 'It is now we must send him to his reckless father.
From him only can he get his cloth of youth.'
He hurried there, the son of Senzangakhona,
And with unfaltering words he spoke out to his father:
'I have come to fetch the ceremonial gift of my youth!'
25 His father stared at him, disquieted by this reckless bravado.
To rid himself of this fearless youth he slaughtered a beast.
Shaka, seething with grudges, uttered only incoherent words.
That night of the feast
He dreamt of a visitation from the Forefathers.
30 They came to him and said: 'Take courage, Somlilo.
One day you will grow in fame beyond the stars.
You will cast your shadow over nations far beyond the horizon.
Nations of the earth shall sing of you;
Great heroes and heroines shall pay you their tribute.
35 They shall talk of you until the sun falls into eternal darkness.'
Over many years he harboured these words in his mind.
To contain this anger he cried out in an inconsolable outburst.
No longer were his tears those of a child
But of someone who knew the horror of closed lips and moving
40   eyes,

Who had found no warm embrace even from his own parent.
When Shaka arrived at his mother's home he was silent.
He did not speak much of his stay in Zululand.
The day after, before the sun rose from the southern hills,
5   The voices of his playmates exploded from the mountains.
They declaimed his poem of excellence, saying:
'Beautiful one of our clan, of whom they asked Nandi:
"Who is this with whom you enter?"
She said: "I come with a royal spear of Ndaba,
10 The sharp tip of a spear from the nations of Nguniland."
The silent walker, who travels alongside the black inclines,
He said: "I shall cover my eyes to espy the lion,
To spread alarm to his cousins of abasemaLangeni."
He is as huge as the oceans on which the sun rays dance.
15 The cowards and runaways shall choke in his presence,
The great gift that has been bequeathed to our family!
He said: "I am this nourishment for all creatures."
He cast his shadow of Malandela over them.
He made people listen from the open valleys
20 And made their poisonous tongues shrivel like leaves.'
Shaka shot out, bragging of his ancestry of Jama,
His youth blazing like an uncontrollable flame.
The wild men of Hlabisa terrorized all travellers,
But Shaka was not like those who stretched their arms in terror.
25 He woke up with the power-charm in his mouth.
The charm reinforces the mind. He said:
'When you have overcome the sorcerous bandits
People shall emerge and travel freely on earth.'
Thus was Shaka named 'The Fearless Young of the Sacred
30   Snake'.
One day, indeed, he did see a snake climb his leg.
He stared at it, eyeball to eyeball, until it retreated in terror.

Many celebrated and danced at the royal city of Senzangakhona.
Princess Mkhabayi was there.
35 Queen Mkhabi was there.
Langazana was there.
These were the favourites of King Senzangakhona.
It was in these times King Mbengi gave Shaka the heroic poem:
'No longer is he a boy, but a young lion

That breaks the necks of wild buffaloes.
We took the horns to make our smoking pipes and rejoiced.
The black mamba shall arrive.
It shall find the fierce son of Zulu awaiting it!'
5   Shaka's fame spread through these words of praise.
Even the scar in his mind began to heal,
For, indeed, people receive their joys from others.
Shaka was young again and his spirit rose to the sun.
His visions walked their seasons into future times.
10 Under the shade of the mountain
The prophets spoke for their children.
Mkhabayi saw the rays of the sun
And knew then there was born again a royal heir to the
      Forefathers.
15 She watched and listened to his tales of fame:
How he had harassed and chased his challengers.
Even his own friends and relatives scolded him for his madness.
It was said he had inherited the black mood of the snake.
He spoke to trembling plants alone;
20 He shouted and beat their bended branches.

Senzangakhona had long ears for news.
He heard and carefully listened to Shaka's fame.
He wished this honour could go to his favourite sons and
      daughters,
25 Counting amongst them the arrogant Prince Sigujana,
The proud and erratic Prince Dingane, the soft-hearted Prince
      Mhlangana,
The beautiful daughter, Princess Nozinhlanga,
And his heir, Prince Bhakuza.
30 His guilt ate at him like a restless worm.
He knew, too, should this section of his house grow in power
It would cast a threatening shadow over all his children.
When Mkhabayi saw these growing fears
She poured salt on the wound and said:
35 'Son of my father, your reign grows between two hostile winds.
The abasemaLangeni bear you bitter grudges.
Your reign shall overflow with pools of blood.
The sun on which you fix your gaze is setting.
As it sinks it brings with it its fierce night.

It shall take into its bowels the heads of men.'
She spoke like this, spilling out her own anger,
Outraged at the feebleness of Senzangakhona's rule,
Whose power depended on the friendship of the Mthethwa king.
5 To him he always sent softening gifts of friendship.
Mkhabayi's words stung Senzangakhona and in despair
He said to his sister: 'You are like a sorcerer,
Like a witch who prospers from the tears of others.
I boast only the love of the Zulu nation.
10 We are a proud nation; we beg from no one.'
He spoke this way to restore his own faith,
To beg her to give him the fruits of her envied power.
He knew she alone was the voice to whom all paid tribute.
Her visions were like the long tails of lightning.
15 From her mind's branches the traveller crossed the flooded
      rivers.
Mkhabayi said to her brother:
'It does not pay to pride oneself in a limited peace.
Your son, Prince Shaka, grows in reputation and in power.
20 Rumour tells of his courage and intelligence.
Be wise, send your trusted messenger to bring him back.
Before long your own subjects may demand his return.
They may soon rail against you for your acts of cruelty,
Saying: "With Shaka our future could have been a great one." '
25 It was as though she knew the very words uttered by Sojiyisa.
Of Shaka people often whispered behind the unsuspecting king:
'I predicted this boy's future.
His eyes shone in his childhood like those of a lion cub.
If only the king had ignored the venomous tongues of his women
30 We too would have prided ourselves in a great hero.'
Thus they gossiped and talked of the affairs of state.
Adding, too, that Senzangakhona was not like his father, the
      brave King Jama.
Senzangakhona took the beer pot and drank.
35 He pretended he dismissed the claims of his sister, but he was
      troubled.
He said: 'My great sister, this beer pot from which I drink
Is one which was given to me by my father, Jama.
He said to me, "Drink from this beer pot, my son,
40 And never be afraid of the stampede of feet.

Often people rush and whip up dust in all directions,
Invoking others to join them in their haste but to no avail.
They are blinded by their own enthusiasms.
You, wiser than them, must pace behind, watching their
5   footsteps.
Indeed, however fast you may race you will not earn their love.
However much you may give of your treasures and powers
None of this will satisfy their appetites.
They shall enter through the small gate into your royal
10   enclosure,
Breaking the taboos, letting themselves roam at will,
Until finally they shall demand the secrets of your bowels!''
I can still hear the vibrations of my father's voice.
It is only the Ancestors who know how to guide us.
15 It is to them only that I shall humble myself.'
Mkhabayi quickly responded: 'How terrible a thing is ignorance!
The words of the wise change with each generation.
Woe unto those who cling to them even after their era!
The Ancestors, son of my father, feed those who feed themselves.
20 They are like a ceremonial staff from which our strength issues;
With it we cross the deep and treacherous rivers.
The beginnings and endings of our actions
Issue from where we light the flames of our power.
I do not ignore the words of our Forefathers,
25 But I scatter in their fertile fields the seeds of our own
     generation.'
After Mkhabayi had uttered these words she suddenly left.
He sat there alone, grinding the truths of his sister's words.
In vain he tried to uproot them from his mind.
30 They rushed back like torrents flooding an ancient river.

Dawn speared eternally from the horizon.
From the earth are often many things unknown.
Senzangakhona on this day called his councillors and said:
'I am obsessed with some unsettling thoughts.
35 I try to erase them from my mind, but they emerge again.
Everywhere I look I see a vision of my son, Shaka.
I see him standing over me with a sharpened dagger.
It is as if my whole body is bound by a rope.
With each dream he seems to come closer and closer to me,

His mouth frothing with hatred.'
The councillors were all surprised at these words,
For in all these years never had the name of Shaka been
    mentioned.
5 Senzangakhona continued, addressing them:
'When I told Mdlanga, the son of Sobhada, of these things
He said: "Only one solution is there for our nation:
To lure your son to his capture and death."
But how can I destroy my own blood?
10 Do not our great Ancestors say:
"To spill the blood of a relative is an eternal curse to families?"
These wise words I wish to abide by;
But I am also loyal to the living Zulu nation.
Through the slogans of our Forefathers
15 We may yet suffer some irreparable disasters.'
An old man sought to speak after these words.
His face seemed shrunken from a thousand suns.
He said: 'I am old; I have seen many seasons.
If some bandit should say:
20 "I shall kill you or else your children",
I would gladly say: "Kill me, because when they are dead, I am
    dead."
But should it be to save our nation,
It is I who would take a dagger and kill them.
25 For no nation survives if it lives only for the present.
The great task of our time is to protect this seed.
A nation must sacrifice its children to preserve its shrines.'
The old man now breathed as if he had run a race.
Silence travelled through the Assembly like the voices of the
30   night.
To round up his words, the old man finally said:
'Let people say: "Here lies the children of the king
Who died so that the nation might live."
Let them speak for us. Let them speak for our children's
35   children!'
Senzangakhona was silent.
Only his close and longest-serving attendant spoke:
'Indeed, these are beautiful and wise words.
But how often do people get carried away by their thoughts,
40 How many carry out the lessons of their own sermons?

I do see the problems confronting our king.
I suggest Shaka be exiled to distant lands.
For indeed, a plant whose sweet fruits grow in the wilderness
Feeds no one of its succulent juices.
5 It falls to the ground to be eaten only by worms.
So also shall Shaka's fame waste itself in distant lands.'
Scarcely had he finished uttering these words
Than many began to challenge his comments.
It was a dark-looking man of Vumaneni who spoke:
10 'These words come from a mind devoid of maturity.
No one in the Assembly is ignorant of the bravery of Khuzani.
Even when the king said to him: "Enough!
Let the younger men fight the enemy in the front line",
He simply said: "So long as I have strength I shall fight."
15 None could label him a coward who doesn't abide by his words.
Many times he has foretold coming dangers by his wisdom.
Let the truth of his words guide our actions.
A nation survives through the sacrifices of its children.
Had I the power I would take on my shoulders this challenge.'

Book Three: The worst time of exile

*The conflict between the abasemaLangeni and the Zulus is not helped
by Shaka's growing reputation as a fighting youth. Senzangakhona is
jealous of this reputation and his aunt, Princess Mkhabayi, already
sees in Shaka a great future ruler. The abasemaLangeni, angered by
Nandi and her children as a source of conflict, petition the king for
their expulsion. They leave, embittered by this drastic act. They undertake a long and hazardous journey to seek asylum among their cousins,
the Qwabes. The journey is real but is also symbolic of Shaka's transition to manhood. The sun is indicative of the power with which
Shaka shall overcome all odds to become one of the great leaders.*

In the middle of a fierce night, in the season of the black clouds,
Sharpened daggers were raised for the killing.
Screams tore the blue garments of the sky;
On the horns of a sleeping bull voices bellowed into the night.
5   The neighbouring hills echoed: 'Bandits are killing our
        children!'
The fighting clubs crunched the fragile skulls.
Senzangakhona's men roamed in the villages of emaLangeni.
Someone who had sat whispering tales was suddenly silenced.
10   The drunkard who had lain on the ground
Rose from his prostrate garden of stars and fled.
The children of Ngazana shouted a call to battle.
As the young men of emaLangeni hurried to their weapons
Only the footprints of the Zulus marked their devastation.
15   The fighting men of Senzangakhona hurried back to report their
        deeds:
'It is accomplished; your wishes have been fulfilled.'
As they spoke the giant village-city of Ngazana was in flames.
The inhabitants fled to the mountains.
20   Shaka himself escaped only by the kindness of the Ancestors.
Through their love they had forewarned him,
Making his body tremble with pain and imagined battles.
Agitated, he chose to sleep on a secret spot on the outer fence.
In the fray he plunged his knife into an unsuspecting raider
25   And ripped the long strands of his intestines.
Like a log the enemy fell into a long flat stone.

Despite Shaka's feats of courage and many poems of praise
He did not win the love of all.
Many cursed him for fomenting these eternal wars.
30   Angrily they demanded Nandi's exile.
When Shaka heard of these protests, he said to his parent:
'There are still other lands that are open to us.'
As he spoke tears came down his face in big drops of anger.
He vowed: 'I shall come back, I swear by Nomchoba.
35   Then I shall be wearing a blanket of flames like a forest.
My enemies shall sleep lightly on their elbows.
The scars of the wronged never heal.'
Those who saw Nandi depart with her children
Thrust their long necks to spout their venom.

They stabbed her mind with words: 'Nandi gave birth to an
    animal.
His heart is like that of an old black mamba.'
Yes, even the poet says of these days:
5 'They gossiped about you, my lord, the women of Nomgabi,
They sat basking in the sun, saying:
"Shaka shall never rule, he shall never be king."
But he grew up to envelope the earth.'

Ngazana, enfeebled and weakened, bade them farewell.
10 He said to Nandi: 'I am nothing, my Princess,
Your era is the era of uncontrollable whirlwinds.
They shall lift quiet homes from their grounds.
I wish on you a great future.
May you grow to overshadow all your enemies.'
15 Ngazana gave them provisions
And uttered words of supplication to the Forefathers,
Begging them to give them their blessings.
Nandi took her child, Nomchoba, on her back, and said:
'Even when I no longer have strength
20 I shall beg no one for their kindness.'
She spoke defiantly, despite the terrors she knew lay ahead of
    her.

They traversed the evening when it was still tender,
Until it ripened into a night of a million million stars.
25 The earth opened its mouth, letting out the great moon.
It climbed the high cliffs to the left of the forest,
And it dropped its webs of glistening light.
It gave us tales of fantasy, visiting us with dreams.
All days are born of pain from the ocean.
30 The earth disgorges each day from the boundaries of a fierce
    night.
Nandi followed the mountain path
Until, tired, she descended on the house of Lubhadu.
It spread in an open valley, following the bend of a hundred
35   hills.
Here they shouted their greetings on the silent grounds.
It was Zingili of the great Mkhize clan who suddenly emerged.

He was the son of Nonyane of Ndongeni.
Seeing them by the light of the moon, he said:
'No longer do you greet merely to celebrate friendship,
Your shoulders seem slouched from oppressive tiredness.
5   But, alas! here no strangers are welcomed.
I myself am only a traveller saved from my fate by others.
This village is owned by one notorious Lubhadu,
Who is known throughout for his beastliness and wizardry;
Even now he faces charges from many neighbouring regions.
10 Once two young men asked for a place to sleep
But were never seen again.
The instrument that killed them has killed many a traveller
It is said perchance having fought in many wars
He never received the cleansing herbs used to neutralize a man's
15   fierceness.
Even his own family lives in constant fear of him.'
Suddenly a fierce man appeared, shouting and growling at them:
'Who are these who enter my house by night?
Do not the forests have a place for people to sleep?'
20 Nandi, determined to mellow the beast
And concerned, too, for the fate of her children, said softly:
'The great forests are the homes of wild animals.'
The man flicked his eyes, starring at them from head to foot.
Finally he directed them to a large house.
25 They tiptoed as they entered, fearing the lurking shadows.
On the high point of the side pillar hung a giant bag,
Whose secrets all were curious to know.
They guessed that it might contain the medicines of death,
But it was not so; it carried only bones of birds and animals.
30 By hunting these creatures he assuaged his bloodthirstiness.
The strangers sat in fear of his sudden violence.
To break their anxieties, Shaka spoke and said:
'We salute you! We have travelled a long journey,
We are tired, we are hungry, we are dying of thirst.
35 Our bodies ache and wither from the heat of the sun.
We ask you for a place to sleep to ease our aching feet.'
The man frowned as if in anger, but did not answer.
He seemed to struggle with terrible words and fierce thoughts.
Finally he stood up, leaving them perplexed.
40 Not long after a young woman entered their house.

Quietly and with kindness she led them to their sleeping place,
And dished up for them great helpings of food.
They ate fast, not knowing what was to follow.
No sooner had they finished
5 Than sleep descended gently upon their shoulders.
Only Zingili of the Mkhizes paced the house ceaselessly.
'Strange things are going to happen tonight,' he kept mumbling.
He was not mistaken. In the middle of the night
High-pitched voices pierced the air.
10 Someone was following with thundering footsteps.
The young man of the Mkhizes peered through an opening
And saw by moonlight shadows moving restlessly.
It was as if a body was laid down on the ground.
Someone stood astride it and dragged it by the legs.
15 When he reached the upper end of the sprawling grounds
He rubbed off the dust from his hands,
Placing the body against an old wall.
Zingili rushed to wake up the others.
In low tones he recounted the strange episodes.
20 Shaka listened, but before long he was asleep again.
Zingili was puzzled by this calmness.
He slept in terror, as if someone might pounce on them.
Early, at dawn, Shaka woke up and calmly collected their bags.
'Wake up, mother,' he said. 'Let us begin our journey.'
25 Quietly they left by the back gate, through the dumping
        grounds.
They walked a long distance without talking,
No one daring to mention the events of the night.
When they decided to sit and rest it was Zingili who spoke first:
30 'Young man from countries unknown to me, are you brave or
        foolish
To ignore the warnings of danger?'
Shaka turned slowly towards him and said:
'In danger two courses of action are wrong:
35 To act precipitately brings the threat nearer;
To slacken one's alertness enables the enemy to strike.
Heroes are not those who rush to their weapons,
But those who carefully weigh all strategies.
If because of your alarm this night
40 We all had panicked, we would all be dead.

The killers who kill are great cowards;
They only avail themselves of the fear of others.
Panic-stricken, they attack too late or too soon.
It is at this moment that you must strike.
5   This night I saw how outnumbered we were.
Our escape could only have been possible through the
      Ancestors.'
The young man of the Mkhize clan realized then
He did not converse with an immature boy but a seasoned
10   mind.
He turned to Nandi and said:
'Mother, you have given birth to a great man.'
Nandi did not say anything; she only smiled,
Remembering the vision that had named him 'Little Fire'.
15 To calm him she often said: 'Little Fire, your day will
     come.'
Zingili and Nandi shook hands. He followed the path to the
     north.
There the great Dlamini royal clan held sway.
20 Nandi and her children once again set out,
Crossing the little rivers and the wide, open valleys.
They saw mountains that were gaunt with eternal hunger,
As though they could swallow whole nations.
The forests stood forbidding and threatening,
25 Thrusting their night over the earth.
It was as if they would envelope the whole world.
But our earth is often rescued by the great paths of infinity.

Nandi and her children walked past processions of women,
Some were carrying gifts to wedding feasts;
30 Some were singing the great songs of the First Fruit Festival.
They walked until they reached the great village of Mzimela.
From every part of Nguniland kings and princes sought his
     wisdom,
Each luring him with promises of greater wealth.
35 Now they bypassed the village of Ntunwana, famed for his
     courage.
They climbed the Hills of the Tortoise and followed an old path.
Here their shadows ran into a little river
Where bridges of stones were worn smooth by rains.

This was the same stream in which strangers washed their feet.
From here they climbed the hill following the eastern side.
Bordering this were old mountain cairns.
These stood as monuments to all ancient generations.
5 Nandi and her children threw their ceremonial stones and said:
'Let us not be forgotten by generations to come!'
From the low mountainside they saw a young woman
Who danced and sang her songs of joy.
She picked up her own ceremonial stone, and said:
10 'May I join the singers of the song
And the daughters of the dance who came before me!'
On to this mountain cairn another traveller tossed his sacred
        stone.
His movements were slow and his heart was heavy
15 And so were his gestures to the gods.
His stone sought that of others, tumbling slowly to rest there.
Such a day gives birth to great mysteries.
It was with these footsteps they climbed the hill,
And saw the sun conquering the forests of clouds.
20 It flung its flames, swelling their feet with fire.
Travellers who saw them touched their lips in amazement.
For those rejected by fate find no friendship anywhere.
People often asked each other in jest:
'Does the woman who walks alone in the mountain paths
25 Have no brothers and no husband?'
No one answered; no one sang their song.
Still they travelled on, following the path of the ancient routes
And sleeping under the white lights of stars.
From every direction they heard nocturnal voices,
30 For often fear creeps over the body like a poisonous spider.
Sharp screams throttle the night,
Making dawn a vast field of joy, revealing long fibres of the
        forest.
Paths were covered with white clouds of mists.
35 They asked those they met the direction of the city of King
        Khondlo.
'You are, indeed, in the lands of our great king.
We in truth are his messengers.
We are sent to the river to bring the royal charms;
40 With these the high priest shall perform the ancient ceremony,

Cleansing the fearful powers of the dying year.
Throughout the land no one sees the king.
He sits at his sacred house,
Meditating the deeds of the Beautiful Ones, the Ancestors.
5   Then he rises at dawn to make a rainbow.
The year begins with the sign of plentifulness.
The king then enters the round house of voices
There to be anointed with the leopard's oil,
To have his forehead marked with royal signs.
10 He is not for one man but for all generations.
He must learn his lesson from others.
He is the keeper who preserves the people's symbols.
The children of the sun have a star in their eyes;
They stare at the fire; it does not burn their eyelashes.
15 Such power comes from all generations and from the Ancestors.'

Nandi and her children were welcomed among the Qwabes.
King Khondlo opened his heart to them,
Ordering his relative Prince Gendeyana to give them a home.
Gendeyana was like a father to the young Prince Shaka;
20 Shaka in all his life never forgot his love.
Of this association his close brother, Prince Ngwadi, was born.
Nandi and her children found shelter and kindness there.
But not the young Prince Shaka.
Prince Phakathwayo, the heir, often sought to prove his
25   manhood through him.
Jealous of Shaka and yet older, he often made fun of him.
He chose the moment of many eyes and ears
When laughter would ring from his whole obsequious retinue.
Before great crowds he would shout:
30 'Shaka is nothing but a wild man.
He eats with a weapon in one hand, fending the dog with
        another.'
Shaka never forgot these insults.
Abandoning his relatives of the Qwabe clan,
35 He set out to serve as a recruit in the army of the Mthethwas.
His heart swelling with anger and bitterness,
He followed the path they had taken
And travelled on until he passed the emaLangeni regions.
From there he walked past the Ndundulu

And then veered past the small mountain of Nkwenkwe.
Tired, he stopped at the great settlement of Madloku of
    emaNgadini,
Then he travelled on, crossing the Imfule river.

5 Across these grounds he threw a stone he carried in his hand
And said at the cairn: 'May my life make our nation great.'
From the Ancestors he asked for their blessings.
He climbed up, approaching the path to Luwamba.
It was this great man who presented him with a fighting club,
10 Saying: 'May the Ancestors bless you with a successful life.
May you grow up to be as wise and great as Malandela.'
Shaka thanked him and walked on
Finally he reached the village of Prince Mpukunyoni of the
    Mthethwas.
15 This man was the tutor who looked after the king's children.
For Shaka of the Zulus life was never to be the same again.
The shadows of the past dissolved in the new sun.
He grew proud and generous and full of confidence,
For those who are loved never fail.

Book Four: Mthethwa Kingdom and the rise of Shaka

After a period of intrigue, Dingiswayo (formerly Godongwana) ascends the Mthethwa throne, having lived in exile before his father King Jobe died. Dingiswayo creates a confederation of states which acknowledges the Mthethwa state as the central power. It is among the Mthethwas that Shaka learns a great deal about statecraft. He also gets there an opportunity to put into practice some of his military tactics and theories. With the help of Dingiswayo Shaka emerges as a serious, responsible young man, eager to create a powerful, centralized state.

Prince Godongwana was the son of King Jobe of the Mthethwas.
In his youth he was consumed by a desire to rule.
He called on his brother, Prince Tana, and said bluntly:
'Our father is old and no longer can he effectively rule.
5 Complaints come from various parts of the country,
Denouncing the ineptness of his rule.
People are begging us to take over the reins of power.'
Tana pretended these thoughts were new to him,
Though he, too, had heard many such rumours and protests.
10 He said, answering and acting surprised at these ideas:
'These are fearful words about our own father.
After all, though he is old his deeds have not aged.
Those who complain do so only to elicit our approval.
It is we they believe should spill the blood of their king.
15 They protest today, selecting their targets according to the
     times,
Awaiting the moment when we, too, shall rule.
Then they shall begin again with their new denouncements.
Hence always they shall remain rulers above rulers.
20 We should not be swept away by these young rivers
Loosing the sweetness and depth of ancient waterfalls.'
With these words Tana desired to dig deeper into Godongwana's
     heart.
When Godongwana replied his words were round and thoughtful.
25 He said: 'My brother, you know the truth,
Though you still keep it hidden from others.
You know I am speaking thoughts in your own mind.
I know all the rules and plots that go with power.
Often greatness demands to be nourished with blood.
30 If we fail, the nation shall always blame its children.
It shall say of us: "The children of the king never grew.
They were eternally overshadowed by the old regime."
They shall blame us for all the pestilence in the land.
It is for this we must summon up courage and act.'
35 After he had spoken Tana was silent,
His mind preoccupied with many fermenting thoughts.
Finally he said: 'Your words are like a razor's edge
Which, while cutting the boil and relieving the pain,
Slips into the region of the raw flesh.
40 How can I answer them? They are too challenging.

45

Never in my life have I ever had to shed blood.
Even now I fear the eyes that may be watching us.
The leaves themselves seem bent to listen.'
He spoke now in agreement with his brother,
5   Knowing their debates had only been words in the wind.
To allow the mind time to devise its own strategies
And to nourish itself at its own pace.

The children of Jobe were treacherous.
Before their father they bowed very low.
10   In their long robes of leopard skin they hid daggers.
One solemn night of a million stars they met.
Prince Godongwana peered into all the nooks.
Satisfied, he said to his brother: 'It is done!
A trusted young man shall execute our plans.
15   He shall enter his quiet place of sleep with a knife
And cut in two his rope of life.'
It was the son of Somhlola he spoke of.
Even in his childhood he was the favourite of the king.
He roamed freely like the king's own children.
20   He too knew all the deep secrets of the royal city.
Prince Tana commented in whispers:
'Can you truly trust this favourite of the king?
Great affairs must always be concealed under the headrest.
When we have told them to others
25   No longer can they remain our secrets.'
But his brother spoke fervently and with boastful courage:
'This man I could trust though I were in a deep sleep.
Like a true brother he is with unswerving loyalty.'
There was no time for doubts. He now turned to the young
30   man
And carefully retold the story for his brother's hearing.
The young man consented, vowing by the light of dawn
And by its fire it shall see a new reign;
Witnessing with its own eyes thunderous salutations to a new
35   king.
While all this was happening voices broke the night's silence.
It was as though they issued from violent quarrelling.
The door of their house was flung open;
Then entered those who were armed with daggers and spears.

46

They rushed at them in their secret meeting.
Tana was heard amidst the commotion calling out in pain.
Godongwana escaped, creeping alongside a friendly fence,
Passing through the proud regiments of the king's village.
5 He finally entered the quiet place of his sister's residence.
In confused words he spoke of the dead and the dying,
And told her of their encounter with the king's guards.
She reminded him how their father's anger knew no limits.
She urged him: 'Run without stopping,
10 Even when you reach the very ends of the earth.'
As she spoke she saw the bleeding wound on his side.
Godongwana said no more.
Embracing her with tears he fled into distant regions.

He sought asylum among the Hlubis of King Bhungane.
15 Bhungane was feared by all who lived near the Khahlamba
    mountains.
In the safety of this brave and friendly nation
Godongwana lived, still tormented by visions of his home.
He was never at peace.
20 He rejected the compassionate words of friends,
Constantly fighting the shadows of his enemies.
Even on the day he single-handedly killed a lion
People praised his bravery but denounced his fierceness.
He chastised himself for this fame,
25 Thinking how these episodes could reach his father.
Those who praised him only earned his hostility.
In Mthethwaland many still spoke affectionately of him.
In their secret meetings they often protested:
'How can we endure the rule of an old man
30 When the country still boasts of the young and the wise?'
Many kept to themselves the secret of his very existence.
Some had now despaired,
Claiming Godongwana had long died in the wilderness.
Perhaps he felt their desires; perhaps it was only his heart.
35 Yet always he mourned:
'How terrible the fate of a man in exile!
I am a wanderer roaming in foreign lands.
I have earned the name of Dingiswayo, 'The Exiled One'.
Life in exile stole my youth.

Often I have to salute a low breed of upstarts.'
It was as if the Ancestors heard his protests.
A message from Mthethwaland reached him at this very time:
'King Jobe no longer lives.
5   He has gone forever to the land of the Forefathers.'
His heart swelled with tears and memories and regrets.
He sang the songs and poems of his Forefathers.
With both hands upraised in salutation he cried:
'I make this sign to wish you a pleasant journey, my father.
10   May our Forefathers meet you early in the labyrinths of the
        dead.'

The Ancestors, it was said, now directed the fate of the
        Mthethwa nation,
For at this moment there came the Creature-Without-
15   Good-Breeding.
This man desired a short-cut route to Delagoe Bay.
Dingiswayo did not hesitate; he offered himself,
Hoping this way ultimately to reach his home.
At dawn they set out with the Creature-Without-Manners
20   Who spoke ceaselessly of his own country's greatness,
Claiming a high vision given only to those of his race.
As he spoke Dingiswayo paid no heed,
His mind preoccupied only with the affairs of Mthethwaland.
Dingiswayo said to those with him in the 'House of Strangers':
25   'Wake me up before the last cock of dawn.
I desire to reach my home at the earliest moment.'
As the Creature-Without-Manners babbled his endless tales
Others spoke of him in hushed tones.
They suspected he was one with those
30   Who killed the Xhosas at Ncibe river.
Some said he was the same man, known as Mahlekehlathini,
Who raped the daughter of Kali of Mbokazi hills.
On this night they decided to avenge those of Xhosaland.
Overhearing these things, Dingiswayo seized a horse of the
35   Pig-of-the-Sea.
Throughout Mthethwaland it was announced:
'The rightful heir of Jobe has come.'
Like fire the news spread through the land of the Mthethwas.
Dingiswayo's heroic poems were sung everywhere.

Even those who had denounced him rallied to him.
Some spoke of a monster he brought whose head reached the
      skies.
Pandemonium and panic caused laughter in others.
5   Dingiswayo assembled his men, one of whom was an old man,
      who said:
'Since I knew the king's children it is not I you must convince,
But those who demand with doubt to see your scar.'
Dingiswayo raised his cloak, revealing the bite of the angry
10   spear.
He recounted the names of old villages and old families.
Finally he led them to the graves of his Forefathers.
There he sung their great anthems and declaimed their epics.
His face was wet with tears.
15   Those who had known the old days wept also.
He addressed them: 'You, the treasured minds of our nation,
You shall open the way and begin a new era.
Your name shall be praised by all generations to come.'

Mawewe, who was now king by default,
20   Panicked as the numbers of Dingiswayo's followers swelled.
He fled to safer regions but was killed by Dingiswayo's agents.
Dingiswayo quickly mobilised the Mthethwa armies
And infused in them the old spirit of heroes and heroines.
With this courage they ventured to far-distant lands,
25   Entering in triumph many regions of Nguniland.
He vowed: 'I shall break the necks of the troublesome bulls.'
The Mthethwa kingdom became the haven of many harassed
      nations.
From many regions people sang of Dingiswayo's greatness.
30   'Great lord of lords, we come for shelter.
Our lands are infested with marauding bandits and heartless
      rulers.'
There were kings without mercy, like Phungashe, like Zwide;
Who created commotion and fear in all parts of Nguniland.
35   But Dingiswayo welcomed and embraced the fugitives.
He gave them a place of safety.
The Mthethwa empire was known as the region of tranquillity.
Nation after nation applauded his reign.
Even those lurking in the outposts of Delagoe Bay

Sent to him their representatives of trade.
Royal villages emerged in every part of the land;
Nations and peoples crowded his court with tributes of gifts and
    praise.

5   Shaka found a place to rest his mind.
His new home was filled with endless laughter.
Summer sprouts its new leaves from the buds of winter,
The growing lion learns to fight from its parent.
Here Shaka lived with many young men of his own age.
10 Raising his tall frame from the ground, he would say:
'Here I can rest. I feel at last a man among men.
No one here questions anyone's origins.'

Shaka and General Bhuza of his youth's brigade often debated.
It was in this brigade of iziChwe that Shaka planted his thought
15 He often argued: 'Speed determines the outcome of battle.
A great army strikes like lightning and devastates like a
    thunderbolt.'
In his regiment were many famous heroes.
Amongst them was the much-praised Mgobhozi-of-the-
20   Mountain.
With him and Nqoboka, Shaka shared a close friendship.
Enemy armies fled in terror from them.
For these episodes Shaka was named 'The Unbeatable One'.
Of him they said: 'Only speed in flight can save a man.
25 Let such a man carry his hands on his head like a woman.'
Shaka spoke once to Bhuza: 'My lord, great general,
Something haunts my mind and troubles my sleep.
We launch our campaigns in all parts of the land.
Our skill lies only in flinging the long-stemmed spear.'
30 Then such were the wars of our forefathers:
Whenever an army exhausted its supplies
Then such were the wars of our Forefathers:
Whenever an army exhausted its supplies
Then members would flee to join their crowd of spectators.
35 Each side would sing and dance to outdo the other.
Sometimes the two armies would send to the arena their bravest
    men.
It was on one such occasion a Mthethwa general ordered:

'Let the bravest in your army face our bravest man.'
His candidate was a fierce-looking man with muscles of iron.
Many feared him, trusting only to their feet.
No sooner had the general spoken than he began to move,
5 Flexing his muscles and bending his legs like a gigantic tree.
He groaned like a bull that had recently been stung by wasps.
From the opposing side came the Dweller-of-the-Round-
     Mountains.
The clash of weapons, the writhing of muscles,
10 The swivelling movement of arms,
The thundering of feet, the challenging ram,
The clash of heads like two bounding boulders —
The spectators stood entranced by this spectacle.
The wild cry of 'Surrender! The eagle!'; the tears of the rabbit;
15 Crestfallen and defeated they turned back, singing in discord.
It was such half-hearted battles that incensed Shaka.
He uttered doctrines never heard in Mthethwaland before.
'How many times have we gone to battle and returned without
     victory?
20 We conquer and yet come back like the vanquished.
The defeated re-emerge, again and again. They launch new
     wars.
Like the menace of weeds in a fertile field they are.
The weapons we carry are long spears of fragile wood.
25 Each one who can carve carves his own weapon.
Many return empty-handed, having exhausted their supplies of
     iron.
Yet victory must be final.
The enemy must be chased and trapped in his own home.
30 Then he shall not raise his head again.'
As he said these words many listened silently,
Doubting the wisdom of these new ideas
And claiming this strategy was an open gate to bloodshed.
Was it not true, they asked, the king's fame lay in his kindliness?
35 Was it not this that won him many hearts?
Surely, they reasoned, war is for subjugation, not destruction?
Such outrageous assaults against a victim
Might build allies who might rally to his support,
Eager to stem the tide of bitterness
40 And vowing the destroyer should himself be destroyed.

As generals and regiments argued, puzzled by these ideas,
Shaka stood up and picked a long spear from General
  Bhuza's feet.
He broke it in pieces like a light reed and said:
5 'How can anyone fight with this thin-marrowed piece of wood?
How can such feeble twigs support empires and kingdoms?'
Some began to see his persuasive logic.
He continued: 'I ask of you, great general,
Give me your consent to mould my own weapons,
10 To shape my shield with which to parry my enemies.
When I have completed these tasks
Grant that I fight alone, a body of men.
Let them throw their spears at me at will.'
From every side came applause of this imagined battle.
15 Mgobhozi, who trusted in him, stood up and said:
'Brother of the battlefield, we shall be together in that battle.'

When Shaka was granted this wish
He set out to the Mbonambi clans, the makers of intricate iron.
He told the amazed listeners his own ideas:
20 'I want a spear made short and of the toughest wood.
Even as I stab the trunk of a tree, let it remain firm.
I shall pay for such a spear with my choicest beasts.'
As he spoke he pointed to his cattle in the cattle-fold.
Their flesh trembled with fatness.
25 The Mbonambi experts consented but derided these ideas,
Knowing how many believed victory comes from shape of
  weapons.
On the second day the spear-maker summoned him:
'Young man of Zululand, your weapon is done,
30 But one question obsesses me:
How will you use such a spear for missile-battles?'
Shaka smiled and only said:
'Father, I shall not throw my precious spear.
I shall come close to the man and hug him with my weapons.'
35 The old man shook his head, puzzled at these ideas.
He said: 'Take your gift of beasts.
Give me only from those of your future triumphs.
It seems I shall die at the beginning of an era.
I give you my blessing, child of Nguniland.

Let it be your fate to conquer.
But never forget those who prophesied your greatness.'
Shaka departed, his mind in turmoil,
Sensing a generous blessing of the Forefathers.
5 He ran his hand over his weapon,
Caressing the shaft and its blade with his long fingers.
Often he laughed loud as though siezed by some madness.

As he reached his agemates of the iziChwe regiment
A young fighter ran forward, declaiming his poems.
10 It was as though he sensed the fires of war in him.
Shaka said, restraining him:
'I am grateful to you for these words, Sontongela.'
Examining his spear, testing its thrust,
And shaking it in all directions,
15 Shaka commented: 'From this weapon shall come a plan
That shall be parent to all my strategies.
With my black shield I shall cover and hook the enemies,
Taking them with my shadow into their night.
By my sister, I swear, I shall finish them!'
20 They looked at each other, still confused at these words.
He called aside Nqoboka and demonstrated on him his device.
He hooked him and swivelled him around with his shield.
Then he laughed, as if he had discovered a secret.
He said: 'Tomorrow I need someone who can run,
25 Who, with an antelope's speed can cross the whole wide field.
Should he outrun me he shall take all my cattle.'
They accepted this, thinking it only a young man's frivolous
        joke.
Next day at dawn the fleet-footed young men stood boasting,
30 Waiting at the end of a long stretch of land.
Then, suddenly, like two bodies of the wind rushing from the
        south,
Like two antelopes startled by a pack of howling dogs,
Dust rose from their feet, spinning high like wings of clouds.
35 Shaka speeded past a clump of dense foliage,
His feet thundering like a stampede of giraffes,
Until in one loud triumphal cry he reached the regimental
        grounds.
It was then they realized he had discarded his impeding sandals.

He threw himself on the ground,
Laughing triumphantly until his laughter made others laugh.
It was as if his very lungs flapped against his ribs.
He laughed until tears rolled down his face.
5   Catching his breath, he said:
'I held the tail of the whirlwinds!
All hail, children of the king! Great voice of the Ancestral
    Spirits!
I hold the hair of the wind! I hold the men!
10 The roots are torn out of the high mountain!'
Many who listened were baffled by these garbled words
But he kept their secret and their truth in his heart.

Addressing his regimental assembly
He said things that puzzled even the masters of war strategy:
15 'I ask you to listen to me carefully:
I have discovered an unbeatable plan against our enemies.
I repeat, the essence of success in war is speed.
Speed is of the mind and all intricacies of wars.
Speed is of those who meticulously examine the war's arena,
20 Who combine their wisdom with the wisdom of the wiser.
    men.
Through this knowledge the enemy is surrounded.
Speed is of the feet not encumbered by sandals.
Speed is embedded in the shape of my spear.
25 By this our heroes shall reap the enemy in close combat.
As the enemy dissipates its power
And throws all its missiles,
We shall break through their lines,
Turning our clouds of shields into a forest of weapons.
30 We shall rip their naked chests at close quarters.
If we follow this strategy, no enemy shall defeat us,
For all wars are the same, following only laws of battle.'
As he spoke his eyes caught every face in the crowd,
As if from each word he hoped for an ecstatic applause;
35 Nor could he sit in one place.
His very intestines seemed tied into knots,
Many gestured as though to talk but only looked at each other.
Had Shaka not been the favourite-hero of iziChwe regiment
They might have summoned the doctors of war

To heal him of the fierce power that a man inherits from battle.
It was Bhuza, the great general of iziChwe, who spoke:
'Shaka, the mountains of the world seem to constantly call your
    name.
5   Each day you bring us ever-new ideas.
Perhaps it is not our age that shall inherit your wisdom
But a future generation which shall better penetrate your
    visions.
Even though some may see madness in your plans
10 I always discover in them a wisdom beyond our times.
Yet it would be more laudable if they came in limited amounts,
For people prefer to be persuaded slowly about their customs.'
Shaka leapt up and spoke angrily:
'General, I have always hated the shackles of custom.
15 For, after all, in human affairs there are no eternal laws;
Each generation makes a consensus of its own laws.
They do not bind forever those still to be born.
Those who feast on the grounds of others
Often are forced into gestures of friendship they do not desire.
20 But we are the generation that cannot be bypassed.
We shall not be blinded by gifts from feasts.
With our own fire we shall stand above the mountains, as the
    sun.'
Shaka was alarmed at the violence of his own voice.
25 He sat down, his face contorted with rage.
Someone near him nudged him with an elbow,
Trying to restrain him from this haughty dialogue.
But Shaka turned his eyes in fury and was about to speak
When he saw the general looking at him.
30 Shaka knew no one succeeds in a blind clash with leadership;
Nor does it win him credence to ignore the faith of others.
Bhuza said to him: 'I acclaim the penetrating truth of your
    words.
Your visions gallop ahead of our thoughts.
35 With the permission of the Assembly
I shall put these views before the king.'

Their gathering dispersed at once.
Shaka, still in a dark mood, set off in his own solitary direction.
He reached a lone spot where he often sat, meditating.

He walked a few paces till he could see a little hill.
Here he halted, guessing out passages and escape points of the
    hill.
At each route he posted imaginary troops.
5 Some he commanded to move around the hill;
Some he commanded to close the gap of the retreating troops,
So overcome with this victory, he sang a new song.
Thus was born the great war hymn of the Fasimba regiment.
He walked over the hill humming this song.
10 He saw new exits at the sheer sides of the hill
And knew then, despite the imagined victory,
Through an error of judgement many would have lost their lives.
Like this he continued fighting his battles of fantasy
Until at the late-day-cycle he walked home slowly,
15 Still engrossed in his thoughts.

Phungashe was the powerful king of the Buthelezi nation.
He made many a neighbouring nation live in constant fear.
Some fled from him to the sanctuary of towering mountains;
Some ran to the kindly and generous Dingiswayo.
20 One day Phungashe told his war-hungry regiments:
'I shall strike Dingiswayo, the stubborn, indomitable fool.
I shall make him flee, humiliating him among his followers.'
He boasted, believing that having crushed the monster's arms
He shall have broken its body.
25 Phungashe, the wily one, even boasted:
'We shall acquire the authority to rule the earth.
We shall reap freely of its harvests.
All its wealth shall be for our children.'
His army was infused with this crusading spirit.

30 From all distant hills emerged the fierce army of Phungashe.
The high cliffs resounded with slogans of war.
Battle songs echoed like the many voices of thunder.
Even distant kings, like Zwide, sensing the smell of iron, began
    to arm,
35 Though no threat was posed against them.
They hoped when the two giants had drained each other's
    strength
They would intervene to rule the world.

When Dingiswayo heard of Phungashe's impending attack
He roamed the royal grounds restlessly,
Knowing the terror Phungashe often brought with his army.
Dingiswayo had believed peace was settled at last,
5 Yet the earth trembled;
Conflagrations of war leapt into the sky.
Dingiswayo had believed peace was settled at last,
'Tell me again the strategy you spoke of yesterday.
Perhaps this way we may teach this upstart king a lesson.'
10 Yet it was only a day before
He had heaped contempt on these tactics,
Condemning them for their violence,
Denouncing the bloodthirstiness of their authors.
While other regiments sang, ready for battle,
15 IziChwe regiment talked and guffawed,
Elated now that the great king had authorized their plans.
Shaka moved restlessly amongst the crowds,
Making his regiment race till late at night.
Sometimes to emphasize his thoughts he would say:
20 'A great fighter imitates the movements of the wind.
A war is a dance, the other side of the feast.'
It was for this they followed the horns of the moon,
Surrounding imaginary enemies around the body of the hill.

When the two armies faced each other with blood-red eyes,
25 A tall young man of the belligerent Buthelezi nation lurched
        forward.
He danced, the proud one, raising the dust from the arena.
It was as if the wind itself was frightened of him.
Only the turbulent son of Nandi rushed forward.
30 He — 'the fire whose fierce flames cannot be curbed
From whom the challenger retreats in terror —'
Crouched underneath his upraised shield.
In vain the Buthelezi hero tried to stab him with his missiles.
Each one Shaka parried with his black ox-hide shield.
35 He neared him, holding high his uninitiated spear.
When he came close to him
The Buthelezi hero attempted to probe him from a distance,
Thrusting at him his long, quivering spear.
Shaka threw his weapon off course.

He hooked him with his great black shield,
Driving his weapon through the shocked body.
He fell down with his eyes fixed on Shaka,
As if he had waited for this moment for their final meeting.
5　Crowds of spectators shouted in amazement.
Shaka proceeded to attack those with their bundles of spears,
Tearing at them with his initiated spear,
Shouting slogans from the king and his own poems of excellence.
Mgobhozi and Nqoboka, the twins of battle, rushed over,
10　Opening a wide path and confusing the whole enemy army.
The Buthelezis took to their heels
As the fierce iziChwe regiment ran wild after them.
The Mthethwa army flung their spears at them.
It was amidst this pandemonium that Dingiswayo shouted:
15　'Son of Nandi! It is enough!'
He knew now that Phungashe was humbled.
He sought only to stop the uncontrolled killing.
Ndima, the son of Moyeni of the Buthelezi clan, died there.
Bhakuza, the son of King Senzangakhona,
20　Born of the great wife, Mkhabi, died there.
The Mthethwa army was mesmerized by Shaka's performance.
A message came to him from the supreme commander,
　　　Ngomane:
'Son of Senzangakhona, the king demands to see you.'
25　In spite all the hubbub, Shaka was not excited; he knew
Phungashe and his army would attack again.
Before Dingiswayo he humbled himself, lowering his head.
Dingiswayo spoke kindly to him:
'Your bravery I have seen with my own eyes.
30　I saw your strategies reaping substantial fruit.
I wish I could reinforce them through many battles
But I fear their outcome.
Son of Zulu, bloodshed begets bloodshed.
But since I love your courage and mind
35　I give you the regiment of iziChwe to command.
Teach them your own strategies and tactics.
I give you a herd of my best breed of cattle — it is yours.'
Shaka thanked the king, not for the gift
But for the privilege of maturing his plans.
40　He said: 'My lord, I am grateful to you.

Your words far excel any words ever said to me.
You have made me commander over my agemate regiment,
Despite the many heroes who have fought the king's battles.
Only one request I make of you, my lord:
5   Allow me to divide this gift among my brothers of iziChwe
       regiment,
Though custom forbids that the king's gift be given to others.'
Dingiswayo granted Shaka his request commenting:
'Son of Zulu, you are a man amongst men.
10   Great families boast their wealth of innumerable cattle
Which their heroes have reaped from the gifts of war.
How much more noble of you to give when you count only a few
       cattle!'
When Dingiswayo made these comments his councillors were
15   troubled,
Knowing these words were truly directed at them.
They loudly applauded Shaka to hide their own shame.
As Shaka was about to leave the king summoned him back:
'By the way, my son, I have received a strange message.
20   There is a visitor on the way who desires your presence.
He comes to ask that I mourn with him his son.'
Shaka was about to ask (pretending not to know),
When the king crowded him with words and said:
'Your father, Senzangakhona, comes here in summer.'
25   Shaka's face turned dark like the skies of a gathering storm,
But he only said: 'I thank the king for his word.'

The young men of iziChwe regiment danced all night,
Sending their flames of victory to far-distant lands.
No sooner had King Phungashe lost in this battle
30   Than he followed the path of other kings and princes
Who lavished Dingiswayo with gifts.
Shaka himself was elated;
The brotherhood of the iziChwe regiment embraced him
      excitedly.
35   To them he said: 'It is not I who won against Phungashe
But the concentrated power of all our heroes;
And so it shall be in all our wars.
I am rich with gifts from the king, yet these are not mine.

We shall feast on them and pay tribute to our Forefathers.
We shall honour the great past heroes of our nation.
We shall compose poems of excellence to all our fighters.
When we have feasted with meat and beer
5   We shall begin again the new directions of wisdom.
The fame of iziChwe must resound throughout the earth.
Even those who once boasted the sharpness of their weapons
Shall flee in terror from the fierceness of iziChwe regiment.
We must carry our shields until they are feather-light.'
10 As Shaka spoke the iziChwe regiment laughed and celebrated.
The young man who was on his left side side said:
'Tell us, beloved Commander, when shall we marry
If our lives shall be spent in all these battles?'
As he said this others laughed, knowing he only joked.
15 But Shaka did not laugh. He pounced on these words:
'War is not a joke of lovers. Had it been in my power
I would proclaim that none should marry until they matured.
Strict loyalties of families
Often undermine the devotion and sacrifice for the nation.'
20 None took his words seriously,
Only remarking on the strangeness of Shaka's ideas.
Half-mockingly they demanded: 'Give us the wild men.
Even your own great spear is hungry.'
Shaka smiled and said:
25 'Let us sit and eat, my brothers. The meat is tender.
The king has given us his gifts with both hands.'
The young men applauded his words and sang his heroic poem:
'Thunderbolt that fell into the House of Phungashe,
All-spreading-fame, son of Menzi!
30 Shaka, the invincible one, no one can conquer!
Uncontrollable overgrowth, son of Ndaba!
Luxuriant vegetation that grows wild over the village-cities!
Until dawn the flames of the villages overwhelm each other.
Multi-voiced one, who is like a lion!
35 You trespassed on the grounds leading to the villages of Mfene —
The spear whose handle is red with the blood of men.
Eternal movement! Son of Senzangakhona!'
Such were the celebrations of the iziChwe regiment.

Have you ever seen the whirlwinds ripping off the earth,

Tossing up the village-cities into the empty heavens,
Disgorging them on the pathways with their old mealie fields?
Have you ever seen the Thukela river, pleased with itself,
Flowing swollen to the ribs with ancient plants and trees?
5 Like this, too, iziChwe regiment razed to the ground their
      enemies.
Angered, they marched on Khali of the emaMbatheni clan.
They hurried to Ndonda of the Deep River;
They attacked Nyanya of the Great Dlamini clan.
10 They danced high, showing off their invincible weapons.
Kings and kinglets and stubborn princes slept like wild an .nals.
When they heard of their endless victories, they said:
'Shaka must have the magic power anciently promised to man,
Or else he possesses the magic spear of the dead!'
15 From their campaigns the izeChwe regiment received
Great commotions and shoutings of joy.

Shaka, announcing his new venture, said:
'Too often I have heard of the Wild Man of the forest,
Who it is said cuts down travellers with his battle axe.'
20 He spoke of the notorious bandit who lived alone in the forest,
Waylaying passers-by, defiantly reaping all neighbouring fields.
It was said even those spears flung at him
Only grazed his ox-hide skin.
Like twigs that are blown by the wind they fell.
25 Shaka said angrily: 'The country cannot live in peace
So long as there are those who swagger and threaten others,
Who besiege peaceful people in their homes.
Destroyers of families who go unpunished
Make popular acts of lawlessness.'
30 Some tried to restrain him, saying:
Those who do these things are violent animals.
They should not be followed to their sanctuaries.'
It was as if these very words incensed Shaka.
He said: 'By my sister, I swear I shall deal with this madman.'
35 He went on to sharpen his angry spear.
Even Nandi sent a word to try and dissuade him,
But Shaka simply said: 'Not I alone desire the death of this
      beast,
But many who have suffered through his acts of brigandage.

I know many such bullies in my own life.
They exploit the fears of those who flee from them.'

Dawn came rushing from its night.
Many still attempted to dissuade him from this foolhardy act.
5 Even Nomchoba, his sister, wept.
Even Pampatha, his lover, tore herself with sadness.
But Shaka pointed his weapon toward the sun and said:
'That sun shall find me eating sorghum tomorrow!'
The iziChwe regiment sat on a vantage ground,
10 Constantly calling out each other's poems.
Excited they watched the impending clash of skills.
The great giant of the forest emerged like a tired mountain.
He filled the empty skies with his gruff and convulsive laughter.
At his own chosen moment he sat on a big round stone.
15 There he waved his sharp battleaxe.
Shaka came close to him, spitting in every direction with fury.
As he drew within the shadows of the forest giant,
The colossal creature leapt up as if stung by some bee.
Shaka retreated, drawing him out into the ogling crowd.
20 The giant attempted to strike a violent blow
But missed, hitting the bare ground.
Even the earth seemed to bleed from his blow.
Clouds of dust swirled to the high branches of trees.
Shaka wisely let him rise again,
25 For no danger is greater in battle
Than to rush blindly against a half-fallen foe.
Shaka went round and round to lure him onto a lower ground.
The forest giant sprang up as though to heave him down with
  one blow.
30 But Shaka kept on retreating.
Twice, thrice, the bandit attempted to strike at him.
Shaka only jumped aside, escaping the blows.
This game he played until, tired and desperate,
The giant bounded on him with all his might,
35 Burying the head of his battleaxe into the ground.
It was then that Shaka sank his weapon into his enemy's side.
The giant bandit rose, dazed by the blow,
Attempting to regain his strength, but Shaka gave him no
  chance.

He stabbed him again and again with his firm spear.
The giant fell, collapsing on the ground like a huge tree,
Like a boulder coming to rest in a deep valley.
A din of applause echoed into the distant mountains.
5   Even those who had stood afar in fear
Shouted their songs of praise.
Together they shouted Shaka's poems of excellence.
'Great one, who prepared for battle from the forest like a
       madman!
10   Fierce fire, that pierces the eyes of men!'
The poet, unable to control himself, wept.
Crowds gathered, inviting Shaka to their homes.
IziChwe regiment accompanied him with a song —
They sang the ancient song of the heroes.
15   When Dingiswayo heard of this encounter
He shook his head and said: 'This boy is a riddle.
His greatness is yet to startle the world.'
He listened carefully to the accounts of Shaka's skill;
How he had used tactics never thought of before.
20   Dingiswayo then sent a messenger to summon him to the
       Assembly.
Shaka sat there unmoved by all this excitement.
He even thought to himself:
'Could it be that a call to courage is such a rare event?
25   Or is it the times that make people praise what they fear most?
This bandit was an enemy to all peoples.
Those who show fear of him should themselves be prosecuted.'
Yet Shaka did not reveal these feelings to the king.
He told the story until finally Dingiswayo said:
30   'My son, I praise your bravery.
It is not the first time I have been dazzled by your courage.
Like many, my heart celebrates at the very mention of your
       name.
I want your greatness to be honoured for all times.
35   To me such a deed far surpasses the heroic deeds of war.
Because of it many shall rejoice and celebrate their harvests.
I too, have heard how this man terrorized my peaceful subjects.'
Shaka would have dismissed these words of praise
But at what the king said something stirred his heart,
40   For, in truth, even heroes of battle are moved by kindness.

He repeated these words again and again in his heart,
As though they were some melodious song heard in a dream.
Those who saw him felt the ecstasy in his mind.
Nomchoba, who understood the depths of his heart, said to him:
5 'Mlilwana, your life is now attended by the Ancestors.'
Shaka responding, only said: 'It is true.'

Senzangakhona's heart was crushed with sadness:
He mourned continuously for his son Bhakuza.
To console himself he decided at last
10 He must pay the much-heralded visit to Dingiswayo.
He was eager to let him know with how much grief
He maintained their bonds of friendship.
Princess Mkhabayi, on hearing of this long sadness,
Mocked Senzangakhona, and said:
15 'The King is courting disaster by mourning a hero.
Perhaps as he grows older he forgets our customs.
Was it not always a heinous crime to mourn the heroes of
        battle?'
She spoke as though to herself, though her councillor was there.
20 For to the high-born their followers are only shadows.
Senzangakhona sent word ahead of him and said:
'I shall come and see the rich soil of my son's grave,
To make him a Feast of Return with my feet.'

The fat bulls at the royal villages were rounded up for slaughter.
25 Dingiswayo knew what plans he kept in his mind.
Senzangakhona arrived amidst the hubbub of singing and
        dancing.
Large numbers filled the royal arena of oYengweni.
Songs both ancient and modern echoed from the broken cliffs.
30 The upswelling aroma of tender meat
Rose like light grains of soporific drugs.
Kings, to affirm their greatness, often give lavish feasts;
They attempt to overshadow and dazzle others with their power.
They whisper to themselves in private:
35 'He must know how great and endless are my resources.'
It was for this reason Senzangakhona was shown
Powerfully-built young heroes and beautiful women;
He was directed to the village-cities

Which by their size seemed to reach the earth's limits.
On this night he slept a restless sleep,
Keen to satisfy his appetite on all the marvels of power;
He itched to participate in the gala-feast held in his honour.
5   Many nations, adorned with varied dress and colours, hurried
      there.
From all parts of the world came great dancers and singers.
Great poets declaimed the ancient epics from the mountains;
Each competed to be the greatest among all nations.
10   Even Senzangakhona forgot his grief.

On the following day he sat contentedly with a foreign
      potentate,
Watching the vast open space of the dancing grounds.
A poet was heard descending from the mountains,
15   Declaiming the heroic epic of Dingiswayo:
'You were resurrected from the dead like the magic plant,
Originator of a new era, son of Ndaba!
Restless one, like a cow about to give birth to a young calf:
With which friendly one shall it bond itself?
20   It shall be Mbangambi, son of Vuma of eMashobeni,
The spear that took Ndiyane and carried him off to his eternal
      night.
You overwhelmed the white men.
The places you invaded are stricken with silence.'
25   The regiments began to sing the sacred anthems.
Inspired, a tall man danced the sacred dance.
He was the court poet of Senzangakhona.
He now shouted the heroic poem of Senzangakhona:
'Menzi, son of Ndaba!
30   Great commotion that scolds with tears:
You are like Phika of Bulawini,
The buffalo that casts its shadow over the lakes.
You are like the hunters of the Mfekane clans.
You are the possessor of the beautiful eating-mats, Mjokwane.
35   On them the young girls reveal their beautiful fingers.'
The poet celebrated the occasion with these poems,
Speaking slowly, not throwing away his words.
He danced leisurely, turning his body in circles.

He moved gracefully, eager to exhibit his skill.
Even his tuft of feathers waved gently like branches in the
    wind.
The women of the Mthethwas shouted words of praise.
5   They beat the ground close to Senzangakhona;
They whipped his mat of lion skin with bull-tails of heroes.
Thus began the great dance of the regiments!
The echoes of song reverberated to the distant hills.
The dance-songs lifted the beaded heroes from the ground.
10   Plumes of red feathers and crowns of variegated beads sparkled
    in the sun.
A young man of the Mthethwas leaped up into the air.
He danced until the earth itself seemed consumed by
    earthquakes.
15   Its bowels shook, arousing those who were its first inhabitants.
A tumultuous roar of praise was heard from the ecstatic crowd;
Others followed, swaying their bodies like birds of paradise.
After many a dancer had occupied the arena
A young man who was tall and proud and defiant leapt up.
20   It was as if even the wind stopped, to witness.
The spectators stretched their necks like birds of the forest,
Like a crowd of starlings before their flight.
He swayed his body as if he would beat the ground,
As if he would land his long legs on the arena!
25   He reared up, raising his head and looking in all directions.
Through swift movements he pointed his ceremonial stick east
    and west.
Twice he beat the ground with his foot.
Then the shuddering sound of shouting spectators echoed!
30   He pointed to the ground; he pointed to the sky.
He launched his foot high, then crouched to the ground.
He brought it down with a thundering thud.
He shouted, his muscles moving simultaneously with his voice.
His whole body was uplifted by his movements.
35   When he had brought the spectators to an unbridled point of
    ecstasy
He followed the small drum, retreating from the centre.
Everyone watched in amazement this display of skill.
Senzangakhona said to the man next to him:
40   'By my father, this young man is a great dancer.'

Even when they retired to feast he asked Dingiswayo:
'Who was the young man who danced like a spirit?'
Dingiswayo answered playfully and said:
'At the capital of the Mthethwas are many mysteries.
5   In it there are singers and great composers.
Some boast their skills in battle;
Some boast their power of poetry.
Our fame spreads to all parts of the earth.
Yet there are still others who possess all gifts.
10 The young man of great dancing skill is Shaka himself;
This Shaka who fears nothing is your son.'
These words took Senzangakhona by surprise.
He had heard of his great popularity at the Mthethwa capital.
He had seen, too, how Dingiswayo vigorously applauded him.
15 The threats of the diviner's words came back suddenly.
His mind wandered, obsessed by the fate of his rule.
He feared for his favourite son and heir, Sigujana,
Whom he had called 'The great pathway of Ndaba'.
He slept that night a sleep of many horrendous dreams.
20 In the centre of the night he woke up and paced the royal
     grounds.
At times he gazed at the very spot of Shaka's magic dance.
The fearful night cast many strange and fearful images.
He saw the grim future of wars and internecine battles.
25 He saw his own image as he sat among the Ancestors,
A crowd of them sitting there in judgement of his rule,
Accusing him of discarding their own favourite.
He knew then how fierce is the wrath of the gods!

At dawn Shaka arrived at Dingiswayo's royal house.
30 He had been summoned there by the king.
He now spoke to him solemnly and said:
'My son, I have always loved you with all my heart.
I have wished that one day you may inherit your own kingdom,
To take what is rightly yours, and be my true ally and heir.
35 The moment has arrived!
You must display your royal authority,
Dazzling your father and all his trusted councillors.
I leave the manner to you and give you my blessings.'

Shaka thanked the king and said, with pretended humility:
'I would have preferred the king to tell me the way,
For it is he who knows all things.
But for now I can only blunder until I find the right path.
5   Perhaps this way I shall acquire the wisdom of others.'
Dingiswayo noticed that by these words
Shaka only acted to fulfil the demands of custom.
He smiled and said: 'It is so, son of Zulu.
The paths are made by those who walk on them.'
10   At the high point of day Shaka hurried to his father.
The councillors were gathered around their king, drinking beer.
He saluted the king, curious at their first meeting.
Senzangakhona displayed no signs of surprise.
He sent one of his councillors:
15   'Take this beer pot and give it my son to drink.
When he grows he must resemble his Forefathers,
They who never bowed down their heads to the sun.'
Shaka listened carefully to these words,
Eager to unravel their inner meanings.
20   He drank slowly, gauging the thoughts of those around the king.
They, too, continuously whispered in the king's ear.
After wiping his mouth, Shaka began to talk:
'I have come to you so that we may return home together.'
It was as though he had thrown a spark of fire to a winter
25   forest.
Senzangakhona hesitated, mumbling unintelligible words.
Finally he said: 'It is true, son of Ndaba.
You must return to your own place of birth.
Nothing would fill me with greater joy
30   But I fear to contradict the advice of our Forefathers,
Who said: "Two bulls cannot live in one fold."
Your brother, Prince Sigujana, is now a mature man.
He has also grown in the hearts of the people.
If I go back with you
35   I shall only cause divisions and quarrels among our people.
I shall be condemned for the conflagrations that would follow.'
While Senzangakhona was thus weighing his words
Shaka suddenly stood up and said:
'My father, permit me to leave.'
40   In vain, the councillors tried to persuade him:

'We implore you to stay with us awhile, royal Prince.'
He simply said: 'Father, I have heard your words.
I have duties to attend to in my regiment; the country is in
    turmoil.
5   Zwide has begun his interminable threats.'
He left suddenly, leaving his shadow lingering in the assembly.
Its power haunted those who sat with the king.
At the place of the great diviner Shaka asked for herbs of power.
The diviner chose a special group,
10 Reserved only for kings in the Ceremony of the Cleansing.
He gave him drugs to set his mind at peace.
He was to put them secretly under his tongue as he spoke.
He also acupunctured his temples, his forehead and his body
    joints,
15 And said to him: 'Wake up with the rising sun
And three times in your mind you must ask for your father's
    power.
Call his name, who is the object of your anger,
Then cut with a knife the king's anthill.'
20 Shaka did as told by the diviner.
On the third day he set out for the great pools of the king.
He had now heard from his informants
How his father, the king, bathed there daily at dawn.
He pretended to his men to be wandering, lost in an alcove.
25 Suddenly he shouted to them: 'Run for your lives!
There is the king having his morning bath!'
Pandemonium broke loose, terrifying the king himself.
Only Shaka stood as if rooted to the ground.
He thrust his eyes at the king, strengthened by the magic herbs.
30 Fear cut through Senzangakhona's mind like a blade.
He said: 'Oh, is it you, my son? Is it you, Shaka?
What can I do to please you, my son?'
He spoke, repeating his words out of fear.
Shaka replied gently and said:
35 'Forgive me, my father, finding you naked.
I took this route only to fulfil the demands of my duty
But still I cannot go without the blessing of my father.
I ask you for the spear you carried at the festival.
It shall be my greatest joy
40 To fight with a weapon given to me by my father.'

Senzangakhona made the same hesitant response:
'My child, yours is the request of a hero.
Only one dilemma faces me: the spear I carried is not mine.
I gave it to Sigujana when he attained his age of manhood.'
5   Shaka stared at him, his eyes red with hurt.
He said: 'So then I shall not have it!
Despite my many battles and heroic honours brought to our
    house?
Though Sigujana possesses many others from my father?
10 Though this is my first and sole request?'
As he uttered these words his voice rose threateningly.
Finally, he said: 'I thank you for your words, my father.
They hurt where they should heal; they bring pain.
Despite this I ask your permission to accompany you,
15 To take you to your royal House of Strangers.
Then I shall feel happy, having acted as guard to my father,
Knowing no bandit or assassin can threaten his life.'
He spoke as if he implied a command.
Senzangakhona scolded those with him and said:
20 'Are the commands of the prince not your commands?'
Without delay, they collected the king's goods
And climbed the little hill to Dingiswayo's 'Residence of Kings'.
For Senzangakhona, this was his saddest journey.
Shaka, his son of many memories, never spoke;
25 He only answered briefly to what was asked of him.
When they arrived at the vast royal grounds
His father said to him: 'I thank you, my son.
"To give birth is to multiply one's self," our Forefathers said.
I wish you to grow and reach beyond the sun.'
30 As they parted Senzangakhona stretched his hand.
When he shook Shaka's hand he was trembling,
The inside of his palm was wet with sweat.
He was only too happy to escape Shaka's power
He hurried to his resting place and there slept
35 Until early at dawn Dingiswayo came to bid him farewell.
As he departed from the oYengweni royal grounds
Even Dingiswayo noticed the weakening of his movements.

Zwide was the king of the Ndwandwes of the Nxumalos.
He was the son of the frightful Queen Ntombazi.

In a house set aside for the purpose
She put the skulls of many famous victims.
Everywhere along the walls gazed skulls of once-great men.
There were the heads of Mlotha of Matshalini;
5   Of Zayi; of Ngudlubela, the once-famous hero of Nguniland.
Queen Ntombazi was, like a wizard, feared by her own children.
It was she who egged Zwide on to interminable battles.
She made him pursue all victims into their fortresses of stone.
Never before in Nguniland was known such a disgrace.
10   A hideous crime it was to drive people away from their homes!
The vanquished must be left to reap their own crops;
They must have their wounds washed by the victor.
This was sacred law of Nguniland.
Perchance it was this blasphemy of the Ancestral laws
15   That made Zwide rave as if possessed by an uncontrollable
       force.
Many nations lived in constant fear of him.
Many people were revolted by his ruthlessness.
Was it not this man who often invited people to a hunt
20   And then, in the midst of all celebrations, slaughtered them?
The poet who records and remembers all these things says of
       Zwide:
'By your secret strategies great heroes have been killed.
The families that were unlucky were destroyed,
25   None dared attack you.
Among the paths, which one does he resemble?
He is like the one that crosses.
Among the trees, which one does he resemble?
He is like the tough essenwood plant.
30   Among the snakes, which one does he resemble?
He is like the sacred snake of the Forefathers.'
The poet tells us Zwide attacked without cause.
Only he lived to reap his own harvest.
Those who watched the openings of the black Mfolozi river
35   Saw Zwide's armies set out to raid all around Nguniland.
He attacked Zwangendaba of the Mncwango clan but suffered
       defeat.

Zwide begged for mercy.
The Mncwangos said to him: 'Go to your own lands.

Take a herd of cattle if hunger be the cause of your wars.'
But Zwide was not appeased;
He raided the peaceful clans of Matshalini
And there obtained the coveted head of Prince Mlotha.

5 Presenting it to Queen Ntombazi, he only said: 'Here it is.'
His armies continuously sang their fearful war song,
Encouraged by their victory and such rituals.

Zwide vowed to remove the proud feather from Dingiswayo's
    head.

10 He claimed: 'With it I shall be master in Nguniland.'
Long had Queen Ntombazi pestered her son,
Saying: 'Strike the snake on its head until it dies!
Should you conquer Dingiswayo utterly
All nations and all peoples of Nguniland shall fear you,

15 For whoever overcomes a feared man is feared himself.'
It was for this Zwide prepared his troops for battle,
Choosing the first and best heroes of many wars.
They vowed to bring back Dingiswayo's coveted feather.
Dingiswayo put his numerous regiments on war-readiness.

20 Not far from the Ndwandwe army the Mthethwa army rested.
From there they made their plans and listened to their spies.
They heard how Zwide's army was massed for a total attack,
As war commanders sorted out their final strategy.
Shaka also offered his own comments:

25 'This is how our battle plan should evolve.
Since they come, confident of their large numbers,
We must select our units, breaking them wisely into sections.
From the reports they seem still to be forming their forces.
It is now, we should attack, cutting out all their supplies.

30 We must attack from left and right directions.
The centre should hold our main fighting force.
Moving swiftly from all sides we should surround them all at
    once.
To gain such speed we must remove the cumbersome sandals —

35 This way we shall possess the lightness of the wind.'
They listened intently to each and every word.
Some ideas they welcomed, some they turned down.
Of their sandals, they found the very thought impractical.
'How,' they asked, 'can our feet survive the hard earth?'

Shaka addressed Ngomane, the commander-in-chief: 'In all our
wars
Not once did we ever teach the enemy a decisive lesson.
Every year we fight the same enemies. Zwide, of all Nguni
5   rulers,
Never received the punishment he deserves.
For the good of all, the abominable Queen Ntombazi must be
destroyed.
Only then shall peace come to Nguniland.'
10 Some concurred, enthused by these far-sighted thoughts.
Dingiswayo finally spoke and said:
'My son, I know the blood of youth spoils for battle.
I know, too, that Zwide is a ruthless and a violent ruler
But still I call for a war of reasonable proportions.'
15 With these words Dingiswayo rejected Shaka's plan of a total
war.
All segments of his army began to move.
The units of Matshalini, who bore a grudge against Zwide,
Turned up in all their numbers.
20 The Hlabisa warriors were there in all their numbers.
The Mzimelas, who never missed a battle, were there.
The iziChwe regiment, led by Shaka, spread out in front.
Yengendlovu veterans speedily followed behind.
Nyakeni regiment followed on the right wing of the army.
25 Shaka headed forward with his regiment
Until he reached Zwide's army from a left side.
His regiment rushed at them, hiving them off from the centre.
While thus disrupted, Yengendlovu descended on them.
The Nyakeni regiment launched its fierce attack from the right.
30 Dingiswayo's army stormed them like a tornado.
Disrupted, Zwide's army fled in all directions.
The iziChwe regiment followed them in hot pursuit,
Eager to inflict on them some lasting wounds.
Dingiswayo's army reassembled, singing their song of victory.
35 Zwide himself was captured. He sat in the centre, trembling
with shock.
On the battlefield lay numerous dead.
The triumphant generals assembled together.
It was there that Dingiswayo said to Shaka:
40 'Yes, my son, we have won our victory.

I thank you for your quick actions and strikes.
Even those who threw cold water on your plans now applaud
    you.
They acclaim the swiftness in battle of iziChwe regiment.
5 It is truly the shield and spear of our nation.'
He spoke cheerfully, no longer burdened by the clouds of war.
Even his voice was raised in gaiety.
He spoke intimately to Shaka: 'Zwide is now in our hands.
Tell me, Nodumehlezi, what fate would you reserve for such a
10   man?'
When he asked this question, Dingiswayo was troubled.
He hoped Shaka would soften and forgive the captive.
He was apprehensive, too, lest Shaka have the true solution.
Shaka answered bluntly: 'My lord, it is you who know best.
15 Were it in my hands, I would stop now the misery of nations.
It is no crime against the Ancestors to kill a bandit.
The blood of Mlotha cries out for revenge.
By this act we may yet appease the hearts of many victims.'
Dingiswayo was quiet as though in deep thought.
20 Finally he said: 'My son, I shall think seriously about your
    words.
For the moment we must drink and praise the Ancestors.'
So it was. Young men whirled into space like autumn leaves.
The whole region reverberated with their voices.
25 From all sides poems of excellence were sung.
Heroes from battle walked the arena like black eagles.
Feasts and songs shook the night until, exhausted, the army
    rested.
But Queen Ntombazi did not sleep. She spat revenge,
30 Cursing the very name of Dingiswayo and denouncing her own
    son.
She vowed: 'One day, son of Jobe, we shall meet!'

At dawn, both armies prepared to return to their homes.
King Dingiswayo now summoned Shaka and said:
35 'I spent the whole night thinking of your words.
I fail to abide by them though I see their truth.
Perhaps by this humiliation Zwide might yet come to his senses.
Indeed, those who expect death are more surprised by life.
Overwhelmed by their good fortune, they celebrate life,

Becoming more generous than the rest of humankind.'
Although Shaka had known and expected these words
He closed his eyes as though absorbed in a painful thought.
'My lord, your decisions are always honourable.
5   They put above all else the welfare of Nguniland.
They are the high truth that should make life peaceful.
But, alas, the country is rife with lawlessness.
The barbarian is seldom deterred by kindness.
To you, great King, I pay my respects.'
10   As he said this he bowed his head and withdrew to his regiment.

Not long after the army's return to Mthethwaland,
A messenger came panting from Zululand, reporting:
'I come with the saddest news of our land.
Our king, Senzangakhona, is dead.'
15   Dingiswayo was shattered; his hands trembled with shock.
He paced the grounds, his mind confused and pained,
For he had desired a close bond between Shaka and his father.
Again and again he asked about the details of the king's death,
How he had died or whether he made any final wish.
20   The messenger answered the anxious king and said:
'Death should be a happy opening into the land of our
      Forefathers;
But his last moments were fearful!
He turned to his wife, Queen Mkabi, and said:
25   "Where is my son, Sigujana?"
In vain they told him he was right there beside him.
He claimed this was a treacherous deceit, for he saw only Shaka.
Raving, he shouted: "He casts his shadow over me.
He stares at me with fierce eyes of the sun."
30   Finally he raised his hand, attempting to hold his son's hand
But he withered and fell to the ground.
The mat on which he slept yielded and embraced his body.
Even today the sounds of mourning echo into the far horizon.
As I travel I carry a heavy burden on my shoulders.'
35   It was as though the messenger would suddenly burst into tears.
Even the much-experienced Dingiswayo looked aside.
No longer was he saddened by Senzangakhona's death alone,
But by the very thought of how close he himself was to death.
He sent a message of condolence to Shaka:

'Those who are dead are forgiven for their crimes.
The message of your father's death fills us with deep pain.
You must prepare to leave before the mourning has ceased.
This way you shall have saved your ancestral kingdom from all
5   strife.
I shall give you the iziChwe regiment to accompany you.
You must enter your home honoured as a true and a great
     prince.'
Shaka came in person to thank the king:
10 'I thank you for the tears with which you accompany me.
To mourn my father creates a strange bond.
Here at Mthethwaland is my home.
Before, we roamed the land, a mockery to beer-drinking parties.
But by your kindness you cared for us.
15 We were like your own children.
No one in this great country can thank you more warmly than I.
You shall never know how deep are the fears of a growing boy.
Only through your own fruitful wanderings
Can you glimpse at the terrors of exile.
20 I have come to thank you, but my words are weak.
In truth, whatever I am issues from your love.
When I walked in the assemblies of men, I was proud;
I feared no one, I followed my own course of action,
Knowing whatever I did would find nourishment in your own
25   wisdom.
You were truly my father, my guardian, my life's direction.
As I depart it is only for a mission ordained by the gods.
I shall return to my own home of peace.
I shall see my brothers of the battlefield yet again.
30 Because of you, I have forgiven my father as a dutiful son must.
I feel taller and greater than all the sadness.
I now leave as you have ordered.
Wherever I am, there always shall be your home.'
Shaka warmly shook Dingiswayo's hand.
35 Dingiswayo stretched out both his arms and embraced him.
Like shepherds who watch the parent-bird in flight,
Like the first scatterings of its nestlings into the woods,
Thus did Dingswayo imagine Shaka's departure.
Moved by the warm words, he brought the revered royal spear
40 And said: 'I applaud your greatness

I raise your name through generations to come.
It was you who helped me build this great kingdom.
Your thoughts may not belong to my age and generation,
Yet they have strengthened and reinforced our own strategies.
5   I may yet discover their truth too late.
Should this happen I shall have no regrets;
For I know I shall have fertilized the greatest era in our history.
This spear I give you is the ceremonial spear of my Forefathers.
It is they who by their wisdom built our nation.
10 I am only an agent of their greatness, a reflection of their
      visions.
They prophesied the oneness of the palm race.
Do not forget the gifts of our Forefathers.
However great our wisdom, we are only the branches of their
15   beginnings.
We begin from the rich soil nourished by them.
I give you my blessings in their sacred name.'
The two great eagles parted.
One sun was shrouded by the night;
20 Another nourished itself till dawn.

Book Five: A revolutionary reveals his strategy

Shaka returns to his country and for the first time he is in a position to implement his ideas. He orders his army to discard the sandals to enable it to attain maximum speed. He introduces the use of scientific methods. He inculcates into his soldiers a strong sense of brotherhood, creating separate military towns. The young men and women must not marry until allowed to do so. Altogether the society is infused with a new sense of discipline and purpose. All this proves effective in the battle against King Phungashe who, to the surprise of everyone, is defeated by Shaka's small army. Shaka incorporates the Buthelezi nation into the Zulu nation. All these activities tend to take him away from his mother, who now feels isolated and would prefer him to settle down and have a family.

News spread among all nations of Nguniland
How king Sigujana survived precariously on his throne.
Prince Shaka sent his messengers to Zululand, who reported:
'There has been no peace since your brother seized the throne.
5   Each of your father's royal houses claims the right to rule;
The whole country threatens to break apart into little
     princedoms.
Clamour grows, demanding the return of the rightful heir.
The regiments are restless; civil war threatens.
10 The great leaders of our nation have broken off with their
     followers.
Impatiently they await their peace-maker and king.'
Shaka sent for the hot-heads of iziChwe regiment.
By their songs of war they made known their presence.
15 They scattered the pockets of resisters to the mountains
And found Sigujana stabbed in between the shoulder blades.
They took his body and threw it into the fast-flowing river.
Everywhere Shaka went he heard the welcome songs.
Feasts were held; drums boomed the ancient dances.

20 Great were the preparations for Shaka's enthronement.
Mountains were filled with the din of ancient anthems.
Beautiful women of the land sat in the shade, braiding their
     hair.
They reaped and crushed the fragrance of young scented flowers.
25 They gossiped about their future in the king's household.
Great processions gathered from all directions.
Red feathers quivered as the heroes hurried to the royal city.
There were those who accompanied the princes and princesses,
Who declaimed their heroic poems, making the horizons
30   tremble.
The children of Senzangakhona hurried there to pledge their
     loyalty.
Their heads were adorned with loury bird feathers.
When all the crowds were gathered
35 Princess Mkhabayi silently entered the arena,
Walking high like a cloud over the mountains.
As she came before the king she peered deep into his eyes.
IziChwe regiments watched intently from their semi-circle
     positions.

Princess Mkhabayi bowed low and shouted the royal salute.
The gathered throngs roared in one great acclamation,
Shouting: 'Bayethe! UyiZulu!' The earth itself shook.
On the right side of the king sat Princess Nomchoba.
5   It was in a place next to her the proud Mkhabayi sat.
She opened her lips as if to speak
But she only gestured to Nomchoba, directing her eyes to Nandi.
Thus the House of Zulu affirmed its bonds.
Mkhabayi by her gesture endorsed the position of the new ruler
10 For she, senior to Senzangakhona, had served as regent.

Shaka stood up, tall and fierce, to address the gathering:
'I have come back to my father's kingdom.
My travels have taught me all I need to know for my task.
I shall enhance the name of our house.
15 Like all who battle against violent storms,
Pulling with all the power in their muscles —
Like such men must our nation fight for a new era.
Let all, from now on, know there is only one king.
Whoever violates the law of the nation endorsed by me shall die.
20 The defenders of our nation shall do as ordered by me.
Absconders from battle shall not be tolerated.
Whoever flees from the enemy
Shall have blasphemed the whole nation of Zululand.
None from the army shall marry unless so permitted by me.
25 From the youngest of the nation to the oldest,
None shall be without knowledge of fighting.
Even young women shall have their own fighting regiments.
Through them our nation shall defend our homes.

Tomorrow our generals must assemble all men eligible for
30   battle.
Those to serve as generals I shall appoint myself on this very
        day.
When the Assembly disperses, all commanders and heads of
        sections
35 Shall assemble at our grounds for new laws and orders.
Finally, all members and citizens,
Wherever they are, whoever they are, whatever they are,
Must know: only bravery shall decide each person's worth.

Everywhere the members of our nation shall walk proud and
    unafraid.
Wherever are our children, there our nation shall be.
From the ruins, from endless wars, shall emerge the great nation
5   of Zululand.
The cities and nations shall be named after the children of
    Zulu.
For now, let us eat; our path is long and our powers infinite.'
A great shout of 'Bayede!' greeted his words.
10 Even the old men who had commented about these new laws,
    saying,
'This land is older than the oldest man,'
Now applauded his great new vision.
They remembered how from time immemorial
15 Raiders and conquerors like King Phungashe, like King Zwide,
Like King Macingwane, had left their cattle-folds and fields in
    ruins.

Shaka now ordered a feast of many of his beasts from
    Mthethwaland.
20 The delicate scent of meat rose in waves to the heavens.
The Forefathers felt its filaments like sweet voices of their
    children.
The dancers shook the earth with merriment.
As all this was happening Shaka retreated aside.
25 From a vantage point he watched the untrained recruits.
He laughed knowlingly as he proceeded to the gathering of
    commanders.
He began addressing them: 'Before dawn tomorrow
All commanders must come to my place of residence.
30 For now you must summon up the most courageous fighters.
Whoever chooses their blood-relations and friends
Shall be fined by me with everything they possess.'
The commanders saluted but were still confused at these
    changes.
35 They still hoped for a full season of celebrations,
For custom demanded they be held, for the length of all
    remembered reigns.

In a round house Shaka sat, discussing with Mgobhozi,

Guessing at this and that of the strategy of wars.
Shaka commented pensively: 'Yes, son of Mgobhozi, the time
    has come!'
As he spoke he ran his hand over the shining blade of his spear.
5   He felt the firmness of its handle,
And said: 'We shall make firewood of our Forefathers' weapons.
We shall make them for throwing at the wild-potato game.'
They laughed and joked together, recalling their adventures,
Until at the appearance of the dawn-heralding star
10   Someone shouted the king's salutations:
'My lord, by your order your heroes have arrived.'
As he announced the commanders moved restlessly on the
    grounds.
Even old commanders came, despite the coolness of the
15   morning.
The king walked through the crowd, examining them.
He pointed to an old man and said: 'You, my father, should
    retire.
Let the young fight the wars.
20   I shall give you a bevy of fat cows for your achievements.
You, too, and you, and you, my grandfather.'
There was great consternation at this drastic act,
For it was customary that when a man got old
He still served in wars, augmenting his wealth according to
25   rank.
For this reason, many clung to their positions of command.

When Shaka had divided his troops into regiments
He addressed the commanders:
'Each member of our army must be proud to be a part of it.
30   I shall put into different age-divisions our regiments.
Each one shall have its own officers.
These must listen and take my final orders.
The laws guiding the regiments must be known to all the
    officers.
35   I give them now; I shall not give them again.
Those who violate them invite only death.
I repeat: those who flee from battle
Shall be sentenced to death by their very act.
No one in all the ranks shall boast scars on his back.

Each man shall carry to battle only one short spear,
Unlike the many cowards who carry an assemblage of weapons,
Who, having thrown away their collection, take to their heels.
Whoever shall lose his spear shall have lost their lives.
5   The enemy we shall pursue to the end.
Each regiment shall have its own runner-boy detachments
To carry all weapons and provisions for each body of fighting
    men,
Thus to preserve their strength for battle.
10 This shall serve as training ground for the young of our nation.
On the day when all regiments shall be assembled
They must enter the arena running at full speed.
They shall start from those distant mountains
And gallop like wild animals pursued by hunters.
15 Even I shall be there, running with them.
The first regiment I name amaWombe.
It is the one to comprise the mature young men of our nation.
The second shall still be uDlambedlu and uJubinqwanga.
The third shall comprise the youngest recruits of the nation.
20 These I shall command personally and call them uFasimba.
All enemies shall live in fear of them.
They shall search the mists and listen to their songs in terror.

A commander is a commander for his bravery and astuteness
And not through birth or status.
25 If you are a leader, it is only through merit.
You possess an experience and knowledge superior to your
    followers.
You are the voice of all those in your regiment.
You are the eyes of the whole nation.
30 Here is Mgobhozi, who shall train you in the skills of war.
Day and night you shall keep your ears open,
Digesting fully and clearly his words and thoughts.
For now, go and summon all the regiments.
Day after tomorrow at the low base of the mountains we shall
35   assemble.'
When he finished many applauded his words, but not all.
The son of Duze, who was known for his courage,
Said: 'My king, we have heard your words, but something
    troubles me;

How can we call all the regiments when the youngest recruits
Still wait in seclusion with their doctors and teachers?'
The whole gathering of commanders was shocked.
'Who dares follow the kings's words with his own?' they scolded.
5   It was the great Shaka who simply laughed
And said: 'Son of Duze, I understand your words.
I can see now you are as brave as you are said to be.
It is men of such courage who earn my admiration.
Commanders who take only instructions
10   Cause disasters and may yet make our whole strategy a
         mockery.
A true commander asks and must be given all necessary truth.
He must raise all questions appropriate to the ultimate strategy.
Thereafter there can only be one decision:
15   This must control all our movements.
Thus your question deserves to be answered:
From this very day never again
Shall the regiments spend time enfeebled at the School of
         Manhood.
20   Instead they shall pierce their ear-lobes —
This symbolizes their readiness for battle.
I want those absent taught all these regulations.
When they return they should be steeped in these laws.'
The whole gathering of commanders was alarmed
25   But could say nothing against these strange ideas.
Old men of the land simply shook their heads,
Knowing these rules violated the most ancient customs.
As everyone dispersed they discussed heatedly the king's new
         laws.
30   Shaka was pleased with this display of confusion,
Since it is known man learns best from unexpected shock.

From various regions regiments assembled at the mountain base.
Among them was the numerous amaWombe regiment,
Followed by the battle-hungry uDlambedlu regiment.
35   As they sang their battle hymns
Jubinqwanga tested their skills on an open ground.
In this gathering only the Fasimba regiment carried the short
         spear,
For they alone had been initiated in the new methods of
40   warfare.

No longer did they wobble like the praying mantis;
Their bodies moved vigorously like those of young bulls.
The Chief Commander called out, announcing Shaka's presence:
'The battleaxe that overwhelms others is in our midst!'
5 The tumult of their saluting voices reached the distant regions,
But Shaka did not wait long for these ceremonies. He said:
'Since you are versed in all the laws,
I shall not repeat them.
The Fasimba regiment must stand behind the rest of the
10   regiments
Others should move a few paces forward.
From here the distance stretches far to my capital.
You must run it as if chased by death.'
He spoke firmly, not showing his earlier indulgence.

15 The commanders in great haste organized the race.
As all the regiments stampeded
The earth itself vibrated as if to yield its centre.
When Jubinqwanga had covered a short distance
The Fasimba regiment followed close to their heels.
20 Though last in the race they whizzed passed them,
Climbing the little hills like a disturbed nest of ants.
The panting regiments hobbled behind on their sandals.
Some were tripping and falling on the brushwood;
Others were sinking and falling on the sand.
25 Still others were trapped in the loosened cords of plants.
It was the Fasimba regiment that reached there first.
After the whole gathering had assembled Shaka addressed them:
'My army must be as fast as the whirlwind.
Through this race I wanted you to see for yourselves
30 How sandals impede a man's speed and movement.
Should the enemy be overwhelmed by our regiments
He may yet regroup and fight again,
But with your speed we shall make such tactics obsolete.
By your swift movements you shall defeat the enemy,
35 Saving large numbers of your own men.
What fights a war is not numbers, nor weapons, but the mind.
From today on our regiments must harden their feet
And throw away the softening sandals.
On the swiftness of our feet depend all our wars.

To train ceaselessly all our fighting men is the key to our
    victory.'
As he spoke he turned to look at a cluster of bull-thorns
Which the Fasimba regiment had been directed to collect.
5   He now rushed to trample on them with his bare feet,
Dancing on them until they lay flattened.
All the regiments joined in the frenzy of this stoic dance.
Finally Shaka called out: 'Enough for today, children of
    Malandela.'
10 He ordered for the regiments large pots of beer.
Young boys shouted their poems of excellence as they roasted
    meat.
Crowds sang the songs of friendship.
When the song of the Mbatha clan was sung
15 It was Shaka himself who went first into the arena.
He moved all over like the body of a buffalo.
He danced until the young and the old were delirious with
    excitement.
Great was the day; great were the bonds that were cemented in
20   this era.

Day after day Shaka went without sleep.
He moved from camp to camp, training and coaxing his army,
Showing his regiments this and that of battle.
Sometimes he called by name those in the regiments he knew;
25 Sometimes he took a shield from a feeble hand
And challenged the opponent to a mock battle.
In all this Shaka's heart still bled with old grudges.
He still remembered those who had humiliated him.
One day he spoke openly to his regiments and said:
30 'Your readiness for battle fills me with joy.
Yet for now I want to tell tales in broad daylight.'
Many were eager to hear the story of his life —
For to many he was like a hero of fantastic legends.
His former enemies lived in fear.
35 Often in gatherings he would spell out their names.
Shaka began his story:
He spoke of the unhappy events of his youth;
He spoke of Hubhu who humiliated him before a group of young
    women;

He spoke of his clansmen who denied him their kinship;
He told them of the crimes of his cousins of emaLangeni;
He spelled out the name of the evil woman who denied them
    water.
5   Thus one incident led to another in quick succession.
'The victim,' our Forefathers say, 'never forgets.'
He laughed mockingly as he watched the terrified eyes of his old
    enemies:
This is no tale like the tales of old —
10   The perpetrators of these crimes still live!
Alas, such a tale is devoid of its true ending.
The evil men seem never to have been punished.
Thus, it is necessary to provide the final episodes.
Generations hereafter should say:
15   "Indeed, this is how such a story should end."
I have summoned a witness so that I may not err.
He pointed to an old man who staggered with age.
His hair was white like the winter flowers on the mountainside.
Slowly he named them one by one,
20   Not sparing even those who were the former king's councillors.
Shaka ordered them to come forward and stand before the
    Assembly.
Among them was a councillor, Mpembeni, who once called his
    family the 'cow's children'.
25   Also was the diviner who had fomented hostilities against
    them.
There, too, was the man who had sought the former king's
    favour
By spreading scandalous rumours against Nandi:
30   'I only did it, my lord, to please those who sent me,
Those who hated you and the mother of our nation.'
Shaka shouted at him angrily, demanding the names of these
    men.
Trembling, the councillor sputtered out even the names of those
35   who were dead.
Seeing the man so overwhelmed with fear, Shaka laughed and
    said:
'Did you let these evil men destroy the reputation of our nation?
Did you sleep in peace while a woman wandered in the
40   wilderness?'

The man was quiet, knowing these barbed words challenged his
    own role.
Shaka finally said: 'Whoever does not intervene in such cruelties
Only spreads the disease of his own cowardice.
5   Such a man is no man; he destroys the reputation and pride of
    our nation.
You, too, are guilty with all your masters.'
He directed the young men to round up all the culprits.
'I have long dreamt of a day like this,
10   To avenge myself against the vermin that cursed my youth.
If any among you still has something to say
Let him speak now before his sun sets.'
'My lord, it is hard to serve faithfully one's king,' commented
    the councillor,
15   'Yet it is clear a man must pay for his past judgement.
Such a man is swept away by the rivers of time.
We, too, father of our nation, share in such a fate.
Our deeds deserve the punishment designed for us by history.
I hold no grudge against my king.
20   To those who shall live hereafter
I ask them to serve our king faithfully.
Nor should they look down on us who failed.
A great era is best understood by those who are not of it.
Long may you live, my lord. Live to give the best to our nation.'
25   The words of this old man moved Shaka deeply
But he did not show it,
For a ruler must rarely show his feelings.
He said: 'These words would have been welcomed
Had they been uttered wisely at the right moment.
30   But today they have lost their meaning.
Indeed, they are bitter as though meant to buy a reputation.
I have one word to say:
May they be fulfilled as from the speaker's own lips.
Yet anyone is guilty who speaks only after the events.'
35   He turned to those in the Assembly and said:
'Perhaps you feel the sad fate of these men.'
One of the king's councillors, who was respected throughout the
    land,
Stood up and said: 'My lord, by the right of the Assembly
40   And the ancient laws of our Forefathers, permit me to speak.

I was there when these things happened.
It was I who opposed the evil talk against the Princess Nandi.
Then, I lost the respect of many in the Assembly.
I know these people and all their past crimes —
5 Yet I believe it was for the king they did these things.
I did then, and still now, blame the king, your father.'
Silence fell on the Assembly,
As though his words had violated some ancient sacred code.
But to this he paid no attention.
10 Instead he continued: 'The crimes of the powerful
Fall on the shoulders of the weak.
It is you who see further than tomorrow,
Whose judgement must accord with the truth of our times.'
Shaka concentrated his mind in silence.
15 Finally he said: 'I thank you for these words.
You are truly a man of greatness.
But my conscience troubles me.
If a nation surrenders its ancestral powers to its rulers,
Shall it not lose the essence of its nationhood?
20 Surely, blaming its kings and its rulers is not enough?
It is for this I seek your final judgement in these matters.
Thus I do not take your argument, father, however persuasive.
I do not seek to avenge myself, or my mother,
But that we should maintain some laws to create a great nation.
25 No nation survives only through its weapons.
A nation's true greatness begins from little truths.
Those who came hereafter must learn these events.
Self-serving men eventually destroy great nations.'
His face was contorted in anger and his voice lost its
30   mellowness:
'I forgive you only because of the great tasks before us.
A new season must be fertilized by old leaves.'

After this event Shaka and Mgobhozi sat discussing future plans.
Mgobhozi said to the king: 'This is how I see things, my lord:
35 If we start off with the weaker nations and overwhelm them
We shall augment the regiments of our Zulu army.
My thoughts focus on those of the abasemaLangeni
Who live in fear of their old crimes against the king.
The guilty often split their ranks,

Terrified at the spectre of their crimes.
In panic they point their fingers at whoever is suspect.
For all this they are easiest to overcome
In truth, the whole of Nguniland shall support your campaign.
5   But for us, my lord, the secret shall be
To give fighting experience to our army.'
The last words hit home in Shaka's mind.
As though roused to some exciting venture
His eyes moved with new warmth.
10 'Your thoughts coincide with mine, Mgobhozi,
My heart still bleeds when I recall
How they sang brutal songs against our family and held us to
    ridicule.
Let our forces surround them by night;
15 Let them be greeted at dawn by the angry eyes of our army.
It must be the uFasimba and amaWombe regiments that should
    lead the attack
Let the two horns, the old and the young, balance each other.
AmaWombe have many times faced enemies in battle;
20 UFasimba regiment is young and full of battle-eagerness.'

In the middle of the darkest night the regiments listened to
    Shaka
As he enumerated in whispers their routes.
He emphasized the need for swiftness in their actions,
25 Ordering them to advance cautiously until they reached the
    gates.
The combined forces would then split in half, rushing on either
    side.
Finally some would encamp on the higher ground and guard the
30 smaller gates.

The great night swallowed the shadows of the regiments;
Only the rhythms of their footfalls echoed in the river.
Sometimes they walked on the anthills, leaving their imprints
    and broken ants,
35 They climbed the little hill, approaching abasemaLangeni,
And there began to split, forming their strategic movements.

Shaka sat waiting until he heard the last cock crowing.

He raised his head and saw the large villages of the
    abasemaLangeni clan.
The sun spread its light from the night into the earth.
A crimson ribbon hung all around the horizon.

5   The eagle, disturbed from its night of peace,
Hovered high over the neighbouring mountains
As though to spy out those who should fill the earth.
The old dog flopped its ears near the cattle-fold,
Casting its eyes and peering at the rising shadows.

10   The Zulu army rose with the morning star.
It was as though they awaited the butterflies of dawn,
To see them fly in all directions and colours.
The glimmering spears caught the light of the sun!
Young men leaped like flashes of lightning from fence to fence.

15   The sons of Sokhulu skirted their way to the dark side of the
    village.
There they combined with the forces of Gebhuza-of-the-side-
    boards.

The grounds of the abasemaLangeni screamed with frightened
20   beasts.
People were suddenly awoken from their sleep;
Slowly the mist of night fell from their eyes.
A woman was heard, her voice wailing to the skies.
The Fasimba and the amaWombe regiments still waited silently.

25   Shaka, the son of Senzangakhona, shouted out their names,
Saying: 'Come out! I have arrived. I said long ago, "I shall be
    back."
Silwane, the son of Zagila, shall prod your memories.
It was he who scolded Sompisi of Vuma as they mocked us.

30   It was the same Sompisi who called out to me once:
"How can a thing like you return against us?"
Those who know of these events must save your homes —
'I mean you, and you, and you, and you, too, Mageza.'
As he spoke Shaka pointed at them with the spear handle.

35   Those who once harassed and humiliated him
Now wept before him, begging for mercy.
They wished the earth's numerous dungeons could swallow
    them.
Shaka looked at them steadily and finally said:

'How despicable a bunch of cowards you are!
Who would have guessed you would crawl and beg for your
    lives?
Even if I were to forgive you for your crimes
5   I would be revolted by your endless pleas and appeals.
For this you shall surely die. Look your last at the sun!
Tell me before you die, why did I deserve so much cruelty?'
He spoke, looking at each of them as though on the verge of
    tears.
10 They gabbled words which neither they nor he could
    understand.
One of them spoke clearly and said:
'As for me, I did only what I was directed to do.
I feared the anger of those older than me.'
15 Shaka smiled as if about to laugh and said:
'Yes, it is so. I remember how you feared bodily harm.
You whimpered and fled at the very sound of the whiplash.
You begged your agemates to let you stay while they challenged
    others.
20 I do forgive you, but I shall teach you how to be brave.
You shall learn how great a burden is cowardice.
At the very first battle we shall fight
It is you who shall be posted at its mouth.'
He spoke as if he was only making fun of him, but he meant it.
25 Those condemned were led to the place of execution
And knocked senseless with a gigantic club and thrown to the
    vultures.
After this a Cleansing Feast was held.
The general announced: 'The king commands that old grudges
30   be forgotten.
Eat and drink for indeed you are the king's relations.'
As he spoke Shaka wandered through the fields with his
    followers.
He gestured and commented on the landmarks of his days of
35   youth.
Great pains keep the memory fresh.

Many danced, celebrating the era of Shaka's return.
How strange are people and their moods!
Often they sing and dance only to hide their fears.

Thus abasamaLangeni danced the great Dance of Healing.
In tribute to him the whole country echoed with festivities.
When all had feasted to their hearts' content
The commander-in-chief summoned home all the Zulu
5   regiments.
Among the abasemaLangeni clan Shaka left a commander;
His task was to teach the new methods of warfare.
Henceforth, they were to boast the great short spear of
      Nodumehlezi.
10 From a distance could be seen the Zulu army departing.
Young men looked with envy at the singing regiments.
They, too, wished they belonged to the growing Zulu army.
The commander posted there infused in them the heroic spirit:
'Tomorrow it shall be you who shall be the nation's heroes.
15 You too shall be the great king's favourites.
But for now you must train without ceasing.
Never wake up at the last crowing of the cock.
Our bodies must come out to the sun. On them it must flow like
      water.'
20 As he spoke a poet's voice declaimed from a distance.
His words reverberated into the distant valleys: 'Great one,
Who is eternally on the lips of the women of Nomgabi.
They endlessly gossiped: "Shaka shall never rule;
He never shall be king."
25 But it was then he grew up to overwhelm the earth!'
Great hymns of triumph echoed from distant regions.

Shaka was proud of this new spirit of fearlessness.
Many sang songs that challenged the belligerent kings of
      Nguniland,
30 Yet Shaka still restrained his over-eager regiments and said:
'Great wars are not fought through zealousness,
But through schemes and strategies born of sleepless nights.'
Throughout Nguniland Shaka's reputation grew,
Attracting smaller and greater nations.
35 Large numbers of emaQungebeni clans arrived.
Their great warriors were eager to be the heroes of the Zulu
      army.
Some were drawn by the thought of easy loot and fame.
Such a man was Shayimpi, son of Shonkweni, of Nogalazela.

He had fought in many fierce wars.
He was solicited by many kings and princes,
He wandered from kingdom to kingdom, but never settled.
Shayimpi was not the only warrior who roamed like this.
5   Many could be seen following the direction of wars in large
        numbers.
Such were those who, on hearing of Shaka's magic name,
Set out for the land of Zululand.
Shaka did not discourage these reckless adventurers,
10   But moulded them into brigades of fearless detachments.
In them he infused a new spirit of brotherhood,
Making them denounce their brigandage by an oath of loyalty.
For Shaka knew disparate loyalties often divide a nation.

Having now reorganized his army and given them the new short
15   spear,
He declared war on the troublesome King Phungashe.
It was the same king who fleeced Senzangakhona through
        endless tributes.
Shaka sent his messenger to him:
20   'Tell him I hear from the babbling voices of the wind
He demands of me a settlement of old scores in battle.
Tell him through the narrow passages of his bird-like throat
We shall make him swallow the swear words he has used against
        our house.'
25   He said this, remembering how Phungashe once said to his
        councillors:
'Have you heard of the wild boy of Dingiswayo
Who now raises his upstart head above those of his superiors?'
The messenger from Shaka announced his mission:
30   'My lord, the son of Senzangakhona says
I should return with the beasts to cleanse his father's house.'
King Phungashe said: 'Here is my answer to your king:
Tell him he, the leather-tanner, bites what he cannot chew.'
When Shaka heard these words he rubbed his hands,
35   Looking at all his regiments with glee.

He said, smilingly: 'Go then, son of Bhejane.
Tell him to prepare for battle. Soon a lion shall kill a mouse,
Says I, who responds without delay like a thunderbolt.

Tell him his defeat shall be a lesson to all arrogant rulers of
    Nguyniland.
They shall know it is unwise to wake the lion from his sleep,
To treat carelessly a growing bull of the House of Jama.'
5 The fierce cry of battle was carried to distant lands;
With trembling voices the shouting women summoned all to
    battle.
Their words were picked up by those who dwelt at the distant
    mountains.
10 Who in turn shouted them to those of the northern regions.
All cried out the same message of war.
From hill to hill, from valley to valley, it resounded.

The same tumultuous cry echoed: 'War is in our gates!'
At the summit of the mountains hung the voices of death.
15 Even animals, dwellers of the river banks, stared in amazement.
They saw, daily, great crowds who came to their homes,
Who bent down to sharpen their spears on the smooth river
    stones.
So great were their numbers that the hills and valleys seemed to
20   yield.
The antelope, frightened, fled into the deep regions of the forest.
King Phungashe inspired his army for battle:
'Let men and women flee from the wrath to come!
Let widows be heard wailing: "Woe unto you, who dared the
25   son of Shenge!" '
As all this was happening Shaka only half slept.
He sat all night planning and plotting new strategies,
Eager now to avenge all the humiliations against his Forefathers.

As the two armies faced each other
30 Shaka ordered the uFasimba regiment to occupy the centre.
Behind them he put the Mbelebele regiment
And spread it in a crescent battle line.
At the tips of each horn of the half-moon formation
He put his two great heroes, Mgobhozi and Mshokobezi.
35 The Zulus raised their shields as if to cover themselves from a
    downpour of rain.
Slowly they moved in a uniform dance of war.
Phungashe's army threw at them a thick hail of spears.

Among them was the famous warrior of flamboyant habits in
   battle.
The Buthelezi poets shouted his poems of excellence!
'Vaulting spear that hits the targets of flesh!'
5   He stood on a small rise perched on a flat boulder.
From there he threw his spears like a collection of pebbles.
Even the winds that carried them whistled in accompaniment.
Sometimes he threw many spears all at once,
Making them sink into many victim's hearts.
10   One such missile started slowly from his hands
And, gaining momentum, it turned, spinning round in flight
Until by its accurate aim it sank its iron tooth into the flesh.
Then it spat a gush of blood, making itself like a fountain.
It was Noduze, the tall son of Prince Langa, who was killed.
15   He was known for his reckless temper.
Of him it was expected that he would fight great wars.
His body was corrugated with many spear wounds.
He, the great hero, said as he lay wounded:
'Brothers of the battlefield, finish me up, I am wounded.
20   I applaud the day whose dawn I see but whose sun I shall never
   see.'
As he spoke others retreated in terror.
It was Shaka who shouted at them,
Harassing them with threats, cajoling others with poems of
25   excellence.
He raised his own great spear and said:
'Noduze, son of Langa, die like a hero!'
As he said these words, he relieved him of his final pain.
The hungry heroes of battle rushed from the two horns of the
30   crescent.
Half surrounding the army of Phungashe, they attacked from all
   sides
Forcing back Phungashe's numerous throngs.
Amidst the front-line heroes was Shaka himself.
35   He was stabbing on all sides, inciting his regiments into battle.

As the battle raged King Phungashe sat at a distance with his
   wives and children,
Having delegated the tasks of battle to his many generals.

Seeing his army disengage he thought it was only to gain
    distance.
The Zulu army had anticipated these tactics.
They crowded them, following them on their heels.
5   Each time Phungashe's army attempted to gain a breathing
        space
The Zulus rushed on them with their avenging spears.
Impeded by shoes they plodded on the ground,
Until the two horns of the Zulu crescent closed in on them.
10   The Zulu fighters were red with the blood of Phungashe's army.
It was as if the slaughter would never stop.
Some fled to the open plains, chased by Shaka's army.
Others fled to their families' regions, chased by Shaka's army.
Still others flung themselves into the precipice.
15   Everywhere Phungashe's men fled in vain.
Realizing the impending defeat, Phungashe fled alongside a
        broken wall.
He took the route that led to King Zwide's regions.
Breathless as he arrived at Zwide's royal residence, he said:
20   'Great King, brother and friend, give me shelter!
I flee from the fierceness of the son of Senzangakhona.
I despised him, thinking him only a boy.
Only recently the Zulus paid tribute to us!
My whole clan of relatives has been killed.
25   The whole great Buthelezi army has been routed.
My village-city has been razed to the ground.
I am now worth only what is on my body.'

He spoke hurriedly, as though someone might yet dispute his
        words.
30   King Zwide opened his mouth in shock and held his hand over
        it.
He said: 'Phungashe, your words overwhelm me.
How can a king as mighty as you be defeated by a mere boy?
Did you listen properly to your messengers?'
35   Phungashe of the Buthelezis shook his head.
It was as though he had beheld a horrifying spectacle.
He said: 'Zwide, son of Langa, it is not from hearsay I speak.
I report what I have seen with my own eyes.'
At this point Zwide decided to say no more.

He sat absorbed in thought,
Imagining the great threats that faced their kingdoms.
Secretly he consoled himself:
'After all, I have a better army than the defeated Phungashe.'
5   While Phungashe slept in the House of Strangers,
Zwide, the son of Langa, stayed awake,
Attempting to unravel the strategies of this battle.
He felt haunted by the very thought of Senzangakhona's proud
    son.
10   To one of his councillors, he said: 'Go to the Great House.
Tell the Female Elephant, my mother, we have a stranger.
She may wish to witness how I shall entertain him.'
Zwide was only making a mockery of Phungashe,
Since he knew the Queen Mother would only demand
15   Phungashe's head.
As the councillor gave his message
She laughed loud like one who knows some secret.
Finally she said: 'Tell the king, my lord, I have heard his word.
Ask him if he has forgotten the race of ants
20   Whose feast would last eternally on so big a head?
The hunger of an ant sets out a million others.
All things become their nourishment.
Through his scruples they may attack even this kingdom.
In desperation they may devour his own bones.'
25   The messenger trembled at this sorceress's conversation.
He knew the life of King Phungashe would soon be
    extinguished.

The heroes of Zululand returned ecstatic with victory.
Their triumphal songs rose in harmony over the little
30   mountains.
Great crowds rushed to meet the triumphant army.
Poems of excellence were chanted everywhere.
Women sang in accompaniment to their children.
At the arena the poet's voice boomed with ancient epics.
35   He sung of Mdlani, of Malandela, of Phunga, of Mageba, of
    Jama.
He sang of the young lion of Senzangakhona.
He shook the hill of cranes with his poems of excellence:
'The bull that bellowed from Mthonjaneni —

All nations heard it.
Dunjwa of Luyengweni heard it, clearly.
So did Mangcegceza, the son of Khali,
The uncontrollable blaze of Mjokwane
5   Which singed all things on its way!
It burnt the sleeping owls at Mdlebe
Until those of Mabedlane were destroyed.
When he passed through the villages of Ndina and Mgovu,
Women who were pregnant aborted.
10 The tender fields were left unfinished.
The precious seed was left in the fields.
People fled in terror!
Old women were abandoned in ruined villages.
Old men were left half-way to their sanctuaries
15 The giant roots were upturned as if by a whirlwind.
He hurried through the villages of Mcobo in the evening.'
Thus did the poet eulogize Shaka's triumph.
Warriors who did not fight in this battle sat and wept:
'I too, shall cross the Thukela river one day.
20 I shall walk on its sands; its waters shall wait for me to pass.'

Shaka was elated with the performance of his new army.
He distributed the fat cows of Phungashe,
Saying: 'People must eat what is theirs.
Through many years Phungashe has robbed and pillaged many
25   homes.'
On this great day Shaka addressed the excited gathering:
'I confer all honour on the uFasimba and the Mbelebele
      regiments.
They are honoured by the living and the dead.
30 On them the whole great nation confers the poems of heroes.
The power of Phungashe has been broken forever!
His voice of terror has been silenced.
His ant-eaters shall dig for the children of the Palm Race.'
He referred to Phungashe's troops now in the Zulu army.
35 Its commanders quickly learnt the new codes of war and
      fraternity.
He said, continuing: 'The nation of the Zulus embodies all
      peoples.
Those of the Buthelezi nation are now part of us.

All must abide by the laws of one nation.
Their share in peace-time and in danger is equal.
Whoever shall show hostility against them
Shall have committed a heinous crime against us.
5   He shall have challenged the living and the dead.'
His words alarmed those of the older generation,
Who thought victory meant the mockery of the defeated
    enemies.
But they were now accustomed to these startling
10   announcements.
Shaka said, continuing: 'I forgive those of the Buthelezi nation,
Who shall accept the full authority of the Zulu nation;
Nor shall I confiscate their possessions.
But the stubborn ones shall get the punishment they deserve.'
15   Even the councillors who had accepted the need for diplomacy
Began to protest; their faces were twisted with doubt.
These men had hoped to amass the wealth from confiscated
    cattle.
But Shaka took only those that had belonged to Phungashe:
20   'I take these cattle for those who were robbed by him.
Let other little kings and upstarts learn their lesson:
It is unwise to walk the land triumphantly like a bull elephant.
People must choose their regions of destruction
And skirt away from the sacred graves of our Forefathers.
25   Our weapons are ever sharp and ready against such wild men.'

Soon after this battle Shaka set out to Mkindini royal city
For there the Princess Nandi, his mother, had demanded his
    presence.
As he arrived he noticed an all-pervasive mood of sadness.
30   He said: 'I came here only because you summoned me.
Nothing besides this would have shaken me.
The country is in turmoil.
From all sides kings and princes prepare for battle.
In the upper regions King Zwide calls for total war.
35   In the north Prince Matiwane of the Ngwanes
Roars loud like a wounded lion.
I hope what you called me for surpasses all these affairs.'
He spoke, staring angrily at Nandi,
Restless as though he wanted her to speak quickly.

But she took her time. . . .
She spoke slowly as if her tongue was in pain.
He himself was forced to control his eagerness.
He asked of things of no consequence.

5   Nandi looked aside and said to her councillor:
'I want the king to be feasted with a hundred head of cattle.
Let the arena be filled with celebrations.
Let this be a great moment of rejoicing.'
The councillor lowered his head, consenting to her.

10   Shaka thought within himself:
'Could I have neglected my mother,
And concentrated only on the affairs of state and wars?
Could it be she invites me to affirm her authority?
Or does she wish to say our bond surpasses all things?'

15   Despite all these misgivings he still felt angry at her.
He was torn between his loyalty to the army and his parent.
He knew a great nation prospers only through ceaseless
      devotion.

In spite of his anger he did not show it.

20   He consoled his mother: 'I have neglected you.
I fell under the spell of battles and affairs of the land.
You chastise me now, making me feel sad.
But it was you, daughter of the Mhlongo clan,
Who often planted in me the anger against our foes.

25   I have avenged myself; I have humiliated your enemies.
I now do what was designed for me by my Ancestors.
Their voices give me no rest and no peace.'
He said this, hoping to dig out the truth from her.
Yet Princess Nandi did not respond.

30   She continued to inquire of this and that in his daily life.
She even asked him to tell her how he vanquished King
      Phungashe.
As he was carried away by talks of battle episodes
Nandi digested the thoughts and words she had not revealed.

35   Suddenly she was made beautiful by her tears.
They fell gently; sometimes were suspended on her cheeks.
Shaka continued narrating these novel things to her.
Sometimes she began singing his poems of excellence,
Rousing in him the memory of past episodes.

Shaka was puzzled by his mother's gloom.
For though he thought his obsessions were her source of anger,
She urged him on to talk of them.
When he was finally tired out
5 Nandi said to him: 'My lord, people are waiting for their king.'
As she said this, voices boomed and echoed on the royal
        grounds.
The feet of dancers thundered at the large arena.
Shaka held himself back, not asking questions.
10 For he knew ideas that are pursued too impatiently
Often are like the tail of the bird of paradise,
Whose feathers snap off in the hand of too eager a hunter.

The celebrations continued uninterrupted for three days long.
Nandi had often sat next to the king but did not speak.
15 She had her eyes constantly fixed on the arena,
Her mind turbulent with memories and her heart beaming with
        joy,
Her face shone with the softness of a new fresh season.
When those who had gathered had fully immersed themselves,
20 Nandi turned to Shaka and said:
'It is enough for now, my child, nor is it the last.
This day has fed the thin ones of yesterday.
Suffering gives birth to the rich earth and all things grow.'
Shaka quietly consented to these words.
25 He realized now this was her day of joy.
When Nandi returned to her house, she said:
'I thank you for celebrating this day with me.
Tomorrow I ask that I complete its pleasures with you;
To have a moment to tell my heart's secrets,
30 For in truth I am getting old.
But pains persist, eating deeper into my heart;
Though often my face is dressed in a convenient mask,
Yet I still continue to suffer.
You know the fierce scars that mark my life;
35 How you and Nomchoba and your younger brother, Ngwadi,
        lived.
Indeed, your little brother scarcely knows about these things.
When you became commander at the Mthethwas
I was scarcely pregnant with him.'

As she said this her face twisted with remembered pains.
Shaka consoled her with all the warmth he could give,
Consenting to her request and promising to do as she
    wished.
5 When he spoke his voice was soft and his face was turned away
As though to hide his own pain from her.

The following day the sun rose in all its splendour;
People wandered off in all directions.
They were not cursed with the fate of Nandi of the Mhlogos,
10 She who had never dreamed their simple dreams,
Still broken, still harassed by nightmare visions.
The pockets of her eyes were touched with darkness.
When she heard Shaka's approaching footsteps
She sharpened her words, preparing her challenging questions.
15 Stung by her experiences of many years, she had lived as a
    recluse.
She said to her councillors:
'I ask you to leave me alone with my lord.
Let us talk of things known only to us.'
20 Shaka, the tall one of Nguniland, entered.
When he sat down and rested, Nandi began to speak,
Saying: 'I called you to empty all in my heart.
In every pain that befell me in the past
It was you who were my hope and deep vision.
25 When your fame grew at the royal court of the Mthethwas
I rejoiced at your many heroic deeds.
Only this faith sustained me:
You would go back to rule in your own kingdom.
Like others, I wished you all my blessings for your future rule.
30 But when it finally came
I was left like a plant in a heap of decaying leaves:
I withered amidst the plenty of your kingdom.
As I am, I am devoid of consolation and true friendship.
My hands are always empty.
35 I begin to envy the happy women of other lands,
They who feel the eternal warmth in their hands.
They hear a voice emerging from their backs,
Unlike myself who continues to carry a silent stone,
Hearing no new voice heralding the future.

I lured you here so that you might see the plenty that is mine.
I hoped you would see how this abundance
Hangs over my house, haunting me as though I were a mad
    woman.
5 I am like someone who suffers loneliness amidst their own
    families.
I ask you: may I rejoice in a voice that is yours?
May I be made human by the warmth of your child?
Make me able to walk proudly like all other women.'
10 It was as though a thunderclap had struck,
Making all things flee in terror.
Shaka's lips quivered. He spoke only in half-finished words:
'Mother, I hear your deep and powerful thoughts.
It is a challenge greater than that of wars.
15 My head is confused by these unusual words from you.
Often I have parried with these thoughts as though I was
    bewitched by them.
This was not because I could not see the answers,
But because I was frightened lest I should tread on your
20   dreams.
I knew, too, how deeply your heart desired what I cannot give.
Even when I gave you all, my conscience still troubled me.
Indeed, I, too, in your position would yearn for as much:
To have joy in hearing the speech of my children's children.
25 But then my failure to give is not of my doing.
It is the task given to me by my Forefathers
To enhance the name of their ancient nation.
It is threatened by many gangster kings.
As long as I am still building this nation
30 I must postpone the joys of my domestic life.
I fear lest my ligaments be eaten by such a progeny,
For a strong man often weakens after having children.
His knees, his whole body, tenses and collapses.
He begins to have fear of death for his children's sake.
35 It is for this same reason I have forbidden my soldiers to marry.
It is through these very children you desire
That the enemies of our nation shall create dissension.
They shall split our nation before it has put down its roots.
We shall be like all kings who are in constant fear of their
40   children.

Such was the case with my own father, Dingiswayo.
Such has been the fate of such men as King Macingwane,
Who have had to murder their own children in broad daylight.'
As Shaka spoke he remembered from his own life
5   How once he had hated his own father, Senzangakhona.
How this feeling had consumed him silently day and night.
He recalled how Godongwana and Tana
Planned the death of their own father, King Jobe.
He knew, too, of the many rulers whose sons
10 Settled their disputes through the murder of their own fathers.
Though Nandi now confirmed what she had always feared
She still felt pained and saddened by it.
The wilderness of the old is often inhabited by disembodied
      voices;
15 Old memories trail like sounds heard distantly in a dream.
Only their children's children break the silence.
Nandi listened intently to Shaka's words.
She said: 'I am not prepared to argue.
I do not wish even to follow up your words with mine.
20 I believe in your thoughts, even if they be unpleasant to me.
Yet I still fear their eternal power.
They are like the abundant waters of the ocean
Whose vast regions show no growing forests,
Nor do they nourish the summer fields of our lands.
25 Bitter they are, nor can they quench our thirst.
Yet I must wish you the warm hands of the Ancestral Fathers.
In your power I shall always see a growth that is ours.
Our house shall be like a great mountain range
On whose shoulders your image shall dazzle like the sun,
30 But it may be my destiny only to watch from a distance.'
Such were the biting words of Nandi.
From these comments Shaka realized
How his achievements had undermined their relationship.
Their old bonds had been broken, manifesting only new
35   directions.
Generations divide and the sun blazes into the womb of night.
A new generation leaps into the eye of the mountain,
Lighting a new fire for the new dawn of tomorrow.

Book Six: The end of an era — Dingiswayo dies

Shaka's life now takes a turn. He assumes the responsibilities not only of power but also of the personal welfare of people he has known. Mbiya, who looked after him in the days of exile, dies (historically Mbiya died after Dingiswayo's death). Dingiswayo himself needs Shaka's advice, though he is still reluctant to embark on the total war advocated by Shaka. Dingiswayo attacks Matiwane. with Shaka's force as the main thrust of battle. Matiwane is captured. Against Shaka's advice Dingiswayo releases him, only to let him roam and cause greater destruction. He is attacked by Zwide, whose ambition is to rule the whole of Nguniland as a private family domain. The saddest event is the murder of Dingiswayo by Zwide, which ends the hopes of an era of peaceful transition to all embracing Nguni nationhood. His murder sets the stage for a confrontation between Shaka and Zwide and the decision concerning the hegemony of Nguniland.

King Phakathayo, the son of Khondlo, was an ambitious ruler.
He cast his eyes to distant lands, restless at the thought of
    conquest..
But he was not like Zwide or Matiwane,
5 Who desired to subordinate all the nations of the earth,
Causing great panic amongst smaller and larger nations.
A word came to Shaka of Senzangakhona, saying
Dingiswayo now considered these two rulers a threat to peace.
Once again they had begun to sharpen their spears.
10 Simultaneously the messenger gave a message that disturbed
    Shaka:
'I have come, too, to tell you about your father, Prince Mbiya,
Whose life may close with the closing of this very day.
He calls you to listen to his last words of life.
15 He says he shall not let them dry in his lips before you come.
You his son must inherit his thoughts.
Yet King Dingiswayo says he awaits you with such tears
As will consume a man in his old age.
It is too long since he last heard your words of wisdom.
20 He implores you to plan with him against gangster rulers.

He prepares for action against Zwide and the wild Matiwane.
These wolves eat the bones in our cattle-folds.
They capture the young lamb and retreat into the forest.'
The messenger spoke in a calm voice, knowing
5 It is improper to rush through the telling of important news.
Shaka was stunned by these words.
He hurried through the affairs of the land in a daze.
For it was this great man, Prince Mbiya,
Who at the Mthethwas treated him with kindness and love.
10 Like a bull pampering a young bull calf,
Licking it with the tip of its tongue,
Teaching it the delicate movements of fighting.

Shaka sent word to his mother, Princess Nandi, and said:
'I go to revive a life at the ruins.
15 Mbiya is on the verge of dying.
Perhaps even now he is no more.'
Shaka traversed the mountains and valleys of the Mthethwas,
Accompanied by the fierce uFasimba regiment.
When they arrived at the grounds of the great Mbiya
20 Crowds were talking in subdued tones.
As Shaka entered the house
It was as if he had brought a magic herb.
The old man reared up and began to speak:
'I was waiting for you, my child, Nodumenhlezi.
25 The time for me to leave draws near.
I go now to rest with my Forefathers;
I hear them calling me each passing moment.
I am glad I found a unique and fruitful plant
Which I nourished when it was young,
30 Until now I see it begin to feed the nations of the earth.
I can see the eagle climb into the sky.
When it reaches the high point of heaven
It spreads its shadow,
Casting it over worlds never known before.'
35 Shaka, eager to hide his own concern,
Said: 'Father, do not speak as if you are dying.
We still have great doctors in the land.
I shall summon the very best of them.
What will people say,

Seeing you depart without sharing in your son's feast?'
The old man's mind wandered. He smiled and said:
'No one man has seen the earth from its birth
And lived to see it mature into old age.
5   Grant me peace, my child, that I may pass to my Forefathers.
A beautiful lamp burns away with the morning.
By the love of the Ancestors, may it be so.
I ask you to accompany me to the verge of the night.
Even now the king awaits you with your wisdom.
10 Go to him so that as I sleep
I shall know no enemy tramples on our place of rest.
I shall listen to the eternal voices of our land
And hear the bellowing of our beasts in the fields.
This peace I ask from you, Nodumenhlezi, when I am no more.'
15 He spoke, breathing deeply,
Like someone who had received unpleasant news.
Shaka's face darkened, his mind absorbed in Mbiya's words.
He stretched out his hand to him, and said:
'Father, I ask you for your blessing.
20 There are too many tasks on my shoulders.
With this hand, and your permission, I shall break new paths.'
As he spoke, Mbiya stretched out his weakened hand.
Holding Shaka's hand and cupping it
He said to him: 'I want you to leave me
25 And rush to heed the king's word at oYengweni royal city.'

There were heroes celebrating on the royal grounds.
Many Shaka had known from his days of youth.
King Dingiswayo went to meet him half-way and said:
'So, you have come Shaka who is invincible.
30 I knew you would not sink into paralysing sadness
At a time when the troops are waiting for your leadership.'
He spoke, focusing his mind on Mbiya's death,
Whose suddenness had cut off Shaka's tenderness of youth.
He said, consoling him: 'You are blessed, my child.
35 All the unhappy hearts turn to you!
Such a person shall live eternally.
I, too, hope you might fill your home with joy.
For, indeed, you have two homes.
Both call equally for your warmth.

I mourn your sadness, which is mine.
Mbiya was a man I could truly trust.
Through him I realized we are the weeds of the past.
We shall wither in the fields, fertilizing the new plants.
5 It is you, Nodumenhlezi, who shall raise new life from our ruins.
You shall build capitals that shall far surpass ours.
For this reason our last efforts must open new paths,
Leaving the hoe in your hands.
I am haunted by thoughts of impending disasters.
10 To fight them we require men of courage.'
As he spoke these words Shaka nodded in assent.
He said: 'My lord, we shall not throw away
The great gifts that have come from your hands.
Whatever we shall be, it is with your nourishment.
15 We shall acclaim your era in all our efforts.'
Dingiswayo, eager to suppress this effusive praise,
Said: 'Son of Senzangakhona, I am old.
Do not decieve yourself with these thoughts.
I, in all the period of my reign, knew
20 It was you whose vision would bring eternal peace.
Once I believed (infused with hollow dreams)
That kings and princes of Nguniland would embrace my vision,
Surrendering their petty quarrels to a new bond of friendship.
But I have now seen and known the truth:
25 No one gives up their spoils of war except through war.
As long as they possess the power
People shall always flex their muscles in battle.
As I say these words I feel a deep pain
For they affirm the disintegration of my dreams.
30 The failure of someone who can no longer change
Surpasses all failures by its sadness.
Even though I now admit the truth of your words
My heart is heavy with thoughts of what could have been.
I continue to cling to my illusions.
35 I shall die, known only as the foolish ruler of the Mthethwas.
But I am not a fool, nor am I a coward.
I do not denounce war for fear of dying in battle.
For this I still grasp the truth of your triumphs.
I only feared the terrors that wars bring to families.
40 I knew by a common effort our land could be one,

Yet it is your vision that has the truth in it.'
Dingiswayo quickly checked himself from this low mood.
He said to Shaka: 'I did not invite you, my son,
To burden you with the ramblings of an old man,
5   Who may seem wise only after his years of glory.
I called you because of problems that give me no rest.
Zwide, the son of Ntombazi, is restless again.
Day after day he challenges me to war.
I fear this might be my final battle.
10   I shall fight with my own strategy, while you fight with yours.
Let these two arms of battle prove their power.
Let those who report the devastations of wars
Forever observe the two aspects of battle.
Perhaps, tired of slaughter,
15   Generations to come may yet return to my grave,
To wake me up to speak once again my words of wisdom.
Here is my plan then, Nodumenhlezi of Nguniland.
I shall first attack the short-tempered Matiwane of the Ngwanes.
My spies tell me this hunchbacked dwarf
20   Bristles with tricks and schemes and distasteful stratagems.
He is feared and hated even by the hospitable Hlubis.
Many nations flee in great numbers from him.
His army raids Nguniland and the gentle Sotho nations.
It is said the calf skin he wears is marked with magic signs.
25   Because of this, his nation lives without friends.
When nations hear of his approach
They seize their belongings and flee from him.
The head of the black mamba must be crushed!
Only this way can we bring peace:
30   I want us to surround this horrid snake
Before it strikes and kills another unwary bird.'
Shaka listened, thrilled at the prospect of humiliating Matiwane.
Indeed, it had been too long since he had tried his new
        strategies.
35   In his mind he began to see the forming regiments
And the eager young heroes crowding the mountain tops.
He said: 'My king, I thank you for trusting me.
Your faith in me does not wither with the years.
You continue to give me ever-expanding regions to guard.
40   I shall do as you have commanded.

My troops are always battle-ready.
They await whatever word comes from you.
When I have made all the funeral rites for my father, Mbiya,
I shall wash my feet with dew,
5   Rushing early at dawn to fulfil your wishes.
Above all, I request that these preparations
Be known only to you and a few commanders.
Indeed, it is true that Matiwane is a wily ruler.
On hearing of our preparations
10 He may yet devise some new tricks —
Perhaps raise a gigantic army from his satellite nations.
Our attack may yet be confronted with a formidable army.
A devastating thunderbolt travels silently, my lord.'
Thus they concluded their affairs and plans of war.
15 They embraced, keeping dark their secrets.
But both were sad, knowing Mbiya had danced his last dance.
Neither did he hear the great new battle song,
Nor see the heroes don their battle array.
Dying, he said: 'I am satisfied with what I have heard.
20 I know no nation shall rule over us.'
When he slept in the ancient anthill
His heart sang the songs of joy.

Such was the time when the Zulu allies prepared for battle.
The Mthethwa regiments assembled from all parts of the land:
25 Many kings and princes talked ceaselessly of these preparations.
Zwide himself kept aloof, only watching in readiness,
Knowing the victor shall yet face
His freshly launched regiments.
The secrets of Dingiswayo and Shaka were secrets no longer!
30 Through Matiwane's many spies
News exploded, telling of the plot against him.
He approached the Hlubis to shelter his children and wealth.
With pride he drove there the thousands of stolen beasts.
Their dust, the ancient poets say, clouded the sun.
35 The Hlubis bowed to his will in fear,
Knowing his wars followed the heat of his anger.

The son of Senzangakhona launched his regiments,
Setting them to follow close to the Mthethwa army.

They crossed the clear waters of the white Mfolozi.
Dingiswayo's army trudged on, approaching the Mthshali
    territories.
Like a great swarm of fierce bees they were.
5   Even the sun seemed dimmed by their dust.
It is said at this moment Shaka commented to Dingiswayo:
'My lord, I have many times restrained myself from saying this.
In this war it seems there is only one possible way.
Our task is to break the stubborn tree mercilessly in the middle.
10 For should we only gently bend it
We shall have scattered many seeds of bitterness.
I know this has always been my request to you
But today I feel it with greater conviction.'
Even then the indolent son of Jobe, Dingiswayo,
15 Still hoped to fight only to frighten the enemy.
Shaka, irritated by this, said:
'It is not for myself that I want this decisive battle,
But to protect the glory of all your achievements.
Indeed, the older you get, the more fierce the challenges against
20   you.
Rulers now threaten your very home and loyal allies.
It won't be long before they take advantage of your kindness.'
He spoke as though he had divined the future.
Dingiswayo reluctantly consented to Shaka's words
25 But desired him to await the outcome of this battle.

When the two armies clashed
Shaka, grandson of Jama, rushed ahead of others.
He swayed his shield as if moved by some spirit.
The Zulu heroes leaped and followed close to him
30 As the afternoon opened its wings of crimson.
The Matiwane army was scattering in all directions.
Each Zulu regiment chased groups of fleeing enemy soldiers.
It was after this decisive triumph
That Dingiswayo spoke to the captured prince:
35 'I mourn for your men who died in vain,
Who were lured by you with promises of loot.
They shall now be nourishment only for the vultures.
Because of those you scattered and terrorized,
Because of the nations whose widows mourn your destructions,

Because of the ruins of homes and fields unattended
I should sentence you to death without mercy.
Indeed I would win the applause of many nations.
My own troops demand your execution.
5   But, despite your dreadful crimes, I still believe,
I still hope, a man of such wisdom and intelligence
May yet learn and put down his weapons of destruction.
It must be you who protect the smaller nations,
Lifting your great wings to shelter them from the sun.
10 I leave you to go with your own people
To build a new city that shall be your home of peace.
There I shall visit you myself.
We shall drink and feast as brothers.
Then all nations shall applaud the great country of Nguniland.'
15 As he spoke Matiwane pretended to listen attentively
But his heart was closed.
He swore revenge for his son who died in this war.
Prince Matiwane's mind was restless.
He yearned to rain havoc on Queen Mantantisi,
20 A fierce woman who personally led the baTlokwa armies.
She raided and terrorized the Maluti nations of the Sothos.
She chased the Fukengs and the Kwenas.
Prince Matiwane often harassed these nations, too.
He did not spare the Thembus and the Xhosas of Ngqika —
25 All southern nations sought alliances against this bandit prince.
He roamed like one consumed by ulcers.
It was at this moment he decided to fight without end,
Hating the superior voice of Dingiswayo as it sang to him.
He said within himself: 'I am not to be dressed down like a boy.
30 I am the descendant of the great line of ancient kings.'

The regiments of the Mthethwa army returned home.
They sang alongside the brave regiments of the Zulus.
For each other they sang their ancient songs.
Only Shaka was reserved as others frolicked and danced to
35   victory.
He still cursed the failure to fight for an outright victory.
He saw, too, how Matiwane did not take heed of Dingiswayo's
     words

But patronized him like a senile old man.
Shaka was sad, too, that his words fell on deaf ears.
He realized how hard it is to kill the wasteful habit of frequent
     wars.
5 Indeed, he saw how kings and leaders favoured each other,
Sparing each other's lives while the fighting men perished.

The Mthethwa army veered off toward Mthethwaland.
Poems of excellence given to Shaka by Dingiswayo
Still echo now down through the ages.
10 The poet's voice was heard reverberating from the high cliffs,
Declaiming Dingiswayo's poem of excellence:
'The slow-climbing sun of Mdlala —
When it rose the morning stars warned each other.
One was of Ntombazi; another was of Langa!
15 Round calabashes that are bought
Are beautiful like the sun!
He came down the mountain
On which no beast ever descended
Only the millipedes tumbled down!
20 Black one, who is like the rich fields of mud!
You are as huge as the giant tree at the hilltop
You are like the young of the buck!
Pathfinder, who opened the way to Ntumeni and eShowe cities.
The great bird returned by the landmarks of tall trees.
25 It passed your settlements of Sigubudu.
Black one, who ate the bride's gift of cattle.
The great stampede that flattened the tall grass.
Even now the hill of Zaza is still disturbed
For it had not seen any herd of elephants!
30 You will hear them tell you, Sombageya, saying:
"The fields of sorghum are ripe at the Biyelas
Because you captured the wife of Xubuzela,
Then captured Nodumo, the son of Donda, the son of Shiya.
He captured Mangxango of Donda of Shiya.
35 He took away Valelisani from the same place of Shiya.
He captured Mlovu of Ngogwana of the same clan of Shiya.
Lion-hearted one, who is feared even by his in-laws!
You destroyed the houses of your in-laws!" '
The poet continued narrating this poem till the sun set.

His words are like dew in the middle of the night.
They make nests in the open mountain tops.
The mountains show their caverns to the heavens and declaim
    with him.
5   There were feasts and ceremonies throughout the land.
Those who returned with victory were welcomed with songs.
They slept, praising the eternal peace in the land of the
    Mthethwas.
It was as though this great day should never pass,
10 But must always feed people with its fullness.
Even Zwide and all the children of Ntombazi envied them,
Fearing, too, lest when they had been fed with ambition
They might desire the green pastures of the Nxumalos,
Threatening to seize their possessions and lands.

15 Matiwane now returned to his home, his mind raw with pain.
He chastised himself for this ignominious defeat.
He rushed to the large settlements of the Mthimkulus,
Eager to assuage his pain.
He hoped to recover the cattle hidden from Dingiswayo.
20 But, alas! The defeated are mats on which everyone tramples.
The Hlubis sent him a message:
'You shall not get your fat cows.
They have lived in our folds and partaken of their nourishments
They are the prize for our kindness to your children.'
25 When he heard this he frothed, his mouth trembling with anger.
He said: 'Must I be the plaything of such a little man?'
Using the remnants of his defeated army, he attacked,
Routing Prince Mthimkhulu and his army,
Killing his sons and setting others to flight.
30 The vultures came and feasted.
Prince Mthimkhulu fled to Prince Mpangazitha and pleaded:
'Child of our great clan,
The children of your Forefathers have been killed by Matiwane.
Give us shelter and protection from this fierce bandit.'
35 The once-proud Prince Mthimkhulu was broken.

At this very moment Zwide launched a fierce attack on
    Matiwane,
Breaking his army from all sides,

Sending him running to the southern regions.
All along his path Matiwane opened a trail of grief,
Destroying many an ancient settlement of the Sotho nations.
Thus the homes of Queen Mantantisi were destroyed.
5 In the ruins only bats and rats roamed.
The great Hlubis retreated to the southern regions.
In turn they set those before them in flight.
It is said not one man could swallow
Soon after the name of Prince Matiwane had been mentioned.
10 Many took their few possessions and fled,
Matiwane of the Ngwanes was fearful.
The rivers over which he stood threatened the passer-by with
    terrors.
He planted the Age of the Great Disturbance.
15 Many were forced to flee before they reaped their harvest,
Leaving their rich fields to feed Matiwane's multitudes.
There was the Age of Plenty followed by the Age of Destruction
Nation after nation fled from him.
He entered their settlements from all sides.
20 In fury he razed their homes to the ground,
Leaving whole regions stalked by hunger.
No wonder many spoke of Dingiswayo with contempt, saying
It was he, with his love of praise and personal fame,
Who let loose the monster on others.
25 Some composed songs of hatred against Matiwane,
Recounting how his hordes were repulsed by the Thembus of
    Ngoza.

Matiwane lost his favourite son and the feared General
    Nomtholwane.
30 Thus, scared and disturbed, he changed course.
Searching for a place of temporary settlement,
He roamed the lands of the great King Moshoeshoe of the
    Sothos,
Who invited him and said:
35 'It is enough! In my lands you can find a place of refuge.
You shall receive from me a large gift of cattle,
If hunger be the reason for your roaming.
The nations of the Palm Race must face only the foreign
    enemies.

Besides, a brave man needs a mountain for his monument.'

In Nguniland Queen Ntombazi raved in anger.
She warned: 'I shall not rest
Until I see the son of Jobe staring in eternal silence;
5   Until he faces the sun
With empty sockets like the many little Kings.'
It was for this the feared sorceress
Roamed the grounds, urging her son to capture Dingiswayo.
Had Zwide not overcome and driven away Prince Matiwane?
10 Had he not seized Matiwane's cattle and grazing lands?
Was he not feared even among the southern inhabitants?
Had he not sent Phungashe into eternal night?
Was it not he who was like the whirlwind
That brings the dryness of winter?
15 Dingiswayo fumed at the many treacheries of Zwide
But Zwide knew his weak spot.
He sent Princess Nobenguni, his sister, saying:
'The country of all the Forefathers is surrounded;
From all sides there are hungry leopards.
20 Go to Dingiswayo and say: "I am the daughter of King Langa.
I am tired of the warlike existence under my brother's rule.
I have come to ask for a peaceful place to stay."
Because of his self-love and his desire for fame
He shall give you a special place in his royal home.
25 It is then you shall dig deep into his heart,
Softening it with love and stories of endless fantasy.
Then he shall listen to your commands; they shall become our
      weapons.'
The fearless daughter of Langa consented to her brother.
30 She said defiantly: 'Even if I fail I shall be happier than others.
I shall have served my country and fought for my father's
      house.'

Things did go according to Zwide's wishes.
When Princess Nobenguni of the Nxumalos arrived
35 Dingiswayo welcomed her with a feast, slaughtering the fattest
      bulls.
He sat with her night after night,
Searching for the truth and secrets of Zwide's life.

She spoke to him, befogging his mind with cunning words:
'My lord, I am giving you all that is in my heart
Even though I know those who desert their families
Shall forever be cursed by the gods of their clans.
5   But then our house must prosper through kindness.
My brother, Zwide, no longer has a human heart.
He has treacherously murdered potentates of Nguniland.
I think of Phungashe who came to him seeking only shelter.
Such wickedness has never before been known in Nguniland.
10   The love that is of the House of Langa
Has turned within me and become a phial of poison.
I began to fear even for us who are of his own family,
Lest hungry for fame and power he may soon destroy us.
The hearts of evil people are strange.
15   They pride themselves in ever more bizarre acts.
Zwide is not like you, my lord.
You are gifted with great kindness and wisdom.
You would rather die than destroy your own relatives.
You are like rain that brings growth to crops.'
20   The great old King Dingiswayo was flattered by these words.
He felt sad and sorry for this woman.
Such, indeed, is the fate of those who are old:
They warm in sympathies of the young
Like a fowl sheltering its foundlings.
25   It was for this reason that Princess Nobenguni
Found kindness and love in the royal homes of Dingiswayo.
Even those who remonstrated with the king were rebuked.
Councillors who cast doubt on the wisdom of this action and
       said:
30   'Great king, Zwide is a treacherous ruler;
We fear him; we fear too the cunning of his family,'
Earned only the king's anger.
He likened them in their harshness to Zwide himself.
As he railed and raved against them, Princess Nobenguni
35   listened.
She said, appealing to his kind heart:
'I know no one likes me among the Mthethwas.
I know, too, the crimes of my brother are levelled against me.
Many poison the king's heart against me.'
40   Dingiswayo would be stung by these words.

He would say: 'Whoever hates you hates my very person.'
Yet there were many who daily came to him to protest.

Often Dingiswayo wanted to set out to battle against Zwide,
Eager to break the power and violence of the fierce king.
5   But Princess Nobenguni would approach him with soft words:
'My lord, it should be I who should urge you to this war.
I should personally lead the army against him —
Perhaps, if the gods so desire, open his intestines with a spear.
But it is not he alone who is the child of the Ndwandwe nation.
10 There are many of my family who shall also die.
I ask that in their name the bloody wars be postponed.'
Because of this the generous King would relent,
Surrendering to this seeming concern and kindness.
Indeed, he would praise her to many a listening fool:
15 'The world is full of mysteries.
How can one so kind be born from the same womb as a
      monster?
How can such wisdom reside alongside an evil force?
It is an unbearable experience for her
20 To have witnessed all the slaughter and bloodshed.'
Because of this blindness Dingiswayo was lured
By the wily daughter of the Nxumalos.
She planned and plotted for her brother, Zwide.
Painstakingly she studied all Dingiswayo's movements.
25 With her team of messenger-spies she conveyed the news to
      Zwide,
Informing her brother of all his secret fears and weaknesses.
Often messengers were dispatched as though to soften Zwide's
      heart,
30 Or else to plead with him for his goodwill and forgiveness.

When Zwide had amassed all Dingiswayo's secrets
He attacked the old and kindly Malusi at early dawn.
He knew the death of this honourable man would rouse great
      anger.
35 He suspected, too, that the Mthethwa princess, Malusi's wife,
Conveyed to Dingiswayo his secrets, as did his own sister.
A man of deceit fears the same plots against him.
When Dingiswayo heard of this bizarre killing

He raved and shouted, promising revenge against King Zwide.
Even the words of restraint from Princess Nobenguni
Seemed only to spur him on in his anger.
He shouted: 'Zwide, it is enough!
5   You have defiled the house of my Forefathers!
You have entered it with tears.
If I don't punish you now I am king no more!'
He did not delay but got his army battle-ready.
Zwide had foreseen in him this very response.
10 He prepared his army amidst genial and self-satisfied laughter.
The sadness of his sister haunted Dingiswayo. He could not
        sleep.
He roamed the house, muttering to himself incomprehensible
        words.
15 It was in this mood he sent out his army.
He fed them with his fury like someone
Desiring the annihilation of all that is of his enemy.

The Mthethwa army spread out over the hills.
Hurrying forward to meet its wing of the Zulus.
20 The whole earth seemed silent to listen only to their voices.
Branches of trees drooped mourning for the crimes of men.
When the Mthethwa army approached Zwide's Dlovunga royal
        city
They set up their temporary camps.
25 Dingiswayo did not rest; he roamed everywhere,
Frothing in anger like someone who had taken a bitter herb.
Finally he called his generals and commanders and said:
'I want to go and see Zwide myself.
I want him to know the true ruler of Nguniland is Dingiswayo.
30 I shall not even enter his grounds with an army.'
They listened in disbelief at these words,
Fearing lest Zwide's hypnotic medicines had conquered his
        mind.
They tried hard to restrain their king:
35 'It is better to wait for the Zulus
Or else to launch our army in all its strength.
Let our king not go there alone.
Let him not rush to the wild man of Langa
For indeed, it might be this very trap he has planned for him.'

But these words were like water on a dog's back.
He was determined to confront this evil man,
To tell him with fierce words his crimes against Nguniland.
Such are the follies of those who believe in their own truths,
5 Who deceive themselves that the world is halted by their
    outrage,
Or else driven to new directions by the violence of their words.
Dingiswayo reared up in anger:
'Are there no more heroes among the Mthethwas?
10 Is there none that shall listen to me?
Has Zwide drained all the courage from the once-brave nation?
I want only a few courageous men
To accompany the king of the Mthethwas.'
He took a few paces forward.
15 It was then that they competed for the honour,
Rushing to escort him to the village-city of King Zwide.
Among them were some of the Mthethwa royal clan.
They were only a small body of men
Since Dingiswayo no longer desired to settle issues through
20   battle.
Indeed, he thought such a war could only absolve Zwide,
Making him look like an opponent over superior issues,
Hiding from all the downright wickedness of his crime.
Dingiswayo believed his anger was enough.
25 With it he would crush the evil creature that was Zwide.
When he reached the top Hill of the Goat
He found himself face to face with Zwide's guards.
When they tried to seize him he scolded them, pushing them
    aside,
30 Saying: 'What is this that stands before the king?
Take me at once to your fearful King Zwide.'
They fell back, saluting him with the Mthethwa royal names.
They guided him to the inner sanctuaries of Dlovunga royal city.

Zwide, on hearing of Dingiswayo's arrival,
35 Said: 'Go and tell the king I thank him for this visit.
I give to him my fattest and best cows for a feast.'
Even though Dingiswayo was fuming with anger
His heart softened, thinking perhaps Zwide had chastised
    himself.

He even secretly praised the success of his latest strategy.
Days passed as he waited to see Zwide.
On each day a word came reporting his ill health.
But it was only to confuse and weaken Dingiswayo.
5 Zwide himself began to doubt the success of this plan.
His mother, Queen Ntombazi, daily infused in him her own
    ideas.
Urging him to seize this moment for his final glory.
Zwide's spies reported how closely the Zulus had approached his
10   capital.
It was this that made Zwide panic,
For he knew should Shaka arrive he was bound to attack.
Alarmed at these events, Zwide sent a messenger:
'Go and tell Dingiswayo I command him to my presence!'
15 Dingiswayo reared his royal head and said:
'Who is this who dares summon me, a king?'
He shook his head like an elephant harassed by a wasp.
He threatened all Zwide's agents, his anger befogging his mind;
Even the messengers of Zwide retreated from him in terror.
20 King Dingiswayo set out for Zwide's court,
Eager to confront him and flay him with his fierce words.
He found Zwide surrounded by a large body of his councillors.
Zwide spoke mockingly:
'All hail, King, who has no respect for the sun.
25 You who do not fear the power of the Ancestors,
You enter the front gates and exit through the back.'
As he spoke Dingiswayo realized
How he had let himself into Zwide's hands.
He did not speak many words; he only said:
30 'I believed once our land of Nguniland
Should flourish with a great sense of brotherhood and peace.
I did not see then the worms that infest its very heart.
I am sad, not for fear of death
But for many who shall see the coming of the vultures.'
35 Disturbed by these words, Zwide said:
'Your words are no different from those of many cowards
Who often predict for others their doom.
They threaten them with wild hyenas
Which they claim shall eat their bones.
40 They speak as if those of the earth are meant to live eternally.

But, in truth, the great moment of life is the present.
Before you embark on your journey to the Ancestors,
What last request would you make of us?
Dingiswayo, the son of Jobe, looked at him fiercely.
5   Even those who were staring at him shied away.
Angered, Dingiswayo's escort lurched forward but he restrained
        them.
He loosened a large collar of beads
Which had been made and designed only for him.
10 From his neck it spread covering his chest and shoulders.
By his own orders he had put there numerous colours and
        symbols.
He had said: 'I want it to fall over my shoulders like a cloak.
On the chest and at its centre
15 Let it be like the great red circle of the rising sun.
Its middle must be woven with a black spot of crowded beads
But its outer fringes must be of yellow colours,
Spreading in threads of black and white beads.
In its extreme points let there be the white beads of the river
20   stones,
Whose colours must alternate with the green of our summers.'
Thus Dingiswayo created his emblem of peace and plenty.
The red part was the fire symbolizing the generations of man.
The black spot was the power of Being on which man depends.
25 The various colours of the outer parts were the many happy
        thoughts
Which all generations shall experience on earth.
Dingiswayo took this sacred emblem
And put it gently in Zwide's hands, saying:
30 'Grant me this, Zwide, son of Langa.
When I begin to kick with pain of death
Break this apart, fracturing it in all its segments,
Throwing in all directions its elements of beauty.
Thus shall end the fragments of my dream.
35 I had envisioned the rich bonds to embrace all the children of
        Palm Race.
I have failed.
I have not made a feast for all the children of the sun.
Here is my breast, wide open and unprotected.
40 Do as you will. Plunge into it your blade of power.

Quench the fire that lit the horizons of yesterday!'
His bold words made Zwide look down.
He spoke softly as if consenting to a request.
He said: 'I shall do as you request.
5   Great kings rule over the grave.'
His mind suffered a conflict,
Knowing his mother, Queen Ntombazi, would not forgive,
Yet aware of the ancient saying and truth:
'He who kills in cold blood shall himself be killed in cold blood.'
10 The words of Dingiswayo found their target in his mind.

The great and famed son of Jobe was killed.
It was as if the earth would quake and tilt over all its children.
The death of an innocent man is often registered in the
    firmament.
15 The power of his being sends shudders through the belly of the
    earth.
The numerous wives of Dingiswayo surrounded his body.
Their wails rose as if to explode into the centre of the sun.
Only Queen Ntombazi showered praise on her son:
20 'You have followed the truth of your destiny.
You have accomplished the wishes of your Forefathers.
Now you shall rule without challenge.
You are now the supreme ruler in Nguniland.'
Zwide listened to this excited praise of his parent
25 Yet he knew it was folly to rejoice
For there still were the great Qwabe rulers.
The Thembus still boasted their power over the southern
    regions.
It was for this reason Zwide still sought to build up allies
30 And to reinforce his army against Shaka and the Mthethwa
    army.
He knew Dingiswayo's army spoiled for revenge.
Indeed, when they heard of the murder of their king
They each vowed an oath of blood against Zwide.
35 The great army of Dingiswayo, leaderless, turned back to
    Mthethwaland.

When Shaka heard from the Khumalos
How the great king, Dingiswayo, had been killed by Zwide,

He shed tears and lowered his forehead to the ground.
He vowed to make Zwide and his allies pay for this crime.
He stood at the pass of the Yiwane,
Dreaming and imagining the events of their lives together.
5   'I shall avenge my father!
I swear by my Ancestors, I swear by my sister, Nomchoba.
Zwide, the son of Langa, shall not live for long!'
He turned back his army to Zululand,
Saying to them: 'I have already begun the war-journey.
10 The day that leads to the great battle with Zwide of Langa has
        begun.'
Zwide himself alerted his troops,
Knowing Shaka's revenge would be swift and unpredictable.
He sent a messenger to King Phakathwayo, saying:
15 'Kings and leaders of our stature must stick together.
We must build such bonds as shall guarantee peace between us.
We must knock down upstart rulers
Who seek to create disturbances in Nguniland.'
As these messengers were presenting this message to
20   Phakathwayo
Others were giving assurances to the Thembus,
Promising in Zwide's name to block the routes of the Zulu king.
Zwide now invaded his relatives by marriage, the proud
        Khumalos.
25 He surrounded and killed the handsome Prince Mashobana.
He continued mercilessly killing those who did not bow to his
        rule.
Valleys and river beds were glutted with his victims.
There were large numbers who fled his harassment and rule.
30 It was from these the Zulu nation swelled its numbers.
Among them was Prince Mzilikazi, the son of Mashobana.

Assured of his invincibility, Zwide then sent a message to Shaka
'I still remember the pledge made to me by your father.
Once he promised he would give in marriage the beautiful Zulu
35   princesses.
As your father's heir, I demand this from you.'
Nodumehlezi fumed with anger
And speaking in a thousand syllables all at once, he said:
'Tell him not one of my sisters

Shall marry a creature so old!
He looks like some hard, dried-up cowhide.'
Zwide's pride was hurt. These words gnawed at his mind.
He said: 'I shall teach this boy of Senzangakhona's a lesson.'
5   Shaka knew the strategy he most needed against Zwide,
For if he was to attack successfully
Then he must open up the friendly zones in the southern
    regions.
It was for this that he vanquished the weaker armies
10 And built in this territory a base of friendship and supplies.
Mgobhozi, known as the One-who-Comes-from-the-Moun..in,
Listened intently to Shaka as he said of Zwide:
'I am awaiting for confrontation with Zwide where the elephants
    rest.
15 This war is a decisive one.
Should he defeat our armies
It shall mean the end of our growing nation.
But it shall not be so, however much he may desire it.
He is guilty of a heinous crime: he killed the great king of
20   Nguniland.'
It was at this time that a messenger came to him and said:
'The great royal princes, the sons of Dingiswayo,
Have split the country by their quarrels.
We come to you to request that you assume full authority
25 And direct the affairs of the great house of your father.
It was you he chose to inherit his power.'
Shaka, still confused by their words, agreed reluctantly.
This he did by way of silencing the Mthethwa nobles
But his mind also raced with numerous thoughts:
30 How by a union of the two nations he could create a formidable
    army.
He knew, too, the Mthethwa army had forced the nobles to seek
    his aid.
In the army his name was legend.
35 When the regiments heard Shaka was to lead them
They shouted in a great chorus of joy
For their desire for revenge against Zwide still dominated them —
Indeed only the disputing princes had held them back.
The whole Mthethwa nation sighed with relief,
40 Knowing the era of family quarrels had been ended.

Shaka, having assumed the power of regency,
Now sent a word to the general commander, Ngomane, and
    said:
'Since you are someone whom my father trusted
5   You shall now govern where he ruled,
Looking after his family as if it were your own.
Teach the army to fight in the manner of the fierce iziChwe
    regiment.'
That was how the great Zulu army was born.
10   It set out to unite all fragments into one great nation.

Many Zulu heroes spoiled for battle against Zwide
But Shaka restrained them,
Telling them this was no ordinary war;
It demanded long planning and seasoning of minds.
15   Shaka began to mould his troops, conditioning each mind,
Fashioning them like ancient heroes whose names live in
    legends.

Shaka sent his newly trained teams to examine the war arena.
They surveyed and studied every nook and tarn;
20   They followed the pattern of falling shadows in the evening;
They reported about the shape of mountains;
They brought details of each neighbouring settlement;
They told of the wide open regions near the battle arena.
Many commanders argued and debated,
25   Sifting all aspects and accounts brought in by their informants.
Yet this was only an exercise
For Shaka and a few generals had now worked out their
    ultimate plans.
So great was the movement of peoples to and fro
30   That the famous heroes addressed their spears with these words:
'Great bosom friend, this promises to be a frightful war
Such as must be fought only by the experienced.
Zwide himself prepares his army from all sides.'
Shaka said to them, speaking in whispers:
35   'Of all wars I have ever fought, this is the most dreadful.'
He spoke like this, cracking jokes amongst the gathering of
    heroes.
'Even the Mthethwa warriors are frightened,' he commented.

'Did not Zwide lure and kill their king in their presence?
Such a curse must be exorcised from an army.
Wars are fought not only through numbers
Or the cleverness of strategies but also through beliefs.
5   Thus I asked of Ngomane, the general commander:
He must make a great and memorable feast
To cleanse the army of this violent curse.
Such disgrace can only be cured
By the roar of dying bulls in the cattle-folds.
10   How else can the armies live down their defeat without battle?
We must close off this potency of Zwide's power over us.
Our driving anger is only this:
Zwide killed the greatest and gentlest of kings.
We shall attack him with all our power,
15   Hurling assaults against which he shall have no escape.
Let generations hereafter remember our battle.
Let them never say we let evil men roam freely at large.'
He spoke continuously to the generals and troops alike
Sometimes he called out the names of each man's ancestry,
20   Infusing in them the courage of his own begetters.
For, indeed, the greatest heroes are those who are dead.

One day when Shaka had taken the strengthening medicines
He saw the great Princess Mkhabayi enter his royal city.
She spoke out the thoughts which many had been anticipating:
25   'I have come to you, son of my brother, to wish you all my
         blessings.
In your many wars I have never uttered a single word.
I now must speak, knowing this is your greatest war.
I know you shall confront the fierce witch of Langa
30   Who ate up kings and queens and princes mercilessly.
Should you defeat him you shall have repelled the ocean;
The whole country shall have at last found peace.
Even our Ancestors shall rejoice with us.
From the Forefathers I ask for their blessings.'
35   Shaka lowered his body and said solemnly:
'Most respected and most revered Paternal Mother,
I thank you for these rich and nourishing words.
They give me courage that I still shall build the nation of
         Zulu.

By your guidance and wisdom the Zulu nation has prospered.
Under your shadow I have grown like a tall bamboo plant.
I thank you for your blessings, Great Paternal Mother.
I know you are the messenger of the Ancestral Forefathers.
5   You are the Voice of the Zulus whose clamour brings down a
      mountain.
I shall open the pathways for their harvest
To let the children of Zulu feast to their heart's content.'
The royal princess thanked him for his words.
10   She raised her hand to honour him and her Forefathers.

Book Seven: A military and political genius organises

The first battle against Zwide is one of the greatest tests of Shaka's military genius. Fighting a powerful enemy, he devises several plans that amply demonstrate the superiority of his military concepts and ethics. Not only do the Zulus fight as a body of men united against an enemy, but as a brotherhood. Zwide and his sons, on the other hand, constitute a decadent and powerful aristocracy and it is no surprise that they lose the war through blundering and conceit. Shaka for the first time puts to test his new and elaborate network of agents, thus demonstrating his principle that to fight an enemy one must infiltrate his organization and know his every move. He is helped in this by the arrival of Mzilikazi, who knows Zwide's court intimately.

Once Zwide was as angry as the mouth of an open sky.
While in this state he encountered a demented old man.
When he saw Zwide walking proudly amidst his councillors
The old man laughed uncontrollably.
5   Zwide stopped suddenly as though frightened by this laughter.
One of the councillors in fury set forth after the old man.

He stood over him as if he would stab him with his long spear.
Zwide restrained him : 'Leave him.
Let him explain the reason for his laughter.'
The old man did not stop but let out greater peals of laughter.
5   When he had worn himself out
He saluted Zwide mockingly: 'All hail to our king!
I dreamt you carried a shield over your head.
It was as though you ran over a wide flat terrain.
Close on your heels was a young calf with budding horns.'
10 Zwide questioned him searchingly,
Eager to know the meaning of this dream,
For by now Zwide had succumbed to a secret fear.
He said: 'Who are you?
From what regions do you come?'
15 The old man opened and closed his eyes:
'I am he whose children have all been killed.
I am the relative of Prince Donda of the Khumalo royal clan.
Our valleys and plains are choking with ruins.
Once a king invited us to a hunting feast.
20 We arrived at the royal grounds in all our numbers.
We carried only the light hunting spear,
Believing the occasion only for hunting wild animals.
But how great the prize we paid for our error!
Our children lay crumpled on the ground like earthworms.
25 It was there that all my children were killed.
I am now alone. I am the companion of the dry reeds.
I hear them rattling like a clash of spears.
You, too, must forgive me if I see you in flight from an enemy.
It is only because of the speed that often seizes my mind;
30 For those who know too much suffer madness.
I have seen the horrific death of my kinsmen.
The Great Spirits have told me of a dreadful day to come
When many will flee, exposing their naked shoulder
          blades.
35 Zwide turned away, as if the old man had affirmed some hidden
          fear.
In his conscience the scorpion's eggs hatched their poisonous
          progeny.
He shouted out: 'Kill him! Kill him!'
40 He rushed away as he spoke, not daring to look.

When he arrived at the camp of his chosen troops
He did not speak but walked alone, restlessly.
Finally he spoke in a fierce voice,
Sharpening their minds for the great battle.
5 He said: 'I shall destroy Shaka, the son of Senzangakhona.
I shall fight him as though he were bound in one bundle of
    wood.
I shall make him run as though in a fearful dream.
But this boy has the cleverness of a weasel.
10 Do not underestimate him.
Each man who shall command a regiment
Should know all the movements of battle.
Only our concerned efforts can win this war.
We must fight as one body,
15 Neither rushing nor retreating in fear.
Even when the Zulus attempt to break your centre
You must not retreat nor give way to their onslaughts.
I trust in those who have been seasoned in our victories.
Whoever shall turn to flee shall be executed.
20 I shall kill him myself with my own hands.
I want each regiment to keep advancing.
The war doctor who is to strengthen your minds has come.
He descends from a long line of war doctors,
Their medicines for this war have never been used before.
25 Their power is fresh and new and invincible.'
He spoke as if he now was possessed by feats of war.
His voice was of a bull stung by black ants.
His eagerness for battle had become an illness.
He went personally to the royal prince, Nomahlanjana,
30 And said: 'I order you to command the whole army.
Teach them no one survives, who challenges the House of
    Zwide.
Accompanying you shall be all your brothers —
I mean Prince Mpepha, Prince Nobengula, Prince Sixholoba.
35 They vow: with you as commander, Shaka shall be crushed.
They have rejected all my pleas to stay out of this war
For, indeed, I am old and I loathe to fight with both hands.
A great house must not be swept away all at once;
Its seed must feed a growing season.
40 Yet participation by the royal house shall inspire the regiments,

Making this war a total war fought by kings and princes alike.
I put on your shoulders the protection of your brothers
Do not bring me corpses I am too old to mourn
I cannot endure the grief of losing my children.'
Nomahlanjana responding to his father's request said:
'My father, do not worry yourself.
It is I who am commander of this battle.
I shall return with Shaka's head on my shoulder.
And say: "Here is the conceited boy, the son of Senzangakhona."
He has grown bold because you had spared him.
Have we not the greatest and largest army in the land?
Would he not flee at the very spectacle of their numbers?
After all, he only comes with a small contingent of troops.
They are no more than boys and old men,
Nor do they have our experience in battle.
We shall destroy him; of that I am certain!'
These words infused Zwide with confidence.
He even said: 'I trust you. I trust in your courage.
I know, too, your army is composed of the fiercest of fighters.
Yet you must plan carefully against this treacherous boy.
His courage surpasses that of a cornered elephant.
I send you so that the nation may praise your leadership.
Let not people say: "When their father dies, who shall rule?"
You saw how the subjects of Dingiswayo were tamed,
No sooner than he breathed his last.
The rulers are the fountain from which a nation drinks.'
As he said these words he gave him his last blessing.
Even the war medicines could not surpass this power.
Prince Nomahlanjana's name was hailed everwhere.
Every household and valley echoed with his praise.

Some were meeting and embracing
As though this war was some great festival.
Listen, too, to the poet calling Zwide from the mountains:
'Zwide, son of Langa,' he exclaimed,
'Those you embraced felt the stab of iron.
The families that were unlucky were destroyed —
But you could not be destroyed!'
Battle songs echoed in all the regions of Zululand.
Heroes were those who spoke eagerly of the coming war.

Ndlela, of Sompisis, was training those under his command;
Nzobo was infusing his own unit with great fighting spirit;
Nqoboka, a hero of many wars, brought the Sokhulu clan.
The chief commander, General Mdlaka, was everywhere
5   exhorting the troops.
Shaka boasted openly: 'I pity the children of Zwide.
I am sad for those who will not see the two bulls collide.'
He spoke to Mgobhozi his final words:
'Our army bristles with sparks of war.
10   Even the wild animals that shall eat us
Shall reap our flesh until choked by our numbers.
My heart leaps like that of a child.
I am filled with joy at the Dlamini clan that has joined us.
I am pleased, too, at the high spirits of the Sibiya clan.
15   This is how an army should be — a truly great family.
Such was the spirit once when we set out to battle with
          Nqoboka.
This must be the greatest war ever fought by any two armies.
I know the Ndwandes depend on their large numbers
20   But we must evade this by our own superior strategies.
We must knock out their ankles until they collapse.
It is the only way by which we can conquer.'
Mgobhozi-of-the-Mountain agreed with these comments,
And said: 'My king, we are ready.
25   Each one must set out to be a great fighter.
I confess I no longer can restrain myself.
Many times I have dreamt I was already there.
Sometimes I wake up in the night and rush to my weapons,
Believing the battle is already raging.
30   Then I console myself with sharpening my spear yet again.
Violating the ancient custom
Never to prepare a weapon in the dark,
Since, too, only cowards sharpen their weapons often.
It is you, my lord, I must thank.
35   You have fed my vision with a spectacle of a great day to come.'
Shaka, the great fighter, was enthralled by such enthusiasm.
He desired there and then to set out to battle.
Yet his mind counted every step, searching deep into known
          hazards.
40   He said: 'Mgobhozi, a great day requires painful preparations.

I have worked out my own final strategy
But I want to know what thoughts you have in your own mind.
My first plan is based on this truth:
Our success in this great battle
5   Depends on how our movements are controlled.
No single person must take his own way
Even if the temptation for heroic actions is unbearable.
For, in truth, we shall face a force larger than ours.
It is on their numbers they shall base their own strategy.
10   Thus should our army be broken and disrupted.
The defeat of our smaller forces shall be inevitable.
My second observation is this:
We have no way of attacking with both horns of our army.
Such a tactic would thin out our forces,
15   Overstretching our few numbers against a larger force.
Here, then, is what I have planned:
Our army shall advance until it reaches the hill of Qokli.
This hill is strategically placed,
Occupying as it does the very heart of battle.
20   The Zwide army shall come from the Mhlathuze river,
Eager to cross at its lowest point.
Our forces must stand, blocking the crossways.
At the hill we must build the army in encirclements
To overwhelm whenever we choose with fresh reserves.
25   Surprises often disrupt a superior enemy.
This is my own thinking. . . .'
Mgobhozi-of-the-Mountain was silent,
Pondering over these words and working out his own views.
Finally he said: 'O my lord, it is hard to say anything.
30   It is clear you have thought deeply of these plans and strategies
But something remains unexplained to me.
What if they surround us at the hill,
Penning us in like a herd of cows?
Besides, should they capture all exits and points of retreat
35   They may cause great panic to our army.
For every man fears to be hemmed in by a well armed enemy.
Our army may yet break out in disorderly directions,
Exposing itself to greater danger.'
These comments made Shaka look intently at Mgobhozi.
40   He said: 'Mgobhozi, the question you ask is a searching one.

133

I thought of this myself and was at first puzzled,
Then I realized there is only one way for us to survive:
To be strong, to stand our ground without yielding.
If necessary we may yet break our way through the spears.
5   Since the enemy shall be weakened by thirst
They shall constantly be forced to lose their numbers
Or else fight in extreme desperation.
They shall have problems, too, with their spears,
Which they shall throw at us from lower ground.
10   On such an incline the advantage is ours.
Combining with our old tactic we shall pick them one by one,
Stabbing them as though in a boys' game of wild potatoes.
If we used only the old tactic we would certainly lose
But our new weapon ensures success despite our numbers.
15   Confident of their numbers they shall become reckless,
And attempt to cross the river at its highest tide.
But our army shall be ready for them.
Wars are fought through courage and persistence, son of Msane;
Whoever endures the first fierce assault has won the victory.'
20   Mgobhozi followed these words with his own and said:
'My lord, I now can see your plan clearly.
I make only one request: let me fight in the front line of heroes.
It was this urge which made me once refuse the commanding
      powers.
25   I am a fighter. I desire the enemy at his belly.
I want always to be in the earliest engagement of battle.'
Jokingly Shaka responded:
'Mgobhozi, there are still greater battles before us.
A man must fight and return to hoe his fields.'

30   The regiments of Shaka-of-the-long-white-armlets,
He-whose-arms-are-covered-with-beads-of-the-festivals, began to
      move.
They stirred like a cloud of locusts heading for the north.
From all parts of the land they came.
35   Great heroes sang songs and joked together.
They touched their spears like some ceremonial staff.
They caressed the blades, uttering to them their poems.
The famous hero of Ngcolosi clan stood in the open.
He danced, kicking up clouds of red dust;

He leapt high as though carried by the wind.
He landed on the earth, causing a violent thud.
The moon was encircled by tufts of red-tinted clouds;
Like a great white orifice it spat mists of circling vapours.
5   Even the carrier-boys walked proudly,
Each accompanying the hero he most admired.
After a long and tiring journey the regiments rested.
Here they sat, narrating stories of past glory and future
     strategies.
10   None would have protested had Shaka, like Zwide,
Remained at his capital, guarded by his own home troops.
But he chose to fight with all his regiments.
All night he talked, inciting his army to greater feats of daring,
Listening to each of their views and questions,
15   Making fun of those who showed signs of fear.
The commanders spoke as though with the authority of the king.
There were young men who were possessed by the war spirit.
All night they ran roaring like disturbed buffaloes,
Stabbing at an imaginary enemy and sniffing like bulls.
20   Njikiza, the great hero of Ngcolosi clan, came to Shaka
And in his booming voice he said: 'My lord,
Great protector against our enemies, you are wise.
You are older than all the living people on earth.
I have come to ask you for your permission
25   To feed my fighting club with the skulls of the enemy.
It has been troubling me these days demanding:
"On what shall you feed me tomorrow?"
I come to you, my lord, to ask for a vantage point.
I ask for a point at the ford
30   Where the enemy shall come in large numbers.
I beg only for two heroes who shall block this ford with me.
There, I swear by my father, no enemy shall pass.'
Shaka smiled and said jokingly:
'Your physique alone shall prove a deterrent to the enemy.
35   I give you the pass at the lowest side of the river.
You shall join the unit of Nqoboka.
There, if the enemy dares to cross,
You shall close him in like the teeth of a lion.
Go and rest and sleep a long, good sleep.
40   Tomorrow you shall stand on your feet till evening.

You shall break the skulls of the little men of Nomahlanjana.'
He saluted as if a great joy had entered his mind.
The great hero of the Ngcolosi clan shouted Shaka's epic:
'Butterfly of Phunga and Mageba,
5   Whose body is covered with variegated colours;
Great one, who is like the long shadows of the mountains!
They merge with the night when witches travel freely.
Uncontrollable one, son of Phunga and Mageba.
All hail, my lord, you are the thunderbolt that cannot be
10   escaped!'
He called out like this, walking off to lean on a large stone
       support.
There he let his thoughts wander to the great battles to come.

All night long the carrier boys brought water from the springs.
15   It was as though the hill would turn into a gigantic pool.
It was only at dawn that the commander
Called out to the carrier boys: 'Young men, go to sleep.
Rest and prepare to see the great battle.
Soon you will boast of war episodes you have seen.
20   Tomorrow's dance shall be held for you.'
After Shaka had collected together all strategies
He spoke to the assembled regiments:
'We shall repulse Zwide's army, beating it back mercilessly.
We shall attack wave after wave like ants from an anthill.'

25   At the break of dawn Nqoboka led them.
He was followed closely by the heroes of the Sokhulu clan.
They sang the war songs softly.
They hummed, walking slowly alongside the river.
Even the roar of the river seemed to echo their songs.
30   At the lower ford they stopped.
There they planned to pluck the enemy like some strange water
       fruit.
Ndlela, son of Sompisi, led those under his command.
He pointed his fighting spear in the direction of the Ndwandwe
35   army
And said: 'They shall have no passage in the upper ford.'
How beautiful their muscled bodies as each division
Set out to guard their assigned posts!

The far end of the Qokli hill teemed with eager regiments.
People were like a disturbed nest of giant termites.
Even Mgobhozi was no longer sitting leisurely:
He roamed the place like someone expecting bad news.
5 Only the king's word made him stay in one place.
Had he had his way, he would have been fighting there and
    then.

The day stretched its horizons.
The skies were adorned with red tails of dawn;
10 The sun lashed down on the earth; it lashed on the stone.
The dew vanished suddenly from the blades of grass.
Such sweet scent of the wild plants would soon become drenched
    with blood.
The day lit the distant regions of Mthonjaneni.
15 The great tree near Nkandla weighed heavily over the earth.
The shields of the Ndwandwe army opened;
They were like a huge forest of giant black mushrooms.
Among them were many heroes of famous battles.
They carried with them bundles of long spears.
20 As the army sang its fierce war songs and anthems
Great heroes leisurely sat, taking large helpings of snuff.
They remarked: 'Only the inexperienced rush at the break of
    battle.
Like the early winds they leave no memories.'

25 The morning is always ready to receive.
It desires the soft body of the young plants.
It fertilizes itself with the old stems.
The new season is rich with the nourishment of yesterday's
    feast;
30 It is fertile with kings and rulers and conceited men.
Zwide's army rushed like elephants,
Determined to cross the Mhlathuzi river by their numbers.
But a wise man depends on both mind and body.
Like a calf he sharpens the two sides of his weapons.
35 Great processions of Zwide's army hurried there,
Passing each other and vying with each other in their
    recklessness.
When they reached the fords

Their generals and commanders shouted, mocking the Zulu
    army,
Filling their own troops with joy and a conqueror's laughter.
'There they are, the cowards who shall soon flee from us.'
5 See them! the innumerable regiments of Zwide,
Above their heads they carry their gigantic shields.
Half covered by the river they forge forward into battle.
Many yearned to be the first to kill in battle.
Often such honour belonged to the great clans of the land.
10 Many years afterward people still spoke of them with awe.
The legend never dies!
As they reached the end of the river,
Confident they would soon initiate their weapons,
They collided with the fierce-fighting commander, Ndlela of
15   Sompisi.
His unit stabbed Zwide's army in the naked ribs.
Grown men were seen carried away by the river like swollen
    cows.
Their bellies were torn open and their shields were drowned.
20 They sank slowly like the back of dead bulls.
Yet the waves of Zwide's army came,
The commander realizing should their first line of attack be
    broken,
The whole army would face certain defeat.
25 The Zulus would stab them like a herd of animals.
He restrained the anger and eagerness of the Ndwandwe
    regiments.
The Zulus stood defiantly on their open ground.
In vain the Zwide army threw their forest of missiles.
30 On the southern side Zwide's army faced the same fate.
Njikiza held his fighting club with both hands,
Knocking those who dared climb to the narrow river bed.
Their foreheads caved in like stems of reeds.
He was not alone. With him was the great Nqoboka
35 Who constantly shouted his poems of excellence,
He rushed from side to side, calling out in fury:
'I have killed the plague of Zwide.
I, the son of Nontshiza, who hails from the south.'
They fled from him, but like the wind he rushed after them,
40 Nipping them like the soft buds of tender plants

And pinning them down into the Thukela river.
Sometimes he lured them, allowing them to approach very close,
Then, like an eagle, he would swoop down on them,
Causing them to stumble and fall on large slippery stones.

5   By such strategies their morale was broken.
No longer were the Ndwandwes like the fierce campaigners
Who terrorized all Nguniland.
They wailed and begged as they plunged into the river caves.
The pride of Zwide's army was shattered.

10 When their magic power collapsed, the Zulus boasted with new
        power.

At the midday cycle no triumphant slogans were heard.
Zwide's chief commander called together the Council of
        Generals.

15 Addressing them, he said:
'It is clear it is no easy matter to defeat the Zulus.
They are small in numbers but skilled in stratagems.
Already too many of our best heroes have been killed.
The task of crossing has proved too costly.

20 It is wiser to pull back our army and replan our strategy.
Even as we talk our men have began to lose their thrust,
Yet we must teach the Zulus the Ndwandwe army is
        imperishable!
You, Mlandisi, son of Zibongo, rush and bring us more troops.

25 Tomorrow the fields shall teem with an ever-formidable force.
Their numbers shall send the Zulus panicking with their shields.
They shall find refuge in the mountain fastness like baboons.'
After Nomahlanjana had thus commanded
The troops retreated, falling back from the teacherous river.

30 The Zulu army shouted in triumph.
The great river was choked with the men of Zwide,
Everywhere floated their ballooned bodies.
Hard as they tried to disguise their cause for retreat
(Pretending it was only to refreshen themselves),

35 Shaka knew by the discords of their songs it was in desperation.
He walked among his excited troops, listening with satisfaction
As each commander claimed greater heroic deeds for his unit
        than others.
He cheered them, cajoling them by their heroic poems.

He gave special honour to Njikiza and his men of the fords.
Mgobhozi-of-the-Mountain was still restless,
Eager to fight at the front line of battle.
As the battle raged, he had stood fixed like a pole,
5   Watching only the movements of arms and weapons.
Sometimes he laughed joyfully as Shaka's strategies interlocked.
Shaka entreated him: 'Come with me, Mgobhozi.
We must frequently inspect the battle arena.'
Thus, with a team of Fasimba regiment, they descended on
10   General Ndlela.
They discussed and laughed as if the war was over.
High-spirited, they walked down to Nqoboka.
To him Shaka said: 'Yes, great hero, I did see your
     performance.
15   You still possess the skill with which we fought at the
     Mthethwas.
You checked the war-hungry hounds of Zwide.
It is clear their wounds are too severe to bear.'
The hero of the Sokhulu clan turned to the king and said:
20   'My king, we only do what befits your greatness.
A follower performs as well as his master.
You are the whirlwind that breaks open the fields of summer.
If I die let it be among my brothers of battlefield.
I shall have fought my great war of body and mind.
25   I shall have sheltered our nation with a great shield.'
They hugged each other, recalling their Mthethwa battles.
Then, their exploits were themes of songs and fireside stories.
Shaka thereafter approached Njikiza and said:
'Njikiza, what you have done equals a hundred men.
30   You shall be a legend so long as the Zulu nation lives.
You shall be a theme of songs like ancient heroes.
As the battle begins again, give them no time to rest.
Let the beautiful sun shrink their proud manes of war.
Tomorrow you shall fight until their mothers cry out,
35   "Enough!"'
The great hero of the Zulu army saluted the king and said:
'Ndaba! You set the fields ablaze with inmumerable fires;
Their centres rage even in the rainstorms of the marshes.'

Shaka, proud and confident, watched Zwide's army retreating.

The afternoon stole their shadows and swallowed them.
Often she intervenes to give a man another day.
Embracing those who would have gone forever into the night.
She rolls the leaves of day, preparing the night of fertility.
5   The councils of Prince Nomahlanjana of Zwide whispered all
        night,
Devising plans of how to overcome the obstructing river.

Zulu commanders also sat in seclusion, assessing the events of
        the day.
10   Mgobhozi-of-the-Mountain often intervened,
Giving this and that comment, eager to alert others.
He initiated many plans to cripple the enemy tactics.
Finally Shaka, who had listened attentively, said:
'I have heard and am pleased with your suggested strategies.
15   Even if we may not in this war defeat the enemy totally
We have broken Zwide's power forever.
Whatever we devise should tie up with the successes of
        yesterday.
For whoever has been hit advances with only half his senses.
20   A true fighter must carefully strike again.
By the second blow the clay pot is broken and water spills all
        over.
Yet yesterday's strategy must lose its surprise —
No longer can it keep at bay a persistent enemy.
25   Besides, the Thukela river shall expose its ribs
Opening a path for any tenacious and determined enemy.
We shall no longer be blocking only the fords,
But fighting a long line of storming regiments.
Tomorrow we shall fight a battle of close combat.
30   Everyone should sleep and fill his whole body with new life.
This battle shall be the fiercest.
It shall be fought only by those who are strong and brave.'
The commanders hailed the king's words, and said no more.
Like butterflies they slept, their minds and bodies closed.
35   In the whole field bodies of men were curled.
Sometimes a man would be heard shouting in his dream,
Calling out in terror, causing the whole field of men to stir.
Good-humouredly, others would shout:
'Shut up, Gebedu, the great battle is tomorrow.'

Each man, as he went to sleep, would pull his shield
And put his weapons close to him to the right of him.

Have you seen the stars on a clear night
Like magic white flames hanging from the body of the sky?
5   Have you seen their tremendous light travelling silently to our
      earth?
Have you ever heard the distant noises of the night —
Giant dogs with lions' voices, strange creatures
That call to each other, making the earth like a huge echoing
10   bowl?
Have you ever heard the movement of the night disturbing the
      leaves,
At first creeping softly from a distance, then closer and closer
Until it breaks the branches of the neighbouring plants,
15   Until all around is a blanket of invisible presences?
It was in such a night they slept.
The bright light of the moon fell on them.
Huge bodies of men rolled from side to side.
The king's watchman moved round his grounds like a menacing
20   shadow.
When the dawn-drawing star emerged
He came closer to the king, eager to give him his message,
But fearing the ancient curse and command:
Whoever brings bad news must not speak again
25   For indeed little men often serve as outlets for rulers' troubles.
He summoned up his courage, saluting the king:
'All hail, Jama, son of Ndaba, of Malandela!
I bring news that forebodes ill for our armies.
The high star has exposed the firmness of the river-bed.'
30   As he spoke Shaka stretched his muscles, straightening his body.
He had not fully fallen into sleep.
He said, speaking off-handedly, to Mgobhozi-of-the-Mountain:
'I hope you have heard what the messenger says.
The day has come for all our heroes to celebrate.'
35   When Mgobhozi heard these words
He was startled; he rushed for his weapons and said:
'My lord, I have waited too long for such a day!'

The whole concourse awoke as if in one single effort.

Shaka gave the final orders of the day:
'Great sons of Zululand, prepare for a great battle.
It must end only with the defeat of the enemy.
These are my instructions for today and they shall be obeyed:
5   A section of our young fighters
Shall take the cattle that graze in our southern fields
Driving them fast away through the great plains.
They must not be moved in one single direction
But scattered, emerging from different points,
10 Giving the illusion of a large force in flight.
Seeing them, the enemy shall split its army,
Following each imagined unit in hot pursuit.
But our force must run with the speed of the morning birds.
Heading them off this way shall give us a breathing space.
15 We shall confront a depleted enemy.
In vain they shall try to surround us.
Our army shall repel their forces,
Hitting them at their belly and driving them back.
We shall dig into our position at the hill,
20 Entrenching ourselves in the open space.
It is for this reason I want us to move with lightning speed,
Taking our different points soon after the rising sun.
Those who are defenders of the hill
Shall remain fixed in their locations of yesterday.
25 Let the enemy believe there are only a few of us.
Then by a sudden movement we shall precipitate ourselves on
            them,
Emerging as if from the earth and all parts of the mountain.'
The gathering of commanders was confused by these words
30 But decided to wait and see the unfolding plans.
Some who understood these tactics applauded them.

As daybreak spread over the mountains
The various regiments and units followed their assignments.
Across the Thukela river, in the camp of Prince Nomahlanjana,
35 Could be heard the shouting voices of his war heroes.
Noticing how the river had subsided,
His heart leapt with joy.
He said to his councillors: 'Can you see what I see?
The Zulus are set on a collective death.

They still cling to the mountain fortress like fools.
If I were in their circumstances I would flee.
The river has treacherously opened its gates,
Leaving their little army huddled together,
5   Hiding behind the scattered mounds of stone.
Chasing them to the mountain top we shall trap them like
       cattle.'
As he was making these denigrating comments
A councillor came to him breathless from running.
10   He said: 'Son of the Ndwandwe royal house,
The regiments of the Zulus depart from battle by secret routes!
They drive away their cattle past the thick forests.
Look at the distant plains —
In large numbers they flee with their cattle!'
15   Nomahlanjana stared in disbelief.
He said: 'Indeed, I can see them with my own eyes.
The witches! They only deceive themselves!
Order two sections of our great army
To pursue and swallow them like the jaws of an earthquake.
20   As we descend on them they shall wish they had wings.
I swear by my sister Nozintaba.'
The wild son of Zwide burst out in mocking laughter.
He rubbed his hands together, spoiling for victory.
He roused the fighting spirit of his generals;
25   He roused the fury of his regiments.
They began to sing their great war songs.
The mountains roared with the great anthem of the Ndwandwes
They stamped the ground, pointing their spears to the sun.
The river trembled, jolting the trees on the overhanging
30   mountains.
Its waves raced with reflected images of plants and men.
Shadows and feet swayed with the weapons in water.
The Zulus saw them cross the withered river.
Quickly they retreated to defend the hill sanctuary.
35   The big army of Zwide, like the young of the locust in spring,
Spread over the body of the Qokli hill.
Even the sun, in its gentle maternity,
Seemed now to favour their glistening bodies.
She cast her thousand rays over them.
40   As the army of Zwide advanced

Many a young Zulu fighter would break from his regiment,
Eager to challenge and boast his family's greatness.
Silence hung in the air like cobwebs.
Fear fell on the shoulder blades like insects.
5 Only Shaka watched, gritting his teeth and breathing deeply.
He stared, motionless, as if he saw them in a trance.
Like an overflowing river they came.
They never ceased hurling insults at the Zulu army,
Hoping in this way to draw them to their doom.
10 The young Zulu fighters raved in anger, attempting to break
        through Zwide's army.
They swore and beat the ground; they were like captured wild
        dogs.
As though by some magic herb their bodies burst with new
15   power.
Shaka shouted to his regiments to move in concert:
'Let the enemy enter into the mouth of battle!
Let it lose its control.'
A hero of the Ndwandwe clan rushed forward.
20 He stood in the open space between the two armies,
Challenging the whole Zulu army.
Manyosi, the son of Dlekezele, with anger in his face
Appealed to the king: 'My lord, it is enough!
Give me this dog to kill; let me teach the others a lesson!'
25 Shaka only raised his spear, giving a signal.
It was as if he had let loose a frenzied bull.
The son of Dlekezele bent low under his black shield.
By slow and measured movements he came close to the
        Ndwandwe hero,
30 His face no longer beaming with thankful smiles.
He roared like some fierce animal whose offspring had been
        killed.
The hero of the Ndwandwe army saw this fury and rejoiced.
He said to himself: 'Such fierceness swallows the mind.'
35 For indeed there are those who are blinded by their anger.
Once, twice, the Ndwandwe hero attempted to stab but failed.
With a swaying movement he hurled one chosen missile.
It cut through the many rays of the morning sun,
Searching for the soft regions of the body,
40 But hit the stone-crest like a misguided hatchet.

The persevering hero of the Ndwandwe army only laughed.
He seized the second spear and threw it suddenly.
It spun through the air, singing the songs of death,
Until it landed on the black shield of the Zulu hero.
5 Manyosi, the son of Dlekezele, fell down.
Many thought the sharp iron had found its target.
Izimpohlo regiment screamed loud in shock.
But Manyosi only acted to trick the enemy.
As he drew closer he was met by the firm spear of Manyosi.
10 The Ndwandwe hero cried out, throwing up his hands.
It was then others could see a spear embedded in his ribs.
Manyosi pulled it out, stabbing him again and again.
He raved as though his mind had been entered by the green
    beetle.
15 He turned aside, spitting at Zwide's army,
Still challenging them for a second encounter.
The second fighter of the Ndwandwe army sped forward,
Confident he could overwhelm him after this first tiring battle.
He jumped in all directions, attempting to confuse him.
20 Twice he flung his spear, but suddenly he was stretched on the
    ground.
He attempted to rise once, twice, thrice,
But the earth of the ant pulled him back.
As he lay down gasping for breath
25 He uttered his last dying words!
'I salute you, great hero. Already you have won your battle.'
The Ndwandwe army stood as if paralysed,
As though the whole column feared this one man.
Manyosi finally took a handful of soil and threw it at them.
30 He turned back, returning to the Zulu army,
Reciting the poems conferred on him by Shaka himself.

The fierce sounds of war exploded.
Shaka of Senzangakhona called out to his regiments:
'They have arrived, Zulu of Malandela, they are here!'
35 Responding in consent, they rent the air with their battle-cry:
    'Zulu!'
They ran to Zwide's army like a leopard
Whose claws are loosened to tear strips of flesh,
To rip the belly wide open and pull the intestines.

Sometimes people, sensing their death,
Compete for the last light of the sun.
They demand the final truth from the eyes of the other.
Long, fierce weapons open their fangs.
5 Voices of men fall to the ground.
Their bodies gored with wounds of war they lie limp.
The birds of heaven came closer,
Picking the scattered pieces from the river.
Pulling and dragging them to the sand.
10 They looked in all directions before swallowing
As if this act of carnage offends the whole universe.
The heroes are like hunting dogs on a leash.
They are held until the opportune moment,
When the last dancer catches the eye of the crowd.

15 In the far-distant mountains of Mthonjaneni
The regiments of Zwide chased after the decoy regiments.
Angered by this pursuit, they vowed:
'If ever we close in on them none shall live to tell the tale.'
Endlessly the dust of man and beast swirled into space,
20 Casting a haze over the distant forests.
When the Zulus reached the open plains they pitched camp
And began to feast and prepare for battle.
No sooner had they rested when Zwide's army fell on them.
But Zwide's army, sapped by a long journey and hunger,
25 And fighting on unfamiliar ground, was driven back;
Nor did their main force win the victory of their promise.

At Qokli hill Zwide's over-eager army was cut down by the
      Zulus,
Forcing them back in disorder down the hill.
30 In compact columns the Zulus moved, stabbing them with short
      spears.
Wave after wave of Zwide's army was repulsed.
Over each other and in confusion they tumbled down.
Even by their numbers they crowded the battle arena.
35 Shaka incited his army from all sides.
On one side of the hill were the fierce regiments of General
      Nzobo.
They fought alongside those of the Ntshangase clan.

On the other side was the main body of the Zulu regiments.
Realizing how fiercely the Zulus fought,
Zwide's army fell back onto the river bank
Here was fought the bloodiest battle.
5 The Zulus descended on them in circular waves.
With speed they attacked as if all at once.
The commanders of the Ndwandwe army constantly shouted,
Urging men to battle: 'Fight! Great scion of Langa,
Ferocious army of ancient kings, do not retreat!'
10 But it was all in vain.
In great panic, Prince Nomahlanjana ordered a withdrawal,
Deciding now to plan new bold strategies.
Zwide's army began to cross the river,
Leaving only a few stationed at the lower end of the hill.
15 The Zulus spoiled for a final victory,
Knowing they had broken the pride of Zwide's army.
But their commander called them back:
'Go no further! The pursuit of an enemy forebodes disaster!'
Thus restraining the frenzied heroes, like Njikiza,
20 Who now were shouting the war slogan 'Into the river!'
At the centre of the war arena lay Nomashukumbela.
He, tall and big and fierce,
Had stabbed the enemy from all sides
But now his strength was sapped by the many wounds of battle.
25 His body was covered with thick clots of blood.
He said, looking at his comrades who fought all around him:
'Fight, children of Zulu! I have finished my battle.
It is enough for one man. Zwide shall never win.
Ease my pain with a spear, my brothers of the battlefield.'
30 A companion of his regiment came close to him;
Looking into his eyes with tears, he plunged his spear,
Sending him painlessly into the glorious home of the Ancestors.
Many seethed with anger at the death of Nomashukumbela.
Raising their spears in honour of him, they swore revenge.
35 Ndo, his brother who came after him, wept aloud.
He knelt, gripping his brother's hand close to him.
Only through force was he held back from cutting into
enemy lines.

Aware now of the fury with which the Zulus fought,

Nomahlanjana curbed his forces.
He saw, too, how the hill had served the Zulus well.
Twice, thrice, the Ndwanwe army had attempted to climb
But each time they left the ground littered with the dead.

5 Once more Nomahlanjana summoned all commanders,
Keen to devise yet another new strategy.
He bellowed: 'Let the army climb slowly,
Covering their heads with their shields.
No one must throw their spears into the enemy lines.
10 This way we shall break into their ranks, avoiding the costly
        tactics.
We have done enough to fertilize the mountain.
Our army must disrupt them from the top!'
The generals tried in vain to dissuade him from this plan,
15 Telling him the army lacked knowledge of the close-combat
        methods.
The stubborn prince persisted with his commands,
Ordering them to rush precipitately against the Zulu army.
Zwide's army climbed the hill hurriedly,
20 Resolved to fight and steal from the Zulus their own tactics.
Hungry for battle, they forged their way into the Zulu army.
As the two armies clashed the Zulus opened and stabbed in
        regular rhythm.
As they fought they shouted out their battle calls.
25 The whole day the battle raged.
The Ndwandwes, tormented by thirst
And harassed by the fierce rays of the blazing sun, weakened.
Their generals, approaching Nomahlanjana said:
'Your army shall be decimated by the Zulus;
30 They cannot be dislodged from their mountain fortress.'
They reported how difficult it was to climb the incline.
Often it would collapse, bringing down a thousand boulders.
Faced with a barrage of condemnations
Nomahlanjana ordered the army to return.
35 Yet he was still eager to concoct another plan.
Loathing to submit to failure at the hands of Shaka's army,
He said to the generals:
'I have one last, invincible strategy.
The Zulus, having been drugged by a sense of victory,

Must now be lured out of their fortress,
And be made to follow us in hot pursuit.
Thus in your encounter stay only long enough to draw them out,
Then throw down your weapons as though in terror of them.
5 They shall follow you, unable to resist their chance of revenge.
It is at this moment we shall cut them down,
Loosening their front line from the main force.
To fulfil the demands of our strategy
Our first thrust must withdraw with lightning swiftness,
10 Leaving our army free to kill.
The Zulu army, thus disorganized,
And forced to fight on grounds unfamiliar to them,
Shall be wrenched and broken like the little sparrow's wings.'
The generals were pleased with this plan.
15 They chastised themselves for not thinking of it before.
Once more Zwide's army moved forward,
Confident they might yet empty the hill of the Zulus.
On encounter Zwide's regiments quickly disengaged.
The Zulus followed close on their heels
20 Believing by their speed they could stab and retreat.
It was as if Nomahlanjana had forseen all these errors.
Those on the higher end
Descended in large numbers to chase after Zwide's army,
Shearing the naked flesh with their weapons.
25 Even those who had been restrained from fighting ran amok.
The wave of Zulu fighters burst out in fury.
Even the little boys who carried the fighters' weapons
Scattered in all directions, chasing after them.
It was Shaka who suspected in all this some trickery.
30 Raising his spear and looking in all directions, he shouted:
'The traps of the Ndwandwe army are wide open.
Turn back before their gates close in on you!'
At this command they stopped, leaving the enemy to flee.
But the thrust of the over-zealous fell into the heart of battle.
35 To rescue them Shaka sent the young recruits, but it was too
late.
The enemy stabbed them from all angles.
The Zulus, like a porcupine, fought fiercely from one spot.
Even Zwide's army disengaged in terror, alarmed at their
40 fierceness.

Zwide's men stood back, loathing to be the first to die.
The Zulus thought their fate of death sealed
And only desired to die in glory.
They now climbed in the direction of their hill sanctuary,
5 Running in rhythm as if in a dance of the love-season
And hurrying upwards in an attempt to merge with their army.
The Ndwandwe regiments, realizing this, ran after them.
As the two armies disengaged
Great piles of the dead lay scattered on the ground.
10 Some were still warm as if life itself refused to divide.
The young and old lay lifeless beside each other.
Friend and foe seemed to embrace in death.
The Zulus began to sing their famous anthem.
Zwide's army stood dejectedly, seeing how
15 Their much-praised strategy had faltered.
The generals begged the chief commander to sink his pride,
To let the troops eat and quench their thirst.
They hoped after this they might yet fight again.
Thus Zwide's army retreated far from the scene of battle.
20 There to sit and eat and count their dead.
As they rested Shaka and his commanders watched their every
      move.
He said to Mgobhozi: 'We have finally humiliated Zwide's
      army.
25 It now stands only on one leg.
Should they return again,
It shall only be to avenge their wounds.
Our success now depends on our vigilance
To keep ahead of them in all their new strategies.
30 Each blow from us must be severe, revealing our surprises and
      secrets.
We must not let them regain their power.
As one section of their army confronts our men
Let us deliver to them our final blow,
35 Disrupting each thrust in which they put their hopes.
Their sole aim is now only this:
To dislodge us from the fortress hill.
But it is only through their folly they have failed to do so.
Were I in command of their numerous army
40 I would have attacked from three separate directions,

Forcing those on the hill to fight simultaneously on many fronts.
Our forces would then have been too thinned for their army.
Even if they had failed to win decisively
Our position would have been unbearable.

5 Yet even fools learn in time.
They accumulate disparate bits of knowledge
Until in one limited moment all fires burn at once,
Achieving in a lifetime what others solve in a single moment.
Perhaps even Nomahlanjana may finally see the truth.'

10 As Shaka was speaking the regiments of Zwide
Could be seen in procession, following each other.
No longer did they head for the frontal face of the hill,
But split themselves in different directions.
Some took the circuitous route leading to the northern
15   shoulder;
Some veered in the direction of the southern point.
Shaka, realizing this, called Nqoboka and Ndlela of Sompisi
And said: 'Observe now the new plots of Zwide's army.
Their goal is only to divert us.

20 No sooner shall they go behind the hill
Than they shall whirl back, climbing the little hill,
Attacking us from the rear.
Through this point they hope to break our resistance.
Thus our army shall fight on two main fronts.

25 As they climb the hidden side of the hill
We must meet them with a determined and a fierce assault.
But let them come and enter the mouth of our fortress first.
As they have almost reached the strategic top
Swarm them, let loose our regiments from two flanks.

30 Move with the speed of a hounded buffalo,
Forcing them back to the hill base
And breaking the tail of the attacking forces,
Thus encircling the enemy and cutting off their reinforcements.
Like a python our regiments must swallow them!'

35 Countering the armies of Zwide in their early onslaughts,
Two Zulu regiments rushed on them, swooping down on
        Zwide's army,
Stabbing them from all sides like hunters attacking an elephant.
Confronted with this fierce attack Zwide's army retraced their
40   steps.

But Ndlela's regiment followed them.
The great jaws of Ndlela and Nqoboka met,
Crushing them in like a swallow's bone.
Horrendous groans of war echoed into the approaching night.
5   From all parts of the battlefield raged the fighting madness.
The fierce force of Mgobhozi-of-the-Mountain
Attacked now as if bewitched by some mountain herb.
He called out to his weapon, as he fought:
'Eat, my spear! You have long been waiting!'
10 He whistled and sang a mysterious song.
Once it was whispered he had a bad dream.
His mind had been seized by a fighting Ancestor
Who directed him in all his wars,
Often making him sing to him this song.
15 Many of Zwide's sons were killed there — the heir, Prince
      Nomahlanjana,
Prince Nobengula, Prince Mpepha, Prince Ngobe, Prince
      Ngabeni,
Prince Sixholoba, the handsome Prince Dalingubo: all died
20   there.
Great was the mourning in the House of Ntombazi.
It was as though in a single day many wars were avenged.
The Zulus sang their anthems, bequething to all generations
      their story.
25 The great regiments of uDlambedlu, the fierce iziMpohlo
      regiment,
The stubborn Jubinqwanga, the amaWombe, the iziChwe, the
      uFasimba —
All shall be celebrated in song by their children's children.
30 The repulsed the fierce Amankayiya regiments.
The army of Zwide retreated to make a sacrifice to the dead.

No sooner had Shaka won this breathing space
Than he led his army to the Bulawayo royal city.
As it headed to Zululand it often fought the Ndwandwe army.
35 From mountain sides and bushes the enemy threw their
      missiles.
Mgobhozi-of-the-Mountain was infuriated by these tactics.
He said to Shaka: 'My lord, why should we retreat?

After all, we have outwitted and repulsed the enemy.'
For a while Shaka did not reply.
Then he said: 'It is enough, son of Msane.
People have limits. Their spirits erode with each assault.
5   To fight only to survive blunts the higher purpose of war.
Indeed, since our whole battle was fought from a fortress
We are weakened on the new ground.
We must retreat while our army is still strong,
And our fighters still have no fear of disasters.
10 Besides on our familiar ground no army dares follow us.'
The returning Zulu army filled the routes with their numbers;
The dust of the Mbelebele division choked the northern regions.
Here they had kept watch for an enemy invasion.
In many regions Zwide's army attempted to ambush the Zulus.
15 Unable to fight a full battle they contented themselves only with
      loot.
The ever-growing tide of the Zulu regiments repulsed their
      assaults.

From many fields Zwide's army seized cattle.
20 As it reached the Ndwandwe capital it celebrated this feat.
Furious, Zwide scolded his son, Prince Shemane:
'Must you return only with cattle,
Leaving the young Zulu upstart unconquered?
These beasts bring only a curse to our kingdom.
25 They shall rouse the widows from their sleep.
They are the cattle of death, swelling with the lives of my
      children!
You have lost the battle to the son of Senzangakhona!
He is the victor even though may bring his head!
30 You have left your own brothers to wild animals.
It is as if you are not my son,
I who never returned from battle without victory.
Could you not have avenged your own brothers like all people?
You still come back unashamed, full of song and dance,
35 As though your brothers still live!
From today on you shall never lead my army.
I shall appoint my own new commander
 Zwide's word must never return empty-handed!
You have disgraced our great house of heroes.'

The whole gathering listened in terror as Zwide spoke,
Knowing a parent's wrath brings a curse to his children.
When Prince Shemane tried to give his version,
It only incensed Zwide,
5 For he already knew how carelessly they had directed the army,
How they had defied the words of wiser council,
Indulging themselves in self-glory while thousands perished.
Zwide burst out and said:
'I detest even the cattle confiscated from the Zulus.
10 They are swollen with the bodies of my children!
I shall not take one of them nor eat their meat.
I order that they be let loose to roam untouched over the whole
   country.
Let them bellow to the mountains and valleys my grief!
15 Let them tell the whole earth of my children!
As for the son of Senzangakhona, he shall pay for this!
He shall see the sun turning from west to the east.'
His voice quivered in anger as he spoke.
Yet words are seldom equalled by actions.
20 How could he set out to battle
When his army was torn and scarred by the Zulus?
Had not Shaka lopped off his source of power?
Had he not set in flight their ferocious waves of attacks?
Some of the Ndwandwe princes now conspired against
25   Zwide,
Encouraging the many protests against his tyrannical rule.
For people praise the rulers according to their success
And condemn them when they fail,
Regarding them as holding precariously their future.
30 It is then they begin to look for a new leader.

As the army of the Zulus returned
They sang their great battle hymns and anthems.
Women and children who had hidden in the great Nkandla
   forest emerged.
35 Large groups of families set out to their homes.
Those who had criticized the daring of this campaign
Now effused with ecstatic praise, proclaiming loudly:
'A great king is born! Jama is born again!'
All over the land songs were sung; poems were composed

To celebrate the great episodes of the Qokli battles.
Their themes centred on the many feats of courage.

From the tales of the war and their fame in Nguniland,
The Zulus knew how popular their fight was against Zwide.
5   Shaka, proud of these achievements and eager to encourage his
       army,
Addressed the regiments: 'Great nation of Zulu,
You have shown courage against a superior enemy.
The nations that spoke of you with contempt are chilled by
10   your songs.
Kings and princes shiver in their little thrones.
Enemies flee to hide in the mountain caves.
Heroes like Njikiza of the Ngcolosi clan,
Like Ndlela, the son of Sompisi, like Nqoboka, like Mgobhozi,
15   Have become legends in the songs and tales of distant nations.
These are my brothers with whom I have shared many dangers.
We have broken the boasts of our enemies through our courage.
They came to battle full of conceit;
They returned humbled and covered with wounds.
20   Many enemy heroes are left in the battlefield.
It is your persistence and daring
That shall bring glory to our Zulu nation.
The battle you have fought is only the beginning.
Not only shall Zwide once again raise his head against us,
25   But also the little kings and numerous princes surrounding our
       land.
No man must let his weapons lose their power.
Failure to build a powerful nation
Only breeds a nation of vagabonds on the outskirts.
30   Bees that have been stirred from their nest
Often run amok, stinging the innocent passer-by.
For this reason the sting must be removed from them.
By our invincible power we must make peace for all peoples.
We must be alert for battle.
35   Those who believe in our truth shall be welcomed.
Their harvests shall be protected by our army.
Our lands shall be fertile for all peoples.
But for the moment we must build and be ready for our
       enemies.

Let none among our regiments be rushed into precipitate wars.
Let none pester the nation with calls for senseless raids.
Let no one claim Zwide's war still haunts them,
Alleging possession by the spirit of war.

5   Let such reckless men know they only invite death from me.
There is no heroism in those who terrorize others.
Yet there shall be no coward in Zululand;
Whoever makes this blasphemy against you and your clan —
Bring him to justice!

10   Fine him a large prize of cattle to cleanse your family.
Should such a man persist,
You are empowered by our law to fight him to the death.
By his words he shall have scandalized the great heroes of
      Zululand.

15   To blaspheme those who are revered by our nation,
Who opened new frontiers, is a crime difficult to comprehend!'
From his words people acquired power,
Their minds prepared for new feats of courage.
It was as though these words came from the lips of the

20   Ancestors.
The poet was seized by the spirit of the song, and declaimed:
'You whose routes were furnished by Dunjwa — but they should
      have asked Mbozane.
He was rushing secretly to attack Nomagaga

25   But the cock crowed and awoke the whole village.
The thunderbolt approaches!
Take the children to a hiding place!
Only the adults shall flee on their own!
Dunjwa was crushed into little fragments.

30   He built temporary dwellings near the Thukela river,
Where leopard traps are often laid.'
There were happy sounds of voices heralding a new era.

Had Shaka been like the many rulers of Nguniland
He now would have contented himself with his much-acclaimed

35   victory.
But he was restless, like one possessed by an Ancestor.
He began moulding his army, infusing it with new visions.
It was at this time Prince Mzilikazi arrived, appealing to Shaka:
'My lord, I have lost all I had.

All my close relations have been killed.
My sole possession is now only a bitter heart.
I am young; my blood still boils in my veins.
I want to die in the battlefield.
5 I want to die fighting Zwide of the Ndwandwe nation.
It is you, my lord, who shall allow me to fulfil this task,
Chasing him and stabbing him, demanding my father with every
       wound.
I shall avenge my father, Mashobana, and all the Khumalo
10   children.
I have come to you to request a place to live,
Where I can cleanse myself with cleansing herbs.
When I am done with this ceremony I shall thank my lord.
I know many people shall condemn me,
15 Saying, after all, Zwide is my maternal grand-uncle.
How could I ally against the enemies of my relations?
But you, my lord, whose vision penetrates into the night,
Know how one's elders possess the magic power
So long as they continue to give their love.
20 When they have destroyed your family
The sacred cord that binds you together is broken;
They have turned away from the eyes of humanity.
Their own son must no longer hesitate to kill them.
So, too, with Zwide, who has killed my father.
25 Permit me, then, my lord, to make sacrifices for my father,
To accompany his spirit to its resting place.
Through his many children on earth
Let him trace the echoes of his heroic poems.
Thereafter I shall fight in your army with all my strength.
30 I come to you with only a few followers
Whose task has always been to protect our house.'
Mzilikazi referred to a large herd of cattle
Whose numbers seemed to cover the surrounding hills.
Near to them was a large army of the Khumalo
35   regiments.
Shaka burst with satisfaction at his good fortune.
He knew if Zwide had lost those closest to him
They would reveal all his moods and daily secrets.
He felt a strong bond with Mzilikazi,
40 Remembering how he himself was treated by his relatives

He admired, too, his courage and maturity, despite his tender
    age.
He sent his councillor, ordering him:
'I want you to treat Mashobana with special kindness.
5   Place him on the grounds that closely resemble his former home.
Let him know here in this nation we all are relatives.'
Shaka was pleased within himself,
Knowing how many would follow Mzilikazi's example.
In this way they would enhance his own kingdom's prestige.

10   Shaka invited Prince Mzilikazi and spoke to him privately:
'Son of Mashobana, countries rule only through their weapons.
It is wise to trust those who are your allies,
To strengthen them against all potential enemies.
To enable you to avenge your father (as is the custom)
15   You must narrate patiently all details of Zwide's life.
Let nothing remain untold.
Day after day you must visit me without hestitation,
Giving the secrets and habits of Zwide.
Since many may serve him and yet hate him
20   You must find a way to win their trust,
For from them we shall get all the plots and schemes of Zwide.
They shall furnish us with all the debates of his council.
Through them we shall know the conflicts in Zwide's army,
For to fight a stronger enemy
25   It is necessary to find the source of his strength and weakness.'
Mzilikazi consented to these words and thanked the king.
He vowed: 'My king, there is nothing I cannot do
So long as the blood of my parents cries out for revenge!
My mind is ready and my spirit is willing.
30   Since I came here
I have learnt many things and reflected on many truths.
I have grown to be a man whose vision feeds from others.
You restored my pride; you made me brave;
My humanity grew within me.
35   For indeed it is true, my lord,
All people are courageous so long as life is worthwhile.
When one no longer sees the coming of summer
One surrenders, inviting the relieving power of death.
It is only by the kindness of others that people awaken.

Such has been my good fortune, my lord.
I shall do whatever you order of me.
I shall plant a thousand eyes in Zwide's sanctuaries.
Whenever he wakes or sleeps there shall be your agents.'
5   Mzilikazi's words filled Shaka with joy
For he knew the next battle would be fiercer than the first.
It would be fought only through plots and fiendish stratagems.
He gave praise to the Ancestors,
Thanking them for sending Mzilikazi.
10   He knew Zwide's army would soon be on the march again,
And the next war would decide on the supremacy in Nguniland.
Because of this, kings and princes began building their alliances,
Preparing to serve whoever should be emperor of the whole
     region.
15   Such was the power promised to one who would conquer Zwide.
A new wave of peoples now converged on Zululand,
Eager to build a phalanx of nations against the hated Zwide.
A new section of the Khumalo clan deserted to the Zulu camp.
The Ncubes, the Magubanes, the Khozas all followed suit.
20   The Mthethwas now proclaimed Shaka the true heir of
     Dingiswayo.
At the festivals both anthems were sung.

Elated, Shaka constantly exercised his new army.
Everywhere people talked of the impending war;
25   Generals and commanders encouraged their regiments,
Giving rewards and honours for any unique acts of courage.
Shaka himself often sat in the shade with Mzilikazi,
Listening intently to the strange and varied stories of Zwide.
Zwide never knew how, as he gloried in his rule,
30   The agents of the Zulu king reported his every movement.
Directed and briefed by Mzilikazi, they supplied every detail.
Among Zwide's close officials was Nolugu of the Dlamini clan.
Often he served as Zwide's mouthpiece to his many generals.
To him Zwide confided all his secrets.
35   This same Nolugu was Shaka's chief agent;
From him Mzilikazi sifted and interpreted all reports.
The great Dlamini clan sealed its bonds with the Zulu nation,
Creating an alliance in peace and in battle.
It was through their vast network

The news travelled from region to region.
Beaming with joy, Mzilikazi declared: 'My lord, sun of our
    nation,
News travels fast from the court of Zwide.
5 He is preparing for battle.
The great General Soshangane of the Gasa clan
Has been chosen as chief commander and sole strategist.
Around him I have created a network of agents.
Through them I shall report his most hidden thoughts.
10 Rumour has it Prince Shemane bitterly resents this elevation,
Claiming Soshangane often ingratiates himself with Zwide,
Poisoning his father's mind against him.
The nation of the Nxumalos is divided in half.
Prince Shemane sharpens the tongues of his followers.
15 He denounces the war plans devised by Soshangane,
Who demands the short-spear technique.
He proposes the abandonment of sandals to gain speed.
Indeed, he has adopted all your war methods.
Admonishing the army council he once said:
20 "No bull can fight successfully without short, sharp horns."
General Zwangendaba, known for his stubbornness,
Dismissed these arguments with contempt,
Backing Prince Shemane, whose voice he is.
No one took notice of my father's last words,
25 Who long ago demanded a change in the techniques of battle,
To combine the old and the lethal ones of the iziChwe regiment.
But Prince Shemane, hating more than thinking,
Held on tenaciously to his original ideas.
He feared, too, the growing prestige of Soshangane.
30 Besides, should his popularity be totally eclipsed,
Many might flee the Ndwandwe army.
Knowing this he tries to make mockery of your army and its
    tactics.'
The great son of Senzangakhona digested each of these words.
35 Speaking slowly and deliberately he said:
'Mzilikazi, son of Mashobana, drink —
Share with me my own beer vessel. You are a man.
Through these same agents whisper to Soshangane these words:
"The Zulus live in constant fear.
40 Their fighting tactics are a cause of many quarrels.

Many claim them as the cause of weakness at the Qokli
  battle.
Had the spear-throwing method been used, they say,
The hill slope would have eased their efforts,
5 Sucking into the enemy crowds their missiles."
Tell him: "Shaka faces revolt against his tactics." '
Shaka spoke so convincingly that Mzilikazi himself was alarmed.
He said: 'My lord, is there any truth in these conspiracies?'
Shaka drank from the beer vessel and in time he commented:
10 'In war a word to mislead must be stronger than the truth.
Do as I tell you, son of Mashobana.
One day you shall learn how the world is ruled,
How the follower must borrow from the lips of the master;
How the wise implant rumours through their messengers,
15 Spreading their half-truths through these agents.
Thus their goals and wills are achieved by stratagem.
Let me tell you how rulers stay ahead of their underlings.
Once when I realized how the numbers of diviners multiplied,
Crawling on the ground like new-born lizards,
20 Accusing the great men of the court of conspiracies,
I decided time had come to trick them and end this charade.
As you know, there are many varieties of diviners.
Some act to please and win approval of their rulers;
Still some divine to please those who approach them;
25 Yet few exist who speak the truth.
All these types were everywhere in my court.
People lived in fear of a diviner's accusing finger.
It was then I decided I would eliminate them.
I smeared a goat's blood on the beam of my house
30 And at the break of dawn I raised the alarm.
The diviners of the land turned out in all their numbers.
To my great horror, they set out to choose those close to me.
Throughout the day they picked whomever they pleased.
Late in the afternoon a fierce-looking diviner of the Mdletshe
35   clan
Called out: "My king, I do see the culprit,
But I fear him." "Speak. Let the truth be heard!
The land is infested with men of evil intent," I said.
He raised his divine stick, pointing up to the sun,
40 Uttering words not known in Nguniland and said:

"My king, I see only one man.
This man's hands are spattered with blood.
He is no other than yourself, my lord."
The whole gathering was shocked into deathly silence.

5 It was then I intervened and endorsed his words.
I ordered those who were now proven innocent
To pick up their accusers,
Giving them the same fate that was due to them.
One such diviner had dared to choose Mgobhozi-
10   of-the-Mountain!
Only my furious command stopped the crowds from killing him.
To appease them I ordered him abandoned in the forest.
I knew, too, such men are never without allies:
Often they command numerous teams of agents

15 Who carry distorted stories of me and those close to me.
Thus when he roamed he revealed the names of others.
Herein lies the truth of rulers, son of Mashobana:
By their skills they manoeuvre the strings of power.
They play this and that belief into the minds of others,
20 Feeding them with thoughts whose results they often can
        predict.
They plant their own seeds in the summer fields of the mind —
Indeed, for them the truth is only that which nourishes their
        power.
25 Thus the diviners, assuming this authority, blundered to their
        deaths.
By such games they sought to make the illusion of power real.
Yet the greatest power lies in the populace.
As our forefathers have told us:
30 "A ruler only rules through the people."
So let Zwide rule by the same power that shall destroy him.
When he has accomplished this and that by his cleverness
He shall humble himself before them and say:
"I erred and danced to my own songs."
35 The land of the Zulus has earned its peace.
The people of the Zulu nation spread out with pride,
Knowing there never shall be threats from arbitrary power.
I tell you these stories so that you may learn;
So that you may yet understand the truths of power.'
40 Prince Mzilikazi, the son of Mashabana, stared in amazement,

Alarmed at all these things
Like someone who, believing in the excellence of rulers,
Discovers the essence of their corruption.
He thanked the king: 'I have listened to your words, my lord.
5 They have strengthened the bones of my chest.
Through them I enrich and fertilize my own visions.
I shall keep them in mind for all times.
Through your kindness I yet believe
My father shall return from the land of the Ancestors.'
10 These words revealed his inner pain,
For his injured mind was never at peace.
He plotted ceaselessly against Zwide,
Laying snares and consolidating all secret alliances against him.

Book Eight: The masterful genius of Shaka

This chapter leads to the second war against Zwide. In it Shaka proves himself an outstanding military genius. He elaborates his espionage network to obtain every detail about his enemy. Through this network he initiates events in the enemy camp to suit his military requirements. He organizes a sophisticated strategic retreat. Having ordered all supplies to be destroyed, he almost annihilates Zwide's huge army through starvation and direct attack. Zwide's power is broken forever. This represents a turning point in the balance of power in Nguniland. Except for a few rulers like Macingwane, Shaka is now unchallenged master of the region. Domestic issues loom large: Princess Mkhabayi, the royal aunt, acts as a balancing force between Shaka and his ambitious brothers.

Such was the growing power of the Zulus:
Eastwards it expanded, following the sun's directions.

At the vast village-city of Princess Mkhabayi
The sun opened its inner womb of forgetfulness.
Her mind was said to equal ten men of the Assembly.
Many sought to hear her great and fearless thoughts;
5   Large processions travelled to her royal city of Nquthu.
The great princess often narrated ancient stories of the Zulus.
In mid-thought, she would stare as if she had seen a spirit;
Her ideas flashed like lightning.
She was black like the deep shadows of the forest,
10 Like the eternal powers that hang over the earth.
When she walked her footfalls echoed into water,
Proud and confident like one who fears neither life nor death.
It was because of this people cast down their eyes,
Breaking twigs like children before her.
15 In her presence people waited their turn.
When she spoke only her voice, round and beautiful, was heard:
'Zulu and Qwabe were children of Malandela.
Qwabe, like elder brothers, lacked the zealousness of his brother.
He was slow to think and slow to act.
20 He prided himself only in the glories of his father, King
      Malandela,
Not like Zulu who was always thinking of new things.
Even at the Assembly he was never silent.
His sharp mind grasped the thoughts of others like a scorpion's
25   clasp.
For this he was popular at the Assembly;
Often his absence stirred a protest: "Where is the prince?"
Because of this Qwabe resented his brother,
But still there was nothing he could do,
30 For, indeed, the heir must please;
He must derive his power from the importance of his position.
Not so the unhappy lot of others
Who must strive and survive through intrigue and sharp
     intellect.
35 Zulu, by his alertness, did not enhance his brother's name,
Nor did his followers bow down to their future king.
He was as hard and unbending as a winter cane.
These quarrels threatened to break the bonds of kinship.
The wise King Malandela decided: to preserve peace
40 He must allot Zulu his own special place,

Removing him from the ancient lands and graves of his
    Forefathers.
He said: "My son, take this portion of your father's wealth
And never let it graze in your brother's fields."
5 He gave him his choicest breed of white cattle,
Implanting among them a giant black bull.
Prince Zulu moved with all his wealth to his own region.
He vowed: "By my prosperity these lands would be the envy of
    all."
10 Indeed his prophecy came true.
He nurtured a special stock, which he fed with the softest grass.
As it grazed passers-by stood and watched in awe.
He put his cattle in separate corrals and grazing lands
According to their variety of colours.
15 His royal village became the attraction of many peoples —
Indeed, it was the envy of many princes.
From the collection of followers and admirers
He formed the first home of the Zulu people:
To this day we speak as descendants of this wise prince.
20 So long as there are people on earth, so long shall our nation
    be.'
As she finished talking it was clear to everyone
Shaka was to her mind the reincarnation of this prince.
He fulfilled the promise made to them by the Ancestors.
25 The wily Princess knew no great history is without heroes:
Great countries are those that boast a great Ancestry.
Indeed, artists embellish their past to inspire their children.
For this she sang the song of Zulu and broke into tears:
'Those who worship foreign gods are swallowed by them.
30 The greatness of our land lies in the glory of our children.
As we fight our battles, we create their tales.'
Like the poet who moulded the sacred staff,
Carving it from the ebony plant of the ancient forest,
Thus, too, did the princess tell the tales of the Forefathers.
35 In honour of her the poet said: 'Father of the wily ones,
Crafty daughter of the River Snake,
As you tell a tale you lead a man to his doom!
You overcame the wizards;
You destroyed Mkhongoyiyana near the Mngadi villages;
40 You demolished Bheje amongst the diviners.

Thou vast quagmire of Menzi,
That trapped people and was nourished by them.
This is true of Nohela of Mlilo.
Great fire that burns amongst all the mountains,
5 It seized Nohela and swallowed him.
The cow that bellowed from the hill of Sangoyana,
Its voice boomed and exploded into heaven.
The distant villages of Gwabalanga heard its moaning.
(He was the son, Mndaba of the Khumalo clan).
10 After reaching puberty the young woman spoke no more.
Some began to gossip about her, commenting on her turbulent
      mind.
She caused the hunters to capture the birds without effort.
As they seized them she stared at them in the eye.
15 She opened all the gates for people to enter
But members of her family had to enter through the small gates.
She, the devourer of the magic herbs who surrounded the
      enemies,
The Mhlathuzi river is going to overflow at broad daylight!
20 She, the fieldmouse that opened the paths to the land of
      Malandela,
And said: "Only those of Malandela
Shall travel along these sacred routes.
She said, only they shall take the direction they choose." '

25 As kingdoms grow they breed their own internal enemies,
Spawning those who desire to eat the fruit of power
And extinguish the rays of the sun.
Such was the fate of Shaka's rule.
While acts of heroes blazed with grandeur at the memorial cairn
30 There were those who ached with festering grudges,
Who, like Prince Dingane, often generated hatreds against
      Shaka.
Prince Dingane often swore aloud by his father's sovereignty.
He and Prince Mhlangane never fully acclaimed their brother's
35   rule:
They planted seeds of doubt about his war tactics and reign.
Shaka heard these rumours.
Loyal followers urged him to eliminate these troublesome voices
But Shaka only said: 'These are my brothers.

How can I kill those who are the children of my father?
Besides, who would rule the country should I die in battle?'
Indeed Shaka himself never filled the royal grounds with royal
    issue.
5   His children were secretly given to relatives or removed.
Fearing his displeasure, old women became adept at keeping
    secrets.
Even the King's favourite woman of the Cele clan
Never boasted his child, despite her endless pleas;
10 Nor did the King soften to the tears of Nandi.
Encouraged by the absence of an heir
The princes frantically plotted against their brother.
They spoke to Princess Mkhabayi, hoping to win her sympathy,
But she never swerved: she spoke profusely in praise of Shaka.
15 She proclaimed publicly:
'Shaka is the only ruler who shall make our nation great.
He does not hoard the loot of wars like others
Or breed large numbers of princes and princesses,
Who by their conceit often squander what is rightly of the
20   nation.'
Kingdoms and states and empires are kept intact by their poets —
It is they who embellish their tales, making the future desirable.
Thus, too, did Princess Mkhabayi inspire loyalty to Shaka's rule.
Of the people of Zululand it was said:
25 They walk high with crowns of red feathers on their heads.
They stare into the dome of the sky, unafraid.
From the south, from the north, and from the sun's nocturnal
    home,
People sing the great anthems of the Zulu nation.

30 Day after day the regiments built up their anger against Zwide,
Pointing their spears to his region and composing fierce
    anthems;
Mgobhozi often provoked them with tales of Zwide's rule and
    cruelty.
35 More ardent than others was the uFasimba regiment;
They requested to be the first in battle against Zwide.
It was not long before the sparks of war exploded in
    Nguniland.
Zwide, unable to restrain his anger,

Shouted to the mountains the slogans of war:
'Young boy of Senzangakhona,
You swore at me in the hearing of nations.
I, son of Langa, King of Kings, I heard your blasphemy
5 When you called me an old, dried-up cow-hide;
Yet I was senior to you and as old as your father.
I shall yet tear up the sinews of your youth!'
Though not yet fully prepared for this war,
Shaka set out, vowing: 'I shall cut the tongue of this he-goat.'
10 Shaka said to Mgobhozi: 'Anger is not enough in this war.
I have sent a message to my relatives of the Qwabe clan,
Asking them to give me support against this fierce Zwide.
It is hard for us to tackle this challenge alone —
Our army still suffers the wounds of the Qokli battle.
15 The assault of Zwide would be too heavy on our troops.
Besides, in the south we need an opening for retreat.'
While Mgobhozi agreed with these words
He was not convinced of Shaka's judgement.
He said: 'My lord, I doubt if the Qwabes shall join us.
20 Would they not rather wait the outcome of war?
Remember, my lord, there are ancient grudges in your families.'
While Mgobhozi was talking and arguing against these high
        expectations
A messenger was heard, announcing to the king:
25 'I did go, my lord, to Phakathwayo of the House of Malandela,
Telling him: "My lord of the House of Zulu borrows some
        shields.
The wild man Zwide is out on a rampage again."
King Phalathwayo just laughed, making fun of my words.
30 He said: "Go back to him and say I ask him this question:
Does he not know the custom of Nguniland,
Not to swear at those senior and older than him?
Those who breach the laws should suffer the consequence.
They should be punished even if they be of our house and
35   family.
Tell him these words come from Phakathwayo, the son of
        Khondlo.
Tell him I have, indeed, observed for some time his conceit.
He has scattered and terrorized even those under my
40   protection!"'

It was as though Shaka had been hit on his chest:
He was spitting and swearing inaudible words of anger.
He said: 'I shall teach him. I am the grandson of Jama!
Go back to him, then. Tell him to get ready for battle.
5   I shall not delay, I, Nodumehlezi, the son of Menzi.'
He summoned his army from all the hills and valleys;
Phakathwayo's ears were deafened by the sound of war songs.
Yet it was no war to tell one's grandchildren about.
Soon the Qwabe army was thrown into disarray.
10   Indeed, many had denounced this war,
Saying it would open the door to enemies.
The Zulus returned, still itching for fiercer battles,
Eager to settle their scores against their true enemy, Zwide.
When he heard of the swift defeat of Phakathwayo
15   He said to his supreme commander General Soshangane:
'Do you see how skilfully the boy of Senzangakhona fights?
Had he desired it he would have destroyed the Qwabe nation,
But he only gave a warning blow,
Fighting as though preparing for some ultimate battle;
20   For now many are full of praise,
Lauding his generous gesture of preserving his relatives.
I want you to destroy this growing monster:
I want you to return with his head.
If you fail it is your head I shall demand.'
25   The Ndwandwes prepared for war like numerous teams of
        locusts.
Even the young sharpened their light spears.
Everyone talked once again of this war as a war to end all wars,
Certain it would determine the supreme master of the earth.
30   Many swore no war would ever be so fearful.
It was said from the battlefields only messengers should survive.
From the poet, generations thereafter shall ask:
'What great issues could provoke so fearful a war?'
Of the War-of-the-Hurricanes he shall only shed tears:
35   Old age and time shall seal his mouth.

The Zulu regiments swarmed like flying ants after rains,
Eager to challenge and defeat Zwide's army.
Shaka now launched his army in all directions;
He sent a command to the regions of the battlefield,

Ordering the season's harvest to be reaped at once.
Every grain and food-store was to be razed to the ground and
    burnt.
Nothing was to remain in all the summer fields.
5   Shaka knew as he planned these stratagems
Zwide's army carried no supplies
But relied on the loot extorted from the conquered peoples.
Shaka's army carried its own provisions through the young
    carrier boys.
10 No sooner had the two armies come close to each other
Than Shaka shouted a battle command to all Zulu generals,
Ordering them to disengage with speed and to retreat.
The Ndwande army followed, bewildered by this action,
Thinking perchance the large Zwide army
15 Had intimidated the unprepared Zulu army.
Up and down the smaller and larger hills they chased after
    them,
At intervals accelerating their speed but beaten down by the
    sun,
20 Their sandalled feet blistered from the hot earth.
The fingers of hunger restrained their zeal.
Everywhere they found only burnt harvests.
They charged into every grain pit
Like dogs famished for a full five-day cycle.
25 They were like hens digging frantically after rains.
Trapped, they still followed the Zulu army.
Across a winding stream they halted.
There they conferred on the ways to overtake the Zulu army,
But the Zulus launched endless forays and attacks.
30 General Soshangane spoke his concern to General Zwangendaba:
'I think I can see what snares they are laying for us —
As our army is drained by exhaustion they shall attack full-scale.
Go to all our regiments and announce to them:
"The Zulus fight to protect large stores of grain and meat."
35 Then each man shall fight, hoping to gain by his effort.'
General Zwangendaba conveyed this message
Though he knew it was only to keep up their spirits.
The Zulus spread their lines around them, singing their battle
    songs.
40 The Ndwandwe army milled together in confusion.

Without warning they suddenly scattered in all directions,
Disrupting the commander's schemes and stratagems.
Shaka let loose on them his troops,
Causing further panic among the tired Ndwandwe troops.
5 In disorder they attempted to throw their missiles
But the Zulus crept closer, forcing them onto an incline.
Like winter leaves they fell on the broken ground.
Humiliated and defeated, the Ndwandwes began to retrace their
      steps.
10 The ancient poet enshrined this occasion in the great epic:
'The chaser of men who chases without stopping —
How I loved him as he pursued Zwide, the son of Langa,
Following him from the regions of the rising sun
And making him seek sanctuary in the land of the setting sun.
15 Zwide was the man whose little shoulders he broke in two,
Like an old man surprised by a youth!
Fierce one, whom they announce in terror
As they flee from their homes.'
The poet tells us how General Soshangane
20 Sent word to Zwide, saying:
'Your army has been lost to Shaka of Senzangakhona.'
Soshangane himself broke off from Zwide,
Inviting all forces hostile to him to desert the ageing monarch.
He crossed the plains to the north,
25 Where he set up the great Gasa kingdom.
But the grudges of battle die hard:
There the Zulu army pursued him many years after.
It was as though Soshangane had blasphemed the king's name,
So great was the eagerness to bring him to justice.
30 Only Zwangendaba returned with the depleted army.
Ahead of him Shaka sent a section of his own army
Who, by singing Zwide's victory songs, lured them to their
      defeat.
The Mbonambi and Siphezi regiments set Zwide's capital in
35   flames,
Sending the troublesome ruler to flee for his life.
Thus was avenged the many peoples and rulers
Whom Ntombazi had kept for ridicule in her house.
It was this macabre house that was kept intact;
40 Here the Zulus ceremonially buried all Zwide's victims,

Performing all rites appropriate to them.
From every direction anthems of victory were sung.
The regiments shouted their battle call: 'Zulu power is eternal.'
From the lands of the setting sun
5 The voice of triumph travelled to the regions of the rising sun.
King Macingwane of the Chunus shook on his throne.

Listen to the heroes as they narrate their tales of battle.
Zulu, the son of Nogandaya of the Zungu clan said to
          Mgobhozi:
10 'We attacked them at night when they hoped to sleep,
Believing we, too, should rest like all armies of Nguniland
Who never attack in darkness.
Confused and blinded by night, each man stabbed the one next
          to him.
15 Only with the star of dawn did we return to our camp.
Vakaza, the son Heshane, Msinga, the son of Noti,
Vumazwe, the brave son of the Zondi family,
Moyeni who was loved by women: all died there.
Mgobhozi of-the-Mountain could see clearly the truth of this
20   episode.
He said: 'We have succeeded in digging out the root of an evil
          tree —
What remains are only little plants.
Their stems shall be cut by the little boys.'
25 He referred to the little kingdoms that bordered the south.

No celebration in the whole history of the Zululand
Shall exceed in glory the one held on this occasion.
Even old ladies constantly spoke of it in awe.
Festival songs were no longer sung with the voices of children
30 But combined those of the Ndwandwe and the Mthethwa
          nations.
Through these the Zulu nation swelled in numbers;
Even their dances affected a multitude of styles.
Thus many stared in wonderment as the dancer of the Jali clan
35 Moved slowly, thrusting his foot forward,
While tall young men circled him in snake movements.
At intervals they touched the ground with their toes.
Finally ten thousand troops entered the arena!

Even the Ancestors heard their dancing,
For the Forefathers always rejoice in our joys.
They stand at the passes of their divine mountains, watching us,
Happy to see the huge rounds of our feasts.
5   Was it not known to everyone
That Dingiswayo's spirit was there,
Celebrating with his children the downfall of his enemy?
Was it not acknowledged by Jama's children
That his spirit saw with pride the fulfilment of his dream?
10   Shaka caused many eyes to stare as he emerged,
Adorned for the festival in colours of triumph.
On his shoulders were epaulettes of the soft otter skin
And on his head was the long feather of the loury bird.
He carried a large white shield centred with a deep black spot.
15   The poet, inspired by this spectacle, declaimed:
'The glorious feather that bends over beyond the Nkandla forest,
Arching to devour the crowds of men!'
The majesty that was Shaka was embellished with white tails;
His arms were covered with ivory amulets.
20   As he stood facing the noonday sun his body glistened,
Radiating the secrets of mind and contentment.
All around him sat the royal women:
Next to Shaka sat Nandi, the Queen Mother.
Her body was covered in a long robe of leopard skin;
25   Her arms were round, full and gentle.
On them were ornaments bequeathed by queens and kings of
      many lands
Who sought favours and protection from her son.
Princess Mkhabayi sat near her own regiments
30   Who were famed everywhere for their fierceness.
The great ministers of the land sat in a circle around the king,
Their headrings glistening from the sun's fire.
The poets of the land sang their new songs,
Each declaiming the great episodes of battles.
35   They commented in turn on the epic-histories of the Zulu
      nation;
They sang of the great heroes of ancient times;
They sang the old poems of Jubinqwanga;
Yet none could surpass in skill Magolwane,
40   Who was the beautiful voice of the Ancestral Spirit.

He scattered words like sparks of fire.
He beat the ground with his ceremonial stick.
His voice trembled and boomed to the cliffs.
He sang the great epics:
5   'The black thunderhead of Mageba
That roared over the mountains of Nomangci —
It exploded behind the village of Kuqhobekeni
And the bellies of men were chilled.
It seized the shields of the Maphela and the Mankayiya
10   regiments.
The little melons were left half eaten by iziMpaka regiment.
He seized Nomahlanjana, the son of Zwide, of the Mapheleni
          regiment;
He swallowed up Nobengula, the son of Zwide, of the
15   Mapheleni regiment;
He killed Mpepha, the son of Zwide, of the Mapheleni regiment;
He killed Dayingubo, the son of Zwide, of the Mapheleni
          regiment;
He seized Sonsukwana, the son of Zwide, of the Mapheleni
20   regiment;
He eliminated Zwide's wife of Lubongo clan;
He destroyed Mtimona, the son of Gaga, of the Mapheleni
          regiment;
He killed Mhondo-phumela-kwezinde of the Mapheleni
25   regiment;
He killed Ndengezi-mashumi of the Mapheleni regiment;
He destroyed Sihlamthini among those of Zwide;
He killed Nqwangube, the son of Lundiyane.
He was our hero, as he turned his shield in all directions.
30   Come back, Great Destroyer, it is enough!'
As Magolwane declaimed his epic
Great crowds acclaimed and cheered his words.
Their voices resounded from a distance like a waterfall:
They were like a million singers heard all at once.
35   The evening, with its many vessels, brings together the singing
          voices.
The teller of tales sits on the mountainside,
Listening and humming his song in homage;
From many hills, the poems of excellence are sung.
40   The night feeds the dream and those of future times.

From the upper regions the teller of tales speaks:
'We sing a new great song:
From the power of life, each generation gives birth
Until by the thickness of their numbers their dust darkens the
5   sun.
Someone is pregnant.
The child shall rejoice in what is to come
A son of our nation follows the dark path to the forest.
He shall open the way for the children;
10 Because of him the sun shall wait,
Lingering in the east until he has arrived.
To accompany him it opens its giant centre,
Exposing the path into the end of the earth.
Our nation shall live and multiply forever.
15 We are the Children of the Palm Race.'
Such were the songs of the oracle
But no one was listening,
Except one young boy whose body he entered,
Generating in it a great power,
20 Binding his lips until the Forefathers had spoken.

In the remote regions people celebrated.
They sang of Mbonambi, of Ntenjana, of Siphezi,
Of uFasimba, of Jubinqwanga, of amaWombe, of uDlambedlu
      regiments.
25 They composed songs and poems about their heroes.
General Mdlaka was the theme of many songs and legends;
For his skill in battle he was nicknmaed 'Shaka's spirit'.
It was said he laughed loud as he fought in battle.
Of all commanders none inspired to greater acts of courage
30   than he.
Boy detachments swore by his name:
They vowed to equal and surpass their seniors in all things.

Women regiments danced to their own battle songs.
Young men and women sang from distant hills:
35 'Our land shall stretch beyond the horizon.
Of what use is fear?
Great is the feast in Zululand — let all people come.
Listen to the women singing across the river.

They are the women of Baqulusi regions.
They sing of the festival.
They give warning to Macingwane of Luboko.
They threaten Mvelase of the Thembus.'
5   Such were the songs that cemented the bonds of clans and
          nations.
Those who narrate tales of ancient times tell us
Despite all this Nandi still yearned for her own grandchild.
When she heard how Mbuzikazi of the Cele clan
10 Might yet bear the king a child
She made elaborate plans to save it.
She said: 'I shall steal this child and make it my own.
I shall bring it up secretly under my care,
Nourishing it as I did my own children.'
15 Nandi sent a message to the king:
'I suffer constantly from ill health.
Of all the royal women
I trust the gentle and kindly daughter of the Cele clan;
I ask that in this condition she alone attends me.'
20 By such a ruse she hoped to hide this pregnancy.
Months passed; people began whispering;
Words of gossip spread like a new season's crop.
It was Mbopha's wife who exposed the secrets.
She said to her husband, the chief of the royal household:
25 'It seems many surprises shall come from Nandi's household.
I am a woman. I know the craftiness of other women.
I know a woman when her body has become beautiful.
Such is the state of the favourite woman of the king.
The king himself seems ignorant of this truth.
30 He does not know his household grows in secret.'
She planted these words in the sharp ears of Mbopha,
Knowing he craved to be the king's most favoured councillor.
He was weak and flatterable.
No sooner had this been whispered to his ear
35 Than he hurried to report to the king:
'My lord, I bring news that is disturbing to me.
To speak of it I must expose the secrets of your right hand,
But I speak only to fulfil the duties of my office.
I love my king sincerely:
40 I know our whole future depends on him.

It is our task to do as ordered.
By your laws many nations have been brought together —
To follow them is to fulfil the vision of our greatness;
To overlook them is to destroy our very nation.
5   For this reason I am bound to tell all secrets
Though our Forefathers have said:
"Affairs of families hurt only the outsider." '
Thus did Mbopha throw words to soften the king.
Shaka's eyes moved, keen to know Mbopha's story
10 Even before Mbopha could tell it.
For rulers often prefer to be ahead of their underlings.
Through their eyes they learn the secrets of their subjects.
Shaka spoke slowly and carefully:
'Mbopha, son of Sithayi, I have put you above everyone,
15 Trusting you and believing in you.
I did not ask you to distinguish for me what deserves my
        judgement.
These rumours have already reached my ears
But I waited for you to tell me the whole truth.
20 Thus, I order you no longer to swallow words;
Indeed, much more important affairs demand my attention.'
Mbopha was restless; he still spoke in fragmented thoughts:
'My lord, I am frightened to tell the truth,
Yet I have the command of my king.
25 By your command I speak of the Female Elephant, Mother
        Nandi.
She and the beloved daughter of the Cele clan
Hide from you a secret child born to your house.'
It was as if something had stabbed the king.
30 He stood up suddenly and said:
'Mbopha, son of Sithayi, do you know what you are saying?
Have you got the full truth of this tale?'
Mbopha shivered, alarmed at this reaction.
He was like someone who had uttered words of war.
35 Mbopha's sweat ran over his face;
He moved his cold buttocks from side to side.
The great son of Senzangakhona filled the house with anger.
He spoke to Mbopha solemnly and said:
'Son of Sithayi, I want you to leave me alone.
40 I want to put into place my thoughts.

Such news is too heavy for my shoulders.
Go, before my anger overwhelms me,
Choosing you to thrust its whirlwind blade,
Thus making me a target of blame among the Zulu people.'
5 As he spoke, his mind seethed like a volcano.
He groaned like a young tiger at its first kill.
He sat alone on one side of the house, brooding,
His thoughts racing like a pain.
For the first time in the whole span of his life
10 His desires had been flagrantly violated by his parent.
His house seemed enveloped in darkness.
He laughed at the many thoughts that came to his mind.
All day long Shaka kept alone.
Even Mgobhozi never got near to assuage his mind.
15 It was as though he was dressing for some festival.
As he stepped on to the open ground,
'Go to my mother. Tell her before the sun sets tomorrow
I shall have arrived at the grounds of her royal residence.'

No sooner had the early morning spread its seeds of light
20 Than Shaka began bedecking his elaborate adornments.
It was as though he was dressing for some festival.
As he stepped on to the open ground,
His very footfalls seemed to echo his inner thoughts.
He was slow of movement and slow of speech.
25 With a small army of bodyguards he travelled through
        mountains and valleys.
In the whole journey he seldom spoke.
At Nandi's royal city he rested, eager to put together his words.
After his respite he headed for Nandi's special residence.
30 There she waited for him;
She sat leisurely on a multi-coloured mat.
With a stammer he began to speak to her,
His anger choking him:
'Mother, many times I have endured great pains
35 But never have I ever faced so great a challenge.
The one closest to me has betrayed me!
Mbopha tells me you harbour what shall be the death of our
        house.

A child, supposedly mine, has been kept away from me;
Yet I am still convinced never could my parent act against me.
What example would I be setting for the army?
What wise general would ask of his men what he himself would
5   not do?
Yet something deeper eats into my mind:
Of all living beings you are the only one I truly trust,
Nor have I criticized or condemned your own deeds
But of late you have opened the doors to my enemies.
10 Perhaps in my deeds I was blinded by my heart
When I vowed never to allow enemies to cross our path.
I ask you to give me some richer explanation!
How have I erred? How have I wronged you?'
The old, experienced Nandi calmly answered:
15 'Shaka, my son, no one is gifted in all things.
You have many types of knowledge and experiences
But one aspect still remains obscure to you:
The heart that yearns to fulfil its dreams and fantasies.
It is not out of evil that people act against others,
20 But love sometimes obscures itself in acts of cruelty.
The older I get the greater are my concerns.
Thus by my own love I am weakened.
I had hoped when these two voices sing to each other
The dynasty of your house shall nourish forever our land.
25 I live alone, despite all the abundance;
I have never had peace since I first spoke to you.
But all that I utter now is not enough.
Only one thing troubles me above all else:
I fear Mbopha; I fear him as I fear a snake.
30 Often I feel he shall bring great tears to our house.
Even now our talks no longer have meaning
Since, by his orders, he has killed the very child I loved.
Such a man is dangerous!
He kills today; he shall always thirst for more blood.'
35 Shaka was quiet, his mind deeply absorbed in thought.
He was uncertain whether to condemn Mbopha utterly
Or to uphold his act as one of devotion to his master.
Besides, by this deed he had weakened his own case;
Yet a dutiful councillor must elevate the nation's laws.
40 Having sorted out his thoughts he said:

'I understand the deep truths in your words.
I endorse them, too, in accordance with your thinking.
But there are still other demands of power
Whose laws and rules remain obscure to you.
5   The command of our Ancestors demands acts greater than
       ourselves.
I am a king, who must rule over many nations of Zululand.
It is by these laws I myself must abide.
They must extend beyond the circumstance of self.
10 I have ordered the army not to marry except by special
       command.
I, too, must follow these laws, whatever the consequences.
I must elevate the glory that attends to our nation and army.
If I fail and choose only what satisfies my own appetite,
15 Then there shall be greater disasters than ever before.
It would be better if the nation of Zululand
Had not been roused in its nest of peace.
People follow the example of their heroes;
They imitate the image that best fulfils their fantasies.
20 Should I fail, the nation itself shall disintegrate.
I explain all this only because it is you.
To follow the heart is noble,
Yet it does not rule the thoughts and minds of men.
Often it doubts, it hesitates and abounds in self-recrimination.
25 Yet a leader must act decisively where others flee in terror.
He must walk unafraid and unintimidated by all shadows.
These things must inspire others to greater triumphs.
Our spirits no longer follow the same path.
Yours suffers the emptiness of plenty
30 But mine is the spirit of a restless traveller.
It must forever be thrilled by the strangeness of things.
Your own visions bear their own truth —
Perhaps this way they nourish their own worlds.
It is possible that your fears about Mbopha are true,
35 But I have no way to remove him as the nation's honoured
       councillor.
His task is to see what I cannot see,
To be the nation's agent and to protect its king.
What would the nation say
40 If, because of my own whim, I removed him from power?

Will people not complain: "This is no ruler of people.
He succumbs to his parent and follows personal fears."
I cannot follow the heat of my anger
And say, because of his deed Mbopha must die.
5 Besides, whoever shall assume his power
Shall abide by the same rules and the same authority.
It is wiser, then, to retain the man whose mind I know
Than to seek those whose hearts take time to fathom.
I ask you, then, to see things with my eyes
10 In the same way I have always championed your truth,
Even though at times it cut against my plans and feelings.'
As he spoke Nandi stared at him kindly and said:
'Mlilwana, you shall escape any trap laid for you.
For in truth you sense the desires and needs of people.
15 You sift and weigh all acts of men.
I love you, my son, despite all the pains I suffer for it.
But know I have the heart of a woman.
All this enthusiasm about wars does not excite me.
Even though I listen and praise these battles and heroes
20 It is only to fulfil what is highest in your mind.
I thank you for your insight into my desire for a child.
This understanding alone nourishes me with deep fulfilment.
It is this I treasure above all else;
It shall yet console me in my loneliest moments.'
25 Shaka hugged his parent to remove the sadness in her eyes.
Even Nandi wept tears of joy.
While Shaka displayed all this affection
His mind had not forgotten Mbopha's unsolicited act.
He remembered now many strange incidents:
30 How Mbopha would be heard laughing at Dingane's residence,
Then next he would be heard at the home of Prince Mhlangana.
Many reported their suspicions to the king
But Shaka knew: men in positions of authority
Often attract to them many secret enemies.
35 Through their arrogance they became detestable to all.
Such had become of Mbopha, the son of Sithayi.
He swelled with conceit, avoiding those whom he once
    honoured.
He opened and closed the royal gates at will,
40 Deciding who should see the king and when.

Abusing his power, he spread the hostile words of the princes,
Creating a spate of poisonous talk.
Shaka, learning of these stories, approached Mkhabayi.
Speaking solemnly he said:
5 'Great and wise one, you were here before us.
I ask you to share with me your great wisdom.
My brothers are always criticizing my actions
Despite all I have done for them.
As the head of our house I have given them all they need.
10 Their complaints are never spoken directly to me
But are secretly conveyed to those who are not members of our
        family;
Yet I have vowed to them our family together must rule,
Giving to each other the harshest and the best advice.
15 Even now I hesitate to rush into things,
Yet all their violent words begin to challenge my authority
And make us appear a family in dissension.'
The wily daughter of Jama, assuming her composure, said:
'Shaka, my son, listen to me.
20 There is no ruler in this world without fault.
Your brothers criticize only out of love,
Proud of the family you share together.
In truth, this is how they elicit the truth from your enemies.
Above all, they never can be wiser than you.
25 Even as they criticize your actions
They know it is only to enhance their own reputations.
You should only laugh at whatever talk is reported to you.
Words often assume a fierceness when reported by others.'
Through such words did Mkhabayi restore the peace in the
30   family.
She was not like Nandi of the Mhlongos.
She took pleasure in accompanying her regiments with a song;
She declaimed the great epics of her Forefathers and heroes.
Her warm and friendly words consoled Shaka's heart.
35 He said to Mgobhozi: 'It is true, in all large families
The young frequently challenge their elders,
Yet the strong bonds of family survive.'
As he spoke many pleasant thoughts passed through his mind.

Book Nine: The political visionary at work

After conquering his most persistent and formidable challenger, King Zwide, Shaka now concentrates on the consolidation of the internal structure of Zululand. The advent of Prince Zihlandlo amply demonstrates his political theories which go beyond military preoccupations. The internal structure must be based not only on a common citizenship, but also on firm and decisive social ideology. The state must strive for universal participation and involvement and must make its resources available to all its citizens. Justice assumes a new dimension; no longer is it personal, but national. There are still powerful challenges like the Chunus and Thembus, who must be eliminated if central authority is to be preserved. A historically significant break occurs when Mzilikazi departs.

Once there was a king whose name was Macingwane, son of
    Jama.
He was a brave ruler and ruled over the fierce Chunu nation.
On hearing of the defeat of Zwide, he vowed:
5   'However many kings may flee from the Zulu upstart
There is one ruler who shall never surrender.
It is I, who am born of the ancient rulers,
I, the son of Jama, of Luboko, of Nyanda.'
Kings and princes were seeking amalgamation into the Zulu
10   nation.
Even quarrels of distant princes were settled in Zulu courts —
Such was the case with Prince Sihayo of the Nyuswa clan.
He came to protest against his brother:
'Prince Mgabi has usurped the authority due to me,
15   Yet it is I who am born of the senior house.'
For several days this dispute was debated in Shaka's court
Until Sihayo was judged the rightful heir.
Thus the royal poet says of Shaka:
'You hurried through the regions of Nomangci in the high
20   plains.
Rushing to settle the family quarrels among the Nyuswa princes.
Nothing much was at stake among the Nyuswas

But only a few castor oil plants.
They said: "How can these insects wait for the doves?"
He came and destroyed them both.'
Prince Sihayo, the poet tells us, failed to win Shaka's affection.
5   Of him Shaka commented: 'He possesses only a quick tongue.
He never speaks anything of substance;
Before the Assembly he puts many conflicting stories.'

Everywhere were feats and festivals in Zululand.
Listen to the words of the great poet who was there,
10 Who saw with his own eyes the celebration of the new era:
'You rushed to conquer in distant places.
You attacked King Phungashe of the Buthelezi nation;
You attacked Sondaba of Mthandeni royal city as he sat in
      council;
15 You attacked Mangcengceza of the Mbatha clan;
You attacked Dladlama of the Majola clan;
You conquered Nxaba the son of Mbhekane.
Wild one, who, as he sits brooding, swells like a mountain —
He has his weapons ready on his knees.'
20 Generations to come shall listen to the ancient poet,
Envying those who saw the procession of heroes,
Who followed the Song of the Festival,
Who set out adorned with black and white and red ceremonial
      shields.
25 It was these crowds that saw Prince Zihlandlo arrive;
With his many followers he entered the royal city.
He proceeded to ask the Great Ruler of Bulawayo for a place to
      live.
Those who saw him tell us he was admired by men and women
30   alike.
His skin was smooth like a river-boulder;
Its hue was yellow like a ripe fruit of mazwenda plant.
His speech was careful and slow.
He was like those born of great heroes.
35 Shaka himself watched this man with a surprised admiration,
Observing his alertness, intelligence and calm.
He looked him up and down
As rulers do, to imprison the spirit of a subject.
He said ultimately: 'Tell me, son of the Mkhize clan,

What is it that brings you to our lands?
Are you not a member of King Zikodze's clan?
In truth would you not be closer in blood to King Zwide?
I do not mean to urge you to follow this man to the north,
5 But are there no others closer to your family?'
Shaka spoke this way only jokingly since he had liked him.
Prince Zihlandlo said: 'King of kings, ruler of many lands,
You whose shadow overwhelms those of the mountains!
The elephants huddle together as the storms threaten.
10 They retire to their shelter of the mountains,
It is you who protects the heads of fugitives.
Though Zwide has fled, he shall only win temporary peace;
Nothing shall save him from the wrath to come.
Thunder never stops amassing its power;
15 Sometimes even in winter it strikes, burning up the dry plants.
I have come to you to drink from your wisdom.
I am by breeding and training a warrior,
Yet I hate to fight continuous and fruitless wars.
I have heard with envy the stories of the armies you command;
20 How by their skill they have crushed even superior enemies.
Throughout Nguniland and beyond your voice is heard.
You speak of the Palm Race that must be one.
I have come to ask to serve towards this goal:
I desire Bulawayo city to be the capital of all nations.
25 To this end I am prepared to die.
All nations must find a home in our land.'
For the first time Shaka heard someone
Who spoke and saw clearly as his own vision.
Indeed, there were many heroes in Zululand,
30 Some reputed and honoured for their wisdom,
But none had grasped Shaka's vision as clearly as the Mkhize
      nobleman.
He was admired for his generosity and warmth of heart;
He led all the children of Mavovo in harmony
35 And fed them all alike like a great parent.
Knowing all these reports, Shaka responded warmly to him,
Causing everyone to stare in consternation.
He said: 'Son of Gubhela, I thank you for these great words.
They fill me with deep satisfaction by their wisdom and
40   meaning.

Of the many great people I have met
I yet have to encounter one whose vision is as close to mine.
Even Mgobhozi, my fighting comrade,
Fails to equal a vision as far reaching as yours.

5   Your thoughts thrust beyond the terror of the battlefield.
One day nations shall no longer fight each other
But share a common brotherhood.
I present you to the Assembly;
At all times you shall be my brother.'

10   Those who desired to be the king's favourites
Only grinned at hearing these words.
They were puzzled by the suddeness of these bonds:
'Friendship of rulers follow the winds,' they said.
Consoling themselves, they sneered:

15   'One day such loves rise into the sky,
Then suddenly they tumble down into dust.'

Tears of joy were seen in the noble descendant of Mavovo.
He said: 'My lord, it would have been enough
To be one of your humble followers

20   But to be named your brother is my greatest honour.
I have never known a coward in all my family;
You too, my lord, shall find this trust not misplaced.
We shall be loyal even when none shall be.'
As Zihlandlo stood there, uttering these words,

25   Many held him in great reverence,
For many princes had yearned to be as loved by the king as he.
Many rulers were to flock to his residence for protection.
The poet has said of him:
'Wild fire of Ndaba! You whose back is covered with scars.

30   Beast of Somazwi that has five feet!
Beloved one, who is our hero of Sijibeni.
Fierce-looking one, who is like the tough mtungwa plant!
Those who don't know you would flee from you
But we who know you would look in amazement,

35   We of Sijiba would laugh until we fall flat on the ground,
And wonder what made them decamp so speedily.
We shall say: "What danger did they see in the father of
          Nongamulana?" '
Once Shaka said of Zihlandlo: 'No one is like him

No one is as generous as my brother, Zihlandlo.
Even when he is left with one cow he shall give it away,
Yet the cattle-folds of other men burst with wealth.
I ask myself: how do they prosper in so vast a nation?
5 How do they stare in the face those who live in scarcity?'
As he spoke many shivered in terror,
Knowing how his mood changed like the wind;
Of it people were never certain.
Seeing this, he said: 'Tell me, chidren of Zulu,
10 Is there a man or woman in all Zululand
Who can ever give without hesitation, even a pinch of snuff?'
Those at the Assembly turned to look at each other
As though each could give an answer.
Finally all agreed no such man or woman existed.
15 They said, indeed it was the custom to refuse before giving.
Shaka turned his face puzzled and contorted
And said: 'Citizens of Zululand, these words anger me.
I want you, Siwisa, to send word throughout the land
Order my messengers to ask from each person a pinch of snuff.
20 Whoever shall give without hesitating must be brought to me.
The habit of refusing what is possessed is certainly evil;
It only covers the stinginess of the giver.
By these tricks it discourages people from asking.'
Throughout the day the messengers scouted the land.
25 Everywhere they begged for a pinch of snuff
But each one was initially refused.
It was not until late in the evening
When one man took out his snuff box and gave generously.
The king's messengers were astounded by this strange act.
30 They asked the astonished man: 'Tell us, you of distant lands,
Why do you give without the customary act of refusing?'
He replied, feeling strange and discomfited by these questions:
'Since my childhood this has been my habit.
I never refuse things that I possess,
35 Nor do I see any cause to lie when I have the snuff to give.
This very custom seems only a camouflage for stinginess.'
The king's messengers took a few helpings of snuff.
It coursed through their veins, taking away their tiredness.
Finally, revealing their identity, they said:
40 'We are the messengers of the great king.'

The stranger shivered, not knowing
What crime he might have committed against custom.
In vain he asked them the cause for this summoning.
At last he stood before the king, his knees trembling,
5   His eyes red with anxiety.
Shaka, realizing how this event had unsettled him,
Spoke to him kindly: 'Why do you give without refusing,
When by ancient custom the whole nation hesitates with its
        gifts?'
10 In a state of terror the man answered haltingly.
His words stuck to his tongue:
'O, my lord, son of Ndaba,
I have a troublesome hand whose impulse is always to give.
It is this sickness that haunts me,
15 Compelling me not to hoard whatever I possess
But to share it willingly with all peoples.
I am now bereft of all my wealth
For whoever comes to my house has the right to all I possess.
It is this that has made me violate our ancient customs.'
20 The king, addressing the Assembly and lowering his voice said:
'I have now met someone I have always desired to know.
You are not like others, who grab and seize,
Eager to possess the whole world,
You are like the heroes who have fought our many wars.
25 I give you a hundred herd of cattle from among the Mncinci.'
He spoke of his milky-white herd, known throughout Zululand.
By this act the whole nation sang the praises of this man.
Many now desired the company of strangers,
Hoping amongst them may lurk the secret messengers of the
30   king.
Even the poor received large gifts of beasts and grain.

Our Forefathers sat telling tales of their past.
They debated and argued over many mysteries of life.
The king sat with the councillors, making jokes and laughing
35   happily.
From afar could be heard the boom of their laughter.
Thus was peace manifest in the land of our Forefathers.
From many regions people came to sit and talk at the Assembly.

One such man, a poor man, once came to the Assembly.
In vain the councillors remonstrated with him and said:
'Your problem could be solved by many regional governors.'
But he insisted: 'I want to speak personally to my king:
5   I want him to know the truth of my life.'
Shaka heard this fierce debate and said:
'Let the man speak. Is he not, too, of the Zulu nation?
A great nation is governed by all its peoples.
Is it not our boast that minds can solve all problems?
10   What kind of wisdom avoids the little issues of the land?
By what power does it claim to solve the affairs of the world?'
Humiliated, they allowed this stranger before the king.
In truth those who worship at the feet of the great
Often abuse their authority with the violence of their words,
15   Detesting the ease with which others have access to their
        masters,
Recalling too their own fierce struggles to power.
The stranger approached slowly, as if fearing some treachery.
He saluted, crouching low before the king:
20   'My lord, I thank the sun that shines in all regions.
It has made the tender plants grow beside the tall trees.
I am here to ask my lord to mourn with me the destruction of
        my life.
My story begins in the days of my youth.
25   Then I said to my elder brother, presenting a beautiful woman:
"Son of my father, you are now the head of our house.
Since our father's death at the battle of Qokli
Our interests and welfare are only in your hands.
I am still young; I shall go and fight all the king's wars.
30   This girl whose love I shall cherish in every field
Stands at the gates of our house to fulfil our father's wish.
Look after her for me; protect her from all dangers;
Treat her as if she were already in our house."
I said this, hoping he would assuage her aching heart,
35   For, in truth, women severed from their men suffer a deep
        loneliness.
I fought the wars of the king, trusting in my brother,
Believing he would never betray the one to bring honour to our
        family.
40   Indeed, I yearned within myself for the day

When my king should say: "You have fought many great
    battles.
It is time you took a wife to marry."
Such a day, indeed, did come.
5   I rejoiced, proud to be called upon to do like my brother:
To raise a family and fulfil the wishes of our Forefathers.
No sooner had I married this wife
Than I saw her swelling faster than is normal for humans.
Then I realized our house had been blasphemed:
10 It was my brother who had gone ahead of me.
Nor was that the end of this hideous story.
One day this same woman decided to leave.
She headed straight for my brother's house.
He had undermined all my efforts and devotion to my country,
15 Telling her I was a failure.
All the wealth of our house was only through his efforts.
Thus disgusted, the woman left me
I inherited all the extinguished fires of the house.
These, my lord, were all my tribulations.
20 It is why I ask for a judgement
Which shall restore my dignity in the house of my father.
You know the rights and wrongs of such injuries.
It is why I travelled these many days
To put the case myself before my king.
25 Whatever is your judgement, it shall heal my wounds.
You alone have the interests of all the people at heart.'
When he finished he breathed deeply, awaiting a word from the
    king.
Shaka looked sternly at the Assembly:
30 'Nation of Zulu, this case is ripe for your judgement.'
On this occasion, in attendance were many important men of
    the land —
Governors, generals and heroes of many battles.
But they did not speak.
35 A frail old man, with a trembling voice, finally stood up to
    speak.
His hair ash-white, like a burnt-up forest,
He spoke hesitatingly, his words disjointed.
He said: 'I am old; I lived in the old days of King Jama.
40 Nothing that happens should any longer surprise me

But what I have heard today truly astonishes me.
It is clear nothing is below the dignity of the Assembly.
The man who stands before us attests to this truth.
Little men still suffer the injustice of the men of power,
5 Though we have enacted the strictest laws against it.
Let it never happen that as we suffer and die in the battlefield
Some men stay behind to violate our families.
This shall only lead to decay in our nation.
I myself feel this brother deserves the most exemplary
10   punishment,
Such a punishment as would be a lesson to others.'
All members of the Assembly were silent, listening only to his
       voice.
Only Shaka questioned him further:
15 'I do understand the direction of your judgement,
But what shall be the fate of this woman?
Has she not been the cause of this disintegration?'
It was the same old man who replied:
'I still want to complete my thoughts.
20 I want to fulfil the requests asked of us by Jama.
The man from the distant regions has spoken the truth, my lord.
No one can speak such words,
Knowing to lie before the nation means death.
Only the woman's crime concerns us now.
25 A woman in Zululand is the mother of our nation;
By her magic hand she plants new seeds.
Her corruption corrupts the whole nation;
In her is both the power of life and destruction.
Kings of Zwide's reputation were destroyed by their mothers.
30 King Ndzungunya of the Ngwanes, it was said, was often
Restrained by a wise and far-seeing woman.
In our own nation of Zululand the dignity and greatness of
       women
Speaks loudly through the Queen Mother and the Princess
35   Mkhabayi.
Thus this woman deserves even greater punishment than this
       man.'
The words of the old man were never challenged.
The king at once sent his messengers to bring all parties to
40   court.

After a long debate the Assembly gave its judgement.
Shaka turned to the complainant and said:
'Are you satisfied that your complaints have been justly settled?
Would your tears be recompensed through their deaths?'
5 He saluted the king, consenting to these words,
Uncertain lest his harsh judgement be turned against him.
Even the Assembly looked at him in disgust,
For whoever wishes death on a relative is hated by all.
Shaka said, continuing: 'It is up to you, members of the
10   Assembly.
It is you who must give the final word.'
The old man spoke again and said:
'My lord, once again, I ask for your indulgence.
Give us your own word and guidance.
15 A case of such importance demands your judgement.'
The condemned man intervened to plead his case and said:
'I have destroyed the name of my father's house.
I violated the sacred laws of our nation.
Through the living and the dead I ask for your forgiveness.
20 Sometimes a power beyond our control
Draws us mercilessly onto the treacherous cliff.
At the edge, we lose the paths-of-return-and-reason.
Thus too was my fate.
In vain I attempted to restrain myself.
25 My crime is clear, I admit to it.
Perhaps with my death others shall learn their lesson.
Only one request I make from the king:
Let other nations who hear of our judgements
Say:"Punishments of death are meted out only to men."
30 This is all I request from the great Assembly.'
As he finished one man followed up his words:
'Admission of a crime disqualifies one to judge the fate of others.
Had you maintained the nation's pride as you now proclaim
You would have spared us the consequences of these debates.'
35 To these words many in the Assembly agreed.
Summarizing the case, the king said:
'From your judgement a sentence of death has been passed.
I want only to endorse your words.
It is clear this woman, too, must die.
40 She must suffer for her own part in this grisly crime.

She, as a part of the nation's regiments,
Know how serious it is to betray those in battle;
She has violated the sacred code protecting families.
Whoever succumbs to the body's simple invitations
5   Violates the human laws and becomes no more than a beast.
It is such a person who must be termed a killer
For he kills the very essence of what makes a nation great.
Man and woman share the same guilt.
I want this creature of which she is pregnant to be seen.
10 I want the cause of this treachery to be known
When she has died.
Let the monster that has destroyed the families be exposed.
Perhaps what is born of two criminals only resembles their crime.
It is born against the dreams of the dead and the living.'
15 After the king had spoken there was a deathly silence.
Even the prosecutor was alarmed at these words.
He said attempting to water down the king's comments:
'My lord, we have heard your words.
By their endorsement they finalize our judgement.
20 Yet we also are men and must always express our truth.
Thus your reign, through us, shall live eternally.
No king is king except through the people.
It is true, indeed, these two deserve their punishment;
Yet the nation may be repulsed at such an outrageous act.
25 To cut up the womb of a woman is hideous,
For such a spectacle has no cleansing herbs.'
Shaka quickly reacted to these words:
'It is through such fears people fail to execute justice.
Through cowardice they tremble at the spectacle of things
30   unknown.
Has anyone ever died from seeing the secrets of a woman's
       womb?
Yet you foresee disasters that no story can confirm.
All the men from this Assembly
35 Must see for themselves how a child stays in the womb.
No one is allowed thereafter to take any cleansing herbs!
Let us see, then, the truth of these terrifying plagues.'
After these words no one dared oppose the king.
Many looked in horror at the spectacle before them
40 But none dared show their feelings of terror.

They recited to themselves: 'A dead body cannot kill.'
Only Shaka followed with his eyes every detail.
Finally he said: 'At last I have seen
How an infant lies in its mother's womb.'
5 He turned away and fell into deep thought.
He wandered off, as if obsessed by some mysterious memory.

The fame of King Macingwane spread in all directions
As he challenged Shaka's much dreaded armies.
Yet he constantly retreated to the southern regions,
10 Fearing lest the Zulus should make a sudden attack.
Shaka said these provocations should be paid in full.
The story is told by Bhakuza, the son of Mafohloza, of the
 Mpanza clan.
He tells us he saw with his own eyes the preparations for war:
15 'The cause of war began with the words of King Ngoza of the
 Thembus,
Who spoke scathingly of Shaka at his Assembly.
He sent to him a gift of broken reeds,
Saying: "These cannot even be shaken by your footfalls."
20 Shaka enraged, sent Sigwegwe, saying:
"Go to him and say when there is a new moon
He must look up at the sky above his royal city.
Whatever he shall behold shall be Shaka's glimmering spears."
After this the Thembus and the Chunus combined together.
25 They set out to attack from two angles.
The Chunus were to block the passages of the Mzinyathi river,
To drive back the Zulu army from this vantage point.
The Thembus were to fight from the mountains of Hlakazi.
The Zulus divided their army into two sections,
30 One led by the great supreme commander, General Mdlaka,
Another led by the brave General Ndlela and General Nzobo.
This latter wing was to face the Thembus of Ngoza.
It was here that the large number of Thembu war heroes
 assembled.
35 The Thembus stood on the plains like a forest,
For in truth the Thembus are no cowards.
They never easily retreat from battle.
It was by these tactics they had defeated the Khuzes and the
 Mbathas,

And beaten the stubborn troops of the Sitholes and the Ntulis.
Had it not been for the Zulu army
They would have destroyed many of the southern nations;
But Shaka's tactics closed in on them.
5   The Zulus overwhelmed them, burning down their houses
And seizing their numerous cattle and sheep.
As this war raged Shaka sat watching from a vantage point,
Awaiting the news of the battle of eQhudeni.
It was at that time Jobe of the Sithole clan approached him
10 And, mistaking him for a friend, said:
'The great Chunu and the Thembu armies
Shall teach the Zulu upstart the lesson of his life.
Up to now he has triumphed only against old men like Zwide.'
Shaka looked down as this man babbled.
15 He even consented to his words and said:
'I wish them all the blessings of the Ancestors.'
At that very moment a messenger came to him with this news:
'My lord, we have lost the battle!'
Shaka fumed and raved, asking more questions than could be
20   answered.
In great speed he hurried to the battlefield, leaving the Sithole
        man.
When the Zulus heard the poet declaiming Shaka's heroic epic
They began to sing their famed battle hymn.
25 Veering back via the mountain of Thulaneni,
They attempted to surround the Chunu army from behind.
But the Chunus had seized this moment to flee,
Knowing the defeat of the Thembus would mean their sure
        destruction.
30 They followed now the route southwards to the Mzimkhulu
        river.
Everywhere along their path
They left large groups of ageing settlers.
The Chunus were bitter against the Thembus,
35 Blaming them for putting up a weak resistance.
To this day these grudges persist.
Shaka fumed at this uncertain victory.
He ordered the army to follow the Chunus,
Harassing them and speeding up their retreat.
40 The Chunus wrought destruction on all those in their path,

Raising the spectre of former chaos in Nguniland.
Shaka's army pursued them relentlessly to the southern regions.
On their way the Zulus passed through the lands of the
    Phephethas
5 Who lived on the impregnable fortress of Phisweni.
From all sides the mountain gaped and fell in sheer faces.
Only the top was a vast flat ground.
This strange mountain was known as the Fortress of the
    Phephethas.
10 It was impregnable to all passing armies.
From safe points they mocked and hurled boulders on all
    armies.
Boasting, their prince, Mshika of Khondlwane,
Would parade his wealth of beautiful women and fat cows.
15 The hungry Chunus had attempted to climb the mountain in
    vain.
Even the Zulus looked in amazement at these restless creatures.
The Phephethas pulled out their tongues and rolled down big
    boulders,
20 Sometimes killing a group of unsuspecting boy carriers.
Still the war generals demanded that the army proceeds;
They spoke strongly to Shaka:
'How can the great Zulu army spend time with these wild men?
Besides, only cowardice has driven them to their shelter.'
25 But Shaka, in friendly collusion with Mzilikazi, resisted.
He proposed elaborate routes of attack,
Still disturbed by the memories of Qokli battle.
He said: 'We now can solve the riddle
Of how Zwide could have dislodged us from the hill.
30 Indeed, their tactic recalls to mind our own.'
The great generals were taken aback at this comparison,
Thinking their strategies superior to those of fugitives.
Shaka began to walk, following the whole base of the mountain.
Sometimes he threw large stones downwards and upwards,
35 Ordering cattle to be forced up the mountainside.

For five days he studied the strategy, as the army camped.
The generals were puzzled by this obsession;
They knew some unexpected plan would emerge.
Mzilikazi and other young commanders constantly hailed him.

Suddenly Shaka's ideas exploded in one great shout.
He was ecstatic, like a child.
He said to Mgobhozi: 'We have got them! I swear by
    Nomchoba.'
5   He ordered that ropes be plaited,
At the end of which would be tied a rough stone.
These they would hook to the branches and roots of trees
And, through them, hitch themselves
While covering their bodies with an umbrella of fighting shields.
10 This way they would climb the hazardous mountain.
The great ancient poet, reporting on this feat, says:
'You plaited a long rope and climbed into heaven.'
The Phephethas were filled with awe
As they watched in amazement the Zulus defying all obstacles.
15 One section followed the route
Where the sheer face of the mountain would challenge the
    nimblest of animals.
When the Phephethas discovered this
They rained on them a barrage of huge boulders and missiles.
20 Stone after stone echoed on the upraised shields.
The Zulus patiently inched their way up the hazardous
    mountain.
Shaka watched admiringly as his centipede army scaled the
    cliffs,
25 Angry and aching with the Phephethas' missiles.
The Zulus rushed on them, pursuing them like butterflies.
From a distance could be heard the wails of fleeing men.
Over the whole plain of the mountain top they ran,
Sometimes hurling themselves down the spine-chilling cliffs,
30 Sometimes turning back to seek their numerous hiding places.
Even the birds of the forest streamed in terror,
Fleeing from both men and missiles.
The vultures patiently circled the forests.
Mzilikazi distinguished himself in this battle;
35 He ran fighting like one possessed.
As he descended from the mountain he called out:
'I return to you, great black centipede!
You, the knot which they untied while singing a song!'
After this short diversion the army proceeded on its journey.
40 Many argued and talked of the episodes of this battle,

Some commenting directly on Mzilikazi's fighting skill.
Only Mgobhozi regretted that he had been too lazy to join the
      battle.

The hills echoed with the laughter of the Zulu army.
5   At the southernmost point the army rested.
Shaka addressed them: 'My brothers, our journey is now
      pointless.
Everywhere we go we find only those who acknowledge our
      authority.
10 Zulu power no longer issues from conquest
But from a bond of an all-embracing nationhood.
We must turn back to our homes.
Perhaps in the north Soshangane and his lot need a lesson.'

At Bulawayo they sang and danced for the returning army.
15 Shaka was still eager to consolidate the nation's boundaries.
He said to his war councillors: 'Our easy life
Shall soon undermine our fighting spirit.
I want you, Mzilikazi, to head to the north
And there establish peace among the quarrelling nations,
20 And subdue the troublesome people of Ranisi
Who have caused endless wars among friendly nations.
You shall seize from them all the loot of cattle
And return it to its original owners.'
The king spoke to Mzilikazi with great warmth and friendliness.
25 He said: 'I give you my own battle axe, Mzilikazi,
So that when you pass the ruins of your native country
You may raise it and pray for the guidance of your Ancestors.
I give you this so that wherever you are
You may know I shall always honour those who are our brave
30   heroes.'
Mzilikazi of Mashobana was moved by this act.
He said, his eyes wet with tears:
'My lord, I do not know what great things I have done,
What great heroism I have displayed.
35 That I should deserve a gift most coveted by all heroes of
      Zululand?
Long ago you sheltered me when I was orphaned and now you
      honour me.

The journey I undertake now
Seems dictated by the Great Will of the Ancestors.
My heart still burns with hatred at the heinous crime of Zwide.
If my lord grants, I shall go further in search of him,
5 Then I shall walk tall, having revenged my father and my
      family.
Shaka put his hand on Mzilikazi's shoulder
And said: 'Wherever you are, there the Zulu nation shall be.
Go as the sun falls away into the night.
10 When dawn breaks from the mountains tomorrow
Let it behold the fields you have planted for our nation.'
It was as if Shaka knew this was their last meeting.
Perchance he had sensed in him the restlessness of youth.
They both looked at each other as if to share a long-kept secret,
15 Like an elder humouring a youth.

Mzilikazi followed the route to the north,
And there set to flight the troublesome Rakosi.
In vain Mzilikazi attempted to capture the bandit princes.
Their villages and hideouts were left standing as wide-open
20   ruins,
The skies were lit by their fires.
Mzilikazi collected the abandonded cattle,
Driving them in their thousands to the southern regions.
While he campaigned a great meeting assembled at Bulawayo.
25 The king's agents had returned,
Reporting how Soshangane in the north had carved a giant
      kingdom.
On deserting Zwide he took the eastern routes of legend,
For, indeed, ancient tales are often told about this region.
30 Zwangendaba, too, had followed the same route, veering further
      north.
There he bore children and lived as a powerful potentate.
To the north Shaka retained close bonds only with the Ngwane
      state.
35 To maintain these friendships
The Zulus and the Ngwanes kept a constant flow of emissaries,
For as the Ngwane rulers pulled together disparate nations,
This same belief dominated the Zulu court.
Common policies led to marital bonds.

Through feasts and festivals the two nations cemented their
    friendships.
On one such festival King Sobhuza visited Shaka's royal city
And there he was feasted and pampered by him.
5 King Sobhuza himself frequently spoke of these visits,
Pronouncing his admiration for Shaka's beliefs.
He would tell his army: 'The Palm Race belongs to one nation.
The Zulu lion and I are brothers.'
He had once set out to the north, hunting for Zwangendaba,
10 Believing through his defeat peace would be restored in the
    region.
But Zwangendaba fled further north,
For to such men there is no boundary.
Shaka often listened to reports about these turbulent regions.
15 He wished for a test of strength against these bandit armies.
Through the iziMpangele regiment led by Mzilikazi,
He hoped these probes could be made,
Yet he hesitated awaiting the full truth of their alliance,
For a good commander never wastes his men on tests of
20   strength.
At this same period a messenger came panting to the court:
'Great ruler of many nations and lands,
Our vast nation has been challenged by a boy of no
    consequence.
25 The son of Mashobana has seized all the king's cattle,
Absconding with them to the remote regions.
Even now he skirts the borders of the empire fearing your anger.
We are here as fugitives from his dissident army,
Loathing to violate the king's command.
30 In vain we attempted to reason with him,
Telling him such acts only court disasters.
He opened his hands and said: "Let those who wish to return
    leave."
The cattle he took from all the northern bandits
35 He has distributed among his rebellious army.'
Shaka of Senzangakhona sighed and simply said:
'O my child, Mzilikazi, you have soiled over my head!'
He was paralysed by this treachery.
Indeed, he thought even of the wealth he would have gladly
40   given away

If only it would have fulfilled Mzilikazi's dreams.
He sent a message ordering that Mzilikazi be left unmolested;
Still hoping his conscience might yet disturb him
For to Shaka's mind such acts bordered on banditry.
5 Many in the Assembly strongly condemned this crime,
Claiming such action, if unpunished, could soon be followed by
     others,
Bringing about chaos and many dissident kingdoms.
Through the clamour of such members of the Assembly and
10   army
Shaka was forced to send for the young iziMpohlo regiment.
He said: 'Bring back the son of Mashobana.
Let me talk to him man to man.
Perchance his deed comes of a noble desire
15 To avenge himself on the hordes of Zwide's army and his
     followers.
I know Mzilikazi from his days of immature youth and pain.
Then he could not stop mourning his father.
Perhaps in time he will learn how rich are bonds of
20   brotherhood.'

The iziMpohlo regiment set out amidst the splash of summer
     rains.
Some thought this a sign of disaster.
When they returned, defeated, Shaka commented:
25 'As I said, Mzilikazi of Mashobana is a better general than
     many.
I want this affair to proceed no further.
He shall now be our signal branch
Wherever the wild winds of Soshangane and others begin to
30   blow.'
The men of the Assembly were horrified at these words.
Such indulgence had never been witnessed.
For, in truth, appropriating the king's cattle was itself a heinous
     crime.
35 Secretly Shaka hoped Mzilikazi's army would open the north
And, through his fugitive army, test the distant armies.
Yet the clamour against the king's leniency grew.
Bluntly the generals said: 'Mzilikazi has offended the whole
     army.

By defeating the iziMpohlo regiment
He has reared the heads of many would-be bandits.'
Shaka, consenting to their anger and realizing these dangers,
    said:
5   'The great Mbelebele must now attack.
Let them cut the bowels of Mzilikazi's army.
Let them spare none of the offending dissenters.
Whoever is told of this episode must know:
To violate my orders in battle means death!
10   But only one man I want to deal with personally:
Should you find him alive, hold him for me.
Bring him here to explain the reason for this treachery.'
Thus began the fearful exodus of the dreaded Mbelebele
    division.
15   Descending on him, they launched their attacks full force.
It was no easy task. Many times Mzilikazi's army fought back.
Until, weakened and desperate, they sought a way to escape.
It was Mlusi, Shaka's messenger, who, following secret orders,
Left open his flank to allow the escape of Mzilikazi's army.
20   He shook his head in amazement as he saw them follow
    this opening.
He said a silent prayer: 'Run, son of Mashobana.
Your good fortune is endless!'
Mzilikazi fled, following the northernmost route,
25   Passing through the regions of the great Pedi nation.
The narrators of legends tell us: the great King Moshoeshoe
Invited him to his lands as he veered southwards,
Disturbing the peace and causing panic among the settled
    nations.
30   The great king ordered that food and cattle be given to him,
Hoping in this way to tame him and cure him of his
    fierceness.
By the same methods the generous king
Had hoped to tame the restless Matiwane and the destitute
35   Boers.
But Mzilikazi, like the others, spurned this goodwill.
Fearing the wrath of Shaka and others,
He forged northwards into the land of the friendly Tshwanas.
Raiding them constantly he set his new settlement among the
40   Kalangas.

There he ultimately established the feared kingdom of the
     Ndebele.
How true, the sayings of our Forefathers:
'One fierce general can subjugate many peaceful nations.'
5 Mzilikazi proclaimed to his followers:
'I shall build here a royal city
Which I shall name Bulawayo after that of my King, Shaka.
In this way I shall celebrate our undying bonds of friendship.
On my death it shall remain always a reminder of our times.
10 It shall fulfil Shaka's great dream:
To let all nations know the greatness of our nation.
At the break of dawn over the mountains
Men and women of the Palm Race shall be heard singing our
     songs.'
15 To this day his prophecies constantly unveil their truth.
The land of the Palm Race boasts of its children.
Our nations, says the poet, shall yet drink from the same
     calabash.

The regiments of the Mbelebele returned, singing triumphantly.
20 Shaka himself was pleased with these events.
He said: 'I know wherever he is he shall build a great nation.'
As this was happening a messenger rushed through the vast
     plains
Where the grass was green, tall and supple;
25 He sang his song of victory ceaselessly:
'I am carried by the high wind, my lord.
I come to report how our great general, Mdlaka,
Has broken the conceit of Macingwane utterly.'
The messenger of good news hurried
30 While Mdlaka's army followed the lower end of the Khahlamba
     mountains,
Forging on through Ntambamhlophe and Mangweni mountains,
And tracing its routes through the valleys of Magangangozi.
They harassed the wandering army of Matiwane
35 Where it had fled to the mountain fortress.
Mdlaka's army outflanked it, running through the hills.
Only by the kindness of the Ancestors did Matiwane escape.
A segment of his army headed for Zululand,
To ask there for a place to settle.

They denounced the ruthlessness of their former leader.
Shaka, on hearing their sad story was kind to them,
He gave them land and cattle to feed their children.
Many could not believe these were the same people
5   From whom many nations had fled in terror.

Great was the occasion
When large numbers converged on the capital,
Shouting in praise of the returning general, Mdlaka.
When he approached the king he bowed low and said:
10   'My lord, I am ready to die for our land.
I ask you, grant me this: to die fighting in the battle-field!
I request the noble death of a hero.
Let me sing the king's poems of excellence to my last breath.
This, my king, is my most coveted desire.'
15   It was as if his mind had travelled ahead of him.
To hear the great debates of Bulawayo
For many had demanded a special place for him at the
        Assembly.
They said: 'General Mdlaka should be retired from all minor
20   battles.
He must be made to live as one of the king's close advisers,
Giving the nation the benefit of his great wisdom.'
But such admirers did not share the impulse of his visions,
Nor did they fully understand
25   The more he won battles the more he desired to fight.
His courage and persistence made him feared and hated;
His humility and mind earned him deep rancour from the
        ambitious.
Some would have rejoiced at his death in battle
30   But some loaded him with poems of praise,
Desiring their own youth to emulate this great hero.

Book Ten: The white strangers

For the first time Shaka officially meets a delegation of white traders. Shaka sees them from a very realistic angle. He studies their habits and weapons, seeing them as a desperate but still human species. After an assassination attempt on him they ask to tend his wounds and immediately use this occasion to ask for land. He gives them land which for him will also serve as a settlement from which to study them. He intends that whatever he learns of them and from them must strengthen his army. He also wishes for an agreement with King George that will define their spheres of influence. Accordingly, he sends a delegation. He knows, however, that this is only to buy time. Meantime, in response to a request from King Moshoeshoe for protection against the hated bandit, Prince Matiwane, Shaka sends the great generalisimo, Mdlaka, to rout the beast.

For many years there were rumours of the arrival of the
    Pumpkin Race.
In truth, the teller of tales informs us
It was the great King Sobhuza who, in a dream, foresaw these
5   events.
He solemnly told his councillors, at the Assembly:
'Through a vision I saw nations emerging from the ocean.
They resemble us but in appearance are the colour of
    pumpkin-porridge.
10 They speak a language no different from that of nestling birds,
Quick and given to staccato sounds like wild animals.
They are rude of manner and are without any graces or
    refinement.
They carry a long stick of fire.
15 With this they kill and loot from many nations.
Sometimes they seize even children for their sea-bound
    furnaces —
A veritable race of robbers and cannibals!'
Those at the Assembly were deeply disturbed by this horrific
20   dream.
Some denounced the prevalence of dreams,

Certain no such dream would ever come true.
But there were others who affirmed its truth,
Claiming their own story-tellers had told them as much.
It was clear the great king was not alone in these dreams.
5   The narrators of ancient tales tells us:
'Once as the sea lay calm, throwing off only trembling waves,
A strange race emerged from the ocean.
Their hair hung down like husks of maize.
Against them many a mother warned her curious child,
10   Telling her how once a young boy stared at them,
Eager to see the truth of their form.
But as they neared they began to chase after him.
Only by remembering the advice of Mkhulu was he saved.
To him he had said: "There are creatures out to kill and rob.
15   These Nanabahules are a threat to every man.
By asking for water and food they prepare to seize whole
         villages.
For, indeed, they possess insatible appetites.
Should you see them, flee, my grandson, flee for your life.
20   For they run as if they possess the wings of the wind.
To escape them only this stratagem will save you:
Throw chunks of bread (these they never leave),
Which they shall devour like hungry vultures,
To them food is more precious than the human race.
25   They would annihilate whole nations on earth
To feed endlessly their great appetites."
It was this story that saved his life;
As he fled he could hear fierce growlings as they fought for
         bread.'
30   Such stories were prevalent throughout Zululand.
They were known as people-whose-ears-are-shot-through-
         by-the-rays-of-the sun.
Shaka had learnt of them from his many agents.
Many times he had discussed them with Dingiswayo.
35   Mhlope amongst his agents was his chief informant.
He reported to the Assembly:
'O my lord, the country is infested with bad bugs.
Even now they congregate at the mouth of the Mngeni river.
Sent by you, I trailed the new strangers;
40   I mingled amongst the curious crowds,

207

Until I learnt the routine of their lives.
Some indeed have learnt to speak our language.'
One man began to question him intensely:
'It is said these strangers are red in colour
5   And possess long hair like a horse tail.
They wear shoes like our men of old,
Preferring to live in their temporary huts of white skins.'
Mhlope patiently answered: 'It is so,
In truth, their bodies always seem delicate
10 As though they may blister in the hot rays of the sun.
But, indeed, these newcomers are no different from us.'
Shaka intervened and said:
'You talk like ignorant children.
These nations are no different from other nations of the earth.
15 You are the great men of Zululand, nobles of a supreme nation.
These people are scouring the earth in search of food.
Should they come, they should share in the great life of
      Zululand.
Indeed, I want you, Mbikwane, to go to the Thungulu region
20   and invite them.
Our nation's wealth feeds all peoples.
We must learn the truth of their distant lands.'
Shaka paid no more attention to this matter.
He sent a word to his aunt, Princess Mawa,
25 Asking her to receive in his name these new strangers.
It was following these orders
That Mbikwane hurried to the sea coast,
Eager to extend the king's invitation to the race of the glowing
      ears.
30 Shaka constantly sought details of their lives and country.
It was, indeed, by a great stroke of luck
That at this very time Hlambamanzi of Xhosaland sought
    refuge.
He reported on the new strangers' habits and lives.
35 He told how they came to Xhosaland without food or cattle
But seized or bought these with useless trinkets.
'Sometimes they would steal the cattle from the shepherds.
It was these beasts,' said Hlambamanzi of Xhosaland,
'That were later paid for with blood,
40 Soon the strangers claimed the whole region.

It is not only cattle we have lost,
But the rich grazing lands of our Forefathers.
Their hunger for land is insatiable.'
Because of these disputes he said he himself was exiled;
5 Caught as he retrieved the spotted cattle of his family,
In iron leggings he was sent to the Island of Stones,
Known otherwise as Island of Robin.
But then he was only a boy.
When they ultimately set him free
10 He was sold to passers-by like a sheep
Offered only a choice between eternal servitude and the Island
    of Stone.
In this new slavery he was to serve the cruel and ugly Owen.
Heartless and unmindful of the yearnings of a man for his
15   family,
He gave him to yet another stranger-traveller,
Commanding him: 'Go with him and serve him as interpreter
    and servant.'
'It was to this self-styled Hambakahle (Go-Well)
20 That I was sold to as a slave.
Sailing through the rough southern seas
We were flung in all directions until a dragon-wave lifted us,
Throwing us into the night of her endless pools.
It was I, Hlambamanzi, who saved the lives of many,
25 Yet by this act I brought on myself the anger of the foreigners.
When we all assembled on the seashore
They claimed it was my unwillingness to leave that angered the
    sea;
They insulted me despite my age,
30 Slapping me on my face like a child.
Yet in all this I knew my Ancestors were with me.
It was they, too, who had boiled the high-waves of the ocean.
The foreigner in desperation had overplayed his power.
I therefore decided to leave,
35 Seeking refuge from the greatest king of the Palm Race.'

Mbikwane and the Strangers followed the path to the north.
They crossed the Amatigulu river and rested at Nyezane.
Then they passed the large villages of Ntotheleni.
Many spectators and families gazed at them in amazement,

Seeing the elaborate paraphernalia they wore.
Soon they passed the royal village of Princess Mawa,
Heading for Mlalazi region near the Ngoye mountain.
They stopped there and rested at the Mhlathuze region.
5   From there they proceeded to the great capital of Bulawayo;.
From all sides it seemed flooded with long rays of the sun.
There were people from all regions of Zululand.
The Strangers heard the great poets declaim the king's epics.
He sang of him who had vanquished many enemies;
10   He spoke of the nations that had allied together;
He prophesied: 'By their power they shall repulse the invaders!'
The Strangers never ceased to ask questions.
As they rested under a giant shade at the gates of
        Bulawayo.
15   They bowed their heads in obeisance to the great ruler.
From all sides came numerous troops in war regalia.
Mbikwane of the Mthethwas now shouted his presentation:
'Zulu of Malandela, you who are the terror of evil men,
You, whose mind thrusts its light like the rays of the sun,
20   I have arrived. I have come by your command.
I present to you these little humble men from foreign lands.
They, through-whose-ears-pass-the-rays-of-the-sun,
They come to ask for your listening ear, Black One.
By your power you receive pleas from many lands.'
25   He turned to them for affirmation of his words
And shouted: 'Do you pay obeisance to the king of kings?'
Mbikwane then gave them the gifts of elephant tusks,
Performing the ceremony of friendly exchange.
The King beat the two shields of his attendants.
30   By this sign he commanded the Assembly to disperse,
Leaving only Hlambamanzi and himself to talk to the Strangers.
To their horror they saw it was the same man they once
        enslaved.
Stricken with guilt and fear they spoke slowly and cautiously.
35   Shaka ordered for them large pots of beer and meat.
He carefully asked them details of their countries' life and size.
Sometimes they exaggerated to make the day entertaining and
        full of jokes.
Shaka, having pondered on their words, said:
40   'It is my decision that you shall be given all you desire.

In our land the law of the nation reigns supreme.
Whoever observes this law enjoys all the best things of life.
I have ordered a great feast to be held in your honour.
Our custom demands a kindness to strangers.
5 You, as subjects of my brother, King George,
Fear nothing in the great state of Zululand.
There are no robbers and no wanton murderers here.'
Thus began the great dance of Zululand.
Thousands of men and women moved like a great summer
10   forest.
Inspite of all this, Shaka never forgot their secret aims.
He said to Mgobhozi-who-comes-from-the-Mountain:
'We have encountered a race of red ants,
So desperate they would bore into the bowels of stone.
15 It is clear while they speak in soft and round tones
They know what targets they aim for.
It is wise for us patiently to follow their plans,
Then surprise them when they least expect it.
Their eyes are truly those of a desperate people.
20 When a man is a victim of hunger
His whole body is hard; his mind speaks daggers through his
       eyes.
For all these reasons we must study carefully their plans and
       customs.
25 I notice, too, they wear heavy shoes
Which in battle must slow down their speed.
Their feet have been made soft and tender like children's
When I asked them of the life in their lands
They spent much time telling me of their wealth and prosperity,
30 But the prosperous people never leave their homes to roam the
       earth.
Their customs are those of a violent and ruthless race.
Whoever can stand the wails of an incarcerated man,
Enjoys the spectacle of pain.
35 Their weapon of fire
Betrays, only their weakness and cowardice.
It is true that it can kill a man from a distance:
Like a stone that hits someone as he approaches.
Yet it does not have the speed of our regiments.
40 While they reload their fire-throwers

Our fierce army shall have trampled on their heads!
Those they defeated in Xhosaland
Only lost in the battle of speed.
It is with this superior force we shall beat them:
5   As our two armies clash let us combine our techniques with
        theirs.
A group of our men must learn their skills of war.
In battle these shall act as a diversion
But our greatest power lies in us.
10   For those who put too much faith in their weapons are
        doomed.
They are defeated soon when their weapons are broken.
I want my messengers to bring me the real truth about their
        lives.
15   Others must carry my gifts to this King George.
Let them hesitate even if they had planned an early invasion,
Enabling us to learn more about their plans and life;
For to know the ways of your enemy is to possess the power of
        victory.'

20   The whole day the Strangers feasted and sang
Until their stomachs burst with meat.
Each time of day was heralded by new singers and dancers and
        poets.
But at the parting of two nights, amidst the turmoil of
25   celebrations,
A high-pitched voice called out: 'Our king has been stabbed!'
A great stream of blood jetted out from Shaka's forearm.
The Strangers rushed to the councillors,
Telling them they possessed medicines for the wound.
30   They were elated at this chance to show their skills.
They pleaded and appealed to the councillors:
'Permit us to treat the king, our protector and friend.
Our greatest medicines are made for such wounds.'
Through their insistence this was granted to them.
35   They ministered their harsh medicines of war.
Among themselves they debated:
'No opportunity is better than now to ask for land.
Through our gesture the king is obliged to make an equal
        gesture.'

Mqalane, the king's doctor, gave his own medicines,
Making the king chew herbs to kill the pain,
And to raise the secret powers of the mind to heal the wound.
This way he broke the force to succumb to death,
5   And gave him back the magic power of living.
Active, it stunts the powers of decay.
The king's doctor then gave him medicines to neutralize the
      poison.

Crowds shouted and wailed as though the king had died.
10 Many suspected this crime had been committed by Zwide's
      agents
Who, smarting from defeat, had sworn revenge against Shaka.
Some privately accused the king's brothers of collusion.
Like a frenzied crowd, and without waiting for orders,
15 Large numbers set out to attack and rout the last Ndwadwe
      settlements;
Seizing them and piling on them their round stones of anger.
Thus was erected the great Monument of Revenge.
The Strangers began to move freely, feeling honoured by the
20   king's praise,
For the wound had healed quickly.
They now approached the king and said:
'Great Lord of nations, we have stayed already too long.
Having not presented our request for land.
25 We need a place that shall be ours,
Where we shall pay our respect to our own king and
      Ancestors.
We are happy that the king has recovered from his wound
And the nation's enemies have been destroyed.
30 It is our custom to cement bonds of friendships
By putting the sacred right hand on this leaf
Affirming the closeness of families and nations.
By this deed we express our gratitude for your love and
      kindness.'
35 As he spoke his eyes danced in all directions
As though someone would emerge to dispute his words.
He was like a monkey out to steal some winter crop.
He swallowed gulps of saliva and ran his tongue over his lips.
He wrung his wet hands, his eyes still restless.

Shaka tried putting them at ease, for, after all, they were only
    strangers.
He looked at the proffered sheet of paper
And said to Hlambamanzi: 'Interpret it.
5   Let us hear what message it brings.
In truth, I intend to grant them this request
And let them know the earth belongs to all.
It is unwise to use stratagems for what can be obtained by
    agreement.'
10 Hlambamanzi of the Xhosas took the document
And said: 'My lord, here is its silent message:
"I, King of the Zulus, by my own will
And the great powers bequeathed on me by my Ancestors,
I am grateful for the gifts given to me by the White Strangers.
15 I give them the costal harbour
And all the neighbouring regions to the Mdloti river.
This area shall stretch to the regions of Nogqaza.
I give this land to them with all its rivers and forests
And with all that there is in it.
20 I appoint the man Farewell as governor
He must rule and run the land according to white custom.
By this act I express my gratitude to him
For doctoring and saving my life." '
After Hlambamanzi had finished reading this document
25 Shaka looked at all those before him and smiled,
His mind racing ahead of them and their stratagems.
He made them swallow their own deceit.
Great was the occasion when the Strangers prepared to leave.
Shaka said to them: 'Here is my gift of cattle.
30 Greet for me your king and my brother, King George.
Tell him, whoever comes in his name shall be welcomed.
Should you return, know: our gates are ever open to strangers.
I give you these elephant tusks —
They are gifts to you and your families.'
35 Shaka accorded to them these bequests,
Still hoping by kindness and generosity
He might cure them of their greed,
Else convert them to the Zulu religion of generous and selfless
    giving.
40 But such peoples are too far gone in their ways.

Generosity itself stimulates in them new stratagems.
Shaka knew the colonies of lawless adventurers,
Attract many runaways and criminals,
Causing endless disturbances in the region.
5   Thus their land was to be their home and anchor.
He was also eager to observe their plans and habits.
For this he appointed Mbikwane to oversee the settlement.
The Strangers were happy and elated
At what they had obtained,
10   For, indeed, life among foreigners is not like that of the Palm
        Race.
People kill their own friends and relatives for land!
Over the graves of their former allies they erect their
        monuments,
15   But the Palm Race has never heard of such things.
How can one man possess land as though it was life itself?
Is man, then, no longer capable of death?
Is land not the vast endlessness where man lives?
The people of Zululand asked, half amused, half puzzled, by
20   these things.

Following these encounters, the Assembly met.
Shaka addressed them: 'People of Zulu,
Our links with the people of King George are now known to
        you.
25   Their craftiness far surpasses that of Zwide;
With soft words and praise they win their way.
Yet if the great state of Zululand shall embrace all nations,
Then we must win the loyalty of all peoples,
Making out of them loyal and devoted subjects.
30   Thus I gave them land,
Intending to make them, too, men of families.
Their weapons are still something for us to know.
Mbikwane shall administer there our policies and watch over
        them.
35   Having doctored me of my wound,
They seized this indebtedness to demand a gift of land.
Their hearts are as hard as a grinding stone.
They receive for their gifts more than they give.
We must examine carefully their strategies.

Soon they shall be back with more demands.
To their settlement they shall attract many cowards and
      adventurers
But none should disturb them.
5 Let us all observe the laws and customs of their nation.
Through this we shall know their truth
And the disparate loyalties that infest their peoples.
But give me your own views,
Since only through your voices are the children of Zululand
10   heard.'
It was Mgobhozi, the great hero, who stood up and said:
'My lord, I hear your words and their truth I respect.
I know, too, your wisdom has seldom erred;
Yet I feel it wiser to kill at once the fearful vermin.
15 Destroying it now before it devastates our lands and race.
We should put on guard our army
Spreading it all along the coastal region.
Let them find us waiting to fight without mercy.
Each story I have heard about this nation fills me with
20   terror.
What I have seen only affirms my fears.
How is it that no sooner had they arrived
Than the king was wounded?
How is it that they were so ready with their medicines?
25 Being no diviner I cannot give the answers,
But I ask you, members of the great nation's Assembly,
By the power conferred on you by the great nation of Zulu
Have you judged correctly these bloodthirsty foreigners?
Such people dig deep into a nation's life.
30 They strip the wealth and power that once was its greatness.
If what I say seems against the admonitions of my king,
I ask that all the nation's anger be let loose on me.
Yet I shall rejoice if I die for my nation and my king.'
The men of the Assembly shifted places
35 As though stung by some unbearable thought.
It was as if the king himself might suddenly dissolve the
      Assembly
And in anger call Mgobhozi and say:
'You now have exceeded your power of the Assembly.
40 You have usurped my authority, Mgobhozi,

And dared to oppose the visions of my rule.'
But in vain they waited.
Instead he stared high at the pinnacles of mountains,
As though his mind was lost in the horizon.
5   When an old man who sat to his right saw this
He said: 'My lord, I ask you to listen.
Our era faces challenges never known before.
We have no guidance even from our Forefathers.
I applauded the richness of your thoughts
10   When you said it is unwise to rush into action.
Yet I do not dismiss altogether the words of Mgobhozi,
Knowing how great is his bravery in battle.
Indeed, we dare not ignore the truths of what he says.
A bull can only be tamed by a variety of stratagems.
15   On the one hand it is necessary to persuade it;
On the other it is necessary to inflict strong taming blows,
For only when it softens will it follow the direction of its master;
Only then can its slayers cut its jugular vein.
So, too, must be our tactics against this new nation.
20   We must treat them kindly, stretching out both our hands,
Letting them feel our generosity and power
And exposing their strengths and weakness.
I liked the king's words
As he cut the foreigners before the Assembly for their boasts.
25   They praised their weapons
As though to challenge them is to challenge lightning itself.
They spoke as if nothing survives the devastation of their
      armies.
But their weapons could not have won all their battles
30   For, indeed, had it been so they would simply seize our lands.'
The old man reminded the Assembly of the previous day's
      episode
When the strangers rocked the valley with cannon blast,
Hoping to fill the spectators with terror
35   And draw to themselves the power of the gods.
It was at this point Shaka intervened:
'Brave men of Zululand, my heart is filled with joy.
I know now I do not rule this land alone
But with all those whose visions have enriched our land.
40   It is clear there is no division of ideas amongst us.

I praise you for giving thought to things that challenge our
    nation.
It is not the first time I hear of the tricks of the sea nations.
Of their cunning I heard long ago and by my own eyes I am
    witness.
5   With your alertness and that of the nation
Their craftiness shall bring to them only ruination.
Should we ever be duped by them our nation shall disintegrate.
Yet so long as our watchfulness is unrelenting
10   We shall outrun and outdistance all their stratagems.
There is still time for us to learn their ways.
We have not been surprised, like distant nations.
Our great heroes have learnt from their experience in wars.
We shall conquer them both by our courage and planning.
15   Of this white race there are two nations,
Both eternally eager to devour each other.
Our strategy must be to strike a careful blow between them,
Making them turn fiercely against each other;
Thereafter to cement all bonds of the Palm Race.
20   This way we shall defeat and check the invader.
We must bear this in mind:
Nations, like animals, follow the directions of fertile pastures.
They are no more than cliques, holding together to what they
    possess.
25   Should we close our lands to one white race
We shall have driven off the weaker one.
But should we threaten them both
They shall forge bonds, uniting firmly against us.
Thus they shall deprive us of the secret knowledge of their
30   enmity.
For to favour one nation opens the grievances of the other.
Thus one section must build and settle not far from us.
Before long I shall entrap them.
Presenting to them my recruits, I shall say:
35   "White men! Teach them now about your weapons."
They shall have no escape but to bow down to my will.
I ask you, therefore: be patient and hold your anger.
Should the foreigners be alarmed by our calmness
We still have the power to surround and destroy them.

Through the Ancestors, by the adroitness of our heroes,
We shall turn against them like medicine ravaging the stomach.
But as we plan against them they, too, are planning against us.'
The Assembly listened, captivated by these thoughts.
5   Finally they broke out of this serious mood,
Making jokes about the Strangers' habits.
There was one man who said:
'Whenever I see the husks of maize
It is as if I hold their long tufts of hair.
10 I shudder at the very thought of touching the naked cobs of
      maize.'
Another man commented: 'I know now ours is the greatest of
      nations;
Theirs is a story of children fighting over a morsel of food,
15 Or of young shepherds disputing over grazing lands.
Immature at first, such shepherds grow up to tease each other;
They learn to talk of issues more urgent than these,
For, indeed, the world stretches without limit.
Only what is bequeathed by our Forefathers is worth fighting
20   for.'
Such were the asides from the Assembly.
One man was heard to remark:
'Could this nation be an ancient stock of a once proud Palm
      Race,
25 Who by an old curse were turned into albinoes?
Could their wanderings be in search of their ancient roots?'
But the other answered:
'Do not be a fool and look down on these races.
They are no less and no more than us.
30 Perhaps those we have encountered are only fugitives like
      Mzilikazi.
Man only abandons his homeland for a deep reason.'
But these were no more than fireside tales.

Shaka commanded that an Ancestral feast be held
35 To strengthen the ancient bonds of the Zulu nation.
At this very time rumours from the south were rife —
How Matiwane menaced the peaceful nations of the Sothos.
It was this same Matiwane
Who raided and looted the regions of King Moshoeshoe.

But Moshoeshoe had built strong bonds with Shaka;
Often they exchanged gifts and emissaries
As, indeed, those who keep our truths have told us.
The messenger of the Sothos' ruler spoke warmly and said:
5   'My great and noble king, Moshoeshoe of the Basothos,
Who dwells on the high peaks of mountains,
Says everywhere he turns his eyes see only mist and darkness:
Above the horizon there are only heads of Matiwane's armies.
They block the ways to your great capital.
10 Each messenger comes back empty-handed.
The story never changes —
Messengers tell of the same robberies every day.
We have failed to bring to you all your gifts,
Hence my lord has not opened to you his lips of friendship.'
15 Shaka turned to his councillors, his face beaming with joy,
And said, making fun of the whole episode:
'Did you hear how the locusts have begun to devour men?
The beautiful feet of Moshoeshoe no longer reach our gates,
The messenger tells us: some bandit confiscates what is truly
20   ours.
This is a godsend. Our knees were beginning to weaken.
We were beginning to forget the rich experience of battle.
Like old women we sit basking in the sun.
The challenge has been thrown at your feet, Mdlaka.
25 The little upstarts have cast their shadows over your household.
The giant branches of the summer plant are stripped of their
        leaves.'

Matiwane's arrogance had swelled through peacetime.
He roamed the lands, raining destruction on many friendly
30   nations.
Peace for the weak is a disease that undermines their alliances.
No sooner had the king directed these words to Mdlaka
Than he began to turn and twist his face in anger.
Even his old battle wounds began to ache.
35 He recalled many enemies he had subdued.
General Mdlaka could never rest while the battle songs were
        sung;
Often he woke up in the night to sing with distant voices.
When he heard the king throw to him this challenge

He spoke hurriedly and said: 'My lord, you know
How your words ignite the fires of war.
I am always armed to carry out and fulfil your commands.
Whoever dares to challenge your authority
5   Shall be brought down from the mountain.
They shall be consumed by the giant fire of the sun!
I am grateful to you that of all the Zulu heroes
You have chosen me to administer this punishment.
Tomorrow at dawn the winding mists
10   Shall see us emerging from the valleys.
Whoever shall stand in our path shall be swallowed whole.
We shall attack and destroy Matiwane and his bandits.'
Mdlaka spoke as though only in jest
But he knew Matiwane's very name made the army restive.
15   It had waited long to tame this recalcitrant ruler.

The morning came, with her children, from the mountains.
Large processions of regiments were heard shouting their war
     slogans.
Alternating with each other they sang their songs of battle.
20   Shaka stood on the open ground,
Watching them as they marched to battle.
To each of the known heroes he had said:
'Son of the great ancestry, fight like a hungry leopard!'
The army meandered, following the route to the Sotho regions.
25   As they disappeared into the dust of the horizon
Great heroic poems echoed into the distant mountains.
The poet declaimed the king's epic:
'Young calf that climbed over the house of Queen Ntombazi.
They said it was causing an evil omen
30   Whereas it was they who possessed malevolent powers.
The elephant that went on its way;
The Langas followed it,
It turned back and trampled on the crowds of men.
He asked for snuff from Macingwane of eNgonyameni:
35   Macingwane declared he had none.
Thus did he court trouble!
Great power that haunts Macingwane,
Making many people live constantly in fear.

Fear haunts both enemies and friends alike.
He destroyed Bhungane, the son of Mthinkulu of eMahlutshini.'
The epic echoed over the hills like a song
And the commanders could not turn back the poet.
5   The numerous regiments were like bees in flight.

Prince Dingane and Prince Nhlangane resented their role in this
        war.
At every opportunity they protested,
Ridiculing the whole campaign
10   And claiming the king's children should not be exposed to such
        dangers.
They were embittered, too, at being given no powers of
        command.
In self-mockery they called themselves 'the king's policemen'.
15   Shaka had declared to his commanders:
'There shall be no privileges for the king's children.
All men must merit the position they hold in battle.'
Such, too, had been his order when the Zulu clan had protested,
Claiming it was unwise to give Ndlela the position of command
20   Who, after all, was neither royal nor of the Zulu clan.
Indeed, they said, Sompisi, his father, was no more than a
        bandit.
Shaka had stated bluntly: 'Every path leads to Zululand.
No man shall merit from the heroism of others;
25   Only by courage can the power of command be achieved.'
Thus he dismissed the claims of 'high-born' families.
Those who now set out against Matiwane were imbued with
        these words.

See them, the beautiful children of the Palm Race
30   As they climb the rugged ridges of the mountains!
See them as they follow the downward route,
Passing through a path that is overshadowed by giant boulders.
A cluster of resting birds is disturbed;
It sways over the mountains like a long rope
35   Until it meets with others from the south.
In one great swoop it dissolves into the night of cliffs.
Terrified, it seems to speak a human language.

In the evening people tell their tales of battles.
'I have seen the legend with my own eyes:
I have seen Zulu, the son of Nogandaya of the Zungus.
His name is on the lips of children and of heroes.
5 Through his feats of bravery people no longer fear death.'
Of him the great poet said:
'Thunderclap, that struck unexpectedly
Where there was neither thorn trees nor wattle plants.
The thunderstorm that overwhelms like Ntima of Yimaneni.
10 Great hero, whose wounds are manifest on both sides,
Like those of the son of Jobe.
Tumultuous cluster of elephant grass!
Stubborn field that cannot be penetrated,
You ran until you reached Nkilimbeni battle!
15 Spoiler who drank the beer and it fermented!
You, the whey that was left in the pumpkin fields.
Great explosion of fire!
You are like a fly that survives many enemies.
It was you who were dumbfounded
20 At the blasphemy levelled against Dlungwane of Mbelebele!'
It was this brave fighter who now forged ahead of others,
As though fearing Matiwane might escape,
While others hesitated,
Shivering from the snow of the Khahlamba mountains,
25 He threw off his gown of warm sheepskin
And walked into the open arena to dance the battle dance.
With renewed zeal he forged through the mountain passes
And clambered the high ridges of the baboon dwellings.
From the shadowy side of the mountains many fled.
30 The high cliffs spun the battle hymns into the valley.
The Zulu army rested at the friendly territory of Prince Likoele;
Not far from there was the concentration of Matiwane's army.
Mdlaka sent ahead a team of war experts,
Instructing them to study all details of the land and positions.
35 Zulu of Nogandaya bellowed out mockingly:
'Behold the feeble enemy given to us by our king.'
He was restless. Sometimes he made jokes as he sat on a
   vantage stone;
Sometimes he ran and stood on a small hill as though he had
40   gone insane.

Listen now to the great General Mdlaka
As he commands his army into battle.
Listen to the son of Mshiza as he shouts:
'Give them all to me! Let me fight them alone!
5   I bear them a deep grudge! I am bitter against them!
They deterred the sacred gifts of the king!'
The army ran in a stampede, following close to Zulu of
        Nogandaya.
He rushed into the enemy lines, stabbing fiercely,
10   Making Matiwane's army retreat in terror.
It was as though they had beheld some wild animal.
Tired from this effort he walked down to the river
And drank as the war raged on all sides.
In a gesture of contempt he squirted a mouthful into the battle
15   arena.
Suddenly he lept up to them, uttering his poems of excellence
And stabbed the men of Matiwane who dared to challenge him.
He opened the battle centre, spinning his spear in his hand
And chasing the enemy like an angered bull.
20   It was Dingiswayo of the great Ngcobo clan
Who covered his back as a crowd of enemies closed in on him.
Waves of Zulu heroes burst on them like a disturbed ocean:
They drove Matiwane's army onto an upper ridge.
Mdlaka shouted to the army:
25   'Do not attack in strength. Harass them!
Let them crowd together in confused formation,
Then storm their forces, rushing on them
And stabbing them in quick spurts of anger!'
Through these words he set aflame their war madness.
30   Even the carrier boys became restless —
Against orders, they chased after hordes of fleeing men.
Matiwane's army broke and scattered,
Seeking shelter in the many little hills.
Despite its depleted numbers
35   It struck telling blows against those
Who sought to hack their way through the mountain pass.
General Ndlela led a column from the remote side of the
        mountains
And through the rear route attacked Matiwane's army.
40   In disarray some ran into the fierce night of the cliffs;

Some threw off their shields
And ran headlong into the battle lines of the Zulus.
Thus were avenged the many victims of the Sotho nations.

Book Eleven: The two great rulers of the grandeur of Zululand

The defeat of Matiwane having been accomplished, Mdlaka sends messengers to the court of King Moshoeshoe to announce the coming of the Zulu king's emissaries, of whom he is leader. They are treated with every possible kindness by the Sothos, with whom strong bonds now exist. As the army returns to Zululand it cannot at first celebrate its victory because of the illness of Nandi. But Shaka decides to over-look this personal sadness and orders a great welcome feast. The feast symbolically purges Shaka of his gloom but does not cure him. This, in fact, is the beginning of the era, when all the close friends of Shaka die, anticipating his own death. His brothers, particularly Dingane, begin to plot for his assassination, eager to preserve their aristocratic privileges.

The army, singing their triumphal songs,
Drove before them large heads of confiscated cattle.
Under the shadows of the Khahlamba mountains the army
    rested.
5 It was here that General Mdlaka addressed the regiments:
'Great heroes, children of our nation, hero clans of Zululand.
You have now fulfilled the great tasks assigned to you by the
    nation.
May it always be so! May we always conquer!
10 Let the heroes display proudly their crowns of battle.
May those who dare challenge us be devastated by a flash of
    lightning.

Let time remove their dreams of grandeur.
Let their feathers be blown by the wind.
But grant me to praise above all, Zulu of Nogandaya.
Not I alone beheld the fighting skill of this hero,
5   But all the children of Zululand.
He is the "Explosion of Fire!"
"The fly that survives many enemies".'
While he spoke, Zulu, the son of Nogandaya, sat at a distance.
Sometimes he would move a few paces and growl,
10   Raising his hand as though to spite the enemy,
As though he still could see his shadow engaged in battle.
At the battle of Mkilimbeni, it was said,
He arrived in full view of regiments running at full speed.
It was he whom Mdlaka now chose to carry their greetings to
15   King Moshoeshoe.
The messengers set out at dawn to Moshoeshoe's capital,
To announce the Zulu emissaries.
They climbed the Great Mountain through many winding
      passes.
20   It was here many fugitives were received.
On this fortress, too, the Sotho heroes could espy approaching
      enemies.

The heralds of General Mdlaka waited in a large house,
Until the king had completed his round of talks.
25   Finally Moshoeshoe sat solemnly with his advisers and the
      messengers,
Listening to endless stories of Matiwane's brutality against
      nations.
He said: 'You have come to us
30   So that we may consolidate the peace of the Palm Race.
Peace is only possible through our sacrifice and courage.
As I talk the country is infested with the pest of locusts.
Should this plague increase, our land and nations shall be
      destroyed.
35   The greedy nations of the Boers are at large.
They destroy mercilessly, creating their own hamlets in old
      villages.
Many families of baThwa and Xhosa people have been
      annihilated.
40   The wars fought by foreigners are not like ours:

They kill men and women and children.
Sometimes they seize them and turn them into slaves.
From the emissaries of the Xhosa king
I hear their invasions increase every year.
5 Such attacks do not reveal an enemy hungry only for land
But eager to seize and destroy whole nations.
For this reason the Palm Race that seeks shelter from us
Should be given a home and a friendship to heal their wounds.
Tomorrow it is they who shall fight our wars.'
10 As the great king spoke his face was sad and solemn.
It was at this moment that a councillor came,
Announcing the arrival of the emissaries from the great King
    Shaka.
The Zulus declaimed Moshoeshoe's epic poem as they
15   approached.
Crouching low they proffered their salutations.
The great Moshoeshoe said to them:
'Voice of the Great King and Shield of the Palm Race,
I heard how your weapons tore open the enemies of our
20   friendship.
I thank the noble king of many nations.
May the friendship bring to the Palm Race many harvests.
May it nourish the greatness of generations to come.
In all the rich lands may our children multiply.
25 Let them hold in reverence the name of their Ancestors.
Let this day be remembered by all generations.
I shall slaughter for you many of my choicest beasts.
May you, when you reach the great lands of the noble king,
Carry my words as an emblem of brotherhood in your hearts.'
30 King Moshoeshoe spoke these words softly and with great
    warmth.
Not only was he making the gestures of tradition
But through these noble words
He hoped to convey his deep friendship to the Zulu king.
35 People said it was through Ancestral guidance
That the two great houses should give to each other water.
The arena teemed with crowds of dancers and poets,
Who celebrated the defeat of the troublesome Matiwane.
Yes, the mountains tossed to each other their songs.
40 From the echoes of the night came Zulu and Sotho anthems.

The beat of their feet and swaying movements
Cast shadows into the drops of the night.
The moon emerged slowly over Thaba Bosigo.
It threw its white spears into the chasms of the black stones;
5   It covered the face of the cliffs with white sparks of light.
Even after the singers of the festival had gone to sleep
The valley still rang with the enchantment of song. . . .

Such was the great dawn in Lesotho:
A cock crowed, raising its voice to the new day.
10   The envoys of the king of the Zulus departed.
They sang their anthems until they disappeared from sight.
They sang the great themes of the Sotho nations.
When they came close to their encampments
They celebrated with songs from Moshoeshoe's envoys.
15   In one great crescendo all the regiments joined them.
Turning to go in the direction of great Zululand,
They sang and recited great epics of ancient times.
Great waves of their songs surged forward.
The voice of the crier rose and speared through the sky:
20   'The king's army has destroyed the upstart.
It returns, bringing the heroes of Zululand.
The birds of heaven shall feast on our enemies.
When they are satisfied they shall play to our song.
Peace shall nourish all nations.'
25   When the singer uttered these words his eyes were filled with
       tears.
He remembered long ago, when the nation's heroes set out to
       battle.
He was young then, before he was crippled in battle;
30   Then he would run to join his regiment.
Together they would sing until the enemies fled in terror.
As he finished shouting his message
Messengers from the king's capital approached him and said:
'Your words are the words of a happy heart.
35   Indeed, they would fill the whole nation with joy
But their sweetness turns bitter
So long as the news of the illness of the Female Elephant
Hangs loose in the air like a dark winter cloud.
The king carries a heavy load on his shoulders.

For many days he has not been seen.
Every dawn breaks out with graver news.
The whole nation seems in mourning.'
The man was confused and stung with sadness.
5 He was shattered to know
He would not break the pleasant news to his country and king.
He still could hear the last word that set him on his journey,
A clear voice still saying in his ears:
'You shall behold the great ruler of many nations!
10 How wonderful the spectacle when he smiles at you
And says: "My beautiful and great warrior, your achievement is
      great.
You have brought good news by the feet of the antelope." '
He had imagined how as he mentioned the name of Nogandaya,
15 The king himself would recall the past episodes of this great
      hero
And break out with poems of excellence,
Awarding him, the bringer of good news, with a poem and a
      feast:
20 'Eat and wash away the tiredness from your feet.'
Proud, he would say: 'Insignificant as I am,
All the eyes of the nation are focused on me.
Our nation allows everyone their moment of greatness.'
But all these fantasies were crushed cruelly by fate.
25 He stood there before the king's messengers,
Slouched like someone with broken shoulders.
He felt as if the great Ancestral Spirits had deserted him.
He said, speaking slowly and in a low voice:
'I am like someone who on his day of birth
30 Loses the warmth of both parents.
Sad news is as fearful as the night.
The feet of dancers have withered;
The lips must learn to swallow the beautiful words.
They must keep for future times the message of the feast.'
35 News of victory does not excite all families.
Songs and poems of triumph are uttered amidst tears.
The silent memory gnaws secretly like a poisonous plant.
Those whose relatives have died in battle, wither.
The story of war is told in whispers.

From a distance was heard the voice of someone wailing.
Many thought the Queen Mother had died,
But it was only those who initiate the season of mourning.
By their early grief they anticipate what is to come.
5   The voices of Princess Nomchoba and her followers chilled the
     air.
It was not for her mother alone she grieved,
But her brother, the king, who was crushed by sadness.
The memories of their lives together haunted her,
10 For those who have suffered together keep together;
Their pains travel from one body to another,
Causing simultaneous messages of pain.
Always there is a story that is their own;
By their eyes and lips they speak to each other.
15 Sometimes amidst joyfulness and celebration
They steal out in secret to shed tears together.
Such life-long neighbours of mind are life-spirits of another
     world.
It was because of this Princess Nomchoba, on hearing this
20   news,
Had quickly departed from her home.
She knew she alone could assuage her brother's sadness.
In all their past pains it was Shaka and her mother
Who were the butts of all abuse;
25 For this Nomchoba always put their sadness first.
Shaka remonstrated with his sister and said:
'Do not anticipate the will of the Ancestors.
There are still medicines and great doctors in our land.'
The horizon darkened; clouds gathered like armies for battle;
30 Torrential rains thundered from the mountains;
Throughout the land there hung a threatening silence.
Yet when Shaka heard from his messengers
How General Mdlaka had defeated Matiwane's army
His spirits were elated; he sparkled with new life.
35 He said: 'I knew the son of Nogandaya
Never returns from battle without new honours.
Though my spirit is heavy I shall receive him.'
No sooner had he uttered these words
Than a messenger set out in great speed,
40 Meeting half-way the returning army.

The regiments sang the king's battle song as they neared
    Zululand.
Only Prince Dingane and Prince Mhlangane
Did not share in all this excitement.
5   Indeed, Prince Dingane was enraged and bitter at this war;
He had sustained a deep wound on his forearm.
It scared his mind eternally.
Shaka had said to him as they set out to battle:
'My brother, the wars must be fought by all men of Zululand.'
10 Frightened and angry, he collected those of like minds —
Nobles and commoners who hoped to preserve their positions
Or to gain a new power in a new state.
Prince Dingane decided to avenge himself against his brother.
He and his followers met often, attempting to refine their
15   schemes.
Sometimes new recruits would just listen,
Grinding in their hearts the fruits of revenge
And ready to serve their royal masters.

It was amidst such commotion the attendant announced:
20 'The overseas Strangers request the king's ear.
They desire to bring with them news of great import.
Your representative asks that this be done.
Even if pain and sadness eats the king's mind
He says: "My lord of many nations, the wise say:
25 The tears of those in authority must dry up in their eyes." '
After they had put these words to the king there was deathly
      silence,
People feared lest these words should anger the king;
For those who surround the seats of power live in terror.
30 They survive only by keeping their distance from their masters.
Thus, too, the councillors hesitated,
Hoping the messengers might yet change their minds.
But they stood their ground, demanding the king's ear.
When the message was presented to the king by his
35   councillors
It was mumbled in soft and reverent tones:
'O my lord, the burdens of rulers never end,
But your vast shoulders stretch like those of a mountain.

Each day brings with it new challenges, yet each equals your
    power.
Spread, then, your great shadow.
Let all creatures and all peoples find shelter.
5   I bring the words that nourish themselves from your own words.
The Strangers implore you to grant them your audience.
Respecting you and your orders
We have dared put this matter before you.'
They spoke with special humility, uncertain of the king's
10   response.
Only when they saw his eyes light up did they relax.
Shaka said: 'It is good you told me.
Perhaps this illness may be tamed by foreign medicines.'
Shaka spoke absent-mindedly, as though addressing someone
15   else.

After this news the king's mind was lifted.
He asked rhetorically:
'I had sent an army to fight against Matiwane —
Why have we not heard the full story of its battles?
20   Should our nation be destroyed because its leaders are ailing?
Is the country not run by trusted men of courage?
Where are these men who vowed to serve our land?'
He spoke with a mixture of anger and command.
The Assembly, though flattered by the thought of its power,
25   Were shaken by his manner,
For, in truth, it was how the Assembly felt.
They had been unable to take initiatives.
The king's dominance over the Assembly had been accepted by
    all:
30   Decisions were not meaningful unless endorsed by him.
It was Mgobhozi who spoke first and said:
'My lord, we hear your commands and questions
But we, too, have felt weakened by the king's sadness.
We dare not report the heroism of your army
35   Lest, carried away, we may forget your grief.
The returning army awaits your orders on the border.

Reports tell of their great feats of courage.
They speak of the great battles' of Zulu of Nogandaya.
The army brings beautiful words from Moshoeshoe,
He hails our king and hails your army.'
5 When Mgobhozi spoke these words
Many at the Assembly were filled with pride.
Shaka was silent; he only stared fixedly on the ground.
When he finally raised his head he laughed out loud and
continuously.
10 No one joined in this laughter,
Not knowing what word or thought had provoked it.
Indeed, no one will ever know.
But those who speculate on such things say
The joy of these achievements healed his wound.
15 Like a flash of lightning he saw all at once —
Things eternal. Things temporal.
He felt guilty, too, that his grief exceeded that due to the fallen
heroes.
Perhaps those who say these things speak the truth,
20 For, indeed, soon he began the battle song of the iziChwe
regiment.
The great concourse of the Assembly shouted the song in
accompaniment.
They sang it until tears were seen running down the king's face.
25 The great hero, Mgobhozi-of-the-Mountain
Turned and whispered in the king's ear.
He said, lifting the king's spirits and forging the nation's affairs:
'My lord, the returning heroes must be summoned.'
Because of these words were soon heard
30 The great battle songs of the returning army.
The earth trembled from the beat of their feet.
The voice of the poet burst out, renting the air with words.
He shouted to all winds the king's epic:
'The great fierce power of Ndaba
35 Sits ready for battle:
He has put weapons conveniently on his knees.
No one is certain where he stands,
They are consumed constantly by anxiety.
He does not favour only those of his family.
40 Enemies and relatives fear him alike.

Great power of Ngome!
You crossed and built the Ntontela regiment.
They said he shall never build the Ntontela
But they were mistaken.
5   He dared the ocean but did not cross it.
It was only the Swallow Race that crossed it.
He began his journey at the mid-point of day,
Nor would he fear to start in the afternoon.
He chased a man relentlessly.
10 He chased Mbemba, the son of Gozeni;
He followed him to Silutshana.
He discovered what he thought was a reed-bed for initiates.
He was mistaken: it was not of initiates
But of the Ancestral Spirits at large
15 (They wrought destruction on him)!
The battle axe of Senzangakhona,
Which, as it cuts, accelerates its pace.
He who saw a herd of cattle at the top of the mountain
And brought them down with spears,
20 He rubbed his face with tears!
Lover and shameless bachelor!
Great ruler, who overshadows other rulers at the fords,
All hail! All hail! Thou Black One.'
As the poet declaimed he danced and moved like a boasting
25   warrior.
Sometimes he leapt high into the air;
Sometimes he crouched low like a hunting leopard.
The gathered crowds sang the nation's anthem;
Their voices were solemn like the hum of the Ancestral Spirits.
30 Shaka himself joined the troops and began to dance.
Many said he was possessed by some great, mysterious power.
He turned in a thousand movements like the great river,
His face unsmiling and dark like the black trees of the Nkandla
        forest.
35 His inner pain carried his body like a leaf.
He danced until many felt his pain.
With him wept the great heroes,
Like Ngqengelele, like Ndlela, like Nqoboka.
They entered the arena and danced with him in accompaniment;
40 They moved together as if running into battle.

They danced like this until overtaken by the winds of the
    evening.
The moon was round and rich and full.
It seemed to bring news of long ago
5   Before our Forefathers followed the path into the night.
The mothers' songs enriched the festival;
They ululated in accompaniment to the great anthems.
Late in the night the king rested,
Yet he still thirsted for news of battles against Matiwane.
10   His face lit up with each new episode.

On the following day, as the sun sparkled its ancient light,
Great processions surged forward to the royal grounds,
Eager to see and welcome the famed heroes of the Khahlamba
    mountains.
15   They sang the anthem of Ndaba.
The old men watched in silence with tears of joy.
Many were ornamented with beads and colours.
The great heroes were festooned with garlands of mnyezane
    plant.
20   From all sides came famed councillors of the land:
The sun chose its favourites among them.
It thrust its light on Magaye of the Dibandlela, of the Cele clan.
He was honoured by the whole house of Senzangahkona.
He was tall and his body glistened in the sun with blackness.
25   He was as dark as a cape of rocks from under the cliffs.
He was proud and uncaring and his head was held high to the
    heavens.
Seeing him, you would think he would never die,
Nor would his head succumb to the burden of the earth.
30   There, too, was Ngwane, son of Mepho of the Ngcolosi clan,
So fat his whole body shook in rhythms.
He was known as
'The long-eared one who prefers to fight his own battles,
Who can never be stopped except by scolding.'
35   Ngwane of Mepho lacked the courage of Phahleni of the Dlamini
    clan,
Whose hands were scarred as if by flashes of lightning.
He was a clansman of Sobhuza, king of the Ngwanes.
Before him walked numerous poets:

There was Prince Bhidla of Ngonyama of the Kunene royal
    house,
Who was famed for his wisdom in the laws of nations.
Present also was the great Sotobe, son of Mpangalala.
5 Of him the poet sang:
'Swimmer who used an oxtail to cross the river:
You are like a great ship at sea.'

Among the great heroes sat General Ndlela of Sompisi,
Of whom the poet sang:
10 'Bundle of spears!
He who cannot sleep easily,
His wounds are numerous like huge villages.
The horn-bill that is often the last to fly!
You who are decorated with many colours like a leopard!
15 Survivor of many battles!'

Many of the nation's heroes were there:
The bright feathers everywhere quivered in the wind.
But among all the heroes none excelled in importance General
    Mdlaka.
20 He was the commander over all commanders
And was reputed for having fought in every war.
In festivals numerous poets declaimed his poems.
He turned his head from under his shield-shade
And shared a secret message with a relative.
25 He seemed to say: 'Once more I survived.'
He was loved and respected by all.
He was the favourite of the young recruits.
Often he teased them to great acts of courage.
He did not speak much — he always chose
30 To fight in the front line with young recruits.
Many times he pleaded to be released from his position of
    command.

In this huge gathering was also the great Njikiza,
Known throughout as 'the Inspector of the Deep Lakes'
35 He was the theme of all Ndwandwe orators.
They still queried each other about his feats of the Qokli battle.
The young would tease the old, saying:

'Do not pester us about your glorious wars of yesterday.
Njikiza still lives and boasts your downfall!'
Veterans would stare blankly at each other,
As though to say: 'How can you understand
5   What happened at the battle of Qokli?'
Yes, Prince Maphitha of Sojiyisa was there.
He was of the junior house of Jama
And was governor of the province of the Thembus.
Next to him was Ngomane, once commander of the Mthethwa
10   army.
Because of his kindness Shaka held him in great respect,
Inviting him to be his adviser and friend.
Often they sat and talked together till early morning.
To him Shaka spoke as he was a young boy.
15 It was said in jest: 'Shaka ruled by day; Ngomane ruled by
    night.'

Let your imagination travel into the times of our Forefathers.
See them as they walk on the huge arena:
An endless procession of great men and women of Zululand.
20 How happy is he who saw the great Nomabanga,
Who once stabbed and routed the Ndwandwe army in their
    sleep,
Who there and then was given poems of excellence:
'Great plant that destroyed the Ndwandwe in their sleep!'
25 How beautiful was that day!
Present was the great Nqoboka, son of Langa of Sokhulu clan,
Who had killed many a Ndwandwe hero.

Great numbers of decorated heroes filled the arena:
The councillors and great heroes mingled together.
30 Among them were numerous district and provincial rulers.
At a distance were positioned the nation's regiments,
Each carrying their own emblems and shields.
They were uFasimba with its many young heroes;
Gabangaye, Fojisa, Ndabankulu, Jubinqwanga, Dlambedlu —
35 All of whom made up the numerous iziMpohlo division.
There was Nomdayana, amaPhela, amaKhwenkwe,
iziKwembu, Zimazane, iziNtenjana, iNteke, uMbonambi,
Who together made up the great uMgumanqa division.

Of the women regiments were the famed
Mvuthwamini, Nhlabathi and Ceyane regiments.

On the open grounds could be seen the members of the House of
    Zulu.
5 Among them was Princess Mkhabayi of Jama
Whose feared stare was the talk of all gatherings.
There was Queen Mkabi, daughter of Sodubo of the Nzuza clan.
There was Princess Mawa, twin sister of Princess Mkhabayi;
Princess Nozinhlanga, the eldest daughter of Senzangakhona;
10 Princess Nomqotho of Senzangakhona;
Princess Nomchoba of Senzangakhona, the sister of Shaka.
Princess Nozicubu, the beautiful daughter of Senzangakhona;
Princess Ntikili, the poetess-daughter of Senzangakhona;
Princess Nomaklwa, the tall and beautiful daughter of
15   Senzangakhona;
Of the princes were:
Prince Mhlangana, the quiet son of Senzangakhona;
Prince Mpande, the gentle son of Senzangakhona;
Prince Sigiyana, the fiery-tempered son of Senzangakhona;
20 Prince Sikaka, the bow-legged and stern son of Senzangakhona;
Prince Magwaza, the brave son of Senzangakhona;
Prince Dingane of Senzangakhona, known as 'The doer of
    things';
Prince Nzibe, the wise and brave son of Senzangakhona;
25 Prince Gijima of Senzangakhona, in whose huge residence were
    always feasts.
Many of the princes fought and died in battle.
Some through their own merit, were commanders.

A great silence reigned in the arena
30 As the crowds waited anxiously for the king.
The chests of councillors rose and fell like waves.
Mbopha of Sithayi moved in and out of the royal enclosure,
Making the final round of the arena.
Sometimes he would whisper to General Mdlaka of the Mgazini
35   clan,
Then turn back into the house, attracting a sea of curious eyes.
Suddenly Nomnxamama, the great poet, heralded the king's
    approach.

Shaka emerged, sauntering like a proud bird of summer.
He was adorned in a cluster of loury feathers.
His shoulders were covered with large epaulettes of beads.
He was followed by Mgobhozi-of-the-Mountain.
5   The whole ground thundered with the royal salute of 'Bayede!'
Even the birds that were basking in the sun
Rose in a great array of colours and flew to the sky,
Leaving the earth of people and their joys.
The nation's anthem was heard from all the regiments.
10 It was the Fasimba regiment that led the gathering in song:
The whole crowd sang in one proud voice of triumph:
'You conquered all nations —
Where now shall you send the fighting men?
O! Where else can we find the stubborn rulers?
15 You who conquered all nations, tell us.'
The regiments sang slowly, beating the ground with their feet.
It was said this great feast roused the spirits of Jama
And he came to accompany Shaka, his grandson.
He sat down with him, giving him his power and blessing.
20 The king looked on all sides and smiled,
Satisfied at the numerous heroes and peoples of Zululand.
General Mdlaka saluted,
Calling out the names of the Ancestral heroes:
'Ndaba! You, whose shadow embraces large and smaller nations,
25 You, the great scion of Jama!
I see them! I see the Forefathers close to us.
I call out to them and say: "Jama! You, whose herd of sheep
     have no mercy:
They refused to cross the fords.
30 Anthill, that is surrounded by the heads of men!
Bulbous plant which even farmers can not uproot:
Every year it sprouts again and again from the same field.
Jama is never praised by young women
But by the young girls of Mqekwini."
35 I salute you, my lord, in the name of our great Ancestors.
I salute you in the name of those we left in the mountains.
I salute you in the name of those yet to be born.
We have fulfilled the tasks assigned to us by our king.
We bring the noble presents of King Moshoeshoe of the
40   Basuthos.

To you he asks these warm words of brotherhood to be
    conveyed:
He thanks you for uprooting the troublesome weeds.
He thanks you for silencing the hideous sounds of barking
5   hyenas.
He thanks you, and says through you he will sleep in peace;
He shall walk the paths hitherto infested with thorns!
Even now, my lord, the emissaries from the king
Hurry on their way to your capital.
10 They bring you rich and friendly words from his lips.
I bow to you, scion of Ndaba.
I speak only as the predecessor of those better than me!'
A thunderous roar of 'Bayede!' echoed from the spectators.
Ngomane, the governor of the Mthethwa province, spoke after
15   this address:
'I cannot applaud your words, great warrior,
For such is only the prerogative of my lord.
I put before the nation only what ails us all.
Only for the love of our nation
20 Has the king emerged from the shadows of the night.
The whole nation suffers a great sadness:
The illness of our beloved Mother haunts the whole nation.
The children of Zululand have abandoned their songs of joy;
The nourishment of our lives has been curtailed by winter.
25 The hand that has fed us has been bitten by a poisonous snake!
We see the king now after a long period of absence —
It is only you, General Mdlaka, who have brought him out!'
A loud voice of wailing exploded from the crowd
But Shaka only stared ahead silently.
30 Suddenly he broke out in fury like an angry animal.
He raised his hands and stretched his body, shouting:
'Have the Zulus become a nation of tears?
Have you forgotten that wild lamentations such as these
Bring with them only disasters?
35 Are we not here to acclaim the sacrifices of our heroes?
Are not our heroes left dead in the mountains?'
So great was the silence it seemed a thunderclap had struck the
    ground.
The stabbed lion promenaded up and down the arena,
40 Spearing them with his fierce eyes;

His great stare travelled like balls of fire.
The earth itself seemed frightened of this anger.
There was an old man who doted on Shaka,
Who looked on him as his own child.
5 Yes, the Ancestors implant their word through strange people.
Sometimes they choose a child and make him old;
Sometimes they choose the old and make them young.
Such people are gifted to see into the future times.
The old man peered into him; he saw the round seeds of pain.
10 He saw their roots growing into decay
And turning into a forest!
Tears fell down his face.
It was not because of Shaka's sadness he wept
But because of a fearful dream he had had:
15 Then he had seen the death-companions of the Queen Mother.
He stared at Shaka as he shouted in anger,
Until he suddenly sat down.
Mgobhozi-who-comes-from-the-Mountain said to Mdlaka:
'Tell the story of the great warriors.
20 Let us hear of the heroes who tamed the wild Matiwane.
Why do you make us envious amidst plenty?
Give us full nourishment of these events.'
By his words he brought a light mood to the events:
He hoped to humour the king out of his dark mood!
25 Only he, a warrior and a friend, could play this role.
For those close to each other
Retain for themselves a language for moments of disaster.
They know words they must speak to each other.
Helped by this intervention Ngomane urged Mdlaka to speak.
30 The great general raised his voice gradually and said:
'Words choke me. Too many have come before me
Who had the power to make battles live by their words.
Yet I, too, have the right to speak,
Since history gives birth to history.
35 Yes, I am inspired by their courage.
Through their words, mine are fed by their greatness.
Our journey to battle was hard:
We often traversed high ground and forbidding mountains;
Our routes took us over round bends of broken
40   grounds.

Matiwane placed his army in a depression in the Khahlamba
    mountains.
By our persistence we reached his sanctuary.
We trapped him in his own fortress.
5 After we swallowed all the war herbs
We let loose the young of the lions
To tear apart the tender mountain-buck
In vain Matiwane's army attempted to resist.
From all sides we raided him:
10 Our hungry spears struck at them with the fierceness of the
    rhinoceros.
Great honour must be accorded to our great heroes
Who rushed into battle as if stung by wasps.
The battle fought by Nogandaya comes back clearly to mind.
15 He stabbed until he was tired,
Until he rested beside a pile of enemy dead.
It is he who should receive the honours of war.
I praise him and honour him for my king and nation.'
When Mdlaka had finished speaking
20 Mkhabayi stood up and began the slow boast-dance.
She threw her long string of beads on the commander's feet.
Her action let out a great chorus of joy:
Women began to sing and dance in the arena.
Ululations were heard piercing the high regions of heaven.
25 The regiments began to sing the nation's anthem.
The great ruler stood up and began to dance.
He swayed in slow movements of the sacred songs.
He sang as though to harmonize only with himself.
Finally he shouted out the great battle call.
30 The whole concourse of men responded to him;
Their chests heaved simultaneously like a mighty waterfall,
Like the gigantic waves of the sea tossed by the wind,
Like hands of humanity raised in outrage.
They shouted slogans never heard before.
35 Even the ponderous and portly men stood up and began to
    dance.
Nations often collapse through their indulgence.
Visions of courage often obsess only those who begin epochs.
Thus, too, Shaka still incited his men to greater feats of courage.
40 Mgobhozi danced as if he had learnt a new dance;

He shook the water-logged earth.
Women danced in the arena in boastful turns.
Princess Mkhabayi continued to dance a prayer-dance.
Silently she appealed to the Ancestors to uplift the king's spirit.
5 She thought his mood was caused by the loneliness of power
(His own brothers had their own secret plots).
While these thoughts seethed in her mind
Shaka called out a halt to the dancing:
'It is enough! The Zulu nation shall still be great:
10 Its roots go deep into the earth.
I am elated: behold the great power of the Zulu nation!
I praise and salute those who have fought our wars,
Whom the gods have not deemed necessary to drop their
        weapons,
15 Who still inherit the magic power inherited from our
        Forefathers.
I know through you, Mdlaka, and through you, Zulu of
        Nogandaya,
Through you, Mgobhozi-of-the-Mountains, and through you,
20   Nqoboka,
Through all the great heroes of Zululand —
So long as there is the sun
So long shall the tale of our nation be told,
So long shall they speak of our fearlessness in awe.
25 I praise those who share together these thoughts
And those who are ready to die with me in battle.
Together we have built an eternal mountain.
It is to all the heroes I owe this honour.
I praise heroes of the courage of Ndlela of Sompisi,
30 Of Nkayishana of the Khuzwayo branch of our family,
Of Mpisana, the son of Mnandi, of Zihlandlo of the Mkhize
        clan,
Of Sunduka, the son of Zokufa, of Magaye, the son of Vico.
But how can I count all the heroes of Zululand?
35 They are as many as the stars of the heaven.
Gone is the rivalry of all our related nations.
Gone are all the bickerings of ambitious rulers.
Our heroic regiments have brought peace among all our nations.
King Moshoeshoe of the Basothos is praised
40 He shall be praised for his wisdom by all generations.

243

Let them never say we fought like bulls
Who only fight to test the sharpness of their weapons.
We applaud those who build a home for the children of the
    Palm Race,
5 Who like King Sobhuza of Zikodze have united their nations.
Thus, despite all demands, I never attacked him.
Those who I shall destroy are bandits like Matiwane,
Like Zwide of Langa who cause turmoil and rob our lands.
These are like a fearful plague that wipes out all life.
10 Our peace we owe to the living and the dead.
Those who died in battle live beyond our time:
They are the pride and glory of our nation.
Their widows and children shall be fed by us.
There still remain many wars to fight:
15 No one must sit and indulge in endless feasting
So long as the Soshanganes and the Macingwanes
Still disturb the peace among distant nations.
Every day I see men getting obese
As though the purpose of our rule is to make them prosperous.
20 I shall deal with these, by Monchoba, I swear:
They shall fight until they are grey-haired.'
He spoke these words, agitated, making some of these men
    tremble.
Princess Mkhabayi turned her eyes and looked at her clansmen.
25 Her eyes met those of Prince Dingane.
With him she had shared many secrets.
It was Dingane who had said once to Mkhabayi:
'So long as Shaka lives we shall fight until we are grey-haired.
We shall never stretch our feet and bask in the glories of our
30   Ancestors.'
But such were not the feelings of others in Zululand,
For from all parts of the land there thundered the salute of
    'Bayede!'
The regiments demanded larger wars to fight.

35 When Shaka had given the heroes their war decorations
He released the crowds, letting them break into a festival mood.
Men and women danced furiously in the arena,
Regiments entered the open stage in a great stampede.
They sang the great anthem of the regiments

Raising their short spears they stabbed in mock battles.
Never in all Nguniland had such a spectacle ever been seen.
With solemn movements the women's regiments sang to the
    dead.
5   The poet's voice echoed above the hubbub.
He declaimed the king's epic:
'You destroyed Matiwane of Masumpa of the Ngwane clan;
You captured Sihangu-vuthuka-udaka among the Ngwanes;
You brought Khwelemthini, who lives on high like a bird!
10   You captured Mqabuka
Who is like the hidden side of the mountain!
You brought Ngiyekeni, who frets like a child.
You had external intercourse in a moment of chaos at Nkuna's
    house,
15   He returned with a deep hole caused by Mteli.
You killed Nkuna with a blunt spear,
Causing him to run, injured, to his hiding place.
You went round and round the Phiso mountain in tears.
The cattle of Phisweni broke through in a great stampede.
20   They came and followed you.
The southern wind enters silently, breaking through the main
    door,
Making the occupants bite their lips in terror.
It did not discriminate between the poor and the rich.
25   You who ran along the paths,
Avoiding those that led to Ziwedu.
I saw Ziwedu standing at the gates.
Listen to the words of Ngoboza and Mkhupali:
They say Ngwane is wandering, homeless, in the mountains.
30   Mashongwe of Zibisini had his eyes poked out.
He made him walk up the great ridge of Nkume alone
Until he reached the hills of Hlokohloko.
He brought him back again to Maqwakazi mountain,
Then he let him pass on to Matheku hill.
35   Whirlwind that roars near the assembly,
We shall refuse you the royal salute at emaLangeni villages.
Wild one, whom nobody dares to attack.
The cattle of other people, Shaka, better be left alone.
Often they bring with them endless wars and trouble.
40   Often they carry spears on their tails.

They are like those of Ngobe, the ruler of Sowethu.
When he set out everyone knew it was dawn!
He was like a lion that wakes up with the morning
And devours the cattle of the villages.
5   Busybody that frequented Madilika!
Ferocious one! Luxuriant, uncontrollable vegetation,
Who is like a deep forest that is marred by open spaces!
Mananga often travelled to Jiyampondo;
Mananga was nothing but a councillor in the house of
10   Dibandlela.
Great observer of the south, come and ascertain the north.
Come and see where the whole horizon is the sun!
All-Knowing One who tore open the child from the womb.
Begetter of future times who was like a councillor of Nomgabi.'
15   Thus did the poet Magolwana comment on his greatness.
He jumped high, spinning in the air
As though a branch trembling in the whirlwind.
Sometimes he walked cautiously, swaying like a bunch of
        feathers.
20   Other poets inspired by the same madness followed suit.
The great Nomnxamama joined him.
He declared his poems of excellence.
From all sides came the roar of voices in ecstasy:
Voices echoed, nourishing each other with great episodes.
25   The utterances of poets are like prayers to the Ancestors.
The era of greatness flourishes with the epics of nations.
In their gatherings people spoke in praise of the king:
'He has appointed men of greatness
Who command our wars with skill and courage.
30   How great is that ruler
Who judges a man not for his origins but for his genius!'
Thus they sought to inspire the young
And to infuse in them the spirit of battle.
Everywhere and in every region people talked.
35   Old men and old women mimicked raids on their villages.
They sang heroic epics and songs for their children's children.

Yet not everyone hailed these achievements.
There were those who, eager to exercise greater power,
And devoid of a noble vision, craved only for princely power.

Yet the good of yesterday survive the thief.
Only by their shadows do the usurpers claim the love of the
    sun.
They strut on the grounds attempting to impose their shadows.
5   But the gods punish him who kills for power.
They curse him to go in endless search of nothingness.
They withdraw their children ·
Leaving him to listen only to the words of deceit and half-truths!
Such was the era that now began.
10   The great birds of prey follow the shadows of the night.
They bring words to sing them to the ears of the dead.
The conspirators congregate in the night.
To reinforce their bonds they give each other new names,
Immortalizing grievances suffered by their families.
15   Throughout the land there were poisonous rumours
Claiming the Queen Mother's illness was caused by her
    unhappiness,
Or else that Shaka had exaggerated the whole event
To retrieve his sinking popularity.
20   At the centre of these intrigues were his own brothers.
Dingane never forgot his narrow escape in the war against
    Matiwane.
He requested to visit his aunt Princess Mkhabayi,
She who possessed a thousand eyes
25   And knew the secret directions of the people's minds.
She commanded with the authority of a king;
Even her limbs were thick like those of a warrior.
She reigned supreme in her royal city of ebaQulusini.
She detested those who endlessly broke out in frivolous laughter.
30   To them she would say, looking sternly:
'Bees have a liking for holes that are high.'
She would wake up early at dawn, proclaiming:
'Lest the sun should cast its rays over me.'
Then she would walk to the neighbouring hill
35   Where the ground was covered with a cluster of black stones.
On it were two gigantic trees that thrust their shade into the
    valley.
Here she used to sit and watch the sun rising,
Its soft colour touching her feet.
40   She sat there contentedly, radiating with power,

Sharing her dreams of the night with the sun.
It was there that Dingane approached her.
His arrival was no surprise to her.
She said: 'I was expecting you, son of Mpikase.
5   Like the sea you are restless.
Yet I thought you would never come now
While your wounds are still fresh and raw.'
Princess Mkhabayi spoke these words referring to the stab
    wound
10 He had sustained in the war, and quietly mocking him.
She knew, too, that it was this that irked him.
Often he would say cynically to his listeners:
'How lucky was I on that occasion to come out alive!
Only the Ancestors decreed I should not die.
15 It was there my brother had planned to kill me.'
Mkhabayi spoke kindly to Dingane:
'It seems of late our thoughts often coincide.
What has made them reach this point is not of my doing.
Sometimes those who embark on opposing voyages
20 Reach each other at the confluence of each other's journey.
I want you to speak only that which comes from your heart,
Then I shall map the full course of things as they should be.'
As she spoke she sensed the revenge in Dingane's mind.
She wanted also to know the extent of his thoughts.
25 Indeed, she knew many are carried away by their anger
But in the end they succumb to their masters.
A great anger must never be wasted on one man.
Responding to her, Prince Dingane said:
'I thank you for your words, Great Mother.
30 I am grateful for the trust you have placed in me.
Honourable one, the nation is breaking apart.
Whatever we gained is now being squandered through the
    insanity of war.
The insatiable war-thirst of Shaka gives us no peace.
35 Those who applaud the endless campaigns only do so to please.
We have the right to the destiny of our nation.
We, too, are the children of the king.
No nation was ever built only on wars:
The greatness of a people lies in the richness of their lives.
40 The sacrifice of war is to ensure a better life for their children.

If in every season we set out to fight
Our great nation may soon be bedevilled with rebellions.
Indeed the many foreign generals may yet plot against our
     house.
5 Some trace their descent from the House of Jama.
Surely it is unwise to go on with these wars
When we know no nation dares attack us now.
Even the attack against Matiwane was unnecessary —
It was fought only to enhance Shaka's prestige.
10 Why do we not let Moshoeshoe fight his own wars?
Think how men were killed only for a collection of feathers!
This is not my only complaint.
I am concerned, too, about the nation's heroes:
Why are they forbidden to take wives at will?
15 Many age in the wars and die childless.
Is the future of our nation to be wasted through these wars?'
The great princess merely laughed;
She was amused at seeing someone she once knew
Now matured and arguing the nation's policy as an adult.
20 She stared silently ahead of her and said:
'I do understand your words, Dingane;
They issue from a mind that has searched into many truths.
But I hope you do know the extent of his popularity with the
     troops.
25 People idolize him as the builder of the nation.
They shall never trust anyone who advocates change.'
Dingane seized on these words:
'It is true what you say, Mother,
But then madness is often without eyes.
30 Only a few people are ever truly loyal to their leaders.'
Mkhabayi, unimpressed by this argument, said:
'Do not rush into things, Dingane, my son.
I am old; I have a rich experience of governing people.
I have seen how in some eras loyalty reaches deep
35 And cannot be uprooted even by time.
Besides, it is not easy to plot against Shaka.
With his inner mind he shall sense the whole wicked truth.
He is gifted with a thousand ears and powers.
An era that is desired by many
40 Often matures at its own pace.

The Ancestors themselves protect it by their shadows.
There are many who crave for the same glory you desire.
You must think carefully about these things:
You must search for the truth from all sides.

5   Ask yourself: "Is it my wounds that make me bitter?"
If there be some truth in this, then the Zulu nation is doomed.
A dark day lies ahead of all our children.
Strange as it may sound, I am in full accord with Shaka.
The nation's welfare must override all issues.

10   Great rulers are those who have the power to give and take —
Their right to rule is justified only by their sacrifices.
If Shaka fulfils all the needs of the Zulu nation
Nothing you do or say can persuade people against him.
The importance of governing lies not in feasts and acclaims

15   But in the search for knowledge beyond the present.
It is not history that rescues great rulers from obscurity
But their wisdom, which lays the foundations of future times.
How many lose their power because of too much indulgence!'
These words greatly disturbed Dingane.

20   He felt as if he had put words unwisely and spoken too soon.
He knew also how Mkhabayi's heart underwent changes,
Following always whatever promoted Zulu power.
Of this the poet says:
'The wild rat that opened the paths in the land of Malandela.'

25   Dingane, intent on softening her, said:
'You alone see beyond our visions.
It is you who must give me all relevant directions.
Help me so that I may not act precipitately.
I, too, am impelled by the greater concerns of our nation.'

30   Those who plot together distrust each other.
Dingane sought a guarantee for his aunt's commitment.
He would have preferred her total support,
But as she had spoken kindly of his words
He felt this was enough.

35   Mkhabayi finally said to him:
'I shall think carefully about your words
But you should never rush into things.
There still is time; events may change their course.'
By these words she meant to reinforce him

40   Lest he should leave angry with himself.

Mkhabayi wavered in her own mind;
For, while critical of Shaka's rule,
She still could not embrace Dingane's plans.
Indeed, she knew whichever king was in power
5   Her own position would remain unchanged.
She knew, too, a reckless man only brings greater disaster,
For those eager to be loved never make great rulers!

The earth feels the pains of its children.
It feels the weight of their troubled spirits.
10   Aching bodies breed ominous wounds on the ground;
Deformed power creates its own territory of nightmares.
Man must avoid such pitfalls,
For out of hunger the malevolent spirits wreak destruction on all
        things.
15   Thus were the sad days in the life of Nandi, the daughter of
        Mbengi.
After many years of wandering from region to region,
After she had suffered the humiliations of exile,
After she had tasted the peace and plentifulness of her seasons,
20   The pain had found a home.
Here she is: see her with your own eyes
As she lies on the mat whose reeds speak a secret language.
The voice of Senzangakhona is heard.
The voice of Jama, the fiery-tempered one, echoes.
25   Love did not reach its full bloom of summer.
Often it streaked through the body like a travelling pain.
Through her mind flashed the memories of the kindly
        Mbikwane.
It was he whose image frequented her visions.
30   She thought to herself: 'The great Ancestors have come to fetch
        me.'
She wept as these events overwhelmed her mind.
She felt alone with thoughts she could not share.
She was troubled about her son Shaka.
35   For him she uttered a prayer to the Ancestors:
'Great Forefathers, grant that my child may live a full life.
May he have friends even among the crowds of enemies.'
She was troubled lest he should not live long.
Often she had said to him:

'Mlilwana, you are my only true relative.
You are my brother, my son, my father.'
When hearing this Shaka would retreat to a secluded spot and
    weep.
5   He would say with full certainty:
'Two minds that feel together cannot separate.
The world shall still see the bonds that bind families together!'
It was this, perhaps, that sharpened Shaka's mind.
Even when he danced, he danced fiercely.
10 In the battlefield memories of youth came back constantly,
Making him fight like someone challenged by shadows.
Never did he show his broken spirits in public.
Those who were weak of mind
Often earned from him his contempt.
15 Only those who were kind and generous won his acclaim;
Only those who had the power to wipe out the saddness of others
It was because of this that Nandi was agitated.
She feared lest the pain of her death should overwhelm him,
For only through their bonds had his mind glowed fervently.
20 His genius, orphaned, might wither and die.
Absorbed in these thoughts, she concentrated her gaze on the
    earth
And saw a tuft of her grey hair.
She contrasted each of hers with Shaka's black ones.
25 She felt sad for his youth, knowing from his turbulent life
He may never see the long, majestic shadows of old age.

Nomchoba was often in attendance on her mother.
She directed teams of doctors to various houses and homes.
Every convenient spot was laid down with medicines.
30 Present were the great doctors from Queen Mjatshi's region;
Others came with the great doctor, Mqalane of the Nzusa clan.
Each doctor hoped to establish his lasting honour and name.
Some claimed possession of the potent medicines of the sea;
Nor would they reveal these secrets to others.
35 There were some who squirted their magic force to the sun,
Calling out its curing powers, to revive a fulsome season.
It was because of this
There was commotion at Nandi's residence,
Yet none knew what truly ate deep into her heart.

Shrouded by the shadows of the past, she ached alone.
She fought the violent battles in her mind,
Remembering how festivals often fertilize the plague.
Often laughter invites a fatal wind.
5 The warm words of Jama that had kept them together lost their
       meaning.
But then people believe what is true, according to their faith:
Only what brings the intended gifts is true.
All people harbour their dreams
10 And through them they rise from their nightmares.
It was for this the great doctor, Mqalane,
Probed deep into her mind, searching for the sources of her
       pains.
He said: 'Let the Female Elephant ease her mind.
15 Let her forgive all those who have wronged her.'
It was these words of Mqalane that alarmed Nandi.
She turned and stared at him intently
And began to recall all her family and relatives.
It was because of this that on the following day at dawn
20 The Queen Mother was seen walking out in the open.

After the celebrations Shaka radiated with new life.
To his court came many emissaries,
Some from regions formerly harassed by Matiwane,
Some who had been forced by wars to live like wild animals.
25 Weak rulers advised their subjects to farm only limited fields
Lest their harvests and cattle attract Matiwane's army.
The passage of Matiwane was remembered with tears.
He had wandered everywhere, opening his way with spears.
Again and again he had attacked the Hlubis,
30 Making the proud Mpanzitha a fugitive.
He in turn invaded the Sotho regions of the south,
Clashing with the famed armies of Queen Mantantisi of the
       Tlokwas.
Matiwane himself, having attacked and pushed the Hlubis
35   downwards,
Turned on the Bhele clan south of the Khahlamba mountains.
He seized their numerous cattle and harvests.
Hungry and harassed, his army settled in a mountain fortress.
From here General Mdlaka had dislodged him.

It was from such regions the envoys came to the Zulu court.
Many composed the Zulu ruler's poems in their own language,
Lauding the peace and safety from Matiwane's army.
Shaka felt pleased with all of these events.

5 He called Mdlaka after the campaign against Matiwane and
     said:
'I thank you for eliminating this restless bandit.
The number of people who come to our court
Attest to the fear and destruction he had wrought to the whole
10   region.
They affirm to the peace that is now their heritage.
But there is one thing I would like to hear.
Many who praise our campaigns
Never fail simultaneously to rain curses against Queen
15   Mantantisi.
I always marvel at how men could be terrorized by a woman.
Perhaps there is something in her of which I am ignorant!
She may yet possess magic herbs unknown to us.'
Shaka was only making fun of men who flee from a woman in
20   battle.
Mdlaka said, commenting on Shaka's words:
'My lord, only by your exemplary courage
Have we been able to build our great nation of Zululand.
When I saw your army rush to engage with that of Matiwane
25 I was filled with tears like a child.
It was because of the joy of seeing it in battle
That I knew the army to defeat ours is still to be born.
Many stories are told of this woman.
Even the land of Moshoeshoe is full of her episodes.
30 It is said she fights to protect the throne
Sheltering by these acts her tender son, Prince Skonyela of the
     Tlokwas.
She has conquered many nations,
Fighting and leading her own battles.
35 She has subdued the fierce nation of the Fukengs.
She has put to flight a segment of the proud Kwena nation.
She has routed the peaceful settlements of the Khwakhwa.
But her escapades do not end there, son of Ndaba.

She even conquered the army of the great Moshoeshoe himself.
Only the Hlubis of Mpangazitha defeated her.
The whole southern region of Khahlamba mountains
Curses her very name and ancestry.'
5   Shaka was silent; he shook his head in disbelief.
In a low voice he said: 'Your words startle me, son of Ncidi.
How strange is all this courage in a woman!
But we shall not waste our time on this dust of the age.
If she has lost to the depleted Hlubi army
10 Then she is only a tale for those who like such stories.
Though you say she defeated the noble Moshoeshoe
It is he whom I shall still respect as a hero.
This woman demonstrates how a homeless vagabond
Often possesses greater powers of destruction than peaceful
15   nations.
These barbarian invaders
Conquer and dispossess the rich villages of Man.
A wild collection of desperadoes do not compose a nation,
However numerous their numbers.
20 A true nation is like that of Moshoeshoe,
Which, even if it may suffer temporary defeat,
Its roots go deep and it shall not wither.
Indeed, those who plant and harvest may sometimes be
       overwhelmed
25 But they should not be abandoned to the bandits
Perhaps Moshoeshoe's defeat came as a result of an incompetent
       general
Who commanded a collection of young recruits.
These are now my instructions:
30 Send to Moshoeshoe these words —
Tell him: with a warm heart I have received his words.
They are of a great and noble ruler.
Say explicitly: my troops are committed to defend his lands.'
Mdlaka was pleased with these words,
35 For he himself had loved Moshoeshoe of the Basothos.
He narrated how this great ruler had collected all the wandering
       fugitives
And formed from them a proud and a multitudinous nation.
After many years of wandering and plundering they settled
40   down.

Some who had been his unrelenting enemies were forgiven.
They were given herds of cattle to nourish their children.
Moshoeshoe did not seek to conquer peaceful nations
But those who threatened to invade his lands.
5   His devotion to the Palm Race had seized the imagination of
       many poets.

There was a large gathering of the Council,
Debating and commenting on the affairs of the land,
When an old man approached, trembling as though stricken by
10   some fever.
He saluted the king continuously, as though demanding
       protection.
He said, unlocking his jaws and shouting:
'My lord of nations, I have travelled a long way to tell you my
15   story.
I come from the Beautiful Ones in the land of the Ancestors.
In my dreams I was carried by an angry lion:
I thought it would take me to some spot and crush my bones,
But it carried me gently until we entered into the earth.
20   There, in a giant corridor that leads to the Ancestral home,
We travelled ceaselessly until we reached the centre of the earth
The lion gently put me down on soft ground.
The soil there was red like that of the Ochre mountains
I wandered everywhere, not knowing which direction I should
25   follow.
Finally I reached the lands of the Ancestral regions.
There I saw Mbiya, the son of Soshangane of Kayi.
Still surprised, I heard him greet me warmly:
"Fear nothing, son of Fuzindlu, it is we who have called you.
30   You are in the plentiful region of the Ancestral Forefathers.
The vast plain you see before you is the arena
Where the Ancestral Fathers often meet.
Here they talk of their lives on earth and how you live.
They debate, too, about the requests
35   They receive every day from their children.
Today you have been chosen
To act as the friendly messenger of the Forefathers."
I said to him: "No one can listen to me.
I am neither a hero nor born of a noble family."

But Mbiya said to me: "The Forefathers know what they are
    doing.
You are old and have lived in ancient times.
Your word is more divinely inspired than that of others.
5   You must hurry back and tell all the children of Zululand:
'What is it that has made you live like an impoverished nation?
Smaller nations celebrate greater joys of peace than you.
Are you not the greatest of nations?
Is it not you who must demonstrate what joys attend a great
10   nation?
Make a large feast and pay tribute to the Ancestral Fathers." '
As soon as he finished
He turned away from me, walking fast as if in anger.
Then I saw a long climbing path.
15   This I followed until I found myself standing over the ruins.
When I woke up I waited no longer,
Despite my extreme state of tiredness.
I came here to my lord to tell him of the Ancestral command.'
The men of the Assembly looked at each in startled confusion.
20   Each waited for the person next to him to speak.
Finally, as if drawn by some magic power,
They all turned their eyes to the king.
But Shaka did not comment. He only stared at the ground.
His eyes were like those of a drunken man following an ant.
25   Shaka, speaking deliberately and with searching eyes, said:
'I heard your message, you of the house of Fuzindlu.
Your words leap out of your tongue
Like those of someone who has seen a spirit.
I shall call on the nation's high priest to affirm your truth.'
30   Shaka was sceptical of the whole mysterious episode.
When the priest was called
He indeed confirmed the truth of his message.
The king then dismissed the Assembly
And spoke privately to those he trusted.
35   He told them how he still distrusted these claims,
For, indeed, had Mbiya any deep and serious message to give
He would have come to convey it himself.
After all, was Mbiya not like his own father?
Did he not always speak bluntly to him?
40   Did he not tell him to distrust all hearsay?

Why, then, would he choose an unknown old man?
Would he not know he would not believe such a message?
Shaka spoke seriously, giving a word of command:
'You must lead this old man to the mountains.
5   If, indeed, he speaks through the power of the gods
Even the leopards and the lions shall shy away from him.
If at dawn he still lives then I shall believe his word.'

It was because of these instructions they led him to the forest,
There to await for the coming of the morning.
10   Alas, when the dawn eagle spread its wings
It found only his dried-up leather bag.
No sooner had he entered the forest
Than the fierce guardians of the night devoured him.
Shaka reported this event to the Assembly cynically:
15   'The message of the Ancestral Spirits has been swallowed by the
      mountains.
They have silenced the very lips they sent with their word.
Perhaps affairs that are told with such fanfare
Do not issue from the council of the gods but from our enemies.
20   The nation of Zulu shall not listen to false diviners.
Its fame shall only be built on its strength.
Legend shall not say of us, no sooner had we conquered
Than we started basking in the sun like old women.'
The Assembly endorsed these words, commenting:
25   'Such a message was suspect from the start.
Did it not contradict the one given by the king?
Was it not a few months ago that the king told us
How Mbiya had come in a dream and enjoined him, saying:
"The Zulu army should not put down its weapons.
30   From afar a greater enemy appears.
Every day it evolves plots to conquer and to occupy." '
The great heroes were relieved by these decisions.
There was rejoicing and singing in the land of the Zulus.

The Queen Mother had begun to regain her health.
35   Constantly she took long pleasure walks in her gardens.
The king himself now participated in wedding feasts.
It was in this same year he softened the army laws,
Making all commanders answerable to their own regiments.

He enlarged the regimental towns,
Giving to each a vast number of chosen beasts for their feasting.
This way he silenced even the violent tongues
Who had condemned the stern life of the young recruits.
5 Shaka knew of these rumours but had ignored them.
In all Zululand people bustled with new life and new hopes.
Only the illness of Queen Mtaniya disturbed the festivals.
She was Shaka's grandmother and widow of Jama.
Often he would wash her feet, tending to her like a child.
10 Often he would say: 'You make me balance the old and the
      new.'
When Shaka heard the news of her illness
He abandoned all state affairs and headed for her royal
      residence.
15 Simultaneously he sent a word to the white settlers,
Ordering them to provide their medicines.
The first day passed without much startling news;
The second day her pains became unbearable;
The third day the attendants spoke in whispers.
20 Though Shaka had never displayed any fear of death
He felt struck by this power.
Often he asked the White Strangers about the details of her
      condition.
Death itself seemed to fascinate him.
25 When he heard of the final words of despair
He said: 'How much better is the death of a hero in battle
Than that of someone who dies alone, in silence?
This fills even the heart of a warrior with terror.'
Shaka stayed awake all night,
30 Probing into every aspect of her ebbing life.
Only daybreak brought the final verdict.
From all sides were heard the wailings of her attendants.
Voices burst into monstrous sounds of mourning.
Someone ran as if she had gone insane.
35 She called out: 'Our sun has been extinguished!'
Her voice echoed the king's own thoughts.
He walked a few paces until he stood silently under a large
      shade.
This was where Mtaniya used to sit and bask in the sun.
40 Here the king watched shadows fall right round the circle.

He traced the same dry blades of grass he used to watch
And saw the dew sparkling with freshness.
The man who saw Shaka downcast felt sorry for him.
He led him by the arm like a child.
5   This man was Nqgengelele of the great Buthelezi family.
He was alarmed that so great a hero
Should be so broken by the death of an old woman.
Yet few are consoled in their grief by age.
A bond is a presence whose power does not break easily.
10 Was it not the same Shaka
Who had once said a hero defies the fierce wings of death?
Was it not he who often laughed loud whenever danger
        threatened?
Was it not the same man who had helped many others die in
15   peace?
The gathered crowds cursed the powers of death.
Even the White Strangers were consumed by grief,
For indeed people are one throughout the earth:
In the universe and beyond are our own relatives!
20 They, too, wept, recalling the fate of their parents.
The crowds carried Mtaniya, the daughter of Manyelela.
They heard the slow song of the uFasimba regiment;
From the round bowels of the earth it came.
Her spirit turned to the long horizon of the east
25 Where there is the end without end,
Where there are sacred altars and sacred calabashes.
Here, too, are the guardians of our tales.
People who emerge from dawn are blinded by the sun.
Only at the midday cycle do they begin to see.
30 Behind the night are shadows whom we dare not ask for the
        path.
They stand between us and the serene home of our Forefathers.
In their joy our Forefathers hesitate,
Not knowing if it be wise to ask us to follow them.
35 The shield of branches protects the stranger from the sun
But the yellow leaf still falls onto the ground.

The mourners returned, singing,
Avoiding the gardens that were still haunted by her shadows.
Never before had sadness so overwhelmed the king.

His very mind seemed numbed by pain.
Nqoboka knew Shaka's love for his grandparent
But was still incensed by his sadness.
Shaka mourned and reflected on those he had known
5 And saw their images rush through his mind like specks of light.
Speaking loud to his attendant, he asked:
'How was it when you buried your mother, Noziphuku?'
His reply was incoherent; it faded between his teeth.
He was reluctant to say things that might expose his own
10   weakness.
But Shaka insisted, demanding a clear reply.
Finally, the attendant said to him:
'I wept, my lord. I wept until I remembered:
A man must not shed too many tears.
15 Time must touch the wound with its magic herbs.'
Shaka listened as if this voice spoke directly to him; he
     commented:
'Yes, but sorrow does not grow in the same manner in all
     homes.'
20 As he spoke, his mind was fixed on his experience of grief.
Fear travelled in his body like water,
He felt his heart and mind weaken.
He shook his head and said: 'I hear you!'
He stayed there, absorbed in his own thoughts, all day long.
25 The end of the mourning period did not heal Shaka's spirit.
His anguish was no longer for his grandparent alone,
But for others he had known.
Those voices that had spoken gently to him fell into endlessness.
It is said grief begets grief;
30 Yet a word of wisdom must belong to our times.
To such great minds had Shaka turned for truths.
Even at this time it was Mbikwane of Khayi
Who was summoned from his mission in the coastal regions.
The messenger returned only to report that Mbikwane was
35   dying.
Shaka was shattered.
The Assembly attempted in vain to revive his spirits.
Sometimes he would be heard speaking alone in the dark.
To the horror of everyone, he ordered
40 That all his favourite breed of cattle be slaughtered.

With them he made a huge Ancestral sacrifice,
Pleading with the Forefathers to spare those he loved,
Appealing to the Creator of All Things that their return be
      postponed.
5   In truth, it is not proper
That the heart should suffer a double grief.
While the feasting for the Ancestral Fathers was being held
He sat quietly in his own dark house.
He called on his Ancestral Forefathers, Ndaba, Jama, Phunga,
10 And all those before them to come to his aid.
He asked them to help him emerge from the night.
The great doctor, Mqalane, gave him the red drugs.
He washed his feet with green herbs,
Chanting the great songs of the green season.
15 He made the king cast his shadow over the sacred symbol of the
      circle.
Simultaneously the great doctor uttered the sacred words of
      recovery:
'Let the great nation of Zulu grow in strength.
20 Let the sun bring fruitfulness.
Let the bonds that bind us together be eternal.
Let those who plot against us be destroyed.'
As he spoke these words he touched the walls with his hands.
Sometimes he raised his fingers as if in salutation.
25 Then he took the magic tail of Jama's bull and wiped the
      ground.
Finally, he said to the king:
'I ask my lord to cease all commitments to affairs of state.
Let him give his heart and mind the nourishment of happy
30   thoughts.
He must let these magic herbs generate their own powers.
For indeed, my lord, unhappiness is a power.
It is stirred by our own spirits.
The greatest force is from our own body and mind.
35 Through its harmony, and that of others, a new sun is born
And the children of the earth begin a new life again.'
He gave the king the root of the sacred plant,
Asking him to chew it and squirt at the morning sun,
And to call on all the young powers of the new season.
40 It is said all plants listen to the words of their relatives.

The king washed his body with the herbs of light
Whose power often heralds the coming of a great harvest.
· He adorned himself with ceremonial attire.
As he stepped out into the open
5   There was a loud cry of 'Bayede! wiZulu!'
Despite his troubled mind
He felt as though he was lifted by the voice of the Assembly.
He knew then people are a source of power.
He spoke only a few words but his presence excited in them a
10   new season.
He thanked the crowds for the nourishment of his mind.
When he was about to sit, he turned his eyes
And met those of Mgobhozi-of-the-Mountain.
The two great heroes shared the rich moment of their lives
15   together.
All was silence at the Assembly
As the Strangers who had come to mourn the king's
      grandparent arrived.
Shaka watched them as if to trace some secret message in their
20   movements.
He said, addressing his words to the Assembly:
'I greet those who are the subjects of King George.
Our great nation expresses its welcome to them.
We praise them for all the things they have done.
25   We praise those who bequeath the richness of their talents to
      others.
We honour Fynn who tended my grandparent,
Who has kept order and justice among those at the harbour
      region.
30   From today on our regiments shall sit firmly on their shields
Whenever they meet the overseas Strangers.
In this way we shall show our bonds to George's subjects.
We of Zululand fight only those who challenge us
And cause disorder to the whole region of the Palm Race.
35   I thank the Strangers and give them the land adjoining the
      harbour.
This shall be their shelter from the great seas rains.
I want peace between the peoples of Zulu and of George —
All are truly my subjects and live under my protection.
40. These acts of friendship

Shall nourish our lands with great harvests.
Both our nations shall store together their wisdom.
Like us, George seeks to unite all the white nations.
If by this great vision the Palm Race and the White Race unite
5 Then they shall abide by one great law.
For nations turn into bandits
Only when they are without an all-embracing order.
In the name of the Zulu nation and all its allies,
I thank the dogs of King George for mourning with us.
10 We must show them our rich life of Zululand,
And let them teach whatever of their ways
Seems rich and relevant to our nation.
Treat them as friends and honoured guests of our land.'
The king uttered these words with a deep seriousness.
15 His spirits had commanding power.
He spoke slowly as if paying attention to each word and detail.
Those in the Assembly listened in awe.
The Strangers responded with solemn words and said:
'Your words, Lord of Nations, fill us with joy.
20 Ever since we came to your lands
We were treated as if we were your own clansmen.
We have travelled and seen many nations in many lands
But none receive and treat strangers as you do.
We thank you, too, for allowing us to live under your protection.
25 We promise: all we do shall be for peace.
We shall observe the great laws of the land.
Your warm words shall be conveyed to our king.
To him we shall tell of your generosity and kindness.
We come to your capital to mourn
30 Not only from a desire to cement friendship between nations
But to share in the sadness of a relative,
For you are truly this to us.'

The king seemed embarrassed by these words.
He made a joke to ease this serious mood:
35 'Let us drink and be happy
And hear the stories of lands beyond our regions.'
By these words he attempted to suppress his own sadness.
He said: 'Tell me, you of the overseas nations,
What do your wise men say about the beginnings of life?

Do you live guarded by Ancestral Forefathers as we do?'
They itched with the opportunity to spell out their religion,
Even hoping this might win them a much-prized convert.
Fynn, quick to answer, said to the king:

5 'My lord, our religion covers many peoples.
We worship only the all-powerful God of the Heavens,
He who sent his only Son to teach and die for all nations.
It is he who receives and answers all our prayers.
Those who are good at heart go to his place of joy.

10 Those who are evil burn in an eternal fire.
By the guidance of his Son
And the sacrifice he made,
We love and worship him as our Saviour.'
Shaka pondered these words for some time

15 And finally said: 'Our religions are much the same:
We worship Mvelinqangi, the Creator of All Things.
You worship an Almighty who is the Creator of Heaven and
        Earth.
Your Creator and ours are one.

20 They differ only in name.
Your Saviour is no different from our Ancestors,
The Ancestors who are the Great Spirits of our Forefathers.
It is they who have bequeathed to us our great laws.
By their sacrifice they created for us a new world.

25 Of this we are trustees and gave the best for our children.
The Forefathers have made us noble by their deeds.
In praise of them we enhance their names by our own deeds.
They, indeed, died for us to make a better world.
Through their love they intervene on our behalf to the

30   All-Powerful Creator.
Yet the criminals and witches shall not burn in an eternal fire:
Their death is sufficient punishment for them.
How can they be punished after death
When their crimes were committed on our earth?

35 Is it not we who judge their acts?
It is not we who determine the punishment?
How can Mvelinqangi consign his children to an eternal fire?
Our God, Mvelinqangi, forgives them for their crimes,
Since all their deeds are committed in the ignorance of life on

40   earth.

Even I could not punish someone eternally.
Your God seems harsh and cruel.
If I condemn a man to death I do not seek to perpetuate his
    pain;
5 When I make him pay a fine, it is enough.
A man condemned must not be treated like a wild animal
But must be sentenced and allowed to die a wholesome death.'
The Strangers were puzzled by these comments.
Gently they said: 'My lord, we do not agree.
10 A man is more valuable alive than dead.
It is better he suffers in confinement
And is able to set out again to a new life.'
Shaka shook his head, speaking deliberately:
'The life of a man is not of the body, but of the spirit.
15 If he lives, he must stand up and recite the heroic poems of his
    family,
Knowing his deeds and those of his clan are admirable.
There should be no one to remind him of his crime.'
He said, continuing to comment on the religion of the Palm
20   Race:
'It is clear each nation must appeal through its own Ancestors.
Should it abandon them and follow the customs of foreigners,
It would soon succumb and be enslaved by them;
It would lose the power to challenge its enemies.
25 It is for this I praise the religion you hold
For it enshrines the demands of your own nation.'
Promptly they sought to dispute these words:
'It is not so, my lord.
Our religion comes from nations other than ours.
30 As we were enhanced by it we sought to share its brotherhood
    with others.'
Shaka calmly answered and said:
'I hear you, but, in truth, when you spread this religion
You include in it those who are your own Ancestors.'
35 Without answering, they stared silently at each other.
Shaka continued and said: 'The Ancestors prefer their own
    children.
When we prepare the weapons bequeathed to us by them
We call on their names and make such sacrifices as will befit
40   their honour.

After this we choose our own destiny.
Only when we fail do we turn to them.
Every man trusts in the loyalty of his own family.
When there is a war to be waged
5 It is the families that are summoned first.
Thus, a nation appeals for success through the Spirits of its
      families.
It calls on all those who founded the nation.
To them people sing the sacred hymns and ask for their
10   assistance.
From their inner life the Ancestors still listen to our prayers.
Old generations re-live through us their unfulfilled dreams.
We, their children, inherit the gifts of their achievements.
Those who come after us
15 Shall also inherit the gifts of our sacrifices.
It is for this we must always enrich our heritage.
Generations hereafter must say:
"Here lie the great heroes who enhanced our nation."
The earth belongs to no one:
20 It is for all those who live in it and make it fertile,
Those who shall be here, long after our age.'
This debate continued over a long period.
Sometimes they agreed with the king, sometimes they differed.
Finally Shaka said: 'What law surpasses all other laws?'
25 They all turned, puzzled by this sudden question.
Eventually Farewell said hesitatingly:
'It is the law that demands one should love one's neighbour.
This is the greatest command of our religion.'
Shaka agreed with these words and said:
30 'You speak of things that are true of our life in Zululand.
By the command of our Ancestors, families share with each
      other.
The stranger who travels must be welcomed.
He must be given a comfortable place to sleep;
35 When he embarks again on his journey
He must be given provisions;
For to refuse others in times of plenty debases life itself.
Today, when you travel through the length and breadth of
      Zululand,
40 Everywhere you go you will find food and shelter.'

They consented to these words,
Saying they themselves were witnesses of this truth.
They admitted, too, that this practice
Their own nations still had to learn.
5 There, whenever one man gives shelter
It was made known to all nations.
Referring to the tenets of their religion, they said:
'Such noble acts are fully rewarded in Heaven.'
The Assembly could not contain itself; it burst out laughing.
10 Questioning the Strangers, they asked:
'How do the spirits of the dead ascend to the skies,
Leaving all powers of their lives centred here on earth?'
Laughing at the idea, the wise men commented:
'Only children look for an after-life in the distant skies,
15 Believing there in the high dome live the gods and their
        grandmothers.
But to the old the truth of life issues from the earth.
Beyond our earth are many worlds.
From there inhabitants stare at us from an enveloping night.'
20 These comments led to fierce debates about the universe.
Someone said: 'The earth is the Great Parent.
It is the breast from which humanity is fed.
Till the end of time it boasts the endlessness of its nourishment.
From it many creatures and peoples feed.
25 Thus it is called the Great Parent and Provider.
To fertilize herself she devours her own children,
Nor does she ever cease to give birth to new generations.
Her four circles teem with humanity.
She is the sister to other worlds,
30 For, our Forefathers say, there are many others.
Their fields and valleys are inhabited by peoples like us.
In them are many creatures we have never known.
The wonders of the universe are inconceivable to us.
It is for this reason humanity learns every day.
35 Those of yesterday give us their heroic epics.
By their power and insistence we discover our own truths.
For to know is the gift of the Ancestors.
They give endowment that enriches our paths.
In truth, knowledge is the convergence of all experience.
40 Things of the universe cannot be fully comprehended:

Some we know only by the instrument of our feelings.
Some remain eternally hidden from us.
Some are manifest in things that endure by the power of others;
Some retain their substance and defy all laws of death,
5   Yet others are always born.
They issue constantly from the decay of their parents
And the full cycle of eternal truth is maintained.
Each event is a truth of its past and present.
All things take nourishment from each other's being.
10   The web of being never ends.
The wise keep a place for their Ancestors.
They show the way to generations to come,
Raising the red glow of light from the night.'
It was as if he had cast a spell on them.
15   A deathly silence fell on the Assembly. They all whispered his
       name,
For this was the great Jojo, of the Msane clan.
Many regions sang his praises of wisdom.
Rulers and governors lured him to their courts,
20   Feasts and celebrations heralded his visits.

When this debate was over
Shaka invited the Strangers to his royal enclosure.
There he ordered meat and beer to be served.
He was eager to continue the debate of the Assembly.
25   He said: 'Tell me about the medicines of your land.
Have your doctors discovered the herb of immortal life?
It is not for myself I ask (I have set myself only the death of a
       warrior)
But for all those who are close to me.
30   I am concerned about my father Mbikwane of Soshangane
Who even now is ailing in the iLlovu region.
I am anxious, too, about my mother
Whose health is enfeebled by constant illness.'
He spoke these words softly, in a low voice,
35   Showing deep concern for his relatives and friends.
The Strangers felt the power of his words.
They were reluctant to reply,
Knowing such medicines were nowhere to be found.
Finally they said: 'Lord of Nations, we understand your feelings.

Although we possess many medicines,
We have not yet found the medicine to give eternal life.'
They spoke these words hesitatingly,
Fearing to disappoint the king.
5   Softening the impact of these words,
And inwardly hoping he would still demand their medicines,
      they said:
'Yet we have herbs that turn grey hair black
And restore the appearance of youth in an ageing person.
10   This way, perhaps, even the inner self is rejuvenated.'
Shaka was enthralled by these possibilities.
He said: 'If your medicines can change the hair,
Surely they must bring back the youthful life of the old;
For no medicine cures only one part of the body.
15   By rubbing it everywhere
It would renew the strength to the whole person
And regrow the flesh in all the ageing regions.'
The visitors were alarmed but pleased at these claims.
Shaka said: 'I want you to bring me these medicines.
20   You must not delay; cross the sea on foot if necessary.'
They hesitated, claiming their ships had floundered at the
      harbour,
But promised to use those that were still at sea.
Shaka commanded them:
25   'I rule the great nation of Zulus.
Take whatever numbers you need to repair these boats!'
Seized by this speck of hope Shaka had begun to believe
He might yet save the life of his parent.
The visitors were pleased and elated by the king's words.
30   They spoke of the rich medicines of their land,
How these were mixed to make infinite varieties of cures.
They praised too the great medicines of Zululand,
Requesting that the great Mqalane
Should tell them of these secrets.
35   Mqalane, speaking slowly and deliberately, said:
'There are many types of healers in our land:
There are those who use only herbs to cure the body —
These know only qualities of plants, their roots, and juices;
There are healers who also are diviners —
40   These attempt to heal the mind of its scars.

For, like the body, words and fears injure the mind.
With magic bones and powerful songs they divine the heart's
    secrets.
Diviners do not tell the unknown
But are guided in their search by the Ancestors and strong
    medicines.
It is they, too, who interpret the words of the Ancestors.
While doctors of herbs learn through their masters,
A diviner inherits his gift directly from the Creator.
In addition to these there are many others,
Who excel in their various skills in medicine.
Some claim the power to direct the heaven's thunderbolts,
But I find such powers highly suspect.
Yet I do not doubt man's resources to create and to destroy.
Those who threaten with destruction succeed,
Since they possess the power to weaken others.
Every family has deep hatred of witches and sorcerers:
These are the enemies who live by the power of death.'
Farewell now questioned Mqalane, saying:
'How can one tell who, in truth, is a witch and who is not?'
The great doctor, replying, took his time.
Smiling wryly at what he thought was a childish question, he
    said:
'A witch is known by those who are victims of his words and
    powers.
The magic bones of a diviner are only a guide,
Giving to all a point of focus.
A witch does not keep to himself his evil intent:
He lives and acts and talks like one possessed by a restless
    power.
Often he lives alone, communicating only with wild animals.
But let me continue and tell you of our doctors and medicines:
The greatest doctors seem to have lived in the past —
By their heritage we know a great doctor heals the body and the
    mind.
Diseases and illnesses eat both the body and the mind.
While they manifest themselves with violence in the flesh,
They devastate the fierce healing powers possessed by the mind.
An illness attempts to seize the body totally,
Breaking the balance of control possessed by the mind.

Great medicines deter the speed of decay,
Enabling the mind to assert its power of healing.
Only a balance between the two ensures a cure.
Diviners and doctors together work on the two regions of being.
5 Wars cannot be won through medicines
But by the strength and strategies evolved by man.
A nation's power lies in its weapons and poems.
From our experience there are three aspects to any cure:
They are the body, the mind and the medicine.
10 None of them surpasses the other in power; they act in concert.
Thus, too, those who seek a doctor must be accompanied,
For one's relatives are a source of disease or cure.
All medicines are only a temporary measure.
No one must swear by the medicines he uses;
15 No one guarantees immortal life by his cures,
And so no one ever thanks doctors and healers for their
     medicines.
Not even by their skills can they give life.'
When he said these words
20 The Strangers were alarmed, remembering their own promises.
Shaka spoke at this point: 'Yes, it may be so to us, Mqalane,
But the people of King George have found the herb of eternal
     life;
Through it the body is given a new power of growth.
25 Thus in eternal cycles life revives and never ends.'
Mqalane only said in a few words:
'I shall believe only when I see such medicines, my lord.
For if such powerful medicines existed
They would never leave them behind in their homes.
30 Who would not always carry such cures,
Knowing ageing could seize a man in foreign lands?'
After these exchanges
There was no clear word from the Strangers. They only said:
'Great doctor! Don't you see?
35 Such great medicines can only be kept for our kings and queens.
We are mere messengers of those whom we dare not gaze upon.'
The Strangers thought Shaka would say something in their
     support
But he never commented, letting them talk uninterruptedly.
40 His eyes were focused on their foreheads

As if he saw a shadow that made him uncertain.
What was in Shaka's mind at that moment? People have often
asked.

Book Twelve: The long shadows of death

The tragic events in the life of Shaka accumulate. He is often in a dark mood, particularly because his mother — his twin spirit in the Zulu sense — is constantly ailing. But there are also constant deaths among those he loves, of whom he says, 'Must the shade be seized by the whirlwind?' In the battle against Sikhunyana, Mgobhozi, his old fighting companion, fights his last and greatest battle. His death almost unhinges Shaka's mind. At the same period Mbikwane dies. Shaka, however, emerges from those events strong and heroic. He becomes more reflective about things concerning the exercise of his military genius. His brilliant military innovations have been copied by many rulers and adventurers and have resulted in the creation of many Nguni kingdoms beyond the orbit of immediate Zulu power. Internally, the threat comes from his brothers, who are plotting for his assassination.

In the year of the locust Shaka dreamt a terrible dream.
It was as if he stood alone at the gates of Bulawayo city.
He shouted but no one heard his voice;
Only the winds howled and whistled,
5   Flinging the high branches of the dry msululu plants,
Scattering dry leaves in the great empty arena.
A great roar of voices, as though of a stampeding crowd,
Shot through from all passes of the rugged mountains.
It was as if the whole earth was going to break apart,
10   Splitting itself into fragments.
Every time Shaka gazed into the northern regions

He saw a blaze of fire circling as if to compete with the sun.
In all this chaos he heard the shouting voice of Nandi.
It was as though someone was trapped in a bog.
As he ran in her direction he encountered Mgobhozi,
5 He was holding a spear that was imbedded in his chest.
Shaka attempted to extract it as he ran to his parent.
He heard her scolding voice calling out to him:
'Bury him, Mlilwana, he is already dead!'
He felt tears cover his whole face.
10 Embarrassed he tried to wipe them away
But they poured from his face like rain.
He saw Mgobhozi walking slowly, approaching the gates of
      Bulawayo.
He was declaiming his poems.
15 Suddenly, as if from nowhere,
He heard the singing of the great uFasimba regiment.
It seemed to rise in volume as it approached.
Among these voices he could clearly hear that of Mgobhozi.
From the other side of the fence emerged Mbiya.
20 Mgobhozi now shouted the last words of the epic poem,
Then lay flat on the ground in a pool of blood.
A long procession of regimental dancers picked up his body
And walked away in the direction of a large cattle-fold,
Rousing to a state of madness the black and white bulls.
25 It was this riotous noise that woke him from the dream.
After this nightmare he did not sleep:
He ordered there and then that Mgobhozi be summoned.
The great hero arrived at the royal residence at the crack of
      dawn.
30 He said, making a joke: 'My Lord of Nations,
You woke me up from a night of celebration.'
But Shaka did not laugh;
His face was contorted with sadness and anxiety.
Mgobhozi said: 'What has happened, my lord?
35 I hear no noise of clanging weapons.'
Shaka began narrating his horrible dream.
As he concluded Mgobhozi-of-the-Mountain said to him:
'My lord, it is for you I feel unhappy and sad.
As for me my body and mind are in their best state.
40 You should know, my lord: I shall die in battle like a true hero

My body shall be surrounded by many enemy victims.
Yet your dream is fearful, since it is a king's dream.
Were it of someone else no one would notice.
I only listen to its follies because of my love for you.
5 Had it not been so, I would say:
'These dreams have roots in evil thoughts of the dreamer.
To die running from enemies is a curse every hero fears.'
Shaka was quiet, as though these words did not please him.
He said finally: 'O, Mgobhozi, my brother, I thank the
10   Ancestors —
I thank them that you still live.
I am grateful to them that I can still see you with my own eyes;
This way I, too, can bid you farewell.
My dream was fearful; I am alarmed at its message.
15 I remain alone; the supporting poles against which I lean
Gradually yield to the determined bite of wild ants.'
Mgobhozi was alarmed at these words
For he knew Shaka was not a coward;
Besides, he always possessed some power of prediction.
20 He said to him: 'My lord, give me time to think.
I have just woken up; my mind is still befogged with sleep.
Do not worry too much about this message.
The enemies of our nation may take advantage of our moment of
      weakness.'
25 Shaka, commenting on these words said: 'You have spoken the
      truth, Mgobhozi.
Your words come from a mind that is strong and brave. I
      respect them.
Besides, I know your inner truths as you know mine.
30 It is as though we grew up in one family.'
As they parted they warmly embraced,
Clasping each other's hand until they burst into laughter.

The Assembly sat discussing many affairs of the nation,
But Shaka's mind roamed restlessly.
35 He had complained about the lethargy of the army.
Too long, he said, they had stayed without battle.
Who knows, perhaps he was made uneasy by the ghostly
      shadows
That hovered over the large arena,

Walking there as memories of those he had known.
To Nandi, his mother, he had once said:
'I even fear to depart from your residence of Mkhindini,
As though, when I do, I may turn back to find you no more,
5   To be greeted only by songs of the foolish bird of the brook.'
Even the numerous medicines for his parent did not assuage his
    mind.
To his words Nandi had commented:
'I am only grateful that I have lived to see you grow.
10   Your mind surpasses that of any king who ever lived.
For me that is the only life I ever desired.
But you must always be on the alert:
Watch for people whose jealousy turns them into puff-adders.
Never trust those who are quick to praise:
15   It is no easy task to rule over people.
Such was the case in ancient times and such is your fate today.
You are still young and many years still lie ahead of you.
But only remember: with the growth of kingdoms, enemies
    multiply.'
20   These words ate into Shaka's mind.
He knew he had few friends who would speak without fear,
Or else acknowledge fully the era that had enriched their lives.
Shaka not only had to shoulder the tasks of governing
But also had to quell the endless quarrels among his brothers.
25   No one ever forgives a ruler who fails:
People never put a leader's problems before their own.
Thus each era must embellish itself with its own successes,
Making those who follow look with awe on the feats of their
    Ancestors.
30   Such were the demands on Shaka's life.
But he was no old man with whom to speak;
He was only a young man who still could dance all the dances
    of the young.

It was at this time that a messenger came to Shaka's court,
35   Reporting that the little cockerel of Zwide had begun to flap its
    wings.
For no sooner had Zwide died
Than Sikhunyana of the junior royal house seized power.
It was said of King Zwide he had died a horrible death.

From the wily Queen, Mjantshi, he had a necklace of
    poison-beads;
This he proudly wore, courting his own death.
Prince Sikhunyana then fought and defeated the armies
5 Of Prince Shemane, the rightful heir, Prince Somaphunga and
    Prince Mawewe.
Setting himself up as ruler he began planning his return to
    Zululand.
He hoped, through war, to regain the lands of his Forefathers
10 And there make the necessary sacrifices to win their love.

His chief commander pestered him often:
'Shaka has not set out on a large campaign for many seasons.
Rumour has it that Mqalane, the great king's doctor,
Has advised against further wars and bloodshed.
15 He has told the Zulus that the sun's eclipse
Comes only to warn the conquerors to spare others the fate of
    beasts.
For us, this is the moment to attack,
Routing them while they hang up their weapons.
20 By giving shelter to your brother, Somaphunga,
Shaka intends to split and weaken your family.
He hopes people will say: "Why should we fight and die in
    foreign lands,
While Somaphunga, one of Zwide's sons, lives in Zululand?
25 Are not his followers already settled in our ancient lands?"'
The military chief would say this, referring to reports
Of how Shaka welcomed Zwide's son, Somaphunga,
Giving him food and cattle and his family's ancient lands under
    Malanda.
30 He overlooked and forgave the old quarrels between him and his
    father.
Sikhuyana's chief commander advised him:
'It is no use following your relative, Soshangane, to the north.
People shall always resent having left their ancient homes.
35 Going further than this spells only endless troubles.
Yet, should you stay in this region you shall soon regret it,
For, in truth, many are ready to desert you.
There is only one solution to all this: attack the Zulus!
Push them out of your Forefathers' lands.

Some among them may even join you,
Demanding the return of their own ancient lands.'
Sikhunyana only repeated what he had always said:
'How can I attack the Zulus when they are so powerful?
5   Shall I not be throwing myself into the lion's mouth?
Should I survive, will I not lose even this foreign home?
Shall I not have foolishly stirred the restless bees in their hive?'

The commander-in-chief answered angrily:
'My lord, I am old and experienced.
10   I knew Shaka when he counted only a few followers.
Yet because of his skill and courage
He attacked your father's kingdom and won.
You, too, stand the same chances against him,
For it is said the wrongs of the young are avenged by them;
15   Only those of the old are avenged through fire-brands.
Above all, there are strong rumours from all Zululand
Claiming his brothers constantly plot against him.
No longer is he the popular and undisputed ruler of Zululand.
The attacks of your army could break his power.
20   Even his brothers could take advantage of this
And begin to create centres of resistance against him.'
It was because of all these persuasions
That Sikhunyana began to prepare for battle,
His army relying on the tactic of surprise.

25   A messenger came to the Zulu king's court,
Reporting breathlessly how Sikhunyana's army had attacked the
         borders.
When Shaka heard this he rubbed his hands together with joy.
He was like a child that had been given its first adult gift.
30   There and then he called Mdlaka and Ndlela
And spoke, half to himself half to his listeners:
'How beautiful! The bride has entered our own grounds.
I swear by Nomchoba, the daughter of my father, we shall
         dance.
35   They say Sikhunyana of Zwide has challenged me.
Did I not leave him alone to eat more corn in distant lands?
Did he not learn from the old men of the Ndwandwe nation
How I devastated his war-mongering parent?'

He spoke many different things all at once,
Like someone drugged with the red herbs.
He constantly spat on the ground in an act of contempt.
He said: 'All the regiments must be let loose for this battle.
5 I shall make certain not even his mourners shall stay alive.
In this war even little boys will have a place among heroes;
They shall have the taste of their first great battle.'
General Mdlaka applauded these words:
'Yes, my lord, it is the fate of Sikhunyana.
10 The child has entered the mouth of the lion.
Your army shall celebrate when they hear of this invasion.
I am filled with pity for the son of Zwide.
His Ancestors, for some reason, have deserted him.'
Laughingly, the great son of Sompisi, Ndlela, endorsed these
15   words.
He looked forward to this battle as though it were some festival.

The whole country was seized by a whirlwind war.
Old warriors sang their songs of long-forgotten battles.
The young men shouted to each other their famous war-slogans:
20 'How happy is the man who shall see Sikhunyana!'
Even Njikiza, the son of Cuba, spoke secretly to his battle club:
'My love, Nohlolamazibuko, have you heard?
We are invited to a great dance of the mountains?'
As he spoke he touched its head with his fingers.
25 Then he took it into the sun and, mumbling to himself, he said:
'Let the ants be trapped in its head and body.
To them is given the feast of all cumbersome creatures of earth!'

Everywhere and in every hill echoed the hubbub of war.
As Shaka sat at the Assembly,
30 Discussing with his generals the war strategy against
        Sikhunyana,
A great collection of white flowers were scattered in the arena.
Everywhere at Bulawayo the fence trembled with overhanging
        whiteness.
35 Shaka asked the Strangers-from-across-the-ocean:
'What is the meaning of these flowers in this war?'
They were confused, not knowing what risks they took by
        answering,

Fearing, too, lest they should be seen playing the game of
    diviners.
Shaka, without waiting, said:
'Sikhunyana and his army has retreated.'
5   No sooner had he said this than a messenger arrived,
    announcing:
'Great King of Kings, perhaps because of some fear,
Or perhaps because he heard of the mobilizing of the regiments,
Or else was overwhelmed by the power you cast on your
10   enemies,
Sikhunyana has retreated to the furthest point of our borders!'
The Strangers looked at each other in great consternation.
This news was broadcast to all the regiments;
The following day they set out in hot pursuit.
15   When the Strangers woke up they saw only the women and
    children.

The great concourse of troops moved in the direction of
    Nobamba.
There they stopped at the royal Ancestral graves,
20   To pay tribute to the great heroes of the Zulu nation.
Then they set out in the direction of Phongolo region.
The volume of song was like a river after rains.
The young boy carriers danced and laughed with their heroes.
Shaka ordered Fynn and his followers
25   To bring with them their tents.
He knew Sikhunyana's army would think they were some new
    battle device.
With boyish glee Shaka looked forward to their reactions.
He often referred to these tents jocularly as the 'houses of the
30   wind'.
Young boys made fun of them,
Anticipating in their fireside stories the terrors of battle.
With great speed the troops followed the king,
But soon those ahead of him began to lag,
35   Beaten back by the long march and the heat of the sun.
They constantly demanded a halt.
Shaka was pleased at this chance to invigorate the army.
Finally the army rested near Ntombe,
The valley sheltered by Ndololwane and Ncuke mountains.

At Ndololwane were assembled the many troops of Sikhunyana.
Nqoboka and others stared at them
As though to imply they had been seized by some madness.
Often he had to be restrained from launching his own raid.
5　He slept reluctantly as though dawn would be too long coming.
On the following day a small body of commanders climbed the
　　hill,
Keen to assess the aspects of enemy positions.

Shaka commanded them to follow him to a high vantage point.
10　From there they debated the many sides of the war arena.
On returning, Shaka called together all the army generals:
'We must give due to Sikhunyana, the son of Zwide.
He has amassed an impressive array of battle heroes.
His army seems ready and restless for battle.
15　It is large in numbers and spreads to all strategic points.
We must attack directly, hurling our regiments on him
As though each section was made of a separate army.
By a sudden and swift movement we must reassemble,
Breaking into the thickest centre of his forces.
20　By their formation I know they plan to strike in forays,
Hoping to attack and retreat in swift movements.
We must give them no chance, but attack unceasingly;
Our battle fronts must converge from all sides.
You, Mdlaka, shall command the wing on the furthest end,
25　While one section shall emerge from the near side of the
　　mountain.
Above all, we must overwhelm his army with precipitous
　　attacks.'
They all accepted and applauded this plan.
30　Shaka then turned to speak to the gathering of troops.
He said, addressing them in a strong commanding voice:
'Zulu of Malandela, the enemy is now before you:
Sikhunyana has provoked a cluster of resting wasps.
He comes to us not for a place to live but to attack.
35　With my own eyes
I have seen the troops that make plain his intention.
After the wounds of a bull have been healed
It begins again making its challenges,
Forgetting the punishments inflicted on it by its previous defeats.

What you see before you is a foolish young calf
Whose bravado comes only of ignorance.
Yet a young calf may sometimes inflict a deep wound.
It may even kill an unexpecting bull, hurting its weakest spot.
5 I want us, then, to attack Sikhunyana mercilessly.
I want you, before the end of tomorrow,
To send him scurrying and tripping into the night of cliffs.
We shall make of his cattle a great sacrifice.
Of Sikhunyana's regiments none must survive to tell the tale.
10 The dog that has dared to come to our gates
Must never be allowed to escape alive.
Some foolish nations may yet be tempted to follow this example.
They may think, if Sikhunyana could escape, so could they.
Those in distant lands who follow these tales
15 Must recall with terror the fate of such creatures.
Let them know it is an error even to challenge the children of
    Zulu.
Let them know our heroes sleep alongside their weapons.'
Scarcely had he finished speaking
20 Than the great Sotobe began to shout Shaka's epic.
The fearless Mgobhozi-of-the-Mountain shook his body.
He rushed into the open ground as if seized by some spirit.
He danced his great war dance, thrusting his body in every
    direction
25 And shouting: 'You are dead! You are dead!'
As he stabbed the imaginary enemy he spun all round.
It was as though he fought back a cluster of bees.
When he finished his boast-dance
He called out to the onlooking regiments:
30 'Thus will I stab them as I go through their lines,
The dogs will make only one last cry of pain as I rush on to
    others!'
A deathly silence fell on the spectators,
For when someone prepares for his last and greatest battle
35 It is a heinous crime to try to stop him.
Mgobhozi never had to be persuaded about war.
Even little children as they grew up
Often claimed: 'I shall be like the great Mgobhozi,'
This way eliciting a silent nod from their grandfathers.
40 Mgobhozi often told stories of his episodes;

How once a man was afflicted with a running stomach
At the very mention of his name.
Some believed him; some only said:
'It is one of Mgobhozi's many tales!'
5 Even then everyone was in awe of his courage.
When one young man of the Zimpohlo regiment saw Mgobhozi's
  act
He (like all young cocks
Who, when they feel the new strength in their spurs,
10 Begin to boast of their power, but too soon)
Rushed into the arena dancing and shouting:
'I, the son of Nodada of Sondela, of Mashinini,
I, the black log on which the ibises sit and gaze,
I, the thrower of the spear who follows it —
15 I shall stab them until they speak through their stomachs.
I shall lay my path with their corpses.
I shall make them swallow the dry earth of Nkotheni!'
Those who came from his region applauded him,
But others stood there watching, uncertain of his boast.
20 It was as though they said: 'The future will tell....'

The day of spears broke over the mountains.
Some were to cross the river to join the Ancestors:
It was the day whose lips babbled the names of heroes.
It was the day of the great swear-words.
25 The great concourse of troops began climbing the mountain.
They wound round like a snake on the body of the Ndololwane
  mountain.
Constantly they heard the voice of Shaka shouting:
'They are now in your hands, children of Malandela!'
30 Shaka did not enthuse about this war.
He had seen how Mgobhozi indulged in his hero's dance.
Incidents of his whole dark dream had returned to him:
He recognized the details of this place
As though, indeed, he had been there,
35 Like him who by his previous knowledge can anticipate bogs
  and turns.
Unable to contain himself, he travelled a few paces to a
  remembered spot

And was shocked by the familiar details of plants and trees.
He resolved: 'Here the Ancestors once carried me.'
He spoke to Mgobhozi solemnly and said:
'I am haunted by a fear that disturbs the hearts of parting
     lovers.
5 But there is nothing I can do;
I cannot restrain a hero who prepares for battle.
I know I would only be wasting my words
Should I issue such commands.
10 O, Mgobhozi, those who build great nations
Only do so through those who are their twin spirits.
Were it not for you I would not have survived to build a nation.
But now I see the river by which I first quenched my thirst.
It is threatened by the all-embracing sun.
15 It is covered with dirt and decaying leaves.
I try to drink from it but can only see a thick layer of mud.
I see the rupturing of the sacred bonds.
The time has come for the truth to give its bitter fruit.

Our ancient bonds shall eternally give us power.
20 I shall turn my eyes to the mountain
Where there is the twin of our house.
I shall travel there long after many have forgotten.
My mind shall find a home there among the eagles.
There is not time left, Mgobhozi-of-the-Mountain,
25 Otherwise I would sit down and recall old episodes and battles.
I, too, when I have done all that is required of me by the
     Ancestors
I shall follow your dance and fight the last great fight of
     warriors.
30 Farewell, my brother. Farewell, Mgobhozi.'
As he said this tears welled up in his eyes.
Mgobhozi could not speak at length;
He only declaimed: 'Nodumehlezi, son of Menzi,
Miraculous fighter of numerous battles,
35 Mysterious power no one can strike.
You are like the moving current.
When they whistled they roused the lion from sleep!
I shall fight with your epic on my lips.
It was you who instilled in me the power of a warrior.

284

I shall be glad to die in the battlefield.
I shall rejoice to die for the nation that I love
By its power I was nourished from its beginnings until I grew
    tall.
5 Today no one dares to challenge us
Except fools like Sikhunyana, who recklessly court their own
    death.
I have seen our land becoming the home of many heroes and
    nations.
10 Here, then, is my last word to you:
Watch carefully those who seek only self-glory,
Whose heart always yearns for power.
Latecomers to fame often speak louder than their actions.'
He shook the king's hand and said:
15 'I thank Ndaba, my lord, who guided my hand.
Who knows? I may yet come back from battle!'
They both laughed and smiled with each other
As if in gratitude to the Ancestors for their gift of friendship.

Mgobhozi walked quickly ahead of the army.
20 He did not slow down even as he neared the enemy.
The two armies came to a halt, sizing each other up.
Mgobhozi's lips moved as though uttering the sacred word to
    the Ancestors.
Those next to him heard him declaim the king's poem of
25   excellence:
'Endless theme of the women of Nomgabi!
They sit babbling and gossiping at Mlovini
Saying: "Shaka shall never rule; he shall never be king."
But alas! He grew up to overshadow the earth!
30 The cow that bellowed alone at Mthonjaneni —
All nations heard it.
Dunjwa of Luyengweni heard it.
Mangcengceza of Khali heard it,
Wild fire that devours all things!
35 That burnt the owls of Dlebe regions.
Spreading, it consumed those of Mabedlana.
You cut through Ndima and Mgovu forests.'
Thereafter Mgobhozi was silent
As though he listened to a voice in the distance.

As the two armies stood facing each other, Ndlela commanded
    the Strangers:
'Shoot and frighten them with your guns.'
Many times they fired at the enemy army
5 Until, by a burst of anger, the two armies were locked in fierce
    combat.
The angry warrior was heard shouting:
'I have killed him! Yield to my spear! Yield!'
There was a clanging and ripping of weapons;
10 Thudding sounds, splashing sounds, crackling sounds,
Roaring cries of a thousand voices.
From a vantage point Shaka watched.
He saw the enemy units falling and scattering from Mgobhozi's
    side.
15 Then, from a distance, he saw the wing commanded by Mdlaka.
It attempted to encircle Sikhunyana's army, but Sikhunyana's
    army retreated.
Before long they were locked again in violent combat.
For a long time this shifting and thrusting continued.
20 Sometimes it seemed they would win their chance to retreat,
But the Zulu army, too fast for them, would close in on them.

Mgobhozi seemed to be fighting in two places at once.
If they fell back he lurched onto them, reaping them from all
    sides.
25 If they regrouped he seemed to be the first to enter their centre.
Sometimes he would be heard in the heart of enemy lines
Shouting: 'I have eaten! I have reaped! I have opened his chest!'
Small wonder many retreated in terror from him.
After many encounters his arms began to swell.
30 He sought a clear spot where he could rest.
Not far from him the battle raged. Falling spears whizzed past
    him;
Black shields, white-dotted shields, red shields —
They all fell on each other like giant ferns.
35 After many fierce battles
The Ndwandwe army disengaged, eager to replenish its strength.
But Mdlaka pushed on with his regiments from a higher
    plateau,
Forcing them to fight on two fronts

And making their retreat hazardous.
Mgobhozi now led an accelerated thrust.
He speared from all sides like one blinded by poison;
His path was covered with fallen men of all ages and sizes.
5   As he tangled with a giant man of the Nxumalo junior house,
A young warrior of the Ndwandwe army suddenly stabbed him,
But, despite this wound, he lunged at his challenger and killed
      him.
Weakened, he staggered and fell, planting his weapon on the
10   ground.
He began his final words of a warrior's prayer.
Turning his head in an effort to glance at Shaka, he called out:
'Allow me, great earth, land of my Forefathers,
Let me sleep in peace.
15 I have made them sing our poems of excellence.
The paths of courage are now open for generations to come.'
Once again he attempted to turn in the direction of Shaka, in
      vain.
Losing his strength, his body became one with the earth.

20 The remnant army of Sikhunyana, fled into the forest.
Many returned from battle, open-mouthed with amazement.
The Ndololwane mountain rose like a memorial.
There, many years thereafter, people were to say,
Pointing closed fists to the Ndololwane mountain:
25 'There lies the great Mgobhozi-who-comes-from-the-Mountain.
In its womb is often heard his song.
Heroes tend their sons by his battle song.'

The messenger who rushed to Shaka to report victory
Continuously hummed Mgobhozi's song and his poems of
30   excellence.
Breathlessly he recited his last feats of battle.
It was Shaka who spoke first to the messenger and said:
'I have defeated the son of Zwide
But he has snatched victory from me by killing Mgobhozi.
35 Poems of excellence have fulfilled their truth.
From now on he shall be known as Mgobhozi-
      who-sleeps-in-the-Mountain.'

Shaka spoke reluctantly as though every thought was
    unbearable.
His words were thrown in between long intervals of silence.
Looking at the herds of cattle, he said:
5   'This is not enough to compensate for my brother's life.'
He ordered all the regiments to lift their shields in salutation;
Not one raised his arm half-way.
Many told Mgobhozi's last battle as though it was a tale.
They commented on how, by his final thrust,
10 He had killed the very man who had stabbed him.
Often Mgobhozi had said: 'If outnumbered, a warrior must fight
    fiercely.
If wounded, a fighter must charge like a cornered lion.
His pain must be his ecstasy of battle.'
15 These words were fulfilled:
Mgobhozi fought more fiercely
When his body was marked with spear wounds.
His blood and that of the enemy mingled together.
Many times the enemy thought he had stabbed him fatally,
20 Only to see him rise with greater anger and speed.
The young carrier boys watched this spectacle in disbelief,
Amazed at such endurance and courage.

With a great roar of song, the army now returned to Bulawayo.
Each one spoke of the various jokes and sayings of Mgobhozi.
25 Bitter, the regiments still spoiled for battle.
Passing through the regions of Bheje of the Khumalo clan,
The young Thuli regiment asked to settle with him old scores.
Through this episode they hoped to win their own fame.
In vain the army generals tried to restrain them,
30 Telling them how hard it was to dislodge Bheje from the forest.
Shaka intervened and said:
'Let the young learn their own lesson. Bheje is no easy problem,
Nor is enthusiasm enough to win against him.'
It was after these words of warning that Bheje defeated the
35   boy-regiment.
Even the memory of Mgobhozi's battle did not win them their
    victory.

At this very moment it was reported

288

How the overseas Strangers and mulattos
Had raped and assaulted a woman of the Shezi clan.
Shaka burst out like a thunderbolt.
Spitting on the ground with disgust he called out to Fynn:
5   'By my sister! Have I not treated you with kindness?
Have I not given you privileges deserved only by my heroes?
Must you desecrate the house of my father?'
The strangers bowed, begging for forgiveness, claiming
Only their boyish immaturity had made them commit these
10   heinous crimes.
They claimed such habits had been acquired among foreigners,
For even among the children of George
Such crimes are viewed with disdain.
To this Shaka commented: 'This is the land of the great Zulus!
15   Neither foreign crimes nor crimes learnt from foreigners
Must ever disgrace the great nation of the Zulus!
We tolerate no barbarism and no crime against families.
We fight and die in wars to protect our children;
If the very guardians of nations are the very ones who rape and
20   loot,
Then ours is no longer the Zulu army, but that of Matiwane!
I don't want to kill you with my sacred weapon —
I want you to die cleansing this repulsive crime!
Go now and fight against that stubborn Bheje.
25   I should send you alone to this battle
But you still are strangers deserving some kindness.
You bear the lawlessness and banditry of foreigners.
Your lives have been warped by your customs and homelessness.
I shall send the Mbelebele division to accompany you.
30   Should you come out alive, then thank your Ancestors.
You shall have cleansed this disgrace!'
The Strangers, shamefaced, followed the path to Bheje's fortress.
They were accompanied by the kindly Isaacs
Who, though innocent of this scandal, desired to report their
35   fate.
Fynn remained to plead for forgiveness for all the Strangers.
Shaka instructed the general of the Mbelebele division:
'Let the dogs fight against Bheje alone.
Let the other foreigners learn from them the fate of criminals.
40   Watch carefully how they use their weapons.

The Zulu nation must know all the ways of these foreigners.'
When the army arrived at Bheje's sanctuary
It let the Strangers proceed alone.
In vain they hoped the Zulus would come to their aid.
5 They climbed up the steep mountain of Bheje,
Shooting at every point and aiming at every moving object.
As the echoes of gun shots reverberated
The bandits of Bheje hid behind an array of boulders.
Ceaselessly the volley of gunfire burst on the high mountain
10   range.
Bheje's followers, plucking up courage, emerged from the forest.
They hurled spears and stones,
Causing great commotion and fear among the Strangers.
Suddenly they retreated into the forest.
15 Encouraged by this, the Strangers followed them in single file.
At a high point they discovered a cluster of deserted houses.
With glee they burnt them down,
Hoping by this act to affirm their courage.
An old man emerged and addressed them:
20 'It is enough. No man must lose his home from conquest.'
He offered them a large herd of cattle, saying:
'Take these beasts. They are a symbol of our loyalty.
They affirm our allegiance to Shaka, the king of all nations.
It is he who has spared our lives, letting us live in peace.'
25 Throughout this episode the commander of the Mbelebele
      division
Had sat at a distance, observing and counting the numbers of
      bullets,
Comparing in his mind the tactics of guns and spears,
30 For, in truth, every weapon has its weaknesses.

The Strangers, speaking through Isaacs, said to the old man:
'We want girls to accompany our king and renew his spirits.'
When they received these tributes and gifts
They set out to the king's place of rest.
35 There they pleaded many times in salutation:
'We beg forgiveness from the king.
We appeal to his many hearts for mercy.
We bring to him these gifts from Bheje.
He says he speaks to you with the lips of beautiful women.

They shall accompany you until you enter the gates of
    Bulawayo.'
Shaka laughed and said: 'Bheje is truly a great trickster.
He has chosen for me the oldest and feeblest beasts
5   And left behind the best of his herd.
You, too, were foolish; you did not inspect the hidden valley.
There you would have seen the best beasts of the land.
But let the son of Khumalo enjoy his wealth.
After all, these people are relatives of Mzilikazi.
10   Once they were a great nation, but were destroyed by Zwide.
People must be spared too many tragedies,
Lest with continuous blows they be turned into animals.
Indeed, I have great respect for them as a people.
They have sworn to die near the graves of their Forefathers.'
15   Many already knew Shaka's whims.
His choice of favourites was seldom understood.

The Zulu army now proceeded back to the capital.
They passed through the large settlements of Mlotsha,
Who had earned his fame as the great doctor of the elements.
20   By his power of mind and mysterious medicines
He was said to influence the mood of the seasons.
He could create rain and thunderstorms at will.
He, too, came from the Khumalo clan.
He lived in a sanctuary surrounded by high boulders.
25   When he heard the Zulu army singing close to his settlements
He called out, begging the king for mercy:
'We are not beyond the boundaries of your laws;
We have only retreated, fearing what could happen to our
    families.
30   Should you put us under siege, we and our children would die.
We live here only to learn the secrets of life.
Perhaps by our knowledge we can cure many ills
And acquire the wisdom of things still unknown to us.'
Perhaps the cures needed in the land made Shaka
35   Command: 'Leave Mlotsha in peace.
Is he not, like Bheje, a clansman of Mashobana?
But tell him: let the heavens and medicine be his domain,
So long as he walks on our earth,
He must pay a tribute to feed the army that protects him.'

Shaka spoke in jest, still skeptical of Mlotsha's pursuits
And suspecting it was his loss of power that fed his fantasies.
Amused, the troops considered this whole episode a healthy
    diversion.
5 Since Zwide's times, it was widely known,
The Khumalos had become the theme of children's tales.
Often parents would warn their children of the dangers of the
    night,
Quoting the Khumalos as the bandits to be feared.
10 Such is the fate of once-great nations
Who are driven by the violence of conquerors into the
    wilderness!
By the victor's skill their great legends are distorted
And from the themes of their lives he makes tales of wild
15   animals.
The conqueror's children grow up feeding on their woes
And thus is born the superior race whose truth is only their own.

The Zulus proceeded, driving before them large herds of cattle.
The regiments sang the song composed against Sikhunyana.
20 Many young recruits declaimed the king's poems.
Following the army to the capital,
Women raised their voices, saluting them from all sides.
Throughout the land news spread:
'Victory over Sikhunyana was bought with the life of Mgobhozi.'
25 In all regions where there were encampments of the Zulu army
A great chorus of outrage and grief exploded.

No sooner had Shaka arrived at Bulawayo
Than he proceeded to the villages of the Mgobhozi family.
Here lived many poets and singers and followers.
30 Many came to learn of the great episodes of wars.
Some were eager to see for themselves 'Mgobhozi the
    Warrior'.
When Shaka reached the gates he raised his head
And, looking straight ahead of him at the great house, he called
35   out:
'O, Mgobhozi-who-comes-from-the-Mountain!
The loss of a warrior friend is like the loss of a limb.
From now on the arenas are without the dancer.'

He spoke as if he addressed him in person.
Old memories die hard. They rush at their own pace,
Like the wild wind tossing summer-grass from a distance.

After the king's presence had been announced.
5 Shaka summoned Mgobhozi's eldest son and said to him:
'Your father was a brother closer to me than my own
    blood-brothers.
I came here to tell you he died fighting, as befits a great warrior.
He is mourned by me and all the children of Zululand.
10 You are now the heir to the house of a great man.
The whole nation expects you to follow his footsteps.
Your family shall be looked after by me personally.
I shall send to your home two hundred head of cattle at once.
From these you must eat and ease the pain of his loss.
15 I do not have many words, my child;
We all have died through the death of Mgobhozi.'
Shaka did not stay long.
He drank the beer that was offered to him
And said quietly: 'From this beer vessel my brother drank.
20 I, too, and all the warriors, shall drink.'
He departed to Bulawayo, his spirit low
And his words no more than sighs.

Not long after a messenger came to Bulawayo:
'O my lord, bad news invites bad news.
25 My lips ache from the terrible words they carry.
The news of grief travels up against the river.
I am here, my lord, from the Thungulu regions.
Mbikwane, the father of our nation, is no more!
Early at dawn he took his shield and spear
30 And dressed himself with the adornment of an ancient warrior.
Then he called together all the members of his settlement
And said to them: "You of my family and nation,
Know the time has come for me to depart.
I leave you with the greatest king that ever lived.
35 I have known many kings and princes in my life.
I myself am the son of the great King Khayi,
But he never shall rise above the shadow of my king.
He never shall equal the legend of Shaka the Great,

Shaka the Warrior, Shaka the Thinker, who unravels all secrets!
Forever he shall live on the lips of nations.
The Zwides of this earth shall not equal him.
No king shall outshine the splendour of his sun!
5   As I die my heart is swelling with joy,
Knowing not even time shall destroy our achievements.
Nations shall narrate our story to their children's children.
Here then is my message to my king:
Tell him not to mourn my death —
10   I have fulfilled the duties assigned to me by my nation.
I leave behind me those who shall enrich its life.
I go to rest with my Forefathers.
Too long I have heard them calling me from their home."
As he said these words he bade us all farewell.
15   It is this sorrow I bring to you now, my lord.'
Shaka was quiet for a while,
As though the messenger's first words needed to be repeated.
The veins in his jaws showed prominently.
Then he made a long sigh and loosened his body.
20   He said, speaking to himself:
'Does this mean the whole tree shall die all at once?
Must the shade be seized by the whirlwinds?'
He ordered the messenger to leave him alone
And sat there alone, talking to shadows.
25   It was Mdlaka who decided to defy these orders
And went there to the quiet sanctuary of Shaka's house.
He found him lying down, his head propped by his palm.
Shaka spoke first: 'You came here believing,
Since I have mourned my grandmother Mtaniya,
30   And mourned for my brother Mgobhozi,
And my great father Mbikwane of Khayi,
I shall lose my mind in mourning.
It is not so, Mdlaka. The first sting of pain
Often digs deep into the tender parts of the heart;
35   When the same pain strikes again
It finds the heart strengthened by words of experience;
On the third strike the mind seizes the place of the heart,
Then the song of sorrow becomes only a word to life,
Nurturing all experience and profound wisdom.
40   Though I sit here it does not attest to my sadness,

But to a new era of reflection on all things of life.
I am starting to see new truths.
I know I shall attain new strength and power,
Giving to our nation an everlasting heritage.
5 The death of Mbikwane weighs heavily on me;
He was the first who said warmly to me, "My child".
He was not speaking to me in passing, like others;
He put his hand on my shoulders and invited me to his house.
From him I learned how sometimes the words of madness
10 Issue from the sacred commands of the Ancestors.
He taught me the ruthless courage of battle;
How wars are meaningless unless they bring peace to people.
Once he called me aside and said:
"Nodumehlezi! What you have done is not for your own glory,
15 But for the greatness of our nation."
From him I learned the sacred bonds of a father and a son.
Many praised my courage and heroism
But, in truth, from the great Mbikwane this power I derived.
After my battle with the madman
20 He said to me: "In these homes there are hundreds.
Were it not for your courage
Their children would be roaming in the wilderness."
It was this kindness that extended my vision.
I shall never forget Mbikwane for this kindness.
25 He lived and behaved like a true warrior.
For all this, I am satisfied with my days with Mbikwane.
I do not mourn him any longer.
I have an inner power to digest his deeds.
Mbikwane's funeral must be conducted with dignity:
30 I want two divisions dressed in their full battle regalia.
Mbikwane made us crave for greater things.
These are the true marks of a great hero.'
Mdlaka listened to these words with deep concentration,
Knowing words from Shaka often possessed deeper meanings.
35 From his own vast experience
Mdlaka knew that wars emit the hideous smell of blood,
Making sleep a nightmare of visitations and dreams.
A man must have friends and be nourished beyond the night.
Finally Mdlaka said to him:
40 'My lord, I fail to follow all the truths of our era.

I came to you to assuage your pain,
For Mbikwane was like a root on which many leaves grew.
But now I find myself without words.
I drink from the pool of your wisdom and I am cured.
5   I am possessed by a vision beyond the pain.
What you say enriches our lives
And infuses them with a new sun.
I shall do as you order, my lord, Nodumehlezi.
I only have one word to say:
10 The Strangers have asked for the king's ear.
They request to sing their own funeral songs.
In this way they shall applaud Mbikwane's kindness.
He taught them, they say, things unknown in their own lands.
Should their plea be granted,
15 They shall call on their Ancestors in their own language.'
Shaka, still absorbed in thought, nodded his head in consent.
He said: 'Mdlaka, I grant them this request.
I know this would be the wish of my father Mbikwane.
He often spoke kindly of them, despite some customs
20 We find contemptible in them.
For him I overlooked many things
That are heinous crimes among us.
In Zululand it is not often a man thinks only of his wealth.
Indeed, it is a heinous sin to hoard
25 What must be available to all strangers.
But to them wealth far surpasses the bonds of kinship.
From this all their obsessions originate.'

Listen to the echo of beating feet as they follow each other.
Listen to the great song rising from the river.
30 Funeral anthems reverberate to the lower edge of the Ilovu river.
They follow the route to the resting place of the Mthethwa
        kings.
There Xaba, Madango, Khayi, Jobe, Dingiswayo had found
        their eternal peace.
35 Shaka stood silently under the shade of a large tree,
His mind absorbed in thoughts of things to come.
He saw the cycles of seasons dissolve in a cloud of dust.
He heard the bubbling voices of those who were no more.
The voice of Mbiya came clearly to him

And the words of Mbikwane faded slowly into the distance.
He moved his lips as though talking to them.
At times a soft smile hung on his lips.
By this loyalty the eternal bonds of warriors are maintained.
5   Death is an illusion, a transformation,
Whose truth is revealed to those who keep alive their bonds.
Through sacrifice the living continue to commune with the
     dead,
Yet how lucky we are they do not break through the gates of
10   silence;
We would go insane from the challenge of two uncertain worlds.
These thoughts rushed through Shaka's mind.
They came in a succession of violent dreams.
Every night he dreamed the same people speaking the same
15   words.
He spoke to Mqalane, inquiring if these dreams had a message,
Or if, perhaps, he had omitted to make some sacrifice.
He said to Mqalane:
'I am visited every day by a constant dream.
20   Like a vulture, it seizes my sleep.
Sometimes I see Mbikwane standing before me;
Sometimes it is the body of Mgobhozi that approaches me;
Sometimes I see the Ancestors walking into a distant horizon
And branching there in separate directions
25   As if each one follows a predetermined route.
Often I stand alone under a tree watching them.
The tree is without leaves; it is burdened with red fruits.'
Mqalane was quiet for a while
As though to concentrate on this idea.
30   He said: 'My lord, this is a beautiful dream.
When they take these separate ways
They only go to do the tasks assigned to them by our nation.
These great men you see fulfilled their roles on earth.
I shall give my lord some strengthening herbs
35   To allow him to gaze on the dead with power.
When you again encounter them
You shall embrace as you once embraced.
I shall, by the same medicines, release Mgobhozi
So that he may forget the conflicts of his last battle on earth.
40   You, too, my lord, must wake up early at dawn

And go down to the stream to wash your feet with cleansing
    herbs.
There you must throw your most coveted spear.
As you do speak these words:
5   "Here is my weapon and yours, Mgobhozi-of-the-Mountain."
This same dream shall return to you, devoid of its terrors.
It shall be light on your shoulders.
You will see Mgobhozi as you used to know him.
You will sit and laugh at the old stories and episodes.'
10 Shaka followed these directives,
For, in truth, anxieties are lulled by words of friendship.
Medicines themselves only strengthen the mind,
Guiding it in the precipitous routes of awakening.
It was because of this that when Shaka dreamed again
15 It was as though he danced with the Ancestors in a great
    festival.
Mbikwane himself held him as he often did at the Mthethwas,
And said: 'Rule, my lord, do not worry;
There are still many years ahead of you.'
20 As he said this Mgobhozi suddenly appeared.
In a friendly voice he scolded the king, saying:
'What is troubling you, Nodumehlezi?
Why are you low in spirits like a coward?
Was it not you who taught us to be brave?
25 Who said: "Death is only a scourge of cowards"?'
They both laughed together.
They walked together, following the path into the horizon.
When Shaka woke up he went down to the river.
There he threw his favourite spear and said:
30 'Receive this weapon, Mgobhozi.'
It was as though by this act he invoked all the Ancestors.
On the sharp point of the spear were reflected enemies in flight.

In the following month Shaka emerged from the dark mood.
He often sat in the Assembly discussing episodes of battles.
35 Sometimes he would question a man,
Asking him to draw for him a whole battle strategy.
Yet his stories and themes were now not always about wars;
He spoke, too, of peoples of ancient times;
He spoke of the old kingdom of Sikhulumakathethi,

Once said to be the source of thunder.
He was enthralled by stories of Mabelemade,
The queen of the locusts, the queen of rain and long breasts.
No theme of life escaped his attention.

Book Thirteen: The court intrigues

The ceremonies and celebration only partially lift the spirits of Shaka. The achievement brings with it a certain degree of boredom. This is not helped by the isolation Shaka feels now that those close to him are dead or in the process of dying. His brother, Dingane, perhaps taking advantage of the reduced energy of Shaka's visions ceaselessly plots against him. He assumes a posture of greater hostility against the whites, whom he is impatient to destroy. Unlike Shaka, who is keen to stem the whole tide of invasion through a systematic plan, Dingane would, as indeed he did later, kill any group of them without any proper scheme. Shaka moves his capital from Bulawayo to Dukuza, desiring to leave behind him all the 'ghosts' of the past and also to keep an eye on the white settlement on the coast. He visits Zihlandlo, who from now on is to serve as a close friend to whom he can speak his most delicate thoughts. Zihlandlo is brave, gentle, humane and, above all, intelligent enough not to frustrate the restless genius of Shaka.

Many rumours circulated in the royal city of eBaqulusini
Of how Prince Dingane never ceased visiting his aunt.
Many questioned the reason for these frequent visits
Only to be answered by the alert agents of Princess Mkhabayi
5 Who, by a set strategy, commented:
'The prince is in search of the great truths of ancient times;
He desires to know about his Forefathers.
He, of all the royal children, is not gifted with a quick tongue.

His mind is eternally thirsty for things before and beyond our
    times.
He searches for powers that influence the lives of men.
Being a prince, he has a role in the affairs of the land.
5   For these reasons he constantly
Inquires about Qwabe and Zulu, his great Ancestors.'
Those who cared to listen would listen.
Some said: 'It is the right of the royal clan
To know and understand the ways of their Ancestors.'
10   But this was only to cover what was truly in their minds.
Each was uncertain what lurked in the mind of the other.
Privately many were puzzled by these bonds.
Princess Mkhabayi spoke firmly to Dingane:
'Your patience shows a heart that bears strong convictions.
15   I, too, am beginning to see strange things in your brothers's life.
Every day there are more and more bizarre happenings.
It is said the death of his favourite has unhinged his mind.
Sometimes without explanation he suddenly abandons the
    Assembly.
20   This madness must not enter the famed House of Jama.
Such things may cause alarm amongst our subjects;
Creating fissions that may eat into the nation's centre.
Despite all this I still have faith in him.
Perhaps this dark cloud shall pass,
25   And we may yet see a new and powerful king,
Yes, I still have great faith in him.
He is a king most needed in our times.
Such sharpness of mind only comes as a gift from the Creator.
Only those whose life is bound to a higher truth
30   Can serve as fearlessly as he.
By that I am not criticizing you, Dingane;
I am only speaking in fulfilment of the truth.
I know, too, those who initiate eras,
Know best how to walk the labyrinths in them.
35   You, too, must help your brother and consolidate his power,
For when a house collapses it buries all those in it.'
Dingane reluctantly consented to these words
Though these truths cut deep into his heart and plans.
Mkhabayi had blunted the enthusiasm with which he had come,
40   But he still was eager to control the reins of power.

300

He was critical, too, of the endless fraternizing with the
    Strangers;
He harboured deep suspicions against them,
Bitter, too, that they participated
5   So intimately in the affairs of the court.
He was keen to stage an open confrontation with them.
Unlike Shaka, who advocated skilled plans against them,
He demanded a strike that was immediate and decisive.
Shaka had insisted (as more of their plans were revealed):
10 'It is wiser to build alliances with all their enemies.
This way the runaways and malcontents will rally against them.
One must balance the weapons of one's enemies.
Besides, refugee subjects bring prestige to a nation's honour.
Often the strategies of the enemy are best known by deserters.'
15 It was in pursuit of these strategies
Shaka sent his trusted aides to England, under Sotobe.
To him he had said: 'If the White People want peace
They shall find it everywhere in our land,
But if they plan to invade the land of the Palm Race
20 Then they shall find our young lions ready to devour them.
Put to their king, George, these words and commands:
"The Palm Race desires friendship with all White People."
And yet their whole life is fostered by hunger and thirst for land.
Those who starve live like bandits and cannibals.
25 I want you always to be alert.
We hear in Xhosaland they have caused endless troubles.
Hlambamanzi still suffers from wounds inflicted by them.
His legs, once bound with iron leggings, still ache and bleed.
In truth, this is a nation that works through stratagems:
30 It is a nation that is hungry.'
Shaka said this to Sotobe to strengthen his mind,
To give him the skill with which to present his message
To evade the many traps that may be set against him.
Sotobe listened carefully and promised to learn
35 And speak only the words worthy of a Zulu warrior.

One day Shaka spoke to the overseas Strangers and said:
'I have a thought which obsesses me about your nation.
Often I see your fate tied up with that of the Palm Race.

Our nation and yours must grow in bonds of friendship.
Not only have I heard of your courage and wisdom,
But I have lived to see it with my own eyes.
I want now to send to your king, George, my messengers
5 So that in all your visits you may hold a place of honour.
This way our two nations shall strengthen their alliance.
I want you to convey this to my brother, George.
There is, too, a point of strategy,
Since he must unite the White Race as I have united the Palm
10   Race.
Tell him to assemble all his best commanders and strategists.
Let them listen to these words from my knowledge of his
       weapons.
If his country is constantly flooded with rains
15 Then the powder from his guns shall not work.
It is wise to equip his army with both spears and guns.
Should your king's army use both these tactics
It shall fight and conquer the challenging nations.
Your soldiers shall excel in hand-to-hand combat and other
20   ways.
They shall clear themselves of the charge made by our regiments
That they are cowards who only fight from a distance.
Such cowardly tactics seem to us without respect for life,
For to kill any enemy one must demand knowledge of him.
25 Besides, your favourite war cannons are too cumbersome.
They hold back the progress of an advancing army,
Violating one of the great rules of battle.'
When he said this none replied directly.
They were all eager to speak what would sound wise and
30   profound.
But when they realized their replies might differ,
And thus expose the weaknesses of their strategies,
They decided to make no comment.
Shaka still obsessed with his former demand
35 And holding back his own doubts said:
'I want you to bring the herb of immortality
And win for all the White Races a deep and everlasting
       friendship.'

Two years passed but the Strangers brought no magic herbs.

They constantly claimed their boats had been grounded
And needed repairs and missing parts.
Dingane often commented on these things to Mkhabayi:
'I am disturbed by the policies of Shaka;
5   They shall bring disaster to our whole nation.
I have no faith in the promises of the White Strangers
Every day they come with sweet and round words,
But from them there never is any truth.
Their love for land is like a disease.
10   Whoever loves the soil with such insanity
Must surely have wider plans for the whole earth.
They are truly a nation of witches, by my mother I swear!
They shall bewitch the whole earth.
They claim close friendship to the king
15   But dismiss us who are of his own family.
It is as though they care more for his welfare than us?
Mkhabayi would laugh and say:
'Dingane, son of my brother, I fear your impatience;
Such eagerness blinds one to many obvious pitfalls.
20   How can you know what is in Shaka's mind?
It is as though they care more for his welfare than us.'
Mkhabayi would laugh and say:
It is not through your eagerness you will know the truth,
      Dingane,
25   But through a mind that is calm and can follow every step.
By your excitement you shall know only the obvious.
Hold yourself together. There is still time to learn.'
This was how Princess Mkhabayi stemmed the tide of Dingane's
      anger.
30   These evasive words merely incensed him,
For those whose heart burns with impatience
Never easily abandon their fixed convictions.
When they fail utterly
They amass with greater terror their power of destruction.

35   One day, as the Assembly debated the affairs of the land,
Shaka spoke words that alarmed everyone.
He said: 'I am moving from this capital of Bulawayo.
The grounds of Bulawayo have begun to smell of death!

They have become the place of shadows and voices.
The voices I hear move away from me;
They hang in the wind like the tongues of winter.
Even my enemies seem to close in on me;
5   They search and remember every nook.
I want my capital moved from this fearsome place —
Let it be far away from all the shadows of yesterday.
I want my new capital to be built near the Mvoti river.
This great new home I shall call Dukuza.
10 In it people shall walk like ants in a giant anthill.
So big it must be that many shall lose their way in it.
There festivals and feasts shall affirm the greatness of Zululand.
I do not have much more to say.'
He stood up, casting his tall shadow over the Assembly.
15 Before they could comment on his words
He spoke firmly, saying:
'I have spoken. That is my command.
I swear by Nomchoba it shall be so!'
Soon after the regiments were following these commands.
20 Mqalane requested from the king a private audience.
Sitting leisurely on the ground, he said:
'My lord, I thank you for allowing me to speak my heart.
I thank you too for giving us a new home.
There our great ruler shall rejoice with his nation.
25 I am referring to you, my lord, you who are a mystery,
You, the diviner above all diviners, the oracle above all oracles.
I only make this one request: to fortify with secret powers and
        medicines
The whole arena surrounding this great city.
30 Let me cleanse it with all known purifying medicines.
Each generation that comes must feel its strength and power.
It must hear our voices whenever it walks in your royal city.
Your new place must be the eternal monument to our nation.
I make this request for generations to come.
35 By these ceremonies the power of our nation shall be
        enshrined.'
Shaka laughed softly and said:
'Mqalane, you are endowed with Ancestral powers.
You possess the power of the mind and of the body.
40 Your visions fertilize the deserts.

You must do as the welfare of our nation demands:
Not I, but you, are the spiritual power of our nation.
You know, too, all nations are made powerful by their rituals.
I want this ceremony to be carried out at daybreak.
5   Let your supplication affirm to all the permanence of the Palm
      Race.
I want you to reveal the reasons for this ceremony.
In truth, deeds are often the consequence of strong desires.
There are powers that derive from forces unknown.
10 From Dukuza they shall renew their visions.'
Mqalane, raising his head, thanked the king
But was still puzzled by the secrets in the king's mind.

Throughout the land the king's command was heard.
Small nations, large nations, clans and families
15 All sent their contingents to the Mvoti region.
Great crowds and processions hurried there;
Through routes of mountains and valleys they came.

See them as they converge on the new royal capital;
See them as they mingle with each other from hitherto unknown
20   regions.
Some carried gifts of food; some carried gifts of white stones;
Some brought carefully chosen beams from tall trees;
Some came with round black stones of the mountains.
Such, indeed, was the gift sent by the great and noble King
25   Moshoeshoe,
Who said through his messenger:
'Like the earth that is round and bordered by the four circles,
Like birds that share with each other their prey,
We give to each other whatever is of the earth.'
30 Shaka was pleased with these words.
He commented: 'Moshoeshoe is, indeed, a great and a wise man.'
So great was the enthusiasm of nations and peoples,
They competed with each other to reach the chosen centre.
There were the great and numerous Ngcobos of Vumezitha;
35 There came the Qwabes of the House of Malandela;
There came the Mthethwas of the House of Nyambose;
There came the powerful Buthelezis of the House of Shenge;

There came the powerful Hlubis of the House of Mthimkulu;
There came the numerous Dlaminis of the House of
    Mkhulunkosi;
There came the Luthulis of the House of Ngcolosi.
5 Even the Mkhwanazis of the House of Mpukunyoni were there;
The Ngobeses of the Maqungebeni were there;
The Pedis of the North were there.
The wise and brave King Sobhuza sent his numerous gifts.
The great nations and families built the royal city of Dukuza.
10 People feasted and sang and declaimed their epics.
In the midst of these celebrations a messenger came:
'Zihlandlo, your brother, has prepared in your name a feast.
He requests the king to receive these gifts.
He gives to his king the skin of the lion he killed himself.'
15 Despite the many affairs of the state, Shaka said:
'Go to my brother, Ghubela; tell him I shall come.
Indeed, I desire to rest my mind from the affairs of the land.
Tell him I have heard, too, how men like Boyiya are causing
    trouble,
20 And Nzombane of Matomela, who has caused a scandal.
All shall be duly punished.
Tell him I forgive his brother, Mashukumba,
Whom he has punished accordingly.
Tell him, too, I miss his words of wisdom.
25 I need a place to close my eyes,
To see no more of the past and more of the future.'
The messenger left hurriedly, carrying this good news.
He constantly repeated to himself the words of the king.

When Zihlandlo received these words
30 He sent a message to Sambela, his brother, and said:
'We must stage the greatest feast ever held in Nguniland.
Let us sing the great ancient songs of eMboland.
Let the women of our family spread like mountain flowers.'
Zihlandlo himself slept with Ancestral hymns in his ear.
35 He spoke softly to his them and said:
'I thank the Beautiful Ones for loving their children.
I pay my respects to Ngcwabe who followed the trail of Diza.
You are the jester who is like an impending thunderstorm,
The clouds are unequal on upper and lower regions they hang.

Great ones, whose clan of heroes causes tears.
It was Mkhonto, the son of Magaba and Mbangi, they beheld.
They sharpened the spear on both sides.
Slippery stone, that was of our House of Sijibeni!
5   On it many men have fallen to their deaths.
They slip as they attempt to hold on its slippery sides.
Your tongue was harsh, even against your mother-in-law.
She said in anger: "My child's marriage to them was an error."
You brought Nonkenka and threw him down into the waterfall;
10   You captured Sundu among his sons after a scandal.
The magic herbs were given to Zambe and Nsele.
Zelize and Sambela shared in them,
Nodada, son of Ndaba! Slender one,
Who is like the narrow end of a spear.
15   Wild one, who often is provoked by sounds of battle!
Then no one can restrain him.
The plentifulness of the House of Yengweni:
You met abaMbo clans as they approached from the north.
Generous one, who never tires of giving,
20   You were not like the stingy one of Ngonyameni.
No sooner did he step on a cluster of plants than they withered.
Restless one, who is like a he-goat,
Whose feet are spread sideways.'

Such was the occasion when Shaka visited Zihlandlo:
25   The poet shouted the king's epic from the mist-covered
      mountains;
Women's voices accompanied him in high-pitched ululations.
The bodyguard of young men sang the nation's great
      anthems.
30   The great city of Zihlandlo could be seen from a distance.
Far into its circular centre great processions of women could be
      seen.
The sacred smell of burning fat sprang into the air;
Filling the celebrants with anthems of joyfulness.
35   The king steadily climbed the hill.
As he emerged, the poet declaimed his epic:
'You climbed to the pinnacle of Maqonqgo mountain
And found there a blue monkey and a red goat with a yellow
      muzzle.

Proud possessor of a basking lizard of eNkandla forest!
Dlungwane, who devoured the cattle of the wanderers,
You seized the cattle possessed by Mandeku at Mlambo region;
You punished the smart ones of Mbengi.
5   You stabbed a milking cow soon after they set fire to the grazing
        lands.
Whoever so chooses may dare challenge him in his own home,
The bird that devoured other birds!
While still swelling with others it seized others.
10 He, who is as huge as his own vast territories,
He, who is first among all the great Ancestors,
Like the giant mountains of Sondude,
Under which the Ndwandwes and the Nxumalos sat,
Like the giant tree that is perched on Maqhwakaza ridge.
15 Give him one cow so that he may learn the game of milking!
Give him a hoe so that he may learn to dig,
He, whose chest expands like a fortress!
Glorious one, son of Ndaba!
You have a defender among those of abasemaLangeni.
20 Surreptitiously I watch you my lord
My eyes are filled with tears.
It is as if I am looking at a poisonous euphorbia tree.
The great crooked rook of Mdlaka:
It punishes the dancers of the song.
25 Ndaba brings terror among the great cities.
He rears high like the ocean
Which roars and lashes eternally.
Wild one, who is like the unruly ear of an angry elephant,
Like a paste of poisonous millet grains,
30 Like a chasm filled with black centipedes —
You are the dragon! the leopard! the lion!
You are like an old fierce black mamba! You are the elephant!
You are as huge as the tall mountains of Mphehlela and
        Maqhwakazi.
35 Black one!
You, who became powerful as others still indulged themselves!'
When the poet stopped
The anthems of Zululand rose, competing with the wind,
The king entered the arena to a thunderous 'Bayede!'
40 Prince Zihlandlo accompanied him.

On all sides were thick crowds of men and women.
Some wore long, smooth cloaks made of otter skins;
Some wore the patched leather of unusual creatures and animal
    shapes.
5   The bodies of children glistened in the sun with beads.
How beautiful were the women of the Mkhize clan!
How handsome the tall young men of the Mkhize clan!
The colours of their adornments glowed in the setting sun.
Trembling over their shoulders,
10   The sun thrust its last light of the evening.
The rivers echoed as they hurtled into the round holes of stone.
Returning birds headed for the river to drink.
They sang their last songs of the evening.
Darkness descended on the crimson earth,
15   Covering our mountains, our faces, but not our song.
The great light of the moon broke through the early night,
Revealing large crowds of dancers and singers.
From many regiments came the boom of song and the beat of
    feet.
20   Amidst the thunderous echoes of dancing
The poets' voices rose like a great chorus.
Some sang of the ancient heroes of Zululand;
Some sang of the brave heroes of the Mkhize clans;
Some sang of the brave and generous Zihlandlo —
25   A hubbub of voices filled the whole region.
Old warriors sat near the fire, narrating their tales.
When the king had rested, he spoke warmly to Zihlando,
Recalling their episodes together.
So elated was he, many were surprised at this friendliness.
30   He said: 'O, Gubhela. You have built a great place.
You have made this region famous with your wisdom and
    courage.
I hear from my generals you subdued the troublesome Khabelas
And brought Boyiya of Mdakuda of emaDungeni to his knees.
35   You are truly the descendant of Mavovo.
Though I sometimes wonder at your judgement;
You shelter and protect such cowards and fools as Mkhaliphi.
In this you are like my father, Dingiswayo.
He, too, was soft and never knew human boundaries.
40   Yet, by your interventions, you enable me to be kind,

For so long as I rule I can never exhibit my feelings of pity,
Nor let them direct the course of my actions.
A ruler is an image people often imitate:
He must never display the weaknesses that lurk in his mind.'
5   The tall Zihlandlo spoke softly and calmly:
'My lord, whatever I do, I do to enhance your rule.
All eMbo branches spoil for battle from your inspiration.
In all my deeds I only am following the direction of my king.
He alone humbles the stubborn and the troublesome.
10   My role, my lord, is only that of a sweeper.'
As he said this large pots of beer were put before them.
Voices from the feast could be heard singing and talking.
Shaka said to Zihlandlo: 'Let your bodyguards and mine
Go out and have fun while we talk our own affairs.
15   I did not come here to discuss wars,
But to rest and ease my mind.
My rule is open to all peoples of Zululand.
Yet only to you can I speak the truth about my life.'
As the guards left them to join the crowds of dancers,
20   Shaka said, continuing: 'Many matters occupy my mind,
Yet these things I cannot discuss easily.
Too many see me only as a king
But, in truth, the posture of authority often exhausts the mind.
It swallows many of those who could be friends.
25   It was my greatest blow when Mgobhozi died.
It was to him I went to ease my mind.
With him I laughed at the strange things of power.
Then I was able to clear my thoughts
And wash it of all that comes from the lips of scavengers.
30   I am here today to pick up that string again,
To follow it until we who are living
May be able to honour such heroes as Mgobhozi,
Letting their lives and ours stand as a great mountain.
Many say I have imposed too rigid a code of marriage laws
35   And too often I delay the marrying of the regiments.
Even my trusted generals are critical of these laws,
Claiming that a large movement builds up against them.
Indeed, some have said it is one great weakness of our army.
I want to hear from you the truth as known and seen by you.
40   I ask you this, Ghubela, because I trust your fearlessness.

You will not tell me things only please.
Besides, you are my brother and this is your destiny.'
Zihlandlo did not immediately answer;
He concentrated his mind on the king's words
5   And said finally: 'I ask your permission to express my gratitude.
I thank you for honouring my family with your visit,
Even though many poisonous tongues seek to destroy this bond.
I thank you, too, for the great trust you have put in me.
I say this, knowing those who are loyal to rulers
10   Draw to themselves many enemies.
Often they are seen as waiting only to flatter and to please.
I promise you, my lord, I shall give my life to preserve yours.
I do not say this only to echo the words of battle songs
But to speak the truth.
15   Yet I must answer your question with honesty.
Yes, these rumours are true; the complaints are many.
I too say that marriage laws be changed.
I know, there was once a time in Zululand
When the nation needed to build its power for battle.
20   That time, my lord, I feel has passed:
The Zulu nation is huge and powerful.
Should you, then, allow all the young men to marry,
It would only strengthen your rule and raise your name.
People will fight to defend their children and homes.
25   In truth, a man fights not for promises but for things real.
Besides, our population of fighting men will increase.
Should you want to mobilize in strength,
It shall be with the men and women
Born in the era of courage and fearlessness.
30   By their pride they shall scatter all enemies.
The nation shall boast only of its heroes.
A man who has no family is like a wild animal, my lord;
Yet we know from the example of Mgobhozi
A man does not flinch from battle because he has married.
35   In truth, by this act Mgobhozi was given a new spurt of life.
This, then, is how I feel, my lord.
I ask you to open the gates while the bull still has strength.
This alone shall stifle the poisonous tongues of enemies.
Let it not be said: "The Zulus are born of old men."
40   Shaka laughed at these last words and said:

'So, Ghubela, you think the strength of a man
Tells the age of the begetter?
Is it not these old men who have endless children
While we, young men, bear only a few?'

5   Shaka spoke to Zihlandlo in a light and jocular mood
But it was clear these words had moved him. He said:
'I hear your words, Ghubela, and in them there is great truth.
It is necessary always to share ideas; no one knows all things.
It is time the Zulus settled and multiplied.

10   Such thoughts have, in truth, occurred to me
But I have often hesitated and doubted,
For those who initiate things are always conservative.
I was deterred, too, by many who said
The enemy will see in this a sign of weakness,

15   Penetrating our nation by the routes that had been closed to
        him.
From now on I am convinced of the truth!
It only remains for me to choose an appropriate moment
When I shall tell all men and women of Zululand to marry.

20   It must not be said weakness forced us to change.
The day I choose must be an occasion to celebrate a great event.
For whoever changes out of fear invites his own destruction.
When enemies find a point of weakness they never stop;
They seek frantically for many softer spots.

25   Nor do they tire until the whole body is destroyed.
But I have something more to say, son of Mavovo
(I speak to you in deepest trust and confidence):
I deeply suspect my own brothers to be fanning these fires,
Yet it is hard for me to point a finger at my own brothers.

30   Sometimes I think I am only poisoned by reports of people.
No crime is greater than that of killing out of fear.
This is the crime of cowards who often exaggerate the dangers.
It is for this I want to clear my mind of these suspicions.
I know, too, you cannot help much in these affairs

35   But to talk of them opens my mind.'
Slowly and deliberately, Zihlandlo replied: 'My lord, you know
How in my own family my own brother nearly killed me.
Often I had sent him to you with gifts of confiscated cattle
But I did not know he only kept these for himself.

40   Had this truth not come to the open

You might well have thought I had begun to carve my own
    kingdom.
I promptly punished my brother, Mashukumbela;
But I still did not condemn all my brothers.
5 Here is Sambela; I still trust and love him.
The truth then, my lord, is simply this:
In a family there are always many differing thoughts.
As you rightly say, I am reluctant to enter affairs of families,
Yet I cannot deny the jealousies that exist.
10 I was permitted by my king to live and command this territory
But this did not please those of your own family
Who never had such scope and privilege.
Therefore, my lord, before you open your heart
Search in the dark nooks of your house for your enemies.
15 This nation was built by you from its infancy,
Yet they, too, feel: "We must rule in the kingdom of our
    Forefathers."
Are they not also the descendants of Jama and Ndaba?
I do not say your brothers plot against you;
20 Only this: a human being is no better than a beast.
Sometimes it attacks its own master.'
Shaka agreed with these words,
Admitting that such, indeed, was the fate of many rulers.
He said: 'Let us drink and go to our places of rest.
25 Many days and affairs still lie ahead of us.'
They followed this decision and fell to a peaceful sleep.
Their night was one of beautiful words;
Poets all declaimed their poems of excellence.
Zihlandlo dreamt of his Ancestor, Mavovo.
30 He saw large processions proceeding to his Ancestral home.
The forests of Qhudeni were covered with a layer of smoke
And people felt the soft, rich earth with their fingers,
Then they hurried down to the river to wash their feet.
There were numerous flat stones on which small birds roamed.
35 It was as though a voice rose from the deep pool;
Its roar echoed into the river.
The whole valley was seized by a concourse of song.
Amidst this hubbub he heard a strong voice calling him:
'I am your great Ancestor, Langa.
40 Of all our children and those who shall come hereafter

We have chosen you to be the flower
Whose light shall traverse the paths of Lubombo mountains.
Through you we trace our ancient paths.
We travel past the Hluhluwe forest
5   And follow the routes to our relatives of the Dlamini clan.
Through Mavovo our family reaches its destiny
And through you our epics begin again.
We come to give you our blessings and instil you with courage.
Whoever believes in our progeny
10 Shall reap the fruits of its trust and loyalty.
You are not the end of our song:
We shall multiply until we settle near a great river.'
Zihlandlo woke up and covered himself with a lion-cloak.
He walked a few paces to the gates of the cattle-fold
15 And asked the Ancestors to guide him through their mission.
He thanked them for their presence in the celebrations
And appealed to them to enable him
To serve loyally the king and the son of the Palm Race.

A great dawn spread its rays over the earth.
20 In the long blades of grass hung the glistening dew.
The long smell of new seasons seized the earth.
Even the little plants of the dark earth broke through into light.
Great crowds of people emerged from their homes.
At a pool bordered by light and black stones Shaka bathed.
25 He constantly pointed to a neighbouring hill,
Guessing how and where the angle of light would fall.
With precision he told them at what point
The sun would reach a clump of drying shrubs.
All these games he played while the mist still covered the earth.
30 Zihlandlo, having known all these movements, affirmed the
       king's words.
Thus they joked and played with things around them,
Like children who had found a new world.
Even the cliffs and their forms occupied their minds.
35 At times they focused on the crowds of swallows.
Of them Shaka said: 'The speed with which they seize their
       prey
Forebodes the way wars shall be fought in future.

The power of the body must contend against the skill of speed.
It is such a weapon that shall surpass all weapons.
The Strangers possess a dangerous weapon:
Should its power strike without stopping
5   It shall threaten many nations.
We must learn to use it and make our own.
Above all, we must improve on its speed,
Avoiding the need to reload with every strike.
The troops who carry it should proceed ahead of battle,
10 Letting those who follow overwhelm the enemy.'
Thus Shaka's mind wandered, attracted by all he saw.
He said: 'If man lived on grass and soft vegetation,
There never would have been wars.'
Zihlandlo said. 'But lions live like us.
15 They eat meat but still do not wage wars.'
Shaka said. 'Yes, it is so, but only a few of them exist.
If it was only strength that decided the power of territory,
Then the powerful elephant would rule the world.
But these animals live only on vegetation,
20 And of all large creatures they are the friendliest.
In this they show the same nature as cows and goats.'
Thus they talked of various things, coming to no conclusion.
As the sun rose and began to warm the earth,
They joined in the great feasting and dancing.
25 Exciting many curious eyes that followed them;
They revelled in the admiring looks of young, beautiful women.
At this point Zihlandlo said to Shaka:
'How wonderful, my lord, if you included among your royal
        women
30 The beautiful women of the Mkhize family!'
Shaka, making fun of this, said:
'No, Ghubela. Your family is too full of strange happenings.
In the days of your Ancestor, Mavovo, it is said
A young virgin became pregnant without a man.'
35 Prince Zihlandlo laughed and said: 'O, my lord,
It is a story that has been told to us over and over again.
But such tales, my lord, are numerous and they never end.
They are part of each nation and each generation.
We must talk more of things that concern our times.'
40 They walked like this alongside each other

Sometimes they re-enacted great dramatic episodes of their lives;
Sometimes their voices were low
As though to tackle a problem no one should know.
Throughout his stay Shaka was free and elated.

5   The day came when these two friends had to part.
It was a day of warmth and rejoicing.
As the procession reached the gate, Shaka said to Zihlandlo:
'Whoever departs from a place that has given him joy
Carries with him the thoughts that nourish and enrich life.
10 These thoughts speak well of the noble host.'
When Shaka came to Bulawayo he was still elated.
As Mbopha of Sithayi came to meet him, he said, lightheartedly:
'Your restlessness and overt welcome speaks rivers.
Many things must have occurred in my absence.'
15 The great concourse shouted and called out the epics.
There were councillors eager to report the excitement of recent
     events —
How in the southern regions of the Wosiyana clans
Something unknown in all Zululand happened
20 Gcugcwa dared to steal the king's cattle.
Captured, he was brought to Bulawayo to await judgement.
Shaka, on hearing the story, merely said:
'Leave him. We still have a full day tomorrow.
Perhaps he was driven to this heinous crime by hunger.
25 Only from him can we know the truth.'
At daybreak Shaka was still in high spirits.
He walked in the open bubbling with endless thoughts.
When he sat in the Assembly he infused into others this
     warmth.
30 Gcugcwa was brought before the king and the Assembly.
He walked proudly, like someone who had won a battle.
Shaka, noticing this, said to him:
'We greet you, Gcugcwa of the Wosiyana clan.'
Gcugcwa did not respond but looked away at the mountains.
35 The men of the Assembly were alarmed at this insolence.
Gcugcwa affected no respect, neither for the king nor the
     Assembly.
Shaka smiled slightly and greeted him again and again,
But still there was no response from Gcugcwa.

Even the Assembly was restless, fearing the King's anger.
Indeed, they wished they could respond on his behalf,
Or else intervene with soft words of conciliation.
When Gcugcwa finally replied, he spoke defiantly:
5 'My lord, seeing is not one-sided.
As you stand in judgement of me, so shall others.'
The Assembly, hearing these words, were stunned.
They knew Shaka detested such challenges.
He turned aside to one of the councillors and said:
10 'I wish Mgobhozi was here to observe these events.'
When Shaka looked at Gcugcwa again he was in a great fury.
He said: 'Gcugcwa, you have scandalized the Zulu nation:
You took the sacred property of our nation;
Then when I talk to you you answer me only arrogantly!'
15 Shaka ordered that all the stolen cattle be assembled
And penned in the large cattle-fold.
Then he commanded that the thief be tied at the gate.
The furious stampede of cattle!
They howled and bellowed, trampling on him with their massive
20   hoofs.
Their dust rose up, choking the thief and the onlookers.
When this whole event had almost been forgotten
Shaka said: 'I did not punish Gcugcwa for stealing,
But because of the words he directed at the Assembly.
25 The cattle belong to all the peoples of Zululand.
They must always be shared with those who need them.
Why did not this man come to me in broad daylight and ask?
Is it not our custom to give to those who ask?
Had he explained to the Assembly his condition of hunger,
30 He would still be sharing our harvests of the earth.'
Many were surprised that the king felt it necessary to explain.
They thought perchance he directed these words
At those who had recently joined the Assembly.
Had not such people been known as witches in the past?
35 These were all the whispered comments of the Assembly.

Book Fourteen: Laughter like perfumed winds brings grief

*The events that now concern Shaka are mainly domestic and dip-
lomatic. On the diplomatic level, he is keen to consolidate relations
with King George who, his subjects claim, rules over all the White
Races. He knows, however, that the ultimate logic of white presence is
military conflict. In this period the general mood of the Zulu nation is
characterized by a sense of power, maturity, invincibility, and a new
social and political ethic. There is a great deal of cultural activity in
the form of poetry competitions, dances, bullfights and hunting expedi-
tions. This is cut short abruptly by the illness and death of Nandi.
Shaka is almost unhinged by this event, thus demonstrating the crucial
role played by Nandi in Shaka's life.*

    The king was exuberant with life,
    Spreading laughter like perfumed winds of spring —
    Indeed, many songs celebrated this new mood.
    The grandmothers and grandfathers would say:
5   'When a king is as happy as ours
    The nation must gird itself for disasters.'
    The Forefathers said: 'A beautiful day closes with
        thunderstorms.'
    Shaka began again to agitate for an emissary to King George.
10   He summoned the Strangers from their coastal settlement
    And told them which of his men should go.
    Lieutenant King of the White Strangers led the team.
    Of him Shaka said he did not possess the wet lips of a thief.
    He made him commander of the Gibanganye regiment,
15   Thus giving him the status to present his word with authority.
    Those of the Palm Race began to learn of the overseas customs.
    Temporarily they stayed at the home of Hlambamanzi.
    While the boats were being repaired and assembled
    They stood at sea, displaying the name 'Shaka'.
20   In this way the Strangers affirmed their gratitude.
    While all these preparations were happening
    The great capital of Dukuza bustled with new life.
    Even enemies spoke with awe of the name of Shaka.

People of Zululand awaited the meeting of the two great
    monarchs,
For many had begun to admire the humility of the Strangers.

Everywhere there were words praising the rule of Shaka.
His brothers began to distrust their own close friends.
At this very time Shaka sent a word
Ordering a great festival to be held throughout Zululand.
Each family and clan was to make a sacrifice to its Ancestors.
Young men and women had to stage their own gala dance.
Everywhere new songs and new poems were composed.
Shaka himself led the regiments to the mountain;
Here, it was said, King Jama used to gaze at the horizon.
The great concourse of regiments raised their voices and sang.
They circled the mountain, imitating the giant river-snake.
Crowds followed the king to the flat top of the mountain
There to witness the games of strength initiated by Shaka.
People were adorned in their elegant finery,
Walking proudly, like girafes following the path of the forest.
When all the crowds had assembled,
A black bull was let loose into the arena
And ten young men were to kill it with bare hands.
The first team of bullfighters came from the Zimpohlo regiment.
They struggled and tumbled with the black bull in the arena.
The bull roared, advancing fiercely at them.
Some crept close, attempting to hold the violent forehead;
Others followed, stalking each step of the hind legs,
Planning to seize it all at once by a sudden movement,
But by its angry advance it made others retreat.
By simultaneous hold on the hind legs and the head,
They temporarily subdued it.
Jerking itself away from their grasp, it tore open one victim,
Flinging him high as though he was some piece of garment.
Angered, the young men seized it by the horns,
Simultaneously forcing its legs to the ground.
Others now twisted its head, breaking the vital neck bones.
In a loud voice it bellowed out its last beat of life;
The spectators shouted ecstatic slogans of praise.
Yet these challengers had failed since one of their team had
    died.

The next team of challengers came from the Mgumanqa
    regiment.
They flexed their muscles publicly in a boast of strength.
The black and white bull was now let loose;
5   It snorted and bellowed as if its head was filled with fire.
They fell on it with swift, co-ordinated movements.
They broke its power, throwing it on the ground like a log.
But by a sudden movement it threw them off,
Breaking loose and running triumphantly over the wide space.
10 Stopping near an anthill, it sharpened its horns
Throwing aside great clouds of dust.
Once again they attacked,
Pulling its fierce head upwards and twisting its neck;
Others turned its club-like hind legs,
15 Causing it to fall to the ground.
With a concerted effort they broke its neck bones.
A loud cry of pain proclaimed its last breath of life.
The spectators shouted in a great ecstasy of joy,
Acclaiming this display of skill and strength.
20 They called out now for more bull challengers.
Thus was let loose the fierce red bull
Whose shoulders trembled with muscle and power.
Proudly it snorted in all directions.
Suddenly, as if seeing some contemptible creature, it stopped;
25 Its legs quivered as if desiring to run in all directions at once;
Its chest pulsated as though it would burst open.
The team from the Mbelebele regiment inched closer
But by a quick movement the bull turned, its eyes red with
    anger.
30 It shook its long horns, threatening to break through their
    circle,
But the team of Mbelebele regiment closed in on it.
It now rushed to those ahead of it
But those behind it followed closely,
35 Causing it to move cautiously forward.
By a sudden move it broke loose,
Running wild and bellowing loud into the skies.
They all fell, tripping over each other and widening their circle.
Perhaps it was the tree ahead of it that hindered its movement,
40 Enabling the pursuers to turn its head and twist its neck.

It made a loud painful cry as they snatched its life with bare
    hands.
The spectators shouted out their approval.
Yet, it was the uFasimba regiment that won the day.
5   They did not spend much effort —
They rushed on the black bull, giving it no breathing space.
It was as if each one knew which weak spot to attack.
In a short period it was laid on the ground.
One section turned and twisted its head,
10 While others held its long lashing tail.
Still others disabled it through strikes at vital points.
A loud, clear breaking of the neck bone was heard.
The uFasimba team sang their song of triumph
They shouted out their battle calls.
15 The spectators could contain themselves no longer:
They shouted and called out their heroic poems,
Declaiming too the poems of the dead uFasimba heroes.
Shaka praised their swift and concerted actions;
The great mountains echoed with voices of praise.
20 After this event huge fires were lit to roast meat.
A season of plenty and fun dominated throughout Zululand.
In many regions large fires could be seen
Attesting to the feasting of this festival.
From afar could be heard the raised voices singing in the night.
25 By their songs they invited others,
Until the whole nation seemed absorbed in song;
Mbiya's desires seemed now fulfilled.
Women wore their chosen feathers of birds of paradise,
Blending the beauty of their adornments with those of the king.
30 He was tall and splendid in his white and green epaulettes of
    beads.

Shaka constantly heard rumours of a secret kept by his mother.
In truth, Nomazibuko, one of the royal women,
Had given birth to a boy whom she kept with Nomagwebu.
35 Nomagwebu secretly nurtured the king's child.
Of this boy Nandi said: 'I know my child will love this one;
He may at last accede to my request.
I shall look after him until he is grown.
When he reaches maturity I shall place him before the king.

Though he detests the idea of boy-children, he shall love him.
This child shall live to console me in my old age.
When I die I shall know the line of our family continues.'
To make the king less suspicious
5   It was said Nandi had adopted an orphaned child.
When Shaka arrived at Mkhindini royal city he said,
Commenting on this affair: 'I have heard many rumours —
How your love once again centres on a young boy.
I want to see for myself this strange creature.
10   I know whatever you love prospers.
Let me share and be part to this great event.'
Nandi tried to ignore this probe and said lightly:
'O, my child, someone wants to destroy our bond.
They overlook even the grievous state of my health.
15   What is so wrong for me to have something to love?
Is my old age not assuaged by the presence of children?
Sit down and tell me more about your life.
Your heart may yet be healed of its hurts;
Even my tired mind may find in you its peace.
20   In truth, I do not know any child who is not of our family.
All the children that are here are under my care.
Why should this one be separated from others?'
Shaka sat down, his eyes wandering in many directions.
He said: 'Indeed, Mother, how is it that this one is unknown to
25   me?
He seems to be your own secret child.
Ngwadi, my brother, has children and I know them all;
Nomchoba has children and I love them all.
If this one is kept away from me, how can I love him?'
30   Nandi summoned up courage and looked Shaka straight in the
      eye,
And said: 'I shall show you this beautiful child.
I shall tell you how he differs from others.
He is the one I have waited for these many years.
35   Should you cause him harm,
You shall have killed me.'
Shaka spoke kindly to Nandi and said:
'Never say such words: they are poisonous.
If this child is your favourite, he is my favourite also.'
40   Shaka was still uncertain if the child was his.

He still believed in the vows and promises made long ago.
Nandi called out to her attendant
And asked her to fetch the young son of Nomagwebu.
The attendant was alarmed at this command,
5   Knowing how often she had vowed to keep this secret.
She quietly said: 'So, let the truth be known.'
No sooner had the boy arrived
Than he began to cry hysterically, without control.
With his little arms he flapped the air.
10 Shaka simply said: 'Yes, Mother, I have seen enough.
I know now this is, indeed, your child.'
As he spoke he was looking directly at the forehead.
He stretched his hand and touched its fingers.
His eyes were focused on its tear-filled eyes;
15 His mind seemed absorbed on its features.
Nandi spoke softly to Shaka and said:
'My child, I ask you, give me this child.
Never have I asked you for anything in vain.
On this request centres all our lives together;
20 I desire a place where I shall live with my own family,
Where I shall see them grow and multiply.'
Nandi pleaded for this young boy
Hoping she would give to him a full life.
Shaka said: 'Your pain cuts deep:
25 It runs through my bowels like a spear.
I shall do as you have requested.
But acts of love are only given in exchange.
Grant me this then, exile him and his family
Where only you shall know this truth.
30 Let him live with someone of our clan of Zulu.
Mark his temple with three consecutive accents.
This way I, too, shall find him,
There too you shall possess your special own garden.
I do this only to console you;
35 Had it been in my power I would close my eyes,
Giving the decision to over-zealous councillors like Mbopha.'
Nandi quickly commented on these words and said:
'Do not let your tongue speak such things.
My feet are tired.
40 I no longer can travel to see my own great Mlilwana at Dukuza.

I content myself only with imagining his life.
You talk as though you don't see how advanced my age is.
Who knows? I may not have too long to live.'
Shaka quickly followed up on these words:
5   'Do not say such things lest evil things befall us.
I have told you often,
The Strangers shall bring you the herb of immortal life.
From it you shall gain new strength;
Through its power you shall live many years.'
10   Nandi stared with suprise, still not believing these claims.
Alarmed that her son clung to these hopes,
She laughed sympathetically and said:
'O Mlilwana, my child, listen to me.
I have already had a thousand years on earth.
15   The richness of my life far surpasses that of many families.
I have seen you grow from infancy to become my lord and
       master.
You have lived to gaze on the foreheads of our enemies.
All my wishes have been fulfilled:
20   There is nothing I still yearn for in life.
The medicines of foreigners speak only of your wishes
But we must always punctuate our hopes with reason.
I thank you again for your desires;
They are rich possessions I shall always treasure.
25   I thank the Ancestors, the Great Forefathers,
Who have guided you and enriched all our lives with life.'
They quietly embraced and words came through their eyes.
Nandi invited Shaka to a dish of rich buttermilk.
She said: 'Eat with me and let us never forget to share our lives
30   To give to each other more than we get.'
Such were their joys on the day,
Princess Nomchoba, finding them in this mood, said:
'I came here to see the daughter of the Langa family.
From the whispering winds I hear she no longer sleeps.
35   She is heard all night long playing with her witches' cat.
All hail, King of the Nation! all hail, my lord!'
Nomchoba only said this to poke fun at her brother.
Shaka responded in the same vein and said:
'I greet the Princess, whose tears never end.
40   She is heralded by rains and early grasshoppers.'

Continuously they teased each other this way
Until a whole day's rejoicing ended in song.

On the following day Shaka requested of Nandi the right to
    leave.
5 Perhaps the great daughter of the Langas was only acting
When she burst out, shouting angrily and saying:
'Too many years have I lived alone in this abandoned region,
Nor do I have the warmth of those I bore in my own womb.
I am a laughing stock to all passers-by
10 With smiles on their faces they point to my giant villages.
On a day when my children come to see me
They only stay long enough to leave their haunting shadows.
Then let that nation fall apart
If it depends only on one mind to rule:
15 Let this be a lesson to all councillors.
Why can't the man who has given a full life to others
Himself have his own share of a joyful life?'
Shaka simply laughed and said calmly:
'O mother, a fierce bull terrorizes even in its old age.
20 Nothing demands my presence at the capital.
If it be your wish, I shall stay to your heart's content.
Throughout the land there are numerous feasts and festivals.
I want now our nation to loosen its knots
No one should say the nation of Zulu knows no joy of life.
25 Besides, a ruler who is always in a hurry
Only invites to himself the winds of disaster.
All these things I know from experience.
My youth has ended and I am old and wise.'
The old Princess Nandi was pleased with his words.
30 Beaming with joy, she held him and kissed him on his cheeks.
In all the days he spent with Nandi
They talked and laughed only as members of one family.
Nandi ordered Ngwadi to come to this reunion.
The words of joy they shared together
35 Shall remain eternally as echoes from their times.
They shall nourish the secret thoughts of the child of our era.
Someone shall yet be awakened from his sleep
And be made to wander in the quietness of the night.
He shall be heard mumbling to himself.

'Where are they? Where are the Beautiful Ones?
Where is Nandi of Nguga?
Where is Shaka, the great son of Senzangakhona?
Where is the gentle Princess Nomchoba?
5   Where are all those who have nourished our nation?'
He shall stand alone beside a giant tree
And hear their voices humming incomprehensibly in the wind.
He shall see them as shadows clustered together.
He shall hear the clear voice of Nandi of Zululand.
10 Then he shall begin to tell their story and say:
'At the great mountain of Maqhwakazi
I have seen a pyramid of stones.
Let all nations know we are eternal;
Like a mountain cairn we rise forever and ever.'
15 Such joys often travel throughout our land,
Infusing the young with wisdom and the old with youth.
Summer bloomed its fruits before the eyes of the sky.
The stems were banded together with their lush fullness.
In all the open savannahs the cattle and sheep and goats
20   grazed. . . .'

Young men followed large teams of young women
As they sauntered through the hills with bridegrooms' gifts.
In the clear pools of summer they washed their feet;
Even old men look young on wedding days.
25 Such was the commotion in the land
When Shaka finally departed for the royal city of Dukuza.
Attendants walked beside him;
Sheltering him with shields against the blazing sun.
From a distance coils of thunderclouds formed on the horizon.
30 The trees dropped their lower leaves.
The king's royal feather swayed gently.
People began to sing. They sang a new song:
'We who give birth to men of greatness,
We look this way and point to the sun;
35 We look that way and point to the sun;
We look north, east, south, and west, we see the sun.
The sun hangs over the great cities of our nation.
At eBaqulusini it nourishes the earth;
At Mkhindini it matures the season's millet.

Bulawayo is the home of Dlungwane;
Dukuza, is the home of Malandela.'
From the poet were heard episodes of great battles:
'Great fierce power,
5   That looms like a mountain as it spreads the feast,
You who are ever ready for battle!
Great collection of boulders, that are like those of Nkandla.
The hawk that ascended the hills of Nzwakele.
In the land of Khushwayo he was as bright as daylight.
10 Shaka found two wild animals:
Confronting each other between Nsuze and Thukela.
Those two animals were Thondolozi and Sihayo.
When he arrived he threw a shield between them and they
        disengaged.
15 He seized the cattle that were meant for weddings —
Even now he still gets fat from them.
The porcupine, that stabbed the delicate ones
Between the regions of Nzawu and Magaye;
Morning star of Mjokwane, that trails across the sky:
20 It stands by its tail.
It is embedded in the high heavens!'
The whole region resounded with songs and poems.
Long processions brought their harvests to Dukuza
Shaka roamed restlessly in the new city.
25 He said to Prince Magaye, the son of Dibandlela:
'South of the Mvoti river I shall build the camps of Gibabanye.
North of Dukuza I shall build the camps of Bhekenya.
On the coastal region shall be the camps of Mgumanqa.
This regiment shall keep watch over the Strangers.
30 Shaka was still eager to go back to Bulawayo.
He still felt unfamiliar with the surroundings at Dukuza
And yearned for the spectacular sights of Bulawayo.
He invited Magaye to the great hunt at Bulawayo.

Nomazibuko and her child fled and were never seen again.
35 Some said she settled in the southern regions of Mkhomazi river;
Some claim she was seen in the land of the Mpondos.
No one will ever know the ultimate truth!
What is known is how Mpampatha remained the king's only
        favourite;

She was favoured by the king for her mind and calmness.
She now looked after Nandi.
When it was her turn to love she gave all without reserve;
By her tenderness she made the pains disappear.
5   She spoke openly, without fear.
Her words often haunted her listeners with their sharpness.
She was no lover of flattery.
Her beauty lay in her power to please when she chose to please.
It was she, too, who witnessed Nandi's final illness.
10 She had seen her fall after a short spell of dizziness.
That day when Nandi woke
Her body was hot as though touched by circles of fire.
She was sweating and breathing heavily; her chest hissed.
To her attendants she kept repeating:
15 'Under no circumstances must you tell Shaka, my son.'
Thus two months passed, while her illness worsened;
Yet she still demanded the truth be hidden from her son.
For such are those possessed of deep love,
They fight alone, sparing us their extremes of pain.
20 Repulsing the furious missiles directed at us by fate.
We hold onto their shoulders to be carried away by their dream.
Perhaps because of these strong thoughts
Shaka was disturbed in spirit during his whole stay at
        Bulawayo.
25 To Prince Zihlandlo, who had visited him, he said:
'A strange thought constantly nags at my mind.
Often I see myself at the Mthethwas.
There is a clear outline of every stone that I knew.
The whole region where I lived assumes a new life.
30 There are voices of people long dead;
They pass softly as if carried by the wind.
Then I see red forests of Mthunduluka fruit;
A sequence of bird song then emerges from a distance.
It is not from a dream these visions come
35 But from a strange state of awakening.
It is as though I am about to travel.'
Zihlandlo replied to him softly and gently:
'This often happens when the mind is elated,
And so it is: after these many months, you are happy again.
40 The new capital of Dukuza speaks of a new life.

It fills your spirit with new fears and joys.
The same restlessness seized your mind
When long ago you left the Mthethwa capital.'
Shaka said: 'Mkhize, your words speak to the inner mind.
5 As our Forefathers say: "A great doctor is he who can listen,
Who hears the urgent words of someone else's wounds."
Each man is burdened with fears
Against them he constantly wages his own battles
No man lives totally by the laws of knowing.
10 Whoever claims to know all things is a liar.'
Zihlandlo listened, fascinated by these words,
Wondering what truly went on in Shaka's mind.
He thought: 'How strange the tenants of power.
Was Shaka not the man to whom everyone listened in awe?
15 Was he not the very same man
Who by his courage stood firmly on the ground
As others curled in fear of an eclipsing sun?
But does he not now display childish fears?'
Zihlando returned to his home, overawed by these things.
20 He mused on how Shaka had many facets to his genius.
To his attendant he commented, as though concluding a
        thought:
'The king's mind is like a disease that does not heal.'

Perhaps it was only to distract his mind;
25 Perhaps he meant to celebrate the new life at Dukuza,
Or perhaps he meant to give the army an excercise in
        strategy —
Shaka ordered the greatest hunt ever held in Zululand.
He promised the successful man the high honours of war.
30 Thus everywhere matured men and young men were seen
Sitting by the river, sharpening their favourite hunting spears.
Many sang the great songs of the hunting season.
You would have thought there was some new impending war.
Many were seized by the fever of the hunt;
35 They composed songs and staged dramas for it.
Those who hit their targets acquired new poems.
Those who missed were given the idiot's songs.
It was as though the whole Zulu army was to go out to hunt.
The young recruits followed their chosen leaders,

Watching and listening as if to some detail of battle strategy.
The young huntsmen were to commandeer the herds of animals,
Driving them to the trap of the black and white Mfolozi rivers.
They were to close with high thorns in all openings,
5 Making a constant din to drive the game from the points of exit.
Early at dawn, as the dew still covered a man's knee,
The great hunt set out in its variety of names and families.
It sang the ancient hunting song of King Ndaba:
'You hunted in the forests and the forests sang:
10 "All hail! All hail, thou ruler of nations!"
The wilderness teems with bucks —
Gifts of friendship shall be of the meat of antelopes!'
The whole region resounded with hunting poems and songs.
Dogs barked from all sides like a tumultuous chorus.
15 At the meeting point of the white and black Mfolozi rivers
Shaka, together with the Mbelebele regiment, kept watch.
Among them was the great Njikiza of the Ngcolosi clan,
Who often praised his war club:
'There are larger and smaller morsels for all lions.
20 You must not shy away from these games —
Man and animals die in the same manner!'
Shaka commented: 'The elephant is like an assemblage of rocks.
It is better to cut its ligaments with a battleaxe.'
As they joked Njikiza knew Shaka would invent his own
25   strategy.
Thus they whiled away time as they waited.
At a distance Nqoboka sat quietly, chewing the herbs of the
        hunt.
Many secretly wondered what so occupied his mind.
30 In whispers they claimed he saw the shadow of the dead
With whom he shared the thrill of such events.
Once he killed a raving lioness and sat laughing on it.

A great concourse drove herds of animals in the king's direction.
The bedlam of sounds, of animals and people, filled the region.
35 Hunting dogs leaped and barked like branches in the whirlwind.
From afar a great cloud of dust swirled to the heavens.
Large herds of elephants and awkward giraffes beat the ground;
A great commotion of beasts and birds filled the valleys;
Guinea fowls with broken wings screamed to heaven for mercy.

Young boys rained their hunting weapons on them,
Hoping to earn their beads of honour.
The antelopes thrust their limbs into the air;
And by the power of the intestines they leapt above the earth —
5   It was as though some furious wasps had been let loose on
     earth.
As the herd of fleeing animals neared the guards
They turned back again, breaking the lines of their pursuers,
Following the open route to the valley.
10 Still others fell helter-skelter into the sheer of the cliff.
A large herd of elephants was trapped by the river;
It was there that the hunters swooped in on them.
From all sides they stabbed and shouted their hunting songs.
A bull elephant attempted to break through the crowd,
15 Furiously trumpeting and ripping the roots of old trees.
Shaka and Njikiza came running towards them
As though a war had been declared between men and
     elephants.
When Njikiza saw how angrily the elephants charged
20 He lured them, challenging the largest of the herd.
It was then Shaka seized a battleaxe and cut its ligaments.
As it weakened someone stabbed it from the back.
Attempting to flee from its tormenters it charged
But Maphitha of Sojiyisa followed it closely.
25 With a long, shrieking cry it tumbled on the ground.
On hearing the voice of a dying relative the fleeing herd veered
     back,
Confronting the team of pursuing hunters.
In this confusion some chased and some fled;
30 A man of the Khawula clan lost his balance and fell;
A huge bull elephant picked him up and flung him on to a stone.
Encouraged by this, it rushed on Sidada of the Mfekane clan
And crushed him under its massive foot.
At great speed some of the uFasimba regiment descended on it
35 And with fierce blows they stabbed it to death.

Thus did the great hunt progess until late afternoon,
When all sections were ordered to sit and rest.
Only the young continued their pursuit of little creatures.
Some could be seen running across the plains;

Jumping and shouting, attempting to capture the animals with
   their bare hands.
The men of Zululand sat on the open ground.
A high pile of the hunters' kill lay sprawled before them.
5   Young boys rushed hither and thither collecting firewood,
Making large fires on which to roast meat for their elders.
Many tales were told in jest.
Some re-enacted the great episodes of the hunt;
Some began shouting poems of excellence of the great hunters;
10   Some sang songs that were newly composed for the occasion.
From all sides were many voices of celebration.
Above this din were heard the flutes of the Bhele clan.

Ziba of the Dlamini royal clan now began to dance.
It was he who had killed two large kudus alone.
15   Those with him told how on encounter
He stared at the beast, eyeball to eyeball,
Each unable to retreat and driven to a fence of dead wood.
Bending down to pierce him, the beast came charging at him.
Ziba merely slid aside standing behind a large tree;
20   Thus he was able to plunge his hunting knife into its back.
As he triumphantly finished up the beast
A second one emerged from the left side of him.
In a flash he turned and pierced it close to its heart.
He pulled his hunting knife and severed its jugular vein.
25   The two beasts lay before him like two hillocks.
Many who saw this feat fervently acclaimed him.
Conferring on him the emblem of the hunters.
The king, praising him, said: 'You are a great hunter.
You derive your courage and tactics from the Qokli battles.'
30   He said this merely to elevate his act of daring,
For, in truth, Ziba was still only a boy at the time of this battle.

It was amidst all these celebrations
That a messenger came panting to the king and said:
'I come to you with news that paralyses a man's tongue.
35   The Queen Mother of our nation already breathes with extreme
   pain.'
No sooner had he finished saying these words
Than Shaka rose, his eyes flashing like sparks of fire.

It was as though by their light they leaped a thousand
    miles.
His chest trembled as though seized by some convulsions.
His whole physique turned dark, like the earth before a
5   thunderstorm.
The messenger suddenly fell down,
His mouth frothing and his eyes showing only their white.
His body trembled and suddenly he stopped breathing. . . .
It was said his speed had eaten into his heart.
10 The news was spread to all the gathered crowds.
The king commanded that the hunt be ended at once.
With a small section of the uFasimba regiment
He set out to the capital of the ailing Nandi.
Without as much as a stop for water
15 He traversed the valleys and mountains,
Hurrying as if possessed by some spirit.
He slept only lightly by night.
Forging through the tall blades of grass
He by-passed the ancient mountain of the sacred stones.
20 No longer was his power like that of a common soldier,
But an inner force had seized his heart and mind.
In truth, those who receive bad news
Have in them the power to deter its violence.
By their command they can scatter the forces of death,
25 Preventing them from touching too soon the paths of their
      relatives.
As the sun climbed into the high point of the sky
Shaka, with his bodyguard, entered eMkhindini royal city.
At the gates he stood silently,
30 As though temporarily he had forgotten the reason for his
      journey.
The lower clumps of bushes shook
As though to tell each other of the nightmares to come.
The winds carried the voices of the crowds.
35 Shaka proceeded slowly, speaking only inaudible words.
He sat down at a distance from Nandi's house.
To him came Fynn to pay his respects.
He saluted the king and said: 'I fear, my lord,
This illness has beaten all my medicines.
40 We must fortify ourselves and think of the worst, as men.

We must appeal to the Ancestors to postpone the painful
    moment.
I feel the pain which you alone can fully experience.
Though a foreigner, I feel part of your great household.'
5 Shaka never commented; he merely sat and stared,
Focusing only in one direction.
All day he remained on this ground.
The high sun lowered its eye to the west,
Dancing on the bald heads of the old men.
10 No one spoke; only the hearts and minds churned their secrets.
A young boy, who was ignorant of these events,
Wandered into the arena and was startled by the king's
    presence.
He fled in terror, crying out as though he had seen an
15   apparition.
Terrified, adults drew away their children.
The smell of death hovered over the mountains and everywhere.
The royal grounds were stricken with silence.
Suddenly Ngomane's voice broke the quietness of the evening:
20 'Lord of Nations, scion of Jama, of Ndaba,
Of Phunga, of Magaba, of Ntombela, of Nkosinkulu,
Child of the great kings, of Mdlani, of Zulu, of Malandela,
Wild one, who triumphed in many battles —
We have lost at last by the judgement of the eternal circle.
25 The great Mother of our Nation is dead.
We are stripped naked of our cloak for all seasons.
We who were warm and comfortable are turned into orphans.
The earth is covered with our tears.
Where shall we hide from this fearful season?
30 The lion of death has entered our house:
It is trampling freely on our sacred shrines.
We run into the mountains, carrying our grief on our heads.
How enormous the river that swallows our children!'
As he said these words he seemed to mix all sounds.
35 The crowds that were assembled seemed fixed eternally on the
    ground.
Suddenly a great wailing descended on the earth.
The mountains tossed back the voices of crowds.
By a strange power Shaka gained his strength and stood up.
40 He retired to his house

And emerged, adorned in all his battle array.
He stood before his mother's house, tears running down his face,
But he did not wipe them.
Like slow drops of rain they fell onto his shield.
5   He stood like this as though listening to an aching pain.
Unable to control himself, he burst out in a loud voice.
His words travelled through the zone of silence
And settled by their own power on the pinnacles of mountains.
Suddenly a fearful mourning exploded throughout
10   Zululand.
Thousands joined the dark chorus of grief:
It was as though life on earth would end all at once.
All paths to Mkhindini royal city were choked with mourners.
They shouted, they called out the name of Nandi.
15 Messengers scattered to all the distant lands:
The whole earth was seized by one great era of mourning.
Even insects seemed to whistle in sadness.
From all the mountains could be seen clusters of people:
They spread from hill to hill their fierce message of death.
20 A woman's voice shot through into the sky:
'Voice of death, voice of the dark winds,
What nation on earth experiences so much grief?'
Someone heard her and shouted back in response:
'Our death is fearful! The Female Elephant is no more!
25 How terrible the fate of a woman who gives birth to children!
Where shall she sleep? The mountains are bare.
Even the little rivers of Mhlathuze and Mbozama are wailing.
Their mourning rises to the high walls of cliffs;
Their eyes are closed, their ears hear only our song.
30 The stone returns.
It is sterile, it experiences no human warmth.
It has sundered itself from the parent stone.
It has created a heap of black stones.
On them people walk, animals walk,
35 Leaving a memory for generations to come.'
Someone responded: 'What is it that I hear? Is that the wind?
Is our destiny to be turned into voices by grief?
Are we to wander aimlessly, like children of Nozulane?
When the night fell over the earth,
40 Our children fled from the violent winds.

The cloud has covered the heads of my children.
I am carrying the body of my child from the city of
    Bulawayo.
The seasons have let loose the eyeless night.
5   They have left me without a hoe to dig for my children.'
Processions carrying wedding gifts threw them down
And began the hymn of mourning.
Some turned back from their journey,
Trampling on the young plants of the season:
10 'Let me shout with a voice that pierces the sky;
Let the earth seize me by my wings;
Let my eyes and ears be closed so that I may not hear;
Let me make a home for the sad song;
Let our secrets hide their nakedness from the sun.
15 The beetles shall breed and escape with my grief.'

It was as though the whole nation had descended on Mkhindini
    city.
Such grief is only true from the tales of old and passers-by.
It is only to be witnessed by the silent mountains.
20 It chooses a night to bring its message.
Shaka sang a song no one had ever heard before.
His whole body shook and trembled as he sang;
His voice was deep as though from some gorge.
Others began to sing the song, sending its message to all lands.
25 The sun closed her eye and her eyelashes of clouds were like a
    forest.
Over and over the solemn hymn was sung,
Its words intermingled with tears and voices of grief.
Singing this song, Shaka entered the house of Nandi.
30 On her face still was a suspended smile.
When Shaka saw her he bent down and held up her hand:
'I have now seen you and bid you farewell.
I shall not come again to the place of the sun.
Farewell, great multitude of voices!
35 Farewell, great round stone of the Ancestral Forefathers.
I shall not laugh again at the grounds of Mkhindini;
I shall choose my moments of joy in between sadness.'
As he spoke, the veins in his temples shot out.
Princess Nomchoba, who had stood a few paces away,

Now approached him and said;
'As she died she uttered only one word: **Mlilwana**.'
They stared at each other and there was only silence.

Thus began the great mourning for Princess Nandi of the Zulus.
5 Many homes were left in ruins;
Families lived by the code of grief.
Never in all the history of Nguniland was ever such mourning;
Never in all legends had there ever been such sorrow;
Through gatherings and regiments sadness composed her songs.
10 The shadow of Nandi inhabited the nation's arenas.
They multiplied from under the feet of strangers.
The bright sun was choked by the voices of mourning.
Those who bore ancient grudges against each other
Now seized the moment to vent their revenge,
15 Claiming to act in the king's name.
Shaka could not hide his sadness,
Though a king must keep secret his grief.
Even old men were seen in gestures of mourning.
They mourned for the king; they mourned for their children's
20   children.
Fearful was the occasion of Nandi's funeral.
Fierce songs of mourning burst amidst wailings of crowds.
Nandi of Nguga haunted the land like a shadow of a
      mountain.
25 Great gatherings of men and women sang solemn songs of
      mourning.
Each wave sought to excel the other with mourning.
Shaka retreated from the crowds, neither talking nor seeming to
      listen.
30 It was as though all the splendours of yesterday
Would be blotted out at once.
Decay hovered like a vulture over the heads of men.
The nights cut the joys that were once the pride of Nguniland.

Late in the evening, when the sun fell behind the mountains,
35 Shaka came close and examined the face of his dead parent.
When they moved Nandi's body into the grave
Shaka turned away, as though fleeing from a memory.
He stood staring at the red cloud on the horizon;

He surveyed the blankets of the night as they followed each
    other.
He cursed the earth, uttering words of anger.
The crowds drifted, singing the funeral anthems.
5   Shaka sat alone in his house of mourning.
Only Nomchoba came to him and said:
'Son of my father, our mother's death spells disaster.
No one in all life knows the truth of what you feel.
Our family was unique among families
10   Even those who were our relatives detested us.
As it grew it prided itself on its own secrets;
Even those who mourn with us are banned from them.
I only make this one request from you, child of my father:
Let not our house be destroyed in one day.
15   This, indeed, is the wish of our parent.'
Shaka turned and looked at her with kindly eyes.
He said: 'Nomchoba, daughter of my father,
It is I who should be consoling you,
But I failed; my bones were weak.
20   You have woken me from sleep;
By your hand you have tied together the broken tones.'
Shaka began to walk, pacing the house with renewed life.
Indeed, Nomchoba's voice sounded like the voice of Nandi.

It was on this day that Shaka had a visitation.
25   He dreamt that Nandi was scolding him fiercely,
Saying: 'The nation awaits you, Mlilwana.
It is time your feet climbed the mountain.
Do not sink with me into the soft eternal night.
What will those who came before you say?
30   Enemies will begin plotting against you,
Saying you ruled only through the house of abasemaLangeni.
Rise and give your command like a true leader.'
Shaka awoke, trembling and searching for the disembodied
    voice.
35   It was on the following day
He called together all the great councillors of the land
And addressed them: 'Through you I make known to the world
The death of my mother has killed many parts of me.
But so that the nation may have a way to mourn,

I order that this grief be expressed with dignity.
This is the law that befits the mourning of our family.
UFasimba and Jubinqwanga must keep watch over my mother's
grave.
5 But I direct these words to you, Ngomane:
As I am in mourning, I delegate to you all the affairs of state.
It is you and the Assembly that shall speak.
I cannot say more. I must pay my respects to my mother.'
The Assembly saluted, solemnly consenting to these words.
10 Ngomane, speaking for the Assembly, addressed the king:
'O Ndaba, our tears fill up the oceans.
The whole House of Zulu carries a heavy load;
The Assembly and the nation shall always revere the Queen
Mother.
15 To us and all nations her name shall be spoken in whispers;
To her many nations shall sing their songs of praise.
She was the parent who nursed the young.
Today our nation boasts of a thousand nations.
Which woman could boast so much achievement?
20 Were not her visions the sustenance of our nation?
Which woman would not have said:
"It is enough; the power and glory demands that we fight no
more"?
But she said: "Our nation shall prosper through courage and its
25 vision."
For us a great heroine has died;
Her fame shall shine eternally like the sun.
Whoever shall be told the story shall say:
"It was proper the great Zulu nation should mourn."
30 All peoples shall speak only of the one Female Elephant.
She alone gave birth to the king, who is the fountain of our
nation.
There have been two rulers in Zululand:
One gentle, who excelled in her kindness and generosity;
35 Another who rules with wisdom and plans with wisdom.
Such duality has never been known in all history.
Ours shall be sung as the nation of the great heroes and
heroines.'
When he stopped there was a loud shout of 'Bayede!'
40 The Assembly called out: 'Your words are ours, Ngomane.'

At this point Shaka left the Assembly.
They debated now on the various ways to express their
    mourning.
Then proclaimed: 'There shall be no ploughing and no reaping;
5   No cows shall be milked throughout the land;
No man shall sleep with his wife in the year of mourning;
No woman shall be pregnant in the year of mourning;
Lovers shall not visit each other in the year of mourning;
No one shall wear ornaments in the year of mourning.'
10 All these commands were broadcast throughout the land.
Many hailed and praised them,
Eager to display their warm love for their king and the Queen
    Mother.

Many months passed, but messengers still arrived from distant
15   lands;
Some came from Moshoeshoe, the great king of the Basothos;
Some arrived from Sobhuza, the great king of the Ngwanes;
Some came from Queen Mjantshi of Thobela of Pediland.
Some came from kings and princes of little-known kingdoms.

20 After many months of mourning, the love of the people turned
    into bitterness,
For the sight of empty fields speaks disaster to families.
People began to yearn for the happy life of yesterday.
Cattle and goats shrivelled and were emaciated;
25 It was as though the great ancient famine of Madlantule had
    returned.
Even those who had been eager to show off their grief
Now began to make their own secret violations.
But a man's conscience never rests;
30 These same violators set out hunting their own victims.
They ravaged and attacked others to cover their own crimes.
They burnt and destroyed whole villages and settlements.
Huge fires could be seen by night, lighting the skies.
Raiders and vagabonds roamed the country like wild animals.
35 Throughout the land they were known as 'the tears of the king'.
By their power they terrorized whole regions.
They harassed the little men.
The nobles and the heroes, even now, enjoyed their privileges.

It was as though the great Zulu nation
Would collapse and vanish all at once.
The enemies of the king held many secret meetings,
Discussing frequently the impending downfall of Shaka's rule.
5 Prince Dingane approached Princess Mkhabayi once again.
His mind still set on pursuing his secret goals.
Dingane was known for his short-sighted anger and impatience:
His provocations often led to swift and sudden actions.
Thus, armed for an argument, he spoke to his aunt:
10 'Can you not see that the country is falling into ruins?
We all loved Nandi for her kindness,
But if her death means the end of humanity
Then this violates our great Ancestral heritage.
I am certain from all the stories that I hear,
15 And what I myself have seen,
Shaka has been seized by some madness that was heralded at
    his birth.
Those who lived then have told us
When Nandi was pregnant with him she went insane.'
20 The great Zulu princess reared up her head and said:
'Dingane, you speak with the language of children!
Shaka does what he does inspired by a deep pain.
You shall never know the depth of his loss.
You grew up in your mother's house amidst plenty;
25 Today you share in the glory of the empire he alone created.'
Prince Dingane followed up these words and said:
'The nation of the Zulus was not born with the birth of Shaka.
Before him were many of our great Forefathers.
There were Jama, Phunga, Mageba, Mdlani and many others.
30 We who live are the outcome of their heroic past.
We cannot watch the country disintegrate by the hand of one
    man.
We, too, issue from the women who are our mothers.
Shall the whole world be destroyed when they die?'
35 Prince Dingane spoke in great anger;
His whole visage turned dark like a black mamba.
But Princess Mkhabayi spoke calmly and said:
'It is only now that you say something that spells wisdom.
You speak like the true descendant of Jama.
40 Being a ruler demands more than concern with petty things.

If Nandi went insane as she was pregnant with Shaka
It is of no consequence to our present truth.
Besides, this you should never forget:
Shaka is a ruler who is unique in all our history.
5   If the death of Nandi has turned his mind
Then it is a weakness that still attests to his greatness,
For, truly, there is no lover who is without fault.
I command you to know and see these truths as they are.
Besides, you must always know Shaka is your brother.
10 His love for his brothers and sisters is unsurpassed.
Some lesser rulers customarily kill their relatives.
Filled with jealousy, they lay waste their royal cities,
Concocting against them some claim to witchcraft.
It is easy for a ruler to kill whoever stands in his way.
15 Shaka has chosen to be without heir;
Still never did he kill a single one of his family.'
Prince Dingane swallowed words like one who is a stammerer.
He said: 'Yet did I not escape narrowly from Matiwane?'
Mkhabayi, dismissing this often-repeated grudge, said:
20 'Dingane, I know your perennial complaint.
How many times has Shaka survived to fight still other wars?
Yet many rulers only sit at a distance, watching battles.'
Mkhabayi, though critical of Shaka's actions, knew
Dingane would never attain the glory of Shaka's rule.
25 Too often she had to restrain him from precipitate action.
He was like those who, carried away by their own thoughts and
        pride,
Imagine themselves wiser and more gifted than they are.
They are not like those of our house,
30 Who are eternally beautiful, whose actions are blessed,
Who choose by their abundant will their own moment of
        triumph.
Like Nodumehlezi, like all the children of fame
Who are sought by all seasons, their minds are restless.

35 The mourning had spread its sadness throughout the land.
It had sown and reaped the fruits of bitterness
And people were tired and people died.
One such night Prince Zihlandlo visited Shaka,
For every month the great prince visited his king and friend;

This way, he hoped to assuage the pain and heal the wound.
When he arrived at the royal residence, he was tired;
His spirits were low.
He said, speaking despondently to the king:
5 'Son of Ndaba, I am filled with deep sadness.
The nation may yet fall prey to the raids of bandits,
Who in their attacks vow by your name.
While the nation has mourned with you in earnest,
Some, carried away by their own evil nature,
10 Roam the country, terrorizing families and travellers.
Against these, my king must act at once.
By these acts they make our grief look trivial.
The whole country has suffered from such men as Madlebe,
Who wanders through the land with his own army,
15 Strutting about arrogantly, as if he alone feels the grief!
In the village of Sibangani he wiped out everyone,
Accusing even the elders of giving licence to others.
Many are killed by those who seek revenge,
And many a stranger has been chased in error
20 Some have said Madlebe is not alone in these deeds
But has trained a body of men to execute his commands.
In all directions they spread terror and lawlessness.'

It was this terrible story that Zihlandlo told.
When Shaka heard it he closed his eyes
25 As though he had been attacked by some illness:
'These happenings weigh heavily on my shoulders;
Yet I cannot command the mourning to cease in its middle,
Lest I violate the intentions and customs of the nation.
In the words of Mbopha: I shall have rejected
30 The warm hand that raises me from the grave.
I shall have undermined the words of Ngomane.
People may say by a whim I cut short their mourning.
My mother was not mine alone, but of the whole nation.'
Prince Zihlandlo, making his last comment, said:
35 'My lord, I shall speak what lurks in my mind
Only when I return to see my king again.
For the moment, I ask for time to think over these things.
My last word to you, my lord, is this:
Command that these excesses cease.

Order the bandits who use your name to be brought to justice.
Let them stop harassing your loyal and innocent subjects.
I know it is hard to decide which people act in good faith;
But for you, a king, and a great king, the truth is never
5   hidden.
Despite the shadow that haunts your life
You shall still find a way to make life breathe again.'
Perhaps Zihlandlo never saw the full truth of his wound;
For it is said when a man goes through great agonies
10 His mind temporarily ceases to decide its path.
It stumbles, not knowing from what shade it shall drink again.

People were walking about solemnly at Bulawayo city;
Councillors were talking softly as they sat around the king.
Many told stories and tales of ancient kingdoms;
15 Some narrated handed-down episodes of the days of Ndaba.

Like a fierce thunderclap a voice was heard,
Piercing through the silences of the wind and of the people.
It rose, spreading over the whole quiet region of Bulawayo.
It was a long time since someone had uttered the king's poems.
20 The voice called out furiously: 'Dlungwane, son of Ndaba,
Dlungwane, who is of the Mbelebele regiment:
You overwhelmed them at their own cities;
Till daylight their homes tumbled over each other!
Nodomehlezi, son of Menzi,
25 Thou vast region no one can divide like water,
The battleaxe that rose high above others,
Shaka! (I fear to call him by his name
Because Shaka was the king who ruled through battle.)
Whistling one, who is like a lion,
30 Who prepared for battle in the forest like a madman.
This madness seizes the crowds of man and shines in their eyes.
Wild one, son of Sezangakhona,
The stick that is red even on the side of holding —
He conquered Qwabe by overwhelming him.
35 Young black calf of Menzi
That humbled others!'

The councillors who sat with Shaka saw his eyes suddenly light
    up;
They flickered constantly in all directions.
At such moments he often stood, abandoning the Assembly,
5   But on this occasion he did not move.
They all sat high on their round ground stools
Not knowing what reaction would follow
Suddenly he turned to his councillors, and said:
'Who is this who shouts when the country is in mourning?
10   Call him, let him explain the reason for such defiance.'
He paused, drinking from the beer vessel before him.
Still the voice persisted shouting the king's poems;
He repeated the great heroic stanzas
Like someone who had beheld a miracle.
15   He spoke loud as he approached:
'O my lord Ndaba, King of Kings, descendant of Luzumane.
Builder and moulder of our nation,
Fighter who has fought in a hundred battles and wars,
Look outside, my lord: the vultures are having a festival!
20   They toss to each other the pieces of your own nation.
In ancient times Ndaba died, Jama died, Senzangkhona died,
But never in our history has there been so much mourning!
You are killing your own nation, my lord.
What nation shall you rule hereafter?
25   Must a nation be destroyed with the death of its parent?
What story shall she tell to the Spirit of Ndaba,
When behind her she can only hear the wailing?
The land has been devastated by mourning;
It is as though death shall swallow the whole earth.
30   There are no longer crops in the fields.
There are no pumpkins in our gardens.
Bandits roam through the length and breadth of our land.
The little neighbouring kings may yet find us weakened.
I make this plea knowing your love for our nation is deep.
35   I weep for the bulls of Zululand that shall be seized by
    foreigners.
They shall drink the milk that is due to our children!
I weep for your pain that shall sink into our land:
It is time you controlled this pain, my lord.
40   A mourning that never ends opens the house to enemies.

What will happen to Zululand when there are no longer
    children?
Who shall heal our wounds and sing our songs?
It is not the first time someone has died in Zululand.
5 Death is nothing, my lord; only life is real.
My very words sentence me to death,
But if dying I bring life to others,
Then I shall choose to die and live only through their lives.
I shall celebrate through the joys of my lord and king.
10 As I speak, many homes live in fear,
But a king as great as my lord does not rule by fear.
Cease your mourning, my lord, cease your sadness, my king.'
Then he waited for the king to comment, bowing his body.
The king's forehead was creased in anger.
15 He asked him slowly and solemnly: 'What is your name?
How dare you speak to me in these words?'
The stranger answered softly and said:
'I am Gala, the son of Nodada of the Biyela clan.
I have my family settled the other side of the Mpaphala region.'
20 He spoke confidently, without fear.
He only awaited the king's answer to his words.
Shaka now turned to his councillors
And, speaking in great anger he raised his voice,
And said: 'Ngomane! Mpangazitha! Mbopha kaSithayi!
25 Did you hear the words of Gala of Nodada?
Why did you not speak for the nation's welfare?
Are you not its councillors and servants?
Why have you not alerted me to these disasters?'
Each claimed his own reason for failure.
30 Shaka, speaking directly to Gala, said:
'I thank you for my sake and for the whole Zulu nation;
You have released us from the nightmare of grief.
I feel light and free again.
I wish you and your family the blessings of the Ancestors.
35 Never throughout the season of mourning
Have I heard words so soothing as yours.
I honour you with a herd of a hundred black oxen.
Tell all your clansmen and friends: thus a man is rewarded
For his courage.
40 Such acts far surpass those displayed in battle.

They enrich the nation and all its children.
You have infused in me a new life.
When you reach your region, don the head-ring of maturity
And so, too, should all those who are your agemates.
5   You are truly a great man;
Not only do you fight with weapons, but with wisdom.'
From that very day the whole nation called off its mourning.

As the messengers scattered throughout the land
The king followed up with a second order:
10 He would finally move to his new capital of Dukuza.
There he would stage the Ceremony of Return for the Queen
        Mother.
Shaka began to radiate with new life,
Though he still grieved within himself.
15 Sometimes he would suddenly change, withdrawing from
        gatherings.
Many lived in constant fear of these whims,
For soon thereafter he would fall into a deep mood.

It is said no feast in all the history of the Palm Race
20 Shall ever surpass the Queen Mother's Ceremony of Return.
In her honour thousands of cattle were slaughtered;
Many came to eat and dance and laugh with all life.
On the first day long traces of light stretched their crimson
        fingers
25 And the high priest began his sacred rites.
He gave the king the cleansing herbs and purifying drugs.
He made him spurt the mystic water against the sun,
Reinforcing his power of mind and body.
The king, accompanied by the high priest, now retired to the
30   river.
The high priest called out his sacred words and said:
'As you flow away, great river,
Carry with you all the debris of our lives;
Let us sink deep into the bowels of the ocean.
35 Begin again where the source is pure and is of the earth.
This way, too, each generation of humankind begins.
Do not let the sun cut your body over the stone.

347

May your waters give nourishment to the earth.
On the soft shores the seed of our future is buried.'
He took the soil that was mixed with plants
And threw it into the centre of the river.

5   By this rite he called on the earth and water and plants to
        merge.
He said: 'Let the grass not wither from the dead.
Let the animals not die from the power of the dead.
By the great seed of life

10 Let all creatures be nourished from one plant.
Let all people know today is yesterday,
Yesterday is the sacred day to come,
The day that is to come is today.
Let them understand each era comes from the ocean.'

15 Mqalane made the king repeat the sacred words.
When he finished he put on his forehead the mark of the sun,
Making the king declare: 'I swear by all my Ancestors
This land is not mine; all in it belongs to them.
The power to rule is not mine, but for the Forefathers.

20 We, too, are part of the dream.
It shall dream us as we face the lizard.'
These words weighed heavily on Shaka's mind.
It was as though they issued from someone else's lips;
They fell precipitately on their own.

25 They then focused their minds on the sacred stones.

At the royal grounds the regiments began to arrive.
They sang the solemn songs of Return.
When the king reached the royal enclosure
He found all his relatives assembled together.

30 Then was brought to them one large beer pot.
From this the whole family was ordered to drink,
Thus symbolizing the bonds of the House of Malandela,
And linking the minds that are loosened by death.
They all embraced and laughed together.

35 At the vast grounds
There were gift beasts for the Ceremony of Return —
They came from all regions of Zululand.
It was from these the ceremonial bile was taken.
Many were discarded to feed our relatives.

The king emerged bedecked in the royal colours;
He wore his favourite red iNgwele royal beads.
He sat at the upper end of the royal grounds and waited.
It was the old men who began first.
5   They poured out the green bile on his feet,
Symbolizing the rich skies and abundant seasons.
Through the greenness of the sky people shall prosper;
Through the greenness of the ocean people shall be fed;
Through the greenness of the green earth they shall multiply.

10   From afar an old man declaimed the poem of King Jama:
'Jama, son of Ndaba:
He was like the pile of boulders; he was like the stone of Zihlalo,
Which frequently beheld the sharpening of spears.
We of the spear clan found our resting place there.
15   Binder of all things, who is of our House of Legends,
He kept me spellbound from morning to afternoon.
He made the enemy taste the bitter aloe at Mahago,
Yet he gave joy to the little men.
He moved his jaws as though to chew something
20   But it was only to reduce everything into nothingness.'
Inspired, another poet declaimed Senzangakhona's poem:
'Menzi, son of Ndaba,
Fiery one, who scolds with tears!
You are like the wild one of Phiko of Bulawini!
25   The buffalo that casts its shadow over the springs —
He is as great as the great hunter of the Mfekane clan.
Your platters of the festival are beautiful, Mjokwane!
From them eat only young women.
Tall, slender one of delicate movements —
30   Even in the great famine your body was beautiful.'
After this ceremony the regiments circled at a distance,
Paying tribute to the king and all the Zulu heroes.
By their movements they described the nations's Sacred Bond.
Crowds, too, walked in procession, making obeisance to the
35   king,
Making a hero's pledge to the Palm Race.
Following this ceremony there was the slaughtering of sacrificial
      bulls.
The High Priest ordered that the bulls' internal juices

349

Be used for purification and renewal.
For from the stomach life and decay are divided;
Only through decay is growth possible.
New generations feed on the richness of the earth;

5   Their roots extend to the home of the Forefathers.
In the next generation our inheritors shall prosper.
We, too, are the plants that come from broken leaves.
Our anthems shall be sung by the river;
Our children shall drink from the fountains of our legends.

10   The king led the procession to the high point of the mountain
And from there uttered the sacred words,
Scattering the sacred water at the sun's face.
Then he ordered all to discard their garments of mourning.
Great crowds descended into the river to wash their feet.

15   A new anthem of the new season began.
People sang and rejoiced with rich meat and nourishing beer.
Great crowds danced to new songs.
The children of the Palm Race shouted their anthems.
It was as though they had taken a drug of ecstasy.

20   Shaka leapt like a bird at the Renewal dance.
His very movements told the story of his life.
It was as though his father would ask again:
'What young man is this who dances like a spirit?'
He beat the earth, trampling triumphantly on its shoulders.

25   His great song of renewal rose with the high winds.
Some people have the power to look beyond the clouds;
Some people can see into future times;
Some people can hear the solemn voices of ancient times;
Some people can talk to things and make them tremble with life.

30   The old man danced in the open arena,
His mind now befogged by beer and festival ecstasy.
Voices, like a swarm of bees, filled the arena.
People opened their mouths and talked and laughed and sang.
Lovers retreated to their worlds of fantasy.

35   The great cloud of death was dispelled by their song,
Leaving in the open space a beautiful woman.
Her body was smooth and soft and beautiful;
She looked down on the ground tenderly;

She touched the earth that shall bear fruit.
She was all women; she was the mother of our nation.
From the ruins of families come the voices of children.
A new generation is born again to our earth.
5   For, in truth, happiness gives birth to happiness.
Thus did people celebrate the great feast of Return.
From all directions came the rich smell of roasting meat.
Great festivals rouse the spirit of other great festivals;
They nourish the song and the dance.
10   Shaka mingled with the crowds, cracking jokes and abandoning
       himself.
When he came across a crowd of young recruits
He stayed awhile, firming their shoulders, and commenting:
'The calves of Zululand are no longer tender.
15   They desire grounds on which to test their courage.
This one is ready to face grown-up bulls.'
(He referred to a well-built boy of fierce eyes:
He was Bhongoza the son of Mefu of the Ngcobo clan.
He walked with confidence and exuded defiance.)
20   Shaka was in a happy mood.
He simply said: 'Tomorrow, son of Mefu.'

This friendliness did not please his enemies.
They had hoped from this discontent to recruit their allies,
But the whole nation burst into a new mood of revelry,
25   Applauding the king's recovery and composing songs for the
       feast:
'May life be enriched by the gifts of our Forefathers.
May all peoples share the sadness that is of our child.'
With such anthems they danced at the festivals.
30   Shaka, elated by these celebrations, said to Zihlandlo:
'Our era boasts of endless horizons for our nation.
The boil, as it bursts, takes away the pain.
I pay my respects to great men like you,
Who supported me with the elephants' shoulders.
35   They have given new power to our nation;
They have touched the wound with their hands.
By their words of wisdom they have nourished the mind.
Through them I follow the visions of our times.'
Zihlandlo answered gently and calmly:

'My lord, the greatest pain feeds on the mind
But our friends and family are the guardians of our sun.
They are the supporting arms on which our body rests.
It is unwise to thank the mountain for knowing,
5   For only we can bring a language to its silences.
Ours is an endless cycle of ruling and teaching.
Only you, my lord, know the deep truths that are of our future.
We follow the light and stumble on the wisdom of the earth.'
He affirmed his words by a long steady gaze on the ground.
10 Shaka, in order to lighten this mood, said:
"Descendant of Ghubela, let us stretch our hands in pleasure.
In our nation there are still many men of greatness.
Our nation shall live in their wisdom so long as there is life.'
They both laughed and Shaka passed on.
15 He found Nqoboka sitting alone, away from the crowds.
He said in a tone of surprise:
'What strange thoughts occupy your mind?
Why do you sit brooding in peacetime?'
Nqoboka said: 'I am possessed by the voices of the Zulus.
20 The great congregations of people are singing and talking;
Their voices penetrate through to the Ancestral Spirits.
I feel their presence; I feel the presence of the ancient heroes.
Even those who wish us ill dare not speak!
All things speak in praise of your greatness, my lord.
25 Through the years our nation has seen many trials,
Yet none has found us unprepared.
By your wisdom the nation grows like an ancient tree
And through you no winds, no storms, shall uproot this plant.
These thoughts are our heritage to coming generations.
30 As for me, my lord, I am tired of living.
I can no longer vegetate like a child in the cradle.'
Shaka laughed and said: 'Do not rush with these things,
    Nqoboka.
Today is our day of rejoicing; it must complete its cycle.
35 There are still many days to enrich our lives.
Those who, against all custom, failed to mourn with us
Have mocked our grief and laughed at our sadness.'
These words penetrated deep into Nqoboka's mind.
He shook his head pensively and said: 'We shall be there!'

The festival burst with pleasant songs.
The Ancestors heard the voices of their children;
They embraced them and kissed their foreheads.
When the High Priest had poured the purifying medicine
5   He carried the sacred branch of the royal grounds.
He made a solemn prayer, calling the spirit of the Queen
     Mother:
'Here, then, is the nation that loved you.
By their deeds they have shown their grief.
10 They request this in their language of the earth:
Abide by your love; do not forget your own children;
Do not abandon the myriad nations that are your people.
We have earned our pride through your progeny
Make their paths clear; give fruit to their gardens.
15 By these sacred words and through Mvelinqangi, our Creator,
Let all wounds and open scars be healed!'
He then squeezed drops of the life-liquid into the earth.
It was the warm, fresh decay that generates the new season.
When the Assembly had gathered Ngomane stood up to address
20   the crowds,
So excited they gave him the salute due only to the king.
Ngomane spoke: 'I salute the many peoples of Zululand,
They who are as numerous as the locusts.
When they sing the earth itself sings its own songs;
25 When they mourn wild creatures mourn with them.
They stared at the sun and the sun fell into darkness.
I salute my Lord of Nations in the name of the regiments;
I salute you in the name of heroes and families of our nation;
I salute you in the name of the men and women of Zululand.
30 We have mourned the death of the Queen Mother
Until our tears were seen by the distant stars.
Great families and clans and nations have mourned with us.
Our mourning still grows from under our feet —
We shout out against the shadows of death!
35 We implore our Great Ruler to endure his wounds,
To put on them the healing herbs of our Forefathers!
We appeal to them, we appeal to the great Spirits:
Let this horrendous event pass.
Let it not overwhelm our children.
40 Let it not ravish our fields but feed us with courage,

For through this our nation's history is nourished.
May those who are still to be born know:
A nation that possesses the power to mourn
Also commands the great power to love and to live —
5   We, a nation of heroes that subdued the bandit nations,
We, humiliated, conceited rulers of the earth.
We are blasphemed by those who refused to mourn with us,
Who by their acts violated the customs of the Palm Race.
I am talking of such men as Soshangane of the north.
10   I have in mind such rulers as Faku of Ngqungqushe of Nyanga,
Who rules over the Mpondos of the Mzimvubu region.
These rulers must wear the tears they refused to shed with us;
Through them we shall cleanse the death power in our
      weapons.'
15   As Ngomane spoke his voice rose in anger,
And he sought to infuse the same outrage among the crowds.
The assembled gatherings shouted in consent:
'It is ours! This voice of Ngomane speaks for us!'

Such words and such acts lead to war;
20   Because of this the army was soon preparing for battle.
While the land was agog with fresh slogans of battle
Shaka received a messenger from the white settlements
Assuring him his envoys had left for the land of King George.
They carried the royal message:
25   'I, Shaka, Ruler of all the Zulus,
I send this envoy under the authority of General King
Who is the general of Gibabanye regiment.
I send him together with Hlambamanzi, my loyal servant.
I order them to take words of goodwill to King George,
30   Who is known throughout as the Ruler of the White Races.
Let him utter words of friendship through Sotobe.
I request King George, my brother, to look after my envoys.
Let them come back with warm words of brotherhood.
For his services I reward King with warm friendship:
35   I give him the coastal region to administer.
He must govern this province in my name.'
It was because of this
Shaka felt the beginnings of new horizons.
When he heard they had left he made a sacrifice,

Appealing to the Forefathers to safeguard their journey.

At Dukuza royal city the war council met.
Shaka warned the commanders of the challenges of this war:
'Under no circumstances must you take victory for granted.
5   Your supreme concern is to know the army of Faku,
Assessing everything about his lands and peoples
And studying the forests, the rivers and all neighbouring
     mountains.
To achieve this you must send ahead of you teams of agents.
10 Some must come from us and others from the White Strangers
(These can be bribed with cattle and land,
For any man who places himself under a foreign ruler
Shall accept the status and corruptions of that land).'
It was because of these words the lands of Faku
15 Became infested with spies and spurious fugitives.

Book Fifteen: The campaign of cleansing

The war against the Mpondos was never meant to be total but merely punitive. After finding out that the Mpondos employed only guerrilla tactics and did not want to fight an open war, Shaka called off the campaign. One of the losses of this campaign was the death of Manyundela, one of the greatest Zulu heroes. There are many changes that Shaka means to institute after this campaign. For one thing, he intends to consolidate the civilian structure and begin to relax the strict military laws. He still realizes the need to strengthen the Zulu state against possible foreign invasion. Contrary to common belief and propaganda, Shaka strongly disapproves of the occupation of the cape region by the white invaders. The mission to King George was meant to assess the true intentions of the Strangers and to learn about their methods of warfare. Plots are also brewing in earnest against Shaka. People who do not understand the impending turmoil are demanding an end to the interminable wars. The brothers, keen to maintain their

aristocratic privileges, are spearheading the campaign against Shaka. In
all this Shaka finds a close and an understanding friend in Zihlandlo.

Listen to the heroes shouting to each other from mountain tops.
Listen to them as they swear by Faku of Ngqungqushe
Who was not grieved by Nandi's death.
The slogans of war are fearful.
5   With their din they echo through the valleys and cliffs,
Disturbing the peaceful world of animals.
It is said Shaka, inspired by these war songs,
Picked up his weapon and, and, and speaking to it, said:
'And you, Ndomile, you have pestered me long enough;
10 You have called me out of the dream.
Before long you shall dance with me in the battlefield.
You shall say: "Who are these who rejoiced while we
        mourned?" '
Shaka sent messengers to the white settlements,
15 Eager to test their war strategies
And to use their knowledge of the southern regions:
'Help me, loyal friends of the Zulus!
I face a violent revolt in my father's house.
Against me my brother, Ngwadi, has mobilized a formidable
20   army.
He has seized all my favourite breed of cattle.
They must be wrested from him at all costs,
For they symbolize the honour with which our House must
        rule.'
25 But Shaka was privately amused at his own schemes.
He joked about it to Prince Ngwadi himself!
In response a motley group of White Strangers and black
        adventurers
Set out with their favourite weapon — the gun.
30 No sooner had they arrived than Shaka said:
'I have won my battle against my brother Ngwadi,
But since you came determined for battle
We must proceed and wage war against the recalcitrant Faku.
His crime far surpasses that of my brother.
35 He dared to keep away as I mourned my parent,
Nor did he, like others, send me medicines to temper her illness.

Such violations of custom speak of a veritable witch!'
They all consented to his words, having no way to dissent,
Aware of the customs of the Palm Race.

Large numbers of regiments could be seen
5   Eagerly crossing the rivers of the coastal regions,
Stopping to drink, half-way in the coastal regions.
'Sweet are the waters of this river,' they acclaimed.
Shaka, pleased with this river, named it 'the Sweetwaters' river.
Unto this day those who pass there sing the ancient songs.
10   They hear the voices of the dead, as they wash their feet.
They implore the Ancestors to sing with them.
The great Zululand shall rise again!
The army proceeded until it arrived at Hluthankungu,
A region between Fafa and Mthwalume districts.
15   Here it quickly constructed temporary encampments.
Shaka called together the generals and commanders.
Speaking to them seriously and solemnly, he reminded them
How deeply they had penetrated a foreign territory
And how difficult it would be to retreat.
20   Thus they had to rely only on themselves.
He discussed too the reports of spies and informers
Who now arrived in large numbers,
Each telling of his own detailed experience.
Some reported how the Cwangube forest blocked the strategic
25   grounds;
Some described the formations of hills and rivers;
Some reported on the internal disputes between the ruling
      families.
Thus when the army proceeded it was equipped with all
30   details.
General Mdlaka, the son of Ncidi, commanded the southern
      wing.
This was to proceed from the mouth of the Mzimvubu river.
Another section was led by General Manyundela, son of
35   Mabuya.
This section was to descend from the northern regions.
On its downward movement it was to clear the area of enemy
      troops:
These were of the Bhaca and the Thembu nations.

The proud and brave Thembus were ruled by King
    Ngubencuka,
Son of Zona, son of Tondwa, of Dlomo, of Madiba,
Of Hhala, of Dukamanzi, of Xekwa, of Toyi, of Cedwini,
5 Of Bhomoyi, of Mthembu, of Mguti, of Malandela.
The courage of the Thembus was known throughout the
    southern regions.

As the Zulu army proceeded it divided into various strategic
    sections.
10 The gun-carrying flotsam and jetsam of the white settlements
Followed the two wings of the encircling army.
Shaka joined the wing that was led by General Mdlaka.
This made a temporary stop south of the Mzimkhulu river.
From the north the army led by General Manyundela
15 Launched its attacks, causing great panic.
The whites of the Cape prayed incessantly.
They turned to the north where their Ancestors lived.
In the south General Mdlaka searched for the Mpondo army in
    vain.
20 Forewarned, the Mpondos retreated into the forests and
    mountain areas.
So narrow were the passages, only one man could enter.
Angered and frustrated, the Zulu army seized the cattle.
They proceeded to cross the Mzimkhulu and Mtata rivers.
25 Here they searched for the Mpondo army
Until they reached the Cwangube forest.
In it there was a towering hill
And from it could be seen wide open spaces to the horizon.
And here, too, Mdlaka's army prepared for its attacks.
30 They constantly made raids on the Mpondo army,
Sometimes bringing back large herds of captured cattle.
Sometimes they came with teams of captured boys and old men.
In vain the Zulus attempted to find the army's hiding place.
Yet the Mpondo units constantly ambushed the powerful Zulu
35   army.
Sometimes the two armies would fall on each other in a fierce
    battle,
Until by a set strategem the Mpondo's would suddenly vanish.
Because of these uncertain battles

The Zulus returned angry and smarting with battle wounds.

On the remote side of the forest the Mpondo regiments emerged,
Certain the Zulu army had retreated.
But only to attract to themselves the vigilant eyes of spies.
5   Quickly they alerted the waiting generals.
'The children of Faku have come out to the open,' they
     whispered.
No sooner had they said this than a great stampede began,
Spearheaded by the hotheads and the young recruits.
10 But the Mpondo army soon melted away again.
Day after day these uncertain battles continued.
Frustrated, the Zulus seized the few remaining cattle.
Sometimes they reaped the large harvest from the fields.
When Shaka realized the futility of such a war,
15 He called off the whole campaign;
'It is enough. We have scolded them enough for their crimes.
It is unwise to challenge a man
After he has retreated to his hiding place.
Our army is far from its home;
20 Any extended fighting would only break its morale.
If the Mpondo remain in the forest and in the caves
Then they do not intend to fight the Zulu army.'
He sent a firm order commanding all forces to return.
The regiments regrouped from various regions.
25 Those of General Manyundela could be heard afar, singing their
     anthems.
Those of General Mdlaka proceeded slowly to the meeting place,
Still eager to launch one final assault.

All regiments were ordered to feast and to celebrate.
30 From afar many fires sparkled like a million glow-worms.
When General Manyundela's section finally arrived
They sang no triumphant songs.
After a moment of suspended silence their spokesman called out:
'My lord, we may as well be dead.
35 Though we totally defeated the enemy army
The little Bhaca cowards treacherously stabbed our leader!
He had forged ahead of us and disappeared into a clump of
     bushes.

We who had accompanied him called for him in vain.
Finally we found him silenced by the enemy's spear.
At his side lay a large heap of enemy dead.
He had been attacked by them as he assessed the Bhaca
5 positions.'
When Shaka was told of this episode he leapt up
As though he had heard of the killing of a whole regiment.
In a quavering voice he shouted: 'Cowards! Cowards!
You return to me empty-handed without your leader!
10 You report these things with no sign of battle wounds?'
He spoke these words as though they choked him,
As though his very anger would overwhelm him.
In a loud voice he shouted: 'Kill the cowards!'
No word of pleading was heard.
15 They were led to their death as Shaka himself walked away.
He climbed the hill to where other regiments sat.
These had not heard of the fate of the great General
Manyundela.
Shaka sat down and listened intently to each of their episodes
20 As though desiring to take his mind away from this event.
He ordered all the troops to sing the Zulu war anthem
In tribute to the great and brave General Manyundela.

The regiments of Mkhandlwini sang the anthem with special
sadness,
25 For it was they whom Manyundela had commanded through
many wars.
Shaka was restless; he moved from regiment to regiment,
Listening to their stories and making reluctant jokes.
Often he expressed only half-enthusiasm for their feats of
30 bravery.
No longer did he show the excitement of the olden days,
When each story of courage fired his imagination.
Then his whole body would light up
And he would add his own stories, completing them with heroic
35 poems,
Or else there and then confer a title of honour on a hero.
But on this occasion his eyes wandered all over.
He surveyed the gatherings of regiments in deep concentration.
Finally he walked to a group of young carrier boys

And said to Mdlaka, who accompanied him:
'In the future they shall dance their own dance.
From this regiment shall come the greatest heroes:
I shall name it "The Stinging Bees".
5   Like them they shall sting whoever dares provoke them.
Tomorrow I want to proclaim a new order.
I want the regiments to marry at will.
The Zulu nation and army have grown in power.
No longer are our paths filled with uncertainty.
10 Only such dogs as Hlangabeza must be made to mourn,
They who never took heed of all our sorrows,
Violating custom and all obligations of nations!'
These words only confused General Mdlaka
But, knowing the king's many thoughts, he kept quiet.
15 He knew now the army would proceed to the northern regions.
Mdlaka commented: 'I thank you, my lord;
I am grateful to you on behalf of those who desire to marry.
By such weaknesses would your enemies initiate revolt;
Those who seek to destroy a nation are never without reason.
20 I have no one in mind but I speak the truth of all nations.'
Shaka siezed on to these words and said:
'Yes, few keep for long the roots of their truth.
Thus as I listen to your words
I know you have heard some secret.
25 I shall abide by your warnings.
My enemies shall fail so long as I have loyal heroes.
I therefore put to you these sacred words:
Whoever shall destroy us
Shall only succeed through the gate where you stand.
30 Tomorrow you must bear witness to these words.'
Shaka of Senzangakhona spoke boldly,
Satisfied with the victories of his armies.
He sent a word to King Faku of the Mpondos and said:
'Should you send envoys to solicit friendship,
35 There shall be peace between us.'
King Faku responded with friendly words and said:
'I ask you for peace and forgiveness for my omissions.
Brothers often quarrel and even kill each other.
But their disputes, say our Forefathers, must end in song.
40 Your attack on us has caused bloodshed and starvation.

I ask that we open our paths to each other.
Let there be peace among the children of Palm Race.'
Thus he endorsed the policies of many other rulers.
Young men and women and wives of Faku were sent home.
5   The Zulus began to prepare for their return journey.
From all directions their many regiments began to move.

Shaka never knew that as his army prepared to go homewards
The settler general, Dundas, led his troops northwards.
For no sooner had he heard the threats of war
10   Than he mobilized all his followers.
The whole southern region scattered in terror.
Bourke, the commander-in-chief,
Fruitlessly tried to inspire his frightened army.
Some fled beyond the confines of the settlement.
15   They sought citizenship there and beyond.
Troops recruited against their will make poor soldiers:
Such was the fate of the little army of General Dundas.
Had it been its misfortune to encounter the sons of Zululand,
Had they by their foolishness thrown themselves into the
20   beehive,
Their whole tale would have been told only by passing birds!
Widows would have wept against the waves.
Only through the intervention of their Ancestors
Did they encounter that restless wanderer, Matiwane,
25   Who carried his children on his shoulders.
Matiwane's army was crushed and all nations rejoiced.
The Basothos celebrated; the Thembus celebrated; the Hlubis
      celebrated;
The combined armies of the Xhosas and Dundas were praised.
30

Listen with all your ears.
This word is not like the unpleasant ones of yesterday.
It exalts the great deeds of the children of our nation.
This word is not like the unpleasant ones of yesterday.
35   It exalts the great deeds of the children of our nation.
Says my lord: "Such young men as have fought in this war
Have now won the right to marry and have families."
You have made the nation of Zulu great among all nations.
The paths to Zululand are steaming with white mists.

The young shall give the beasts-of-friendship.'
When he finished uttering these words
A great burst of 'Bayede!' rose from the regiments.
Each one spoke to the one next to him and said:
5 'Did you hear the beautiful words of Mdlaka?
Did you hear we have the king's consent to marry?'
So great was the joy among the regiments
That even those who begrudged the king
Joined in the general rejoicing,
10 Sometimes shouting louder to cover their own crimes.
General Mdlaka, speaking in high spirits, continued:
'I can see how these words excite your minds.
Through them you will know the king's desires and truth.
The king did not forbid marriage to pursue some cruel policy,
15 But because he foresaw the future of our nation.
It is now the greatest of all nations.
We have earned our freedom.
We must dilly-dally no longer, lest we be overtaken by the sun.
Let us move with speed to our nest-home of Zululand.'
20 He said these words, poking fun at their enthusiasms.

They shouted in response: 'It is our desire.'
The great Zulu army proceeded, quickening its pace,
Until it reached the boundaries of the Mzimkhulu river,
Where it pitched camp before crossing.
25 The young men were elated at this proclamation.
There was a tall man who was the son of Sonkwankwa,
Who constantly recounted the merits of Nokusa.
She was the centre-fountain of his life.
Many years he had waited; many years they promised each
30   other.
In every battle he narrated how he had seen her.
How she had called him away from danger:
He fought not alone, but with her.
Her voice came through to him like a joyful whisper.
35 Then he would laugh in the thick of battle.
They were twin spirits; they were the voices of the wind.
Through her he acquired the courage to fight without fear.
Beyond the battlefield she stood, waiting for his embrace.
His agemates poked fun at him:

In the middle of the night they would wake him and say:
'We saw Nokusa standing over your forehead.'
Sometimes they would say to him:
'How many are to die tomorrow from the power of Nokusa?'
5 They teased him, knowing from her he derived his fierce power.
As he stabbed he roared like a wild bull.
From his mouth issued only poems of Nokusa.
Thus new songs of lovers were composed.
Young men leaped joyfully over the friendly earth.

10 See them, our Forefathers, in their thousands.
See them as they stop to gaze at the high reeds of the river.
See their beautiful feet before us, walking in the sand.
The deep waters were ready to swallow them.
Shaka directed the army to the shallow parts of the Mzimkhulu
15 river.
Suddenly he saw the angry currents coming full force,
Threatening to drown the crowds of young carrier boys.
He plunged himself into the wide river
And swam until he stood there, chest-high, in the middle.
20 The boys who could not swim hung on the shoulders of the
regiments.
These stood in a long line spanning the length of the river.
Shaka stood there until the last of the boys had crossed.
After this episode he said to General Mdlaka:
25 'Had I not insisted on this course of action
Many of the young men would have been drowned.
Some heroes in our army see these children
As none other than their carriers of baggage and food.
Yet these boys are here for training.
30 From this episode I have decided to dismiss the carrier boys.
Let each man carry his own burden to battle.'
Mdlaka said: 'Yes, my lord, as you rescued these boys from
drowning
I realized then the honour of our nation had been soiled.
35 Many times I wondered what words we would use
To report this disgrace to the nation's parents,
With what humiliation would we have told them:
"We of the Zulu army stood watching our children drowning."

My lord, I do agree with your decision.
The position of authority imposes its own bad habits.
People often turn their partners into slaves,
Forgetting the appropriateness of their common tasks.
5   A great nation counts on all those who are free.
To it belong all the young buds that are still top open;
For, in truth, plants in bloom display a single image.
By these words I praise the noble visions
You bequeathed to our nation.
10   Through you we know: as we grow in power,
So do those who live for their own personal honour.
Thus the army must constantly change its authority.
Let there be no one who considers himself the ultimate hero.
The reputation of our nation lies in families and homes.'
15   Shaka listened carefully to these words of Mdlaka.
They called to mind a familiar nagging thought,
For he himself had begun to think of these same truths.
Shaka said: 'Your words are pregnant with thought and
         meaning.
20   Indeed, since my mother's death there is an emptiness in life.
She was not only a woman but a ruler who ruled with me.
My family is now the nation of Zululand.
With my mother's death my sense of home opens like a wound;
The young of Zululand are not only a promise of our future
25   But are like my own younger brothers.
Allowing the troops to marry
Betray thoughts that have been present in my mind.
Future generations must know we fought for a greater life;
Nor was it for us we took these risks
30   But for them, who shall ennoble the Palm Race.
I have no family; I have no children; but the Zulu nation lives.
It is our nation that shall give birth and multiply for us.'
Mdlaka did not comment; he quietly digested these words.
He knew that those who are troubled desire only to rest.
35   He knew, too, that Shaka was like the wind
Which often lies low at dawn
But, stirred by the feet of men, leaps up to the heavens;
Yet by sunset it falls again quietly on the ground.
Such was the temperament of the great ruler of the Zulus.
40   No sign or symbol or emblem was sacred to him:

Only order and the eternal visions for the Palm Race.

The great movement of regiments seethed through the plains,
Passing through the valleys and climbing the southern hills.
Everywhere large crowds assembled to applaud the returning
5   army.
Indeed, many recruits had come from these regions.
Even little boys had headed south to Mpondoland,
Eager to see the spectacle of the Zulus in battle.
They came back bubbling with many tantalizing stories.
10 Some had adopted the poems of their heroes;
Some sang songs that were learnt from the region of
      Mpondoland;
Some sang the songs of a Baqulusini royal city.

After a long and tiring march
15 The Zulu army now halted near the sea.
It was here that Shaka began to seethe with ideas.
No sooner had he rested than he began to talk fervently,
Pointing to the ocean, he commented to his generals:
'Such are the battle movements the Zulu army shall adopt.'
20 They were all puzzled by these words.
But he continued, somewhat absent-mindedly, and said:
'Like the approach of each giant wave to the seashore,
Like a succession of angry waves —
So must be the measured sequence of our troops.
25 Those ahead must fight in the thick of battle,
Reinforced by the thought of immediate relief;
For no battle is fought spiritedly without hope of reinforcements.
There should be no in-between ground for enemy troops.
Those in front must fight and give way to those who follow.
30 Indeed, such an army can never tire.'
The generals stared at each other, elated at this battle plan.
Though this idea did not differ from their experience
By this illustration they saw the whole strategy clearly.
Thus the poet commented on Shaka and said:
35 'My lord is like a pile of ruined cities.
He rears high like the waves of a stormy sea.
All night long the waves tumble over each other.'
Re-enacting the Mpondo campaign, the poet said:

'You burst open a giant hole in the land of the Mpondo.
Even today that region is still a yawning crater.
You seized the prized beasts of Faku among the Mpondos!
You took those of Ngubowencuge among the Mpondos!
5 You confiscated those of Ncokazi among the Mpondos!
You took those of Ncasana of Majola clan!
You seized those of Macingwane of Ngonyameni!
You confiscated those of Bhugane of a thousand honours!
You took those of the Sothos who wear a dhoti!
10 You seized the beasts of the people of little honour,
Whose hair is plaited in fringes!
The thunderclap that flashed in the land of the Mpondo
Over the great House of Faku, the son of Ngqungqushe —
It flashed and cindered the shields of the Mpondos.
15 The lightning forked and stood at the pass of Nyoka.
He wheeled back only when he reached the maBomyana clan.
Morning star of long rays, the star of Mjokwane —
It stands on its tail, hanging on the dome of the sky.
Two morning stars emerged from heaven;
20 They made danger signals to each other!
Great fierce flame, whose explosions face each other:
One is of Queen Ntombazi; the other is of Queen Nandi.
Oh, my lord, how terrible of you!
You did not spare even those of your maternal uncle,
25 Unforgiving even to your relative Bhebhe, the son of Ncumela!
Many shields come close to each other and embrace.
They are of Gwagaza and Dlakudla of Ntotheleni regiment.
Staff of shining brass of Mjokwane,
That struck the water and it opened into the mud.'
30 The great poet's words reverberated to the heavens.
The uFasimba regiment, elated, began to sing their anthem.
They shouted their slogans calling for greater wars.

Early, at dawn, Shaka summoned his regiments.
All the generals reluctantly responded to this call
35 Except the great General Mdlaka, the son of Ncidi,
Who never once hesitated at a call to battle.
He still yearned for a decisive war.
When Shaka arrived at the arena he angrily addressed the
   regiments:

'Never did I have a wink of sleep.
All night I listened to the discontented voices of our army
And heard the high boasts of the Mpondo army
Claiming: "The Zulus did not dislodge us.
5   We have never been conquered."
Though many bandit nations have been tamed,
There still remain those who would cause disorder
And violate custom and bully the smaller nations.
There are those like Soshangane who still boast their power.
10 Constantly my trusted messengers report
His armies harass the peaceful nations of the north.
The Thongas of the coastal region have had no peace from him.
These disturbances violate the order of our region.
Greater nations may yet be led to endless wars,
15 Bringing back the chaos once experienced in Nguniland.
Soshangane's army is not unlike that of Zwide.
Like Sikhunyana who dared invade our borders,
Disturbing us at our peaceful festivals,
So could he by his bravado seek to enhance his reputation.
20 Because of this we must act swiftly.
We must pluck the wings of the little eagle before it flies,
Before he, too, comes to search for his family's old capitals,
Hoping to revive the rule once held by Zwide.
Soshangane shall always be restless,
25 Like a bird that never builds its nest in one place.
We must strike him and stop his rampage on smaller nations.
Here, too, is an order I want you to observe:
The 'little carrier boys' are carrier boys no more.
They now shall fight in battle like men.
30 Each man from now on shall carry his own baggage.
Even food you will find in plenty wherever you fight.
You must depend on your own resources.
If our Forefathers could survive in their own battles,
Why can't we, whose life is eased by theirs?'
35 He spoke these words in anger,
Still remembering the episodes of the Mzinkhulu river.

Though the generals were alarmed at these changes
They did not oppose him.
They simply said: 'Son of Ndaba, you know best.

You founded the nation; you opened these paths,
So shall by your vision close and open the new directions.'
Shaka was irritated by these words. He said:
'No one builds a nation.

5 Such words betray some secret plots.
Flattery constantly hides some deeper motive.'
Shot by suspicion and their reluctance to proceed to battle,
He stared directly at each one of them.
But the whole concourse of commanders

10 Vowed their loyalty to the king and country.
Each sought to applaud the king's words louder than others.
The great gathering of regiments shouted the royal salute,
Demanding that Soshangane and the Mtshali clan be punished.
For like the Mpondos they, too, had not joined in the mourning.

15 Prince Hlangabeza of the Mtshalis had spit saliva on the ground
As news of Queen Nandi's death was told:
'I shall never mourn for Nandi,' he said.
'Did Shaka ever mourn for my father, Khondlo, when he died?'
It was because of these words that the army attacked him,

20 Taking the supplies they needed for their war against
    Soshangane.

It is said Prince Dingane and Prince Mhlangane met together.
Through a trusted messenger they sent a word to Mbopha,
Telling him of their resentment towards this new campaign.

25 Said Prince Dingane: 'It would not matter if others went to war,
But we are the children of the king.
We must not endlessly be exposed to danger
Indeed, as of late we shall travel like commoners,
Deprived as we shall be of a retinue of baggage carriers.

30 Even food we shall scavenge, wherever we are, like dogs.'
He spoke these words to Mhlangane hurriedly,
As though Mhlangane himself had not known them.
Prince Mhlangane replied to him softly and said:
'I agree with your words, my brother.

35 I, too, was alarmed at these things.
I almost confronted Shaka personally
But restrained myself until our moment of consultation.
What frustrates most is his ever-growing reputation.'

Prince Dingane quietly assured him and said:
'The regiments are composed of ordinary people.
They applaud whoever is king of the day.
Today they praise the man they shall denounce tomorrow.
5   People, my brother, are like water; they follow the gulleys.
If one digs a tunnel the water goes that way.
We, too, must open the lips of those who are silent;
Then we shall hear a volume of protests.
But, above all, keep your own lips sealed.
10 For if we fail to strike at this moment only death awaits us.
We shall either die in foreign lands or in our homes.
Even if Shaka does not by his own hand kill us,
We may yet be killed in the cause of his many campaigns.
If we die in battle it shall only enhance his rule;
15 Indeed, he shall say: "Even my brothers died in battle."
But then the greatness of a man depends on whether he lives or
     not —
It shall not benefit us to earn fame
While the proud vultures pick on our flesh.
20 I am truly tired of wars; I want to be a family man.
If you still hesitate and still follow his commands,
Then, my brother, you shall have only yourself to blame.
Shaka shall never change from his love of wars.
Besides, his mother's death has broken his supporting pillar.
25 Indeed, his tears have already undermined the nation.'
Prince Dingane spoke these words with great vehemence,
Knowing Prince Mhlangane was weak and often had doubts.
He hoped by these words he would entrap him.
As he spoke his eyes were directed at Mhlangane.
30 Hesitatingly, Mhlangane commented on these words:
'I hear your words, my brother.
They bite deep by their meaningfulness.
I only promise this; by my honour as a man,
I shall never tell of things we discuss together.
35 Even when I am overwhelmed by doubts,
I shall come back to you.'
Prince Dingane did not answer but just laughed.
He knew Mhlangane always depended on him.
He laughed at the childishness of Mhlangane.
40 Nothing is sacred to the struggles of power;

Not even the bonds of families and friendships.
Close relations, in madness, slaughter their own clansmen.

Like a huge cloud of locusts the army followed the northward
    direction.
5   Eastwards and westwards it whirled and turned
Like a cluster of winter leaves blown by the wind,
Like a dark cloud of hurrying vultures,
Like a whirlwind carrying pillars and roofs of villages.
Thus it departed from the region of the Mngeni river.
10 The river flows clear and beautiful.
Touched by the lips of the ancient warrior,
It sings the song inherited from the sea.
To this very day Mngeni river sings the song of the Sacred
    Circle.
15 Sometimes it bursts open to feed a new generation,
Making their song the first anthem of the season
And bringing back the story of the ancient hero.
Listen to the echoes of song as the king approaches Dukuza.
Listen to the royal poets reciting to each other the epics.
20 Listen to their voices as they carry the message everywhere.
The poets sing for the return of plenty at the royal city of
    Dukuza.
To the horizon spread the large herds of captured cattle.
They bellow, turning their heads towards Faku's territory.
25 Many sang the great anthems learnt from Mpondoland.
Then was heard the round ringing sound of the Mbelebele
    regiment.
It meandered, following the direction of the Ndosi settlements.
There, people compete with each other in song.
30 Of the Mpondo campaign Princess Mkhabayi constantly asked,
Probing on all issues of the southern strategy.
When she heard of the army that went to attack Soshangane,
She said: 'It is clear Shaka knows the truth of plots against him.
How else could he risk his brothers' lives in two wars?
35 I fear this child; he possesses diabolical powers.'
She spoke these words to her sister, Princess Mawa.
Princess Mkhabayi, said continuing:
It seems we must think in new directions,

For, indeed, we do not know what our brother's son could do;
Nor would it surprise me if he mobilized an old women's
    regiment.
Shaka's cleverness is of evil power.
5 Even when threatened by danger he takes his own time.
He simply sings his own song, believing himself the wisest of
    men.
Of late he seems to toss people around
As though they were some branches loaded with decaying fruit.
10 No longer is there anyone who can restrain him.'
These words alarmed Princess Mawa. She said:
'Do not exaggerate his power.
In this world it is not courage alone that wins,
But a mind that patiently waits for an error.
15 The nation shall rise against all his wars.
We, too, possess the power to cut short his knot of authority.
Our position is unique:
We are not suspects in any game of power;
Whatever we do shall only be for the nation's welfare.'
20 Princess Mkhabayi merely shook her head and said:
'What one does for the nation is not always applauded;
Only time steadily raises its voices for the dead.
That is why our Ancestors have said:
"No one reaps fame in his own lifetime."
25 As long as one lives, life multiplies the race of enemies.
Even by this act they will claim we were hungry for power:
We chose him who would give us authority.
For this reason whatever we do must be carefully thought out.'
She spoke these words, ending their conversation
30 As though she detected some listener.

How beautiful was that time
When the great ruler, Shaka of Senzangakhona, returned.
While the army proceeded to Soshangane
He, the Great One, stayed initiating new changes.
35 The preservers of our ancient legends tell us
He now revealed his plan to re-organize the far-flung regions.
In his discussions with the Assembly
He often said: 'The nation must now have a new order.

The Zulu nation must live a full life.
It must enjoy the fruits of its achievements.
When the army returns from Soshangane
We must proclaim a new law for all young men to marry.
5   I shall send messengers to all neighbouring nations
To tell them: the Palm Race must eat from the same bowl.
I shall yet heal the wounds of the Mpondo nation,
Reminding them our quarrels are only of brothers.
We, the nations of the Palm Race,
10 Shall outwit and stop the vermin of over-the-seas nations.
Their fanatical love for the land threatens the very life of
      humankind.
Should there be time, I shall patiently teach them these lessons.'
The old wise men who heard him shook their heads, and said:
15 'How baffling is the son of Senzangakhona.
He is the ruler who rules with strength and wisdom.
But his mind changes like the strange colours of a chameleon.'
Those present knew also there were complaints of families about
      wars;
20 Some counted many relatives who had been killed in battle.
Our Forefathers say each person is precious to his own family.
Many spoke openly: 'Let our nation enjoy a period of peace,
Or else let a new king be born to rule without war.
Such was the mood among the families of the land.

25 At this period news came of the arrival of King George's
      messengers.
It was followed with yet another piece of startling news:
King, who of all the White Strangers was Shaka's favourite,
Suffered a strange and weakening illness.
30 He lay ailing in the settlement near the Ngcobo region.
Shaka spoke to his friend, Prince Zihlandlo, saying:
'I feel a deep sadness about King, the man I like.
He is the most humane of all the overseas wanderers.
People often comment on him and say:
35 "The heart of King overflows with kindness.
He possesses the generosity of the Palm Race."
He is still young but his mind is of a mature man.
I had hoped one day he would return to his home

And tell his people bout the life in our world.
His early death would only deprive us of his inspired words.
I shall make a sacrifice of two of my best bulls
And plead for his life to the Ancestors.
5 Through him the lives of others may yet be fulfilled.'
Prince Zihlandlo warmly welcomed these words and said:
'I, too, found him full of generosity and humanity.
Often he abandons his group of foreigners
And is heard laughing loud with the young men of our nation.
10 When he was made commander-in-chief of Gabangaye regiment
There was general rejoicing throughout the army.
I applaud your words, my lord.
People are the same throughout the earth;
Indeed, should he die many of his relatives would mourn for
15   him.
Yet it is true no mountain is without a grave.
May he overcome the power of the earth
May he praise the hand that lifted him from the ground!'
Shaka was quiet, as though his mind dwelt on the thought of
20   death,
For often the very word made him pensive.
Raising his head he finally said to Zihlandlo,
'I hear your kind words, you of the Mkhize clan.
Yet I believe he shall not live.
25 It seems whatever I treasure withers suddenly.'
He spoke as though he no longer doubted his words.
Prince Zihlandlo himself made jokes about this,
Eager to dispel these convictions with friendly thoughts;
Yet he himself felt the ominous truth of these words.
30 Unable to bear the pain, he spoke of lighter subjects.
Shaka continued and said: 'I have sent a messenger to the
    Ngcobo region,
Ordering that I be told immediately of his fate.
Meanwhile I await reports from the war against to Soshangane.
35 I told Mdlaka to send all the former carrier boys.
They shall now comprise the iziNyosi regiment.
By a speedy transmission of this message
These young boys shall be here in the arena tomorrow.
Mdlaka's view tallies with mine;
40 But Mdlaka is not like you. His mind is that of a solider.

374

Besides, when I uttered these decisions I was angry,
Having seen how the regiments abuse their power.
Then the punishment fitted the crime.
Yet when I thought of the hardships, these decisions imposed on
5   the army,
I chastised myself, thinking how rashly I may have acted.'
Prince Zihlandlo smiled slightly and said:
'My lord, I follow all the directions of your thoughts;
I appreciate each of their meanings.
10   I saw you as you stood in the middle of the river
And thought to myself how different our nation would be
If all people had the same quick grasp of things as you.
I agree, my lord, to deprive the army of carrier boys
Creates problems for each fighting man;
15   Yet these hardships will be forgotten
And in aftertimes only praise shall be heard.
For, indeed, my lord, you must not build a nation of soldiers,
But one that shall live by the codes of its humanity;
It is its songs of life that must be heard.
20   Our nation must not evolve the habit of rulers,
Making one a special nation, the other a serving nation.
Then our army shall no longer be different from that of
         Matiwane,
Whose sweat is often washed with the tears of others.
25   For these reasons, my lord, I accept your decision.
There is only one comment I would like to make.
It is wrong to speak in anger.
You, the wisest of men, must advise and teach patiently,
For not all peoples are gifted with the same insights.
30   Besides, through haste you violated the authority of the
         Assembly.
Had this decision come from the Assembly
It would have been we who bore the pains of doubt.
Indeed, the errors of the Assembly are forgiven, but not those of
35   rulers.
Our Forefathers have rightfully said:
A great ruler rules only through the approval of his people.
For people detest the laws that are sprung on them.
To this very day we applaud the great King Ndaba,
40   Who said: "I am no king; I am only the nation's mouthpiece.

My thoughts can only be enriched by argument."
I know, too, a ruler who rules in fear does not have long to live.'
Shaka listened intently to Zihlandlo;
He was like a man who had travelled far for wisdom.
5   He said: 'Son of Ghubela, these are profound thoughts.
Great ideas are those that are nourished by others:
They fulfil their truths only in their timely season.
I have sometimes felt contempt for the actions of people,
Which often are cowardly and self-centred.
10   Images of my youth rush back and I decide:
People must be controlled until they learn the higher truth.
But people like you hold me back.
Then I think: it is better to listen to these great men,
To be nourished by them beyond the night.
15   I know now I shall not run this distance alone.
We who are loved by the Ancestors shall nourish our nation;
We shall be the stepping stones for our children.
There is not much time ahead of us, Ghubela.
The races of over-the-ocean have come:
20   Over our heads they have cast their shadows.
If we do not hurry, if we do not block the passages,
Their wiliness shall endanger the whole Palm Race.
In years to come they shall invade the whole region,
Recruiting even old women for their wars.
25   We must paralyse the young of the locust,
Driving them back before they learn to fly.
Because of this we must conquer the Soshangane utterly,
Making the route to our north wide and unhindered,
Enabling our army to move freely against the overseas invaders.
30   We should be the rallying point for all the children of the Palm
      Race.
If we are weak it is through us the region shall finally be
      conquered.
These over-the-ocean people trust only in their guns;
35   For this reason we must increase and strengthen our power.
Indeed, wars are ultimately won through people:
It is through collective actions that enemies are repelled.
People shall break the gun with their hands.'
After Shaka spoke these words, he sighed loudly,
40   As though he had emptied himself of deep harrowing thoughts.

Prince Zihlandlo, the son of Gcwabe, said:
'I repeat my words, my lord:
Your speed of thought excels all in our generation,
Making us seem dull and foolish and lacking in vision.
5   Then you yourself see us only as children.
The words you speak penetrate deep into my mind,
Yet even I had not seen the extent of these truths.'
Shaka did not let him finish these words.
He said: 'It is not wise for one to undermine oneself.
10 It is not true that those who judge look beyond the consequence.
Our task is to strengthen our nation, not to see this truth.'
Prince Zihlandlo tailed onto these words and said:
'The builder, my lord, knows where to find his materials.
To his house often comes many petitions.
15 The man of wisdom seals the lips of those who doubt
      themselves;
His laughter creates new visions for his listeners.
If our nation continues to follow your wisdom, it shall prosper.
It is clear that the crowd shall always be limited;
20 Thus it must constantly be fed with new visions.
People are not always the ones who fail;
Rather, it is the oracles
Who must drink in the farthest springs of future times.
From your truths all peoples of Zululand shall learn.
25 They shall dig the ground with their own hoes.'
Shaka shook his head and said: 'I understand your thoughts,
Even though I may not share their truth.
For many years I shouldered
Those who must grow and live by their own vision.
30 I have lived to see great men;
Some I have accompanied into great battles.
Many men and women have widened my horizons of thought.
No, Ghubela, great heroes breed their own greatness
At the beginning of eras their truth is manifest,
35 They do not wait for large arenas for their battles,
Theirs is not a war of weapons but a war of ideas.
They are like a vast field on which new plants must grow.
Yet they should die to fertilize the ground.'
Zihlandlo then said: 'Ahead of us are challenging times.
40 For us to win totally we must act in concert.

For this reason I ask that we strengthen all aspects of our lives.
Let nothing take us by surprise.'
When this discussion was concluded
The great heroes drank quietly from one large beer pot.
5   Each let his mind wander in its own direction.

On that day the sun blazed even times at the planet of dogs.
Shaka turned to his aide and said:
'Such a day often brings with it some unusual happenings.
Before it sets it shall be loaded with thunderstorms.
10   At that moment our lips shall not speak easily.'
He spoke as if he were only making a joke,
Yet he did feel the overwhelming shadows of the dying.
People heard him speak alone as if to commune with the Spirits.
The sun rose violently into the belly of the sky,
15   Boiling its anger over the heads of bald-headed men.
A huge black bull walked slowly, hanging out its tongue.
Only when the sun peered over the mountains of the afternoon
Did it begin to shed its tails of fire.
It spun its head as though to disappear into the sky.
20   A great wind began to blow,
Making the high branches to bend low to the earth.
Then by a final gesture it flung its seeds onto the ground.
From the distance a coil of black clouds began to assemble,
Piling up until they burst open, letting out floods of rain.
25   It was at this time a messenger arrived:
'My lord, I bring only painful news.'
As the messenger uttered these words
The king's aides looked at each other in amazement.
He continued: 'My Lord of Nations, King is dead.
30   His last words were only in praise of your friendship.
When he realized his moment of dying had come
He said: "On my behalf, praise the king, my lord.
Say I thank him as though I were speaking to my own parent.
Say to him: the Ancestors did not grant me the request to live.
35   I shall die in happiness, accompanied by a great man.
I am thankful for the kindness and the goodwill offered to me;
I thank the generous brotherhood extended to me.
My mission was only half-fulfilled. Had I accomplished it
I would have died a happier man.

I thank him for the mission he conferred on me.
I thank the brotherhood of the Gabangaye regiment."
These words were his last, my lord.
I am here, my king, to tell this painful story.
5   I have no words to soften the blows.'
Thus did Gulana, son of Mdakane, speak,
Knowing this news cut where those of Mbikwane had pierced.
Shaka summoned Zihlandlo to come back at once to Dukuza
      royal city.
10 He now detested the news of death.
Constantly he felt surrounded by these messengers
As though they proclaimed his own approaching death.
From King he had hoped for a deeper truth;
To be able to make a strategy befitting the challenge.
15 When Zihlandlo arrived at Dukuza
His mind told him of the grave events at the royal city.
He found Shaka grave and pensive
As though he was responding to some dark inspiration.
As Zihlandlo saluted Shaka dismissed his aides and councillors.
20 'Ghubela, I called you to tell you the deepest secrets of my
      mind.
I am obsessed with the voices of the dead.
They who were once close to me come back.
I tremble as though death had not been with me all my life.
25 At this very moment I am grappling with news of King's death,
As indeed I knew he would leave us.
It would not matter if this were the last of such news,
But I am like a rotten fruit that attracts many flies.
In my early days I boasted only of my good fortune;
30 The Ancestors then stood by me and drove away the shadows.
Of late I suffer only bad dreams, nightmares and premonitions.
I see those who died many years ago;
I see them as the fearful visage of the Ancestors.
I wake up and see death walking over my shadow.
35 In vain I invoke the aid of the great Ancestral Spirits.
Thoughts long ago forgotten, come back.
I am seized by a desire to have my own progeny,
To have a son and heir
Who shall boast the heroic poems of his own father.
40 Sometimes I even accept the very call of death

And wish I shared the peace of their lives.
Perhaps this way I could talk to my own Ancestor, Jama,
And laugh at the tales of earth with my father, Mbiya.
I would then be freed of all the burdens of power
5   Whose strains have made me old before my time.
I tell you these stories so that we can share them.
King carried for me crucial truths about overseas rule
From these I had hoped to prepare for war or for friendship.
If the foreigners planned wars
10   We would fall on them like a whirlwind,
Disrupting all their carefully planned stratagems.
But it seems the Ancestors have not granted me this boon.
They did not allow the lips to give us their truth.
Nonetheless, this does not forebode our defeat:
15   We still have men like Sotobe who can tell us these secrets.
Their long stay in overseas lands
Must fill their minds with deep and varied experiences.
By this death I am twice the loser.
This man alone could see things through our eyes and his,
20   But now I am left only with the excited men.'
As Shaka spoke, Zihlandlo sat and listened,
Hoping in this way to let the mind wander at will
Until it found its own targets.
For, a true friend does not seize words from the tongue,
25   But waits to receive them in clusters of succulence as they
      emerge.
The mind has its own power to heal itself.
Zihlandlo digested these truths in his mind
He focused on them, though they caused him pain.
30   He was alarmed at the terrors that obsessed the king
They seemed centred still on Nandi's death.
Zihlandlo quietly appealed to the Ancestors for the king's peace.
He stared at his friend, his heart torn with pain.
Often he thought Shaka did not fully live for himself, but for
35   events.
Zihlandlo concentrated his mind on overseas nations;
He saw them as locusts that reap whole fields of corn.
He commented to Shaka, and said:
'I weep for you, my lord. I am sad for our nation.
40   In truth, if such unpleasant seasons come in succession

Even words gradually lose their power.
I feel the terror of all the shadows that hang over you,
But then you are alone, my king.
Your very greatness withers all plants beside you.
5   The future cannot heal yesterday's pains.
It is time to let the next generation handle these affairs.
Let it learn now from its own mistakes,
For, indeed, only those who have failed can succeed.
I ask you to hurry the messages of Sotobe.
10 Listen to his experience while it still troubles his tongue.
It is these superior issues that shall nourish your mind.
You, my lord, are not like other rulers,
Whose deeds are soon forgotten with their age:
You transcend boundaries of time and lands.
15 What we achieved took other nations many eras to accomplish.
Rulers leave their achievements to make their eras great,
But you bundled many years into one single day of greatness.
It is why, despite your pains,
I ask you to multiply your efforts for the nation's sake.
20 Thus, too, shall your terrors disappear.
Summon Sotobe without delay:
Let him tell now the fruits of his mission;
Let him tell us how soon we shall fight the invader.
If this war shall be postponed or never fought
25 It shall depend on the treatment and replies of your emissaries.
You must prepare for the final day
For which you have nourished our great nation.'
These words shot into his mind like a herb.
Shaka was revived both in body and mind;
30 Even the dark wrinkles on his forehead vanished,
Like dawn peeling off the rings of night.
Shaka sighed long and said to Zihlandlo:
'Ghubela, you are truly a brother.
You carry on your lips the message of the gods.
35 Your mind penetrates into the depths of a still lake.
I thank you for these words, Ghubela.
They have cut out the throbbing segment of yesterday.
If I knew there were many who think like you
Then I would stretch my legs and fill my mind with pleasant
40   dreams.

Yet no great journey can be completed in one day.'
He spoke these words, preparing himself for the tasks before
     him.
Refreshed by these thoughts, even his words echoed with
5   warmth.
He now directed his mind to the various strategies of peace and
     war:
In peace-time he would create a nation that was proud and free.
Speaking deliberately and slowly, Zihlandlo said:
10 'The Ancestral Forefathers were wise when they said:
"No one must be praised as long as they live";
For to praise is to conclude the efforts of one man;
It is to elevate him above all others,
Making him free of blame or blemish.
15 No king, no man, can surpass your greatness.
I say this to you only in whispers, lest the winds hear me.
I ask you, therefore, to rest and pull together these powers.
Know by your achievements you have begun an era.
If the Ancestors so grant, you shall test us. Give us your greatest
20   gift:
By this bequest the Zulu nation shall be the greatest amongst
     nations.
Foreign nations of distant lands shall speak of us in awe;
Friendly nations shall send their emissaries.
25 They shall say: "With my own eyes
I have seen the greatness of Zululand."
They shall have seen the abundance and happiness of our
     children.'
Shaka laughed and said to him:
30 'You remind me of my father, Dingiswayo, when you speak in
     this manner.
He often put words carefully, like Mbiya.
Indeed, I have thought of these things;
But serious government demands patient handling.
35 People trained for war are hard:
They take time before they develop the habits of family life.
They require to hear and see for themselves the children.
Yet you have opened my hidden areas of thought.
We must eat and celebrate in preparation for a great tomorrow.'
40 Shaka sent word for a feast to be held

To honour the great Prince Zihlandlo of the Mkhize family.
Mbopha, who was engaged in his own secret schemes,
Became alarmed at these activities
He knew unexpected changes always follow secret meetings.

5   Such was the great feast of the two heroes:
Shaka spread laughter and mirth among the young and the old.
Even enemies sought assurances from their own allies;
Men like Mbopha, the son of Sithayi,
Who counted the days of his king like a cock counting grains.

10   It was during this feast the iziNyosi regiment was announced.
At the royal city of Dukuza there was a great festive mood.
On this very day a message came to Mkhabayi from Dingane,
Saying: 'We are in the northern part of the country.
We turned back from the army bound for Soshangane.

15   To avoid suspicion we informed our commander
We had drunk too strong a medicine and had fallen ill.
We shall wait until we have heard from you.'
Mkhabayi was terrified at these words,
Like someone who suddenly hears the sounds of battle.

20   In a seizure of fierce anger
She spat saliva on the ground, calling them fools.
She was alarmed that they dared trust anyone with such a
    message.
There and then she secretly ordered that the messenger be
25   killed,
Certain that, in terror of the message he carried,
He might babble the whole truth to the king.
As he ambled towards the royal grounds,
Thinking deeply of these events and happenings,

30   He heard a scolding voice shouting behind him.
While still startled, he felt a sharp instrument enter his
    bowels.
With a thud, he fell on to the ground.
As he fell he uttered the king's poems of excellence.

35   Dazed, he only desired by this act a hero's death.
By a sudden flash of thought he saw the whole truth,
And, gurgling the last words, he said:
'Now I see the whole horrendous plot;
Now I know what is to happen to my king.

Why through me? Have my Ancestors deserted me?'
With these final words he died.

At the city of Dukuza the earth shook from the beat of dancing
     feet.
5 Shaka's spirit was lifted by these fresh festivities.
He jumped into the arena and danced like a giraffe.
His whole physique trembled with movement:
It was as though he carried his body in his hands.
Even old men raised their feet, dancing slowly to the ancient
10   songs.
Some were singing, with tears of memories in their eyes.
The feasting did not cease till the morning.
At dawn could be heard voices of those returning to their
     homes.
15 From distant mountains their songs echoed;
From the cliffs their voices woke the birds from their sleep.
The light of the moon travelled to the limits of the horizon.
Only one red-tinted cloud hung loosely in the sky;
It had hung there since the previous noon.
20 Carried by a light wind, it floated slowly to the western regions.
It fixed itself there as though to display its chameleon magic.
Sometimes it turned itself to look like a man;
Sometimes to look like a huge body of an elephant;
Sometimes changing totally to look like the menacing cliffs;
25 Sometimes it stood there like a challenging bull.
Those who were singing paid no attention.
They walked carelessly, shouting and laughing and singing.

In the coastal regions the king's message had been received.
An order had been issued to bury King with his regimental
30   song,
To put his body in a spot always to be remembered.
Thus the wily Fynn and Farewell were left to lead.
They were uneasy about the gifts they carried for the king.
They constantly debated and quarrelled about the wisdom of
35   this action.
When they returned from King's funeral
The shyster Fynn began to inspect the king's gifts.
He was nervous, as they all prepared to go to Dukuza.

Fynn sorted out these trinkets,
Alarmed at their low value,
To enhance his nation's prestige he added his own.
And Shaka had now become impatient for the news of their
5   mission.
The great procession soon began to Dukuza royal city;
It was led by Fynn and Farewell.
After them were many slaves and peoples they had collected.
They deviated, following the route to the regions of Sotobe.
10 The whole crowd finally stopped before the city of Dukuza.
From there they sent word asking for the king's audience.
The messenger found Shaka chatting with the young recruits.
Great laughter greeted his formal address,
For soon after the great feast for Zihlandlo,
15 Shaka received the new recruits with great eagerness.
He constantly poked fun at the rigid shackles of discipline.
The commander of the regiment warmly welcomed these new
     changes;
Thus was Shaka's popularity among the iziNyosi regiment
20   ensured.
Many songs were composed about the episodes of the
     Mzimkhulu river.
Young boys proudly demanded of their seniors:
'I want to fight and die for the king who held me across the
25   river.'
For their battle eagerness they were dubbed 'the nation's
     children'.
Shaka's approach was often heralded with a new anthem:
'We are the children of the nation, we of Zululand!
30 Whoever challenges us shall have touched the mountain
     boulders.
He shall have roused the scorpions from their nest.
He shall have touched a cluster of bees.'
Shaka smiled softly as he walked among them.
35 He was pleased with the heroism of the new regiment.
Often he would sit waiting for the new commanders.
One by one they came to take their spear of authority.
They bowed and shouted the royal salute.
Finally each would lead his own unit to pay tribute to the king;
40 Turning at a distance, they displayed their battle colours.

Demanding there and then to fight their own battles.
They then formed a semi-circle and sang the nation's anthems.
When all the celebrations were over, Shaka addressed them:
'I see before me the future of the Palm Race.
5   I see the great heroes who shall be the pride of our nation.
Let generations hereafter know
We never turned our backs on our enemies.
Amongst us were heroes such as Mgobhozi-of-the-Mountain;
Amongst us was the great Zulu, son of Nogandaya.
10 They were the locusts who infuse terror into the hearts of
        enemies;
They alone were the power that brought us our harvest.
Only through our knowledge of our great past
Can we acquire courage and wisdom.
15 The Zulu nation has fought and won many great wars.
Surrounded by enemies they broke open the hostile
        encirclements,
And built their own shrines and monuments.
Today our nation knows no boundaries except those created by
20   us.
We shall secure homes for all the children of the Palm Race.
You of the iziNyosi regiment, know, your era has begun:
It is you who shall protect the nation's children:
I too demand them from you
25 A nation that is powerful and proud attracts many enemies —
Constantly they prepare and plot against it.
Should they break it they rush to seize its possessions.
The enemies are not to be seen only at the boundaries,
But often penetrate deep into the nation's heart.
30 They make allies of the many once-great families,
Promising to share with them the spoils of a once-great nation.
For all this I liken you to the watchful eyes of bees,
They who day and night guard their homes from enemies.
On the southern regions there is treacherous silence.
35 A nation of overseas peoples has entered the lands of the Palm
        Race:
It is a nation skilled in wily and treacherous strategems.
Stubbornly it persists in gnawing deep into our lands.
From a distance it scans the boundaries of our nations;
40 It is eager to learn all our secrets.

386

Tomorrow it shall no longer take the circuitous route.
Its forces shall come from all sides like a team of vultures.
When this day comes you must be ready.
No longer must you be the raw recruits,
5 But possessed of the fierce power that destroys all enemies.
By your alertness you should surprise the enemy.
I send you in all directions to guard our nation.
Always remember you are born of heroes:
Never live to be a disgrace to your Forefathers.
10 People must never say: "The heroes of the Zulus are dead."
I have spoken at length as though I talk to cowards;
It is only because of the joy from you that makes me speak.
Many shall warn others against provoking the Zulus,
Telling them to keep away from the iziNyosi regiment.
15 I have revived my own regiment through you.
I liken you to the feared regiment of uFasimba.
I repeat to you: many enemies are plotting against us.
When they arrive, run, my children;
Run and sieze them even by their throats.
20 I am talking of the nations with open teeth;
I denounce those who say we have fought enough!
Remind them of my words with your spears!
You shall yet fight many great battles, I swear by my sister.
Your vision has shaken me up from sleep.'
25 As he spoke his voice rose and fell;
No one will ever know whether he spoke in anger or in sadness.
Shaka reminded them of the Zulu heroes,
Who even then were fighting against Soshangane.
He said: 'With them you have formed an undying bond,
30 For whoever fights in battle fights with others.'

It was after this occasion that a messenger came
Reporting how the Strangers and Sotobe awaited the king.
He turned to a councillor next to him and said:
'Let us not delay, lest the worms eat into our feet.
35 We do not know as we sit here
What treacherous schemes the foreigners are plotting.'
He spoke seriously and looked in all directions.
Soon Shaka left the commanders to debate his words.
The whole concourse of the iziNyosi regiment

Fervently discussed the king's new policies.
Endlessly they argued about its finer meanings.
A boy who had become a man,
Having acquired his new regimental membership,
5   Now challenged many who were his seniors.
But the old commander restrained him and said:
'Your time will come. Do not loosen your anger.'
He spoke calmly and in a controlled voice,
For, indeed, the greatest heroes never speak hurriedly of war,
10   Knowing it means death to enemies and friends alike.

Many shall be witnesses of Zulu power and glory.
Shaka, defiant of all dangers, stood before the commanders,
His eyes shot through with confidence.
It was as though he possessed a thousand immobile eyes:
15   He directed his penetrating gaze at every shadow.
Those who were there reported:
'We saw great multitudes of people and troops.'
At that moment a voice called out for silence.
The king addressed them in a high, angry voice:
20   'From now on I dispense with the bodyguard.
I shall not again be surrounded by them,
I shall not be cocooned like a coward.
In my life I fear no death; I fear no one!
Whoever desires to kill me, let him try.
25   I am the son of Ndaba; I am the grandson of Jama.
Many homes are not fenced with spears, then why mine?
Am I not the ruler of people and nations?
Would not all the assassins and murderers
Find the whole nation alert against such bandits?
30   A ruler who is loved fears no enemies.'
It was because of these sharp words
That the royal guard of the Mbelebele regiment was dismissed.
The councillors attempted to remonstrate with the king
But where only answered with violent words:
35   'Have I at any time shown any cowardice?'
By these words he sealed their lips.

The overseas people entered the arena, led by Sotobe.
Shaka invited them to the councillors' meeting place.

He was keen to discuss all these matters in their presence.
Speaking, quickly and impatiently he said:
'I sent you on this mission to fulfil it and return.
After so long I hope you bring rich news.
I hope you bring, too, the elixir of life you claimed you
       possessed.'
They were all silent. Only their tongues swam in the saliva,
Preparing to give some story to excuse their delay.
Sotobe began with a royal address, and said:
'My lord, dreaded lion of the Zulus, of you many live in terror.
Great one, whose greatness is celebrated among distant nations,
Your messengers have returned.
We come back confused and full of misgivings.
We suffered the tormenting recollections of our homes.
Only in your land does the power of humanity and kindness
       prevail:
Plentifulness and selflessness speak of the greatness of its people;
Bravery and courage are beyond the ken of personal glory.
But amongst foreigners cruelty is rife.
I have seen it with my own eyes, my lord.
I have returned to the greatest of the greatest lands;
This land where rule in freedom the children of the Palm Race.
We waited a long period for a word from their king's
       representative.
We were restless and tired after three months of dilly-dallying;
We began to seek ways to escape this confinement.
We threatened to walk on foot to your capital if need be.
At long last we were visited by their commander-in-chief —
The words of the representative and the commander-in-chief
Still ring clear in our ears.
We were cross-questioned: were we true messengers of our king?
How could our own king use the message form of the overseas
       nations?
Why, they asked, did I not approach the representative alone?
Directly they asked of what importance was King to us?
Why had I brought my wife with me?
All these pointed questions they asked; we answered.
We did this only out of respect for the command of our king.
We vowed we should not leave King behind;
We told them he was our commander by your order;

We warned that this endless questioning blasphemed our king.
We were treated as spies not the messengers of our great ruler.
As this debate raged and angry words were exchanged,
King, our commander, entered.
5   It was this that silenced the little man of foreign lands.
We knew then he took advantage of us.
He softened his words, asking us if we had had enough to eat.
It was only through King a word came from the representative
Telling us the message from our king had been conveyed.
10   We were ordered to return with these gifts.
Through them, and in the name of King George, he asks for
      peace.
For the moment, my lord, here ends my story.'
Shaka listened to these words and carefully analysed their
15   meaning.
As they spread the gifts before him
He paid no attention, merely staring at his envoys.
Shaka had heard through his agents
How Fynn had rummaged through his gifts
20   And how he had carefully examined each item.
He said, speaking angrily to Sotobe:
'You have failed! You failed in the mission I sent you on!
You did not examine these gifts,
But let this forward and ever-curious Fynn inspect them.
25   Like a monkey, he is ever peering into forbidden places.
He is no man, nor is he like King,
Who respected the customs and laws of our nation.
How I wish it was he who was talking even now!
He said these words softly and with great sorrow:
30   'The Beautiful Ones lie in the grave.'
Agitated, he turned to look at the presents.
They touched in him some hidden anger and he called out:
'Of what use are all these trinkets?
These gifts are more fitting to children!
35   Before I am seized by an uncontrollable anger
Depart now from my sight.
Only you, Isaacs, shall bring to me these gifts.'
Sotobe and others left unceremoniously.
When Shaka was in the privacy of his house
40   He asked once again the importance of each item.

He said to Isaacs: 'Which one gives immortal life?
Did I not send you to get the elixir of life?'
These words were difficult for Isaacs to answer:
He knew in doing so he would expose his country's weakness
5   And remove from it the awe in which it was falsely held.
Besides, the words of Sotobe had already diminished its
     reputation.
Shaka did not wait for him to answer.
He ordered Issacs to name and describe each item.
10 'This one, my lord, is for a cold.'
'Who said our nation is feeble like yours?
Do we look as if we would succumb to a cold?'
'This one, my lord, shall cure all sores of the body.'
'Who told you our bodies reek with sores like yours?'
15 'This one is for spirits that are low.'
Answering in the same irritated manner, Shaka said:
'Have you seen any Zulus ailing with low spirits?
Are the Zulus not man and creation of life?
The only herb necessary is one to calm them down.
20 That medicine lies in battle, in the festival and in the feast!
Not one of these medicines is needed by us.
Why do you deceive the nations of the earth?
Why do you tell us you possess the elixir of life,
When you know these are only tales to trap the others?'
25 After these words he closed his eyes in an act of contempt,
Dismissing these gifts as useless trinkets.
On opening his eyes he examined the gift sword,
Keen to see how effective it would be in battle.
He touched its blade with his fingers and said:
30 'So! The overseas nations think they are wise!'
Shaka then summoned Sotobe alone,
Eager to know the stratagems of the overseas nations.
He closely questioned him about their customs,
And explained to Sotobe that he spoke angrily
35 Only to keep the foreigners on their toes,
To discourage them from inviting more such adventurers;
For whoever tells of pleasant things in foreign lands
Encourages whole swarms of newcomers.
But those who think they survive by the grace of the Ancestors
40 Discourage the foolish stampede of their kin.

Shaka praised Sotobe for fulfilling his tasks.
He commented on the kindliness and loyalty of King,
Expressing deep sorrow at the death of this trusted man.
He said of them all only King and Isaacs possessed true
5   humanity.
Thus they talked and discussed throughout the night.
Sotobe reported how, on hearing of the Zulu attack in
       Mpondoland,
They mobilized and put together their followers and allies.
10   Indeed, Sotobe continued, it was this presence
That boosted their morale after many months of waiting.
'No sooner had they heard we intended to reach our king
Than King George's representative mellowed.
Everyone began to treat us with kindness.'
15   Shaka laughed at this point, as though he had discovered a
       secret.
He said: 'By my sister! They even sent me a mirror,
As though to direct us to look at our faces like children.
Hlambamanzi, who is experienced in their many ways and
20   customs,
Tells us it is by these simple stratagems they conquered the
       south.'
Speakingly hurriedly he said:
'Yet I would loathe to alert them before I possess their gun.
25   These cowards have, indeed, invented a dangerous weapon.
If some of the regiments learnt its use,
They should be the vanguard as we approach the enemy.'
They continued talking leisurely like this,
Until Shaka said finally: 'Go, Sotobe, and rest.
30   You have fulfilled your mission.
As long as the overseas Stranger is here,
So long shall I maintain the appearance of anger against you.
I shall yet send another team of envoys,
These I shall command to learn the use of guns.'
35   Such was their parting on this day:
Shaka shook Sotobe's hand and uttered his poems of excellence.

Book Sixteen: The plotters assemble

The plot to assassinate Shaka builds up. Its success in all its aspects depends on the trust Shaka places in his brothers. They abandon the campaign against Soshangane with the excuse that they do not feel well. On their arrival they announce their presence to Princess Mkhabayi, who is alarmed at their bungling. Shaka is also surprised that they have returned, but he is in a tolerant mood. He is considering new approaches to government. Tension arises as many abortive plots are hatched against Shaka. One after another they collapse. Meantime, a delegation that had gone to the northern regions is expected. Its return proves opportune for the execution of these plots.

Prince Dingane and Prince Mhlangana, together with their
    followers,
Headed for their royal cities.
Their weapons and hearts spoke the same language.
5   To Princess Mkhabayi they sent word of their whereabouts.
The night whispered until it was overtaken by dawn.
At the great royal city of Mkhabayi few words were spoken;
No one knew who would be the first to strike.
Allies built up on all sides.
10 There were those who played their song for both sides
Who hoped to gain honour from whoever won.
Such a man was Mbopha of Sithayi, the puff-adder.
There were some who desired to serve in the inner circles,
Who helped to spread the rumours concocted by Mkhabayi,
15 Who said it was Shaka himself who had killed his mother!
From house to house they scattered seeds of hatred against
    Shaka.
They spread like the young of the locusts in a tender corn field:
Thus did their lips prepare the ground for the killer.
20 The princes now sent a word to Mkhabayi and said:
'We have arrived. We are ready to undertake our tasks.
Prepare, then, a place where we shall meet in private.
Give this same news to Mbopha, the son of Sithayi.'
The terrible message travelled fast,

Until it was uttered to Mkhabayi.
Simultaneously a messenger hurried to Shaka's court
To deliver a deceitful message from his brothers:
'The king's sons have failed through illness to proceed to battle.
5 They say: "Forgive us for not having fulfilled our tasks.
As long as we live we shall still fight the nation's wars.
For the moment, make allowance for us, who are of your family,
And understand we too desire to make sacrifice to our Ancestors.
We shall plead for all those descended from Ndaba.
10 Above all, we shall pray that your rule be always glorious.
Even our illness may have been imposed on us
To fufil extravagantly the will of the Ancestors." '
When Shaka heard these words he was alarmed,
But he mellowed as he realized he would share in their warm
15 company.
Indeed, he criticized himself for having been too harsh on
them,
For, after all, if they should all die simultaneously in battle
The nation of Zulu may be left without a leader.
20 It was because of these thoughts he sent this friendly message:
'Do not worry; have a full rest.
When you have recovered and have met all the demands of
custom
Share with me the responsibility of power.'
25 He sent a warm word of sympathy and added:
'I would have come to see you myself
But the affairs of the nation call constantly on me.
Even now I am preparing for my mother's Cleansing Feast.
To let her spirit celebrate with us after the years of mourning.'
30 Shaka had, indeed, recently sent an order to his councillors,
Telling them all goodwill and happiness
Should come through sacrifice and feasting
In rememberance of the nation's parent,
All should appeal to the Queen Mother's spirit
35 Imploring her to stand on guard with others,
Protecting all that they had bequeathed and accomplished.
When Shaka's brothers heard this message they were elated.
It was only Mkhabayi who suspected this was a plot,
For, indeed, those who constantly lay traps for others
40 Often are haunted by suspicions.

Even friendly gestures do not inspire in them feelings of love.
They curse and turn their backs on those they mistrust
Until all words and truths are stained by their bitterness.
Thus too were the fierce thoughts of Princess Mkhabayi.
5   She sent an order to her nephews, Dingane and Mhlangana,
Enjoining them not to be swayed by these gestures.
Claiming they were only made to lull them.
She contended he was now frightened,
Knowing he had seized this power without his father's blessing.
10   When the Forefathers said: 'Quarrels of families should be
       avoided.'
They had in mind issues such as this.
For, in time, dissenting families come together;
Then the arbiter bears the brunt of the blame.
15   It is not known whether Mkhabayi, seeing these growing bonds,
Began to fear that the blame would be placed on her.
Again and again she sent messengers to alert Dingane and
       others,
Warning them to be wary of Mbopha himself.
20   It was because of this that when they met
Mkhabayi reiterated her stand and pointed out many of their
       errors.
She told them how by their own folly they could lead to their
       own deaths.
25   Speaking with great vehemence, she said:
'I shall not say too many things.
The times we live in demand people of action:
At this moment we require only those who shall not hesitate.
This country looks up to the the great House of Jama.
30   Unless I am possessed by some madness,
Those I see before me are of the royal House of Jama;
I talk to them with respect and confidence.
I know, too, when they have decided to act
No power and no wind can reverse their directions.
35   They have reared up their heads in time,
Saying: "It is enough; let this family tyranny stop!
The king tramples at will in the house of my father.
He does whatever he wills with the royal children."
I give my second warning, which is my last:

A thunderstorm that has gathered does not spend its force.
It tears the mountains with its fire until all is ashes.
Should houses be destroyed, new ones are built!
Life rebuilds from the centre of the ruins.
5   It plants new fields on the virgin soils.
Thus to you I say: complete what you have started.'
The lips of those who listened moved and trembled,
As though inwardly they uttered her heroic poem:
'The wily one, fearful daughter of the Snake,
10   Which struck its victim while it lulled him with strategems.'
Prince Dingane followed her words with softening comments:
'Great one, we all are here to listen to your commands.
We have come to pay our respects to you.
We have travelled far, escaping narrowly the enemy eyes,
15   It was all to affirm our love for the country.
By your example we have learnt many things;
What you say is treasured in our hearts.
We are here to ask you for the way.
When the bloodthirsty tyrant has been removed
20   We shall let the whole nation celebrate with us.
We are grateful, too, to Mbopha, the honoured son of Sithayi,
Who is the supreme guardian of our nation.
It is he who shall open the gates for us.
Had it been our will, tomorrow would be today;
25   But then a great day is often enshrouded in mists.
The son of Sithayi has come to reveal to us some truths,
For he alone knows best the routes to the opprobrious serpent.'
Dingane turned to Mbopha as he said these words.
Flattered and pleased at this attention, he swelled with pride;
30   He let his mind wander, imagining all his future glory.
Perhaps through self-deception, perhaps through love of power,
He suppressed the advice of our Forefathers, who said:
'He who sponsors a king does not live.'
When he was on the verge of spilling his heart
35   Prince Mhlangana said: 'May I, too, say something?
I am pestered by a nagging voice that refuses to be silenced.
Of late I feel a sadness and pity for my brother, Shaka,
It is as if every day he asks us:
"Children of my father, what are you doing?"
40   It is as if he possessed the power to read our inner thoughts.

His blood shall wail over our houses, crying out for revenge.
People themselves shall never trust us.
Behind us they shall whisper:
"How can the killers of a brother rule a nation?"
5 I am troubled by my conscience.
For it is only the death of his parent
That has temporarily unsettled his mind.
Even the message he has sent us seems to bear the truth,
Testifying to his eternal love for his family.
10 Shaka is, indeed, in a state of deep sadness,
For never once did he ever miss a war.
He personally fought, attesting to his love of the nation:
Staying at home while wars are being fought
Seems strange and contrary to his nature.
15 By these words, I do not put the blame on anyone,
For, indeed, I am here by my own decision and free will.
I only request that we think again of our actions.
For it is not uncommon to assign higher motives to acts
That only fulfil one's own ambitions.'
20 Prince Dingane shifted his position
As though he would reply, but hesitated.
He never got the chance to comment,
For soon Mkhabayi, trembling with rage, spoke:
'Mhlangana! Do you know why you are here?
25 Do you know your very life hangs by the thread?
Do you realize this very gathering may be known to Shaka?
Can you understand you may not live another day?'
She sighed and breathed hard as she uttered these words.
Finally she spoke to him softly and calmly, saying:
30 'Mhlangana, you are ruled by your heart.
It is this weakness that has brought us these disasters.
Had we spoken in outrage long ago
We would have freed ourselves from these problems.
The nation could have been spared the horrendous era.
35 How is it, do you think, that for the mourning to cease
A commoner had to raise his voice before us?
"Enough is enough." he said.
"It is not the first time someone dies."
This truth could not be spoken by us of the royal clan.
40 Instead we indulged him endlessly, consoling the unconsolable!

Even today you still remind us of Nandi's death,
Though through it many a nation's hero and heroine have died!
Do you also want us to follow these victims?'
Mhlangana was now restless.
5   He chastised himself for having uttered such foolish words.
Like many who are weak,
Who, upon hearing words spoken in anger, disavow their beliefs.
Mhlangana pleaded and begged for forgiveness.
'Great Mother, I am ashamed of myself for harbouring these
10   thoughts.
Your words excel all others.
I spoke only in terror of spilling the blood of a relative.
Many families are destroyed by their appetite for bloodshed.'
The wily aunt followed up these words with a friendly comment,
15   Knowing it is necessary to soften the hearts of the frightened.
She knew, too, doubt persists in those
Who have been rushed into action.
She spoke gently to Mhlangana and said:
'No, Mhlangana! It is you who are greater than us.
20   It is always wise to avoid killing one's own relatives
And to look at events from all aspects.
But it is unforgivable in the affairs of state
To let the feelings of pity dominate one's judgement.'
She knew such weaknesses are often a disease,
25   Besetting those who never rule.
Through them the horrid schemes of rulers are exposed;
Through them a whole era may change its course;
And yet they never can hold the strings of power.
Mbopha, the son of Sithayi, requested to speak.
30   It was, indeed, his thoughts that everyone wanted to hear.
He said: 'I am grateful for the trust placed in me.
I am here only to fulfil the tasks of our nation.
I have been loyal to our ruler, Shaka of Senzangakhona.
I shall be loyal to whoever shall assume the power.
35   In the words of the nation's heroine and our beloved Princess,
The nation deserves an era of peace and happiness.
To this end I dedicate myself.
In my judgement, opportunities for action abound.
Of late the king is often alone;
40   He often sits on a round rock below the royal grounds;

Nor is he ever accompanied by a servant or bodyguard.
He has dismissed the guarding troops and close friends.
This to me seems the moment when we should act.
Whoever shall be our chosen performer shall pass through me.
5   When he reaches the king's favourite spot
He shall plunge at him the cold iron.
When the king sits at this spot he is never armed.
I can see no other plan to excel this one.'
They were all quiet as, indeed, this sounded like the best
10   strategem.
It was as though Mbopha narrated what had already happened;
In their imagination they tasted their crime.
They were all horrified.
For, in truth, the victims of murder often speak from their
15   graves —
And how much more, those who are our kinsmen!
Prince Dingane intervened at this point,
Eager to break the poisonous silence, and said:
'This plan seems to meet all our needs,
20   Though I had thought we could use one of the embittered
        women,
Making her the key to execute our plans.
She would hide a short spear, or give him some poison,
Thus earning from us and the nation eternal praise.'
25   Mbopha violently disagreed with this plan,
Since it deprived him of the central role as chief organizer.
He said: 'Shaka is not like other men.
He knows his women and all their weaknesses.
He never sleeps where he has had his joys,
30   Nor does he make any exceptions of the homes of his favourites.'
Princess Mkhabayi focused her fierce eyes on the gathering
And said: 'I have finished, what I came here for is done.
The rest I leave to those who are men.
We agree on all aspects; it is enough!'
35   As she said this she prepared to leave.
Suddenly she stopped half-way,
As though she had remembered something.
'Dingane, I want you to come with me half-way.'
So it was that the pair of them moved in one direction.
40   She said: 'I do not want us to walk too long a distance,

Lest Mhlangana becomes suspicious and bitter.
Here is my last word to you:
It seems your brother is weak;
If you do not follow hard on his footsteps
5   He shall find a reason to retreat altogether.'
Prince Dingane fervently agreed with these words,
And said (happy to damn someone weaker than him):
'Do not bother too much about him;
He is ever changing. One truth remains:
10   He is often the one who urges us to reap Shaka's head.
Should one ignore him
He melts and changes until one's own views are his.
I often plant in him an idea and leave it to germinate.
For however hard he struggles,
15   He ends up with the views implanted in him.
He is like the sun that always ends up in one spot.'
Mkhabayi laughed at this claim of Dingane's.
She bade him farewell and lightly shook his hand.
She thought to herself: 'How Dingane has grown!
20   His courage would frighten an attacking lion.
In him I see qualities of my father, Jama.'

Shaka was sitting at his Assembly place,
Awaiting the news from the great Soshangane campaign.
He was anxious also to hear of the mission of Bantwana and
25   Nxazonke.
These two diplomats led a section of isiYendane regiment
To find the royal feathers beyond the Khahlamba mountains;
Above all, to search for the iron mining centres.
Thus Shaka thought highly of this mission.
30   He desired to know the store of goodwill for the Zulu state
And to create allies out of the small neighbouring kingdoms.
Should this bear fruit, he thought, then these nations
Would accept without war the hegemony of Zululand.
Shaka had spoken plainly the day they departed:
35   'I want you to know how deep are the waters beyond our region.
I assign to you this mission because of your discretion with
      people.
I send you, too, my uncle, because of the dignity of your age.
This, too, is my reason for choosing the oldest regiment.

Your age alone should tell them you are truly the king's envoy.
Should this mission succeed
Then the nations of the Palm Race shall have found their peace.
Our policies shall have won over many nations,
5 Not out of fear but out of good will.
I want you to acquaint my brother Moshoshoe with these truths.
To him you must take gifts from the Zulu nation.
Tell him I have sent you to fetch the royal feathers of the loury
       bird.'
10 Shaka knew by these words King Moshoeshoe would understand
The envoys were sent on a peaceful mission.
Through numerous missions and gifts their trust would be
       affirmed.
From there his messengers would explore the regions of the
15   north,
Where there were remote kingdoms of black rulers,
Such ancient kings and states as those of King Ggari.
The poet said of his greatness and leadership:
'The people have vowed by Mokgadi never to yield.
20 They proclaimed: "In the sacred name of Mokgadi we have
       arrived!"
Dingalo vowed in the name of Kgama and said:
"Only my city shall survive;
To the end of time I shall defend it from all comers!" '
25 In this same region were kingdoms of the Herero and Ovambo;
It was the return of this mission that Shaka now awaited.
He was certain, as he discussed with his few councillors,
Should the mission succeed, the whole region would never be
       the same.
30 Often he spoke directly to his close friends and advisers:
'If there could be friendship among the children of the Palm
       Race
The overseas nations would skirt away from our lands.
Should they by their folly dare enter the home of the black ants,
35 We shall devour them, I swear by my sister,
Until only their bones shall be left in the fields.'

It was now a long time since the overseas team returned,
       empty-handed.
Shaka now desired to send yet another section.

He said, talking to those at the Assembly:
'We shall dispatch a new delegation to the white lands.
The mission that was undertaken by Sotobe was incomplete;
It died half-way through, with the death of its commander,
5   King.
The delegation that follows must learn from yesterday's errors.
Not only must it make contact with the ruler,
But by my directive it must master
All the various laws of the overseas Strangers,
10   Attaining the skill to use and make the gun.
Even though such weapons are only fit for cowards,
Still we must know their points of strength.'
The Assembly applauded these plans,
Knowing on many occassions his views had proven correct.
15   At that very moment Mbopha passed the Assembly.
He bowed low to the king and saluted.
Shaka said, raising his voice:
'I do not see your eyes, son of Sithayi.
Come to me when these affairs have been completed.
20   Let me hear what views you have on my long-lost envoys.
I am concerned now about my uncle, Nxazonke,
Perhaps this journey has sapped all his strength.'
When he said this the Assembly laughed,
Knowing Shaka was only poking fun at his uncle's age.
25   Mbopha said: 'No, my lord, he still lives.
I am certain the life in the north teems with feasts and festivals.
After all, are they not the envoys of the greatest potentate on
    earth?
Besides, whatever happens, my lord shall know before us.'
30   Mbopha said this, referring to the truthful dreams of Shaka.
He was terrified at the evil thoughts in his mind.
Shaka himself sensed something odd in Mbopha's mood.
He thought to himself: 'Mbopha is truly getting familiar.
He even dares to make jokes about my dreams in my presence!
35   He comments loosely on things unbecoming in a subordinate.'
Mbopha soon retired to the house,
Leaving the Assembly debating various affairs of state.
They discussed the many reasons for the delay of Nxazonke's
    mission.
40   Some stated how friendship among those of the Palm Race

Would only be a dream, should this mission fail.
Shaka left the Assembly after all these debates.
He surprised Mbopha in the meeting-house,
As he sat there waiting and concocting his complex schemes,
5   Blending words to parry the penetrating eyes of Shaka.
For such are those whose chests harbour troublesome secrets:
They are ever terrified lest their lips open too suddenly.
Thus they constantly organize and re-organize their words,
Selecting from them those that fit the present mood.
10   Thus, too, Mbopha sat, in an agitated state.
He suddenly shouted the king's heroic epic:
'I salute you, my lord Dlungwana, descendant of Ndaba!
You, the sun that emerged brilliantly
And, as it reached the midday-sky, it exploded with fire!'
15   In his confusion Mbopha confused Shaka's heroic poem
With that of his father, Senzangakhona.
Shaka noticed this but still shelved it in his mind.
He also saw how Mbopha kowtowed lower than ever before.
When he had collected his thoughts he said:
20   'O Mbopha, son of Sithayi, I had a strange dream.
I dreamt you were paying respect to another king.'
It was as if the king had cut him in his intestines.
Shocked by this, he repeated words incessantly:
'I shall never . . . I shall never worship another. . . another
25   ruler.
I would rather die and die like a dog.
There is only one king, my king and lord.
My king is here before me now and always.
What ill luck would lead me to such misfortune?
30   What crime would I have committed against my Ancestors?'
He continued making these endless vows of loyalty
Until Shaka himself felt pity for him and said:
'Do not worry, Mbopha; it is I who know you better.
A dream often follows the direction of one's evil thoughts.
35   No day passes that is without its refuse.
If we followed the meanings of all dreams we would lose our
        truth.
The more one believes in them the more bizarre their
        messages.
40   Perhaps I, too, am jealous of your loyalty.

Having seen you serve faithfully in my household,
I want to believe this loyalty is mine and mine alone.
In truth, this dream enhances your service and greatness.'
As Shaka said these words he toned down his voice,
5   As though to enable the discussion to proceed in a friendly
       spirit.
Mbopha was pleased with this change of mood.
Though still paralysed with fear, he ventured to thank the king.
He moulded his words, commanding them to express a cordial
10   mood;
Only through quiet and softened syllables did he speak.
Shaka followed up with a warm and friendly conversation.
He said casually: 'Tell me, son of Sithayi,
How do you see the affairs of the land?
15   My envoys have delayed too long,
Nor do I hear a word of their approaching arrival.
I am concerned, too, lest their murder precipitates a war.
I had planned that after our northern campaign
The people and the army must rest.
20   It is time we shared the pleasures bequeathed to us by our
       Forefathers.'
Mbopha warmly responded to these words,
Puzzled that the king still trusted him
Yet he hoped Shaka's very obsessions
25   Would take his mind away from their own intrigues.
Mbopha commented as though he was certain about all the
      answers.
Indeed, he hoped if his words were not the truth,
The events must give to them the substance of truth.
30   He said: 'No, my lord, I feel at ease.
My spirits whisper only good news.
It is for this reason they have delayed.
Many great and small rulers seek to pay their respects
And to cement their friendships with our nation.
35   It is customary for a good message to come with a full belly
My lord should not worry his mind with these things.
Who would dare provoke you in your own quiet mountain?
Who would not feast and embrace your envoys?
Are not the children of the great Moshoeshoe our friends?
40   Are not the Ngwanes of Sobhuza our friends and kinsmen?

Who, then, would provoke you unless they were the foolish
    Soshangane?
He, too, shall see our raised stick and flee.'
These words lifted Shaka's spirit,
5   For, indeed, rulers who wait for good news
Feed their minds on the pleasant words of their underlings!
They have the skill to blend the truth with deception.
Their power lies in postponing the unpleasant truth.
Thus Shaka and Mbopha drank in a better mood.
10 The king asked about many affairs concerning the royal
    household.
He inquired, too, about the regions occupied by the Sithayi
    family.
To them Shaka often gave his favourite herd of cattle
15 To thank them for their services to the state.
Even Mbopha wondered, as he sauntered to his home,
Why he was not content with all this glory and honour.
What was it, he asked himself, that could further fulfil his life?
He began to feel contempt for his own plots and thoughts.
20 He said, attempting to grapple with his conscience:
'What good fortune attends a man
Who ties knots against someone who has given him so much?'
It was as though in his drunkenness
He saw clearly a vision of Nandi saying to him:
25 'What are you doing, Mbopha, son of Sithayi?
Whose blood are you spilling in our gates?'
Mbopha looked at his feet closely but it was only mud.
He replied, speaking foolishly:
'I am goaded by Princess Mkhabayi and the royal family.
30 What am I? I am only a servant of the powerful.'
As the voice fell into the winds it called out peremptorily:
'You are a liar, son of Sithayi! You are a liar!'
Like all voices issuing from a troubled mind,
It was swallowed by many others of his own.

35 On one of those days now common to him,
Mbopha was blabbering to himself
When suddenly he heard Shaka's voice beside him:
'Why are you talking to yourself, son of Sithayi?
People who talk loud to themselves often have deep problems.

Is your problem caused by women and family quarrels?'
Mbopha took refuge in these words and said:
'O my lord, it is the truth:
My two main wives have been quarrelling.
5   The senior one swears violently at the other and says:
"We weep for the widow of Dukuza regions,
Whose husband is buried beneath the stone!"
(She implies by this that the other poisoned a rival.)
I cannot tell if I am the one destined for poisoning,
10   Or if it is some victim unknown to me.
Women can make one's mind lose its balance.'
He said these words as he sought sympathy from the king,
For seldom do two men ever disagree about women.
They both laughed and proceeded in their tasks.
15   By a new order the king sent a message to the Strangers,
Telling them to prepare again for a new mission,
To take once more fresh greetings to their King George.
He instructed them to strengthen these bonds between them as
        rulers,
20   Enabling them to fulfil their duties to their nations.
He told them bluntly he did not await only words of underlings.
Shaka knew messages of deputies
Often are full of warmth but devoid of consequence.
They are spoken only to wet the tongues
25   And entertain the wise while deceiving the simple.
Only the master speaks the meaningful words.
For this reason Shaka demanded to hear directly from King
        George.
He summoned John Cane of the White Strangers
30   And instructed him to lead the second mission
And to arrange for training in the use of guns.
Shaka defined the nature of this mission explicitly:
'I want peace between our two nations.
Your King George must lead the White Races
35   As I, too, have built unity among peoples of the Palm Race.
This way there shall be universal peace among peoples.'
Shaka then appointed Mbozamboza and Nomadlambi as
        assistants.
He told them to affirm his goodwill to King George.
40   This team of Shaka's mission was briefed by Sotobe.

He had told them of all the tricks of the south:
How through sweet talk and questioning
The deputies attempted to sabotage these missions.
No sooner had they left Dukuza
5   Than the king sent word to this delegation,
Summoning them back to the royal city.
Shaka's informants had exposed Cane's comments and
      complaints:
How he had not been given any compensation,
10 And was there not for affairs of state, but for trade.
Cane was bitter too that he could not obtain the elephant tusks.
Shaka was alarmed that wealth could exceed loyalty to the state
He said: 'The customs of foreigners are not ours.'
He now summoned the kindly Isaacs to lead the mission.
15 Isaacs was well known in Zululand
At the Assembly he spoke openly without fear.
Sometimes he narrated the stories of his old adventures
When he wandered all over the land as a trader.
He was adopted by Prince Myaka of Mthethwaland.
20 It was Prince Myaka, he said, who taught him about kindness.
Though a foreigner, Myaka had looked after him
Making large feasts in his honour.
Prince Zihlandlo had also invited him.
To honour him, he had slaughtered many herds of cattle.
25 It was he whom Shaka now considered for leadership,
He said whoever must lead these envoys
Should approximate the qualities of King.
Prince Zihlandlo commented on Isaacs and said:
'He does not possess the alertness of King,
30 But his patience and kindness command respect everywhere.
I often forget he is a foreigner or a white man.
Because of his humanity he is suspect to Fynn and others.
Whenever he approaches them they quickly disperse.'
It was these words that fully recommended him to Shaka.
35 As he appointed him to head the second mission, Shaka said:
'I give you the power to lead the delegation to King George.
I erred in giving Cane these powers;
I overlooked the qualities required for this mission.
I am removing him from all positions.

Should you fulfil the demands of this office
You shall receive from me whatever you request.'

Dingane constantly demanded the final day of action,
Fearing lest Mbopha himself should betray them.
5   He often reported how Shaka had begun to sense something;
How he would suddenly ask why they left the young Prince
        Mpande,
Knowing both he and Nzibe depended on their word and
        directive.
10   The others merely brushed this aside
Saying it seemed no more than talk of concern,
Nor did it mean Shaka suspected a conspiracy.
Even Mbopha's comment on Shaka's dream did not move them;
They said it no more deserved attention than a sneeze.
15   Yet it was because of this, Jiji, the son of Myeni,
Who was chosen by Mbopha
To execute this heinous crime, sharpened his short spear.
Jiji bore a grudge against the king:
His brother Sabalaza had been sentenced to death for false
20   divining.
He arrived on a fine, clear day,
Claiming he came to ask for the king's audience and sympathy.
He appealed to Mbopha to grant him this privilege.
They gazed at each other intently to convey their secrets.
25   It was as though Mbopha said:
'May all good fortune attend your mission.'
Mbopha raised his voice, scolding him loudly:
'Who are you to think you could have the king's audience?
Must he abandon the affairs of state for your trivial problems?
30   Is the army not engaged in a life-and-death battle against
        Soshangane?
Stand there, away from me, until I have reported to my king.'
He shouted these words so that everyone could hear,
Or else to let the king, on hearing them, intervene
35   And invite this grim messenger of death.
Yet the king, who was deep in thought, did not respond.
He sat in a far-distant spot, silent like a figure carved in stone.
Perhaps he was thinking of the old battles of Qokli:
Perhaps he recollected the great battles of the Zulu army,

Or pictured himself in battle
As he parried the numerous enemy weapons;
Perhaps he sought to detail the new order for the peoples of
    Zululand.
5 Jiji trembled visibly, nearly losing his murder weapon.
Mbopha saluted, making it seem he resented his task,
And desired the king to reject his request:
'He comes from beyond the Thukela river.'
Mbopha knew as he described this great distance
10 He meant to excite the king's interest
And make him keen to know
What news could bring a man over so long a distance.
Shaka still remembered the occasion of Gala,
When the voice of one man changed the whole course of events.
15 He responded, speaking in a low, round voice,
Like someone who has been wakened from an exhausting dream:
'Let him speak, Mbopha, son of Sithayi.
He has travelled a long distance to speak.
Like me, he may recently have lost a parent.'
20 Shaka said these words as though he had not thought of them,
As though they burst out suddenly from his mind.
Mbopha himself was puzzled by these words.
He retreated to a convenient spot,
Eager to listen to the report of sudden pain and triumph.
25 His ear was alert to every sound;
His heart thundered as though from a giant's footfalls.
He breathed in short, broken intervals.
Many minutes passed without meaningful sounds;
He only heard the exchange of voices.
30 He was trembling with fear and expectation.
He began to hum and grunt a song without meaning
As though to summon his powers of concentration,
Or to direct Jiji's mind without touching.
Desperate, he beat the ground with his large bare foot.
35 Shocked at his own action, he began to collect his senses.
After a long pause he heard Jiji saluting.
He was retreating and moving away from him.
Mbopha strategically moved to meet him.
He hailed him loudly for his good fortune
40 And said: 'How lucky you are to have spoken to the sun!

Tell all your relatives and friends the king is for all people.'
Whispering close to him he said:
'Why did you fail me?'
The man, his voice trembling and his forehead covered with
5   sweat,
Simply said: 'He is fearful!'

When the princes heard of this failure they were filled with terror.
Even the great Princess Mkhabayi was frightened.
She constantly repeated: 'Shaka's power is of Ancestral force.
10 Shaka's power is evil; it is beyond human boundaries!'
She spoke alone, repeating these words to herself constantly.
She was amazed; she could not think of alternatives.
When they met again Mkhabayi was boiling with rage.
Sarcastically she said: 'How do things look now, Dingane,
15   Mhlangane?
The reports tell us Shaka still lives.
He is still king.
The little commoner you sent suddenly lost heart:
He says Shaka is invested with Ancestral powers!
20 But everyone possesses these powers!
They intimidate only those whose forehead is weak,
Who have no will of their own.
If you are wise you will eliminate this man —
Should you fail
25 He shall soon spill out all truths against you.'
It was at this point Mbopha spoke in humbled tones
And said: 'You of Jama, I have since removed this blasphemy.'
Dingane and Mhlangane were alarmed at this swift action.
They had not expected so brutal a decision.
30 Princess Mkhabayi looked at Mbopha with fiery eyes
And said: 'You have tasted blood
And have acquired the power to execute your own decisions!
What if Shaka pursues this man with spies?
What if he discovers he has been suddenly murdered?
35 You have assumed powers beyond your boundaries.
When I say, "This man should be removed,"
I search first for the appropriate day and circumstance.
I know the time has not come when the experience is still fresh;
When he still talks incessantly to all listeners

And they in turn spread his unique news.
His disappearance would speak loud to the whole earth.
If he vanishes before he arrives
Then his relatives, like hunting dogs, shall set out looking for
5 him.
At what point, then, did you get rid of him?'
She spoke sarcastically, unsettling him by these last comments.
Silence sometimes hovers between the shadows of man.
Mbopha babbled and muttered incomprehensible words.
10 He finally said: 'I was carried away by my enthusiasm.
The death squad, Great Princess, killed him on his way home.
I ask for your forgiveness for my short-sightedness.
It was to protect the royal children.'
Such are those who kowtow in high places.
15 Often they are restrained in their recklessness by their masters.
Their eagerness to please often dulls their minds.
Everyone finally brushed aside this incident.
Dingane said: 'What has happened cannot be changed:
The task before us still remains unfulfilled.
20 Our Aunt Mkhabayi has put this aptly: Shaka lives.
We must act soon before our intentions are known.
We must choose a more courageous man.
Shaka overwhelms by his fearlessness and imposing height.
For this reason whoever we choose must have great power.
25 We must strengthen him, too, with magic herbs.'
The daughter of Jama simply laughed at this plan.
She said: 'Your mind concentrates on frills,
Yet the central truth often escapes you.'
Dingane was angry at these humiliating words
30 But kept quiet, fearing to provoke this fierce woman.
Princess Mkhabayi said, continuing: 'You are naive.
You think Shaka would twice indulge in useless domestic talk?
Can you not see his mind is preoccupied with issues of war?
Do you imagine he shall now give ear
35 To fools who overlook their own councils in their regions?
Had it suited his mood he would have sent this fool to battle
  and said:
"You indulge in these trivial things while other men die in
  war?"
40 Here is my own view and suggestion:

It is you, Mbopha, who should undertake this difficult task!'
This word sent shivers through Mbopha's body.
He jumped as though stung by some wasp.
He said repeatedly: 'No! No! Not me, Daughter of the king!
5 I would rather that I myself died.
I swear by my dead father, I fear him like a snake.
Besides, I do not agree with this plan.
He would sense my intention in my very movements.
He is like an accomplished diviner.
10 When I look at him with evil thoughts he turns around to scold
       me,
Even when I try to hide my eyes he simply says:
"Well, Mbopha of Sithayi, what evil thoughts have you in your
       mind?"
15 It is as if my thoughts touch his inner self,
Making themselves visible to him.
I reject this plan and appeal to you to think again,
Unless it be me you intend to kill.'
Mhlangane gestured as if he was going to laugh.
20 He was surprised to see so much fear in someone in such a high
       position.
He restrained himself and said in support of Mbopha's fears:
'It seems the son of Sithayi speaks the truth.
Those who live within the same precinct know the truth about
25   each other;
They share their snuff and dreams.
Thus it is unwise to set up an assassin from the same grounds.
The tasks of each man must be clearly set out.
As I see it, we must begin the whole effort again,
30 Examining again the idea of using his own women.
There must exist among them one whose tongue is smooth,
And whose body is desirable, and who is willing to betray.
Of late there are many problems obsessing his mind.
Should we find such a woman and give her this task,
35 She would serve us with her lips and the feast of dreams.
Let her tell him of the visitations of his parent;
Let her promise him the birth of his own heir;
This way she shall feed his mind with fulfilling fantasies.
No man escapes the joy of a woman's love.
40 Surrendering to him totally, she shall drain him of all his power.

Exhausted, he shall sleep, stretching out like a basking crocodile
Thus opening his chest to the savaging blade.
Tiredness weakens the mind and makes the flesh tender.
Only by this scheme could we succeed.
5 You, Honourable Aunt, tie this plan together,
Inviting one woman for briefing in your court.
Say to Shaka you are ill and need a friendly nurse.'
They were all quiet, thinking out this sole remaining scheme.
Suddenly Mkhabayi shouted: 'I accept!
10 I take all its aspects without reservation.'
The gathering soon dispersed.
Each one felt the impending return of the army:
Should this happen, their plans would be shattered.
Mkhabayi immediately played the game.
15 She sent word to Shaka, saying: 'Son of my brother,
Once some royal woman filled my mind with joy.
Perhaps it was because she had the laughter of youth.
I ask that this woman tend me in my illness.
As you know the sick are healed by love;
20 I ask that she comes at once to assuage my pains.'
When Shaka heard this he was beside himself with joy.
He said: 'Now I know the House of Jama is eternal,
For, in truth, all the royal women should not serve me alone
But enrich the whole House of Malandela.'
25 Pleased with the words of Mkhabayi,
He sent a message to his royal aunt, saying:
'Your illness is suffered by the whole nation.
I would have granted your request
Even if you had asked me for all the royal women.'
30 Shaka sincerely meant these words.
His spirit desired to embrace all his relatives.
He was elated and felt a strong bond with his brothers.
He would say: 'On my right is the nation;
On my left are my clansmen.
35 This is the bond that binds us together.'
He felt as if all his kinsmen displayed a sense of leadership,
It would be easier to share power equally among all citizens.

The daughter of Magiya arrived early at the residence of
    Mkhabayi.

She was frightened as she entered the great house of the royal
    aunt.
Mkhabayi stared at her with full and scorching eyes,
As though she surveyed some fearful porcupine,
5   As though she saw some old, tattered leather skirt.
She did this only to undermine her pride and impose her own
    will.
Mkhabayi made her sit and wait for her.
When she realized how subservient she had become,
10 She asked about her home and clan origin.
But she was only playing a game, since she already knew.
She still desired to tame and weaken her,
For, indeed, those born into humble circumstance
Invite only mockery from the arrogant if they bow low their
15   heads.
By this act they shall eternally serve the violent race of rulers.
She, too, was humbled by the royal aunt;
Gone were her words of boasting.
No longer could she sneer at others,
20 She spoke only in whispers.
When Mkhabayi realized she had been sufficiently mortified,
She softened her voice, embracing her gently,
Like a flower that opens at dawn,
Awaiting eagerly the nourishing rays of the sun
25 And fed by the whole cycle of the rich season;
Like this did Mkhabayi effuse and pamper the young woman.
As she became friendlier she called her 'kindly mother'
And no longer 'Most august Daughter of Jama and Royal Aunt.'
It was then Mkhabayi put her words,
30 Hoping to plant ideas in the rich soil of their friendship.

How terrible was the day
When the young woman betrayed her lover and king,
When she waited and hid her sharpened weapon!
When the king was received with so much love, he was flattered:
35 He loosened his mind and body and began to talk.
As he sat and laughed, Dingane and others plotted and waited.
They hoped for a word to restore them to their former glory.
But Shaka began to suspect her,

Knowing the many quarrels and jealousies among the royal
    women.
As these thoughts stirred in his mind
He cast his searching eyes in all directions;
5 Nor did he reveal what troubled him —
He simply looked closely between the roof beams.
He searched this way without touching,
Until she began to seduce his mind with her body.
She danced, but there was no music.
10 She said: 'Here is your world, my lord.
Walk over it and enter it with beautiful fantasies.
Put in it your dreams that I may dream them alone.
Let them link us together, driving away the unpleasant ones.
The sad ones shall be devoured by the happy ones.
15 Make me praise myself secretly
And say: "I, daughter of the happy one, I give only joy.
I am infinite with joys for my king."
I shall boast to the whole earth and to all the creatures
And tell them my lord gave me the name Mother-of-Joy." '
20 As she spoke she came close to him.
Her whole chest flourished with her breasts.
Shaka forgot the thoughts that had occupied his mind;
A madness of the beautiful night overtook him.
It carried him away to let him play like a child,
25 To make him see their bodies walking round a hill.
There is a moment in childish fantasies
When each one goes in search of the beginning,
Wandering where plants are young and beautiful.
Thus, too, was the dream brought to them by life.
30 But the codes of our House forbid me to say any more. . . .
Only commoners reveal these things.
When they sat basking in the rays of their joys
Shaka cast his eyes everywhere, still searching for the shadows.
He saw the glimmering, sharp point of a spear.
35 It was then Shaka was at peace,
For often doubt and uncertainty unsettle the mind;
A wise man rests only when he has discovered the truth.
Shaka's mind revelled in being quicker than those of his
    opponents.
40 He did not react like the many cowards

Who, when they see danger, flee,
Awakening a host of enemies and inviting greater dangers.
He continued telling many simple tales.
Finally he found reason to leave,
5 Pointing to the many issues that awaited him.
In the quiet moment of reflection he said:
'For now I shall not alarm the royal women;
But one day I shall surprise them
And search the nooks and hideouts of their secrets.
10 I shall unearth the poisonous herbs for their rivals,
And love potions kept for me.'
He discussed these plans with Nqiwane of the great Dlamini
clan:
'Much hatred and rivalry exists among the royal women:
15 Through their intrigues I may myself be poisoned.
Those who have lost their sanity await me with spears.
You, as my doctor and that of the nation,
Spring on them a divining session in my name.
Spill out all that is hidden in these silent homes.'
20 Nqiwane warmly welcomed these words,
And said: 'I, too, had thought of this, my lord,
Seeing how dangerous to your person are the jealousies of
women.
But I restrained myself,
25 Feeling this role could only be authorized by my lord.
I thank you, my lord, for entrusting this task to me.'
It was for this reason a divining session was summoned,
And every house of the royal women was searched.
Many strange creatures and magic herbs were found;
30 Even those who were popular and respected were exposed.
The daughter of Magiya was shamed:
Sharp weapons were found in her possession.
The fierce judgement of the king was ultimately pronounced:
All those guilty of these offences would be sentenced to exile.
35 Thus the pathways were choked with processions of once-royal
women.
Those who trusted in the influence of their families were
rebuffed.
No one dared plead their case.
40 Those who had been conspiring at Shaka's murder

416

Lived in constant terror,
Fearing lest these divinations be Shaka's schemes,
Concocted to hide the truth of what he knew.
The long shadows of a great hero loom like a mountain.
5   They speak and walk and embrace in the homes of the poets.
By their power they leave open the gates of enemies.

Shaka waited for news of his northern campaign.
Sometimes he regretted that he did not go there himself.
He spoke openly to his councillors:
10 'How terrible that I sit here like an old woman,
While the great heroes of Zululand fight in foreign lands.
Such life weakens the mind and eats into one's manhood.'
His unsettled state whetted his mind for news.
He never ceased nagging his council.
15 When he heard of the arrival of the messenger, his eyes lit up.
Through the lips of Tiyane of Manzini, General Mdlaka
     reported:
'Your army vanquished the little army of Hlangabeza.
Digging him out of the western point of the Ngwane kingdom,
20 We then skirted the southern parts of our neighbours
And travelled on until we reached the land of the Pedis.
We passed on, leaving in peace the terrified people of the Pedi
     kingdom,
Then we went through to the southern section of the Sana river.
25 Many times we lost our way in the forest,
But forged stubbornly ahead to Soshangane regions.
Between the Matolo and Nkomazi rivers we had many
     unpleasant mishaps:
Some of our men were poisoned by the terrible mdlebe plant;
30 Others died of the enfeebling malaria.
All these things weakened our army but we did not turn back.
When we reached the lands occupied by Soshangane
We split into two powerful divisions.
One section headed for the state of the Tshopis, near Nyembane;
35 Another forged through the hills of Madolo.
There we found the hiding place of Soshangane's army.
Overwhelmed by the size of our army he had retreated to these
     regions.
We prepared to surround his fortress

So that through hunger we might draw him out to battle.
Both armies scoured the neighbourhood for fresh supplies.
At this point Mdlaka gave me these instructions,
Ordering me to tell my king these developments —
5 Soshangane is no more than an ant.
When an elephant exhales, ants experience an earthquake.
Such is the threat that hangs over Soshangane's head.
The army impatiently awaits a full-scale battle against these
  fugitives.
10 Many of your heroes protest bitterly, frustrated at the lack of a
  decisive battle.
I come to report to you, my lord, these words of Mdlaka.'
Shaka listened to him intently and commented:
'It is clear the Zulus must now rest.
15 There is no army to face our army.
Some flee at hearing songs of battle.
Only the war against overseas nations should concern us now:
We must mobilise all the children of the Palm Race.
Their single-file approach to battle shall be their doom.
20 We shall teach them, their wisdom is only of yesterday.
For now all parts of Zululand must await to feast with our
  army.'
This was the message that was broadcast throughout Zululand.

How beautiful was the entry of Prince Zihlandlo at Dukuza!
25 The king, elated, told him of many adventures of the
  Soshangane campaign.
Narrating the story in a spirited voice, he said:
'It is today I find the truth in the song of Nomlilo, who sang:
"You have conquered all nations, so whom shall you fight?"
30 Once I forbade it, but today I would lead it myself.'
Then, Shaka had indeed scolded the army,
Reproaching it for singing this song
And telling the regiments the words had no truth in them.
But those who wait for the full brightness of the sun
35 Never live to celebrate in the festival
For it is dawn that tells us of the great promise,
In every region was heard the voice of the great poet.
The whole Zulu nation sang of the 'Emblem of the Sacred
  Bond'.

Shaka, beaming with joy, commented to Zihlandlo:
'I feel as if I am as old as the Ancestors.
My life is crowded with events I cannot understand.
I look everywhere and our beginnings astound me.
5   I hear the great song of my grandfather, Jama,
And I know his spirit has accompanied me.
It accompanied me in the small and big wars;
It accompanied me in the wars against Zwide;
It accompanied me in the battle against Macingwane —
10 I feel his presence in all my actions.
His name constantly rings in my ears.
I know I have fulfilled the visions of my Ancestor.
The Ancient Ones celebrate with us!
My friend Mgobhozi has joined the dance of the Foolish Ones.
15 How I wish he were here!
Yet my thoughts are without substance.
I dream too obviously,
He would be fighting in the war against Soshangane.
It is now I would concede to Nandi's request
20 Giving her the gift desired by all parents.
But now I dance alone. It is too late.
I wish only to fight my last battle like all warriors!
I am grateful to these overseas invaders —
They may yet give me a chance for my greatest dance;
25 There we may yet compose our greatest epics.'
Shaka thus rambled on with these different thoughts.
It was as though he desired to begin his life again,
To see once more the growing fame of great heroes.
A true fighter is accompanied by the spirits of the Ancestors;
30 He is pampered by a retinue of Ancestral warriors.
They watch over him, witnessing his great and final battles,
Then they take him away to wash his feet and carry his body.
Zihlandlo made no comments on Shaka's reflections,
For he knew there are pains which do not heal.
35 If indulged with herbs they break out with all their power.
In the early hours of the morning,
After they had spoken all night through,
Shaka took his favourite spear and said to Zihlandlo:
'I give you this spear as a symbol of our friendship.
40 It is a weapon with which I have fought many battles.

Never let this truth pass from your mind.
A friend must always sing for those who cannot sing.
He must dance for those whose feet have withered.'
He spoke these words solemnly and thanked Zihlandlo.
5   As they shook hands and embraced
It was as if they were about to begin a long journey.
Only the Forefathers knew how long it would be before they
    met.

Book Seventeen: The mountain has fallen

Events move with diabolical speed as Shaka's brothers, together with Mbopha, take the initiative to carry out the assassination themselves. It is now clear that Dingane is the leader. Indeed, he later kills his co-conspirators, fearing they may plot against him. The delegation led by Nxazonke is delayed. This provides an opportunity to carry out the plot. As Shaka is questioning the delegation about the reasons for its delay, Mbopha intervenes and, defying all protocol, scolds them violently. In the confusion, and to the astonishment of all in the Assembly, Dingane and Mhlangane appear, armed. Shaka realizes too late the plot against him. He attempts to seize the spear from Mbopha but Mbopha backs off, letting Dingane and Mhlangane kill him. The last words of Shaka warn of the invasion of the whites. Dingane now sets out to kill all those who were friends of Shaka's. Ngwadi, Shaka's brother, and others mobilize an army against Dingane but lose because of their reluctance to embark on a full-scale civil war. So dies Emperor Shaka the Great, leaving behind him inept but ambitious leaders. They bring only disasters on the empire and fail to grasp the military and political exigencies of the situation.

It was on a day similar to the one now above our heads —
Birds flew variously into the four circles of the earth;

The dew fell gently on the ground,
Feeding the soft plants of the earth with growth.
One day they shall grow and bear their own seed.
It was on such a day Princess Mkhabayi spoke her final words.
5 'Dingane! Mhlangane! And you too, Mbopha!
I am going to speak to you plainly.
I am tired of thinking for those who cannot think.
I am tired of endless meetings that are without accomplishment.
I am saying this finally: Shaka must die!
10 You must kill him with your own hands.
Your hesitant actions have resulted in many deaths.
The divining session has claimed many victims.
All your schemes and efforts have failed.
Never again shall I participate in these foolish meetings!
15 It is you, Mbopha, who has easiest access to him:
It is you who should make this first stab.
You, Dingane, and you, Mhlangane, must summon up courage
And walk to him with your weapons.
How do you hope to rule when you are such cowards?
20 When you cannot overcome the power that Shaka possesses?
A true ruler must have no fear.
You, too, must participate in your brother's killing,
For only in this way can you overcome his power.
In truth, Shaka's power can never be destroyed.
25 It will emerge in the hearts of many generations.
They shall make their sacrifice of the black bull in his name.
It is not I who shall be king in this land, but you.
I cannot assist you to tie up all the knots of power;
I must avoid the accusation that I support the weak.
30 Perhaps I should uphold the rule of my son, Shaka,
And stop following weaklings who can never rule.'
These words of Mkhabayi greatly disturbed her nephews;
They suddenly realized their dependence on her.
To humiliate them she suddenly left.
35 Those known for their wisdom believe in their power.
They speak confidently and champion their own truth.
Dingane assumed the mantle of leadership and said
    authoritatively:
'Yes, our aunt speaks the truth.
40 It is enough! We must no longer harbour these fears

But ourselves seize from Shaka the royal power that is ours.
You, Mbopha, prepare for the day when these envoys shall
    return
(I speak of the delegation led by Nxazonke).
5 On that day you shall arrange for their reception at the
    Assembly.
Let them come there to present to the king their message.
It is at this point we shall arrive with our weapons
To end decisively the whole episode of his rule.
10 Let us never meet again in the wild like animals!'
His voice was trembling as though he would faint.
The others stared at each other
As though to say: 'Do you already command as king?'
But, knowing how conscious he was of his shortcomings,
15 They quickly changed their mood and listened attentively.
The plotters parted resolute,
But ashamed of their plans to spill their own relative's blood.
Once every fifteen decades are born the children of the sun.
They are lifted whole, to be part of the Milky Way,
20 And the earth cannot devour them.
Mbopha reported at the dead of night the arrival of the king's
    envoys.
They were full of goodwill messages and gifts for the king.
Shaka, though half-asleep, was excited by this news;
25 He had looked forward to hearing their many episodes.
On that very night he dreamt a strange dream.
He dreamt he saw Mbiya and his mother, Nandi.
They were absorbed in a deep conversation.
Constantly they whispered to each other,
30 But when he came closer, they were suddenly silent.
They turned to him, staring him in the eye.
There and then appeared Mgobhozi-of-the-Mountain.
It was as though they travelled in the old days at the
    Mthethwas,
35 Heading for the base of a familiar mountain.
Mgobhozi said to him, speaking seriously:
'It may be we shall now fight our last battle.
Behind us we shall leave an impregnable fortress.
Those who are our poets shall weep and say:
40 "Few great warriors, few great men lived like them." '

After this episode they shook hands and separated.
Shaka woke up from this dream feeling nostalgic.
He went out and sat on his favourite stone
And saw the moon disappear into the clouds.
5   The stars spread like white flowers, filling the sky.
He heard the voices of people and cows bellowing.
The echoes of the river swallowed the sounds of animals.
He felt his body elated as though it was being lifted into the
     mist;
10 He laughed and laughed alone, laughing with the earth.
The winds did not let the trees go to sleep;
They constantly shook their branches.
His dream gave birth to fantasies and his whole life revived
     again.
15 It was as if some power threatened to invade his mind.
He began to speak loudly to himself.
Thoughts that had never occurred in his mind now troubled
     him:
'Who would rule should I die tomorrow?'
20 He thought of each one of his brothers and said mockingly:
'Perhaps it is Mkhabayi who should rule.'
Finally he said, casting aside these thoughts:
'I am still going to rule.
Only when I am old and senile shall I do as the ancient kings,
25 And have children who shall contend for my head.'
He played with these thoughts in his mind
Until the morning star emerged in the eastern sky.
He was pleased with the light it had planted over Zululand.
He said: 'Accompany our children as they descend from the
30   north.'

Dawn spread its light; the ancient sun hovered over the earth.
It danced like a young woman seized by the spirit of the dance.
Over the rivers it thrust its thin rays.
Its light penetrated into the womb of the mist.
35 Shaka left his house to wash in the open ground.
As he bathed he discussed with his councillors.
He made fun of those who stayed at home as the battles raged.
Despite this joyous mood his heart was troubled;
He wondered what could be the true message of the dream.

Furiously he attempted to break its meaning: one can touch the
    truth
It is said through supreme concentration.
It was for this reason his eyes were constantly moving.
5 When he entered his house
He asked jocularly for the whereabouts of Mbopha.
He remembered how he was ever busy with little things.
Shaka commented and said: 'Among all the people of Zululand
None is as trustworthy and devoted to my welfare as he is.
10 Even his family is deprived of him because of duty.'
The sun rose; the king argued and laughed at the Assembly.
He sat waiting for the envoys.
When the sun had reached the centre of the earth, they came.
Nxazonke made an elaborate royal greeting.
15 He said, beginning to tell their whole extended episode:
'We have arrived, my lord, from your sacred mission.
Our journey was long and pleasant.
Many nations desire close friendship with us.
When we reached the court of Moshoeshoe. . . .'
20 Before they could finish these words, Shaka's mood suddenly
    changed.
He said: 'Your journey was long and extended.
We even contemplated sending a regiment after you.
I hope you bring news that justifies this long stay.
25 You, my uncle, caused me great anxiety.'
They were all dumbfounded at the change of his happy mood.
At that very moment Mbopha suddenly appeared at the
    Assembly.
He was angry and spoke in loud and peremptory voice;
30 He said: 'Who do you think you are?
You dare cause these anxieties to my lord?
You stopped at will in regions of your own pleasure!
You loitered, attending to your own affairs!
Don't you know the king has many concerns?
35 You have become fat from eating meat in your endless travels!'
The Assembly was startled at this impudence.
They scolded Mbopha, telling him the king was still talking.
In a flash Mbopha raised his short spear.
Shaka was incredulous of this insolent behaviour.
40 Mbopha threatened to kill the envoys,

But it was only a diversion:
He turned and stabbed the king.
Admidst the pandemonium and confusion,
Shaka's brothers appeared, accompanied by their followers.
5 They were armed with newly sharpened spears.
They rushed after the king as he attempted to reach for his
        weapon:
They stabbed Shaka of Senzangakhona from all sides.
Blood spurted out even from his mouth.
10 When Shaka realized the truth at the last moment
He smiled and said: 'So, my brothers, you are killing me?
And you, too, Mbopha, son of Sithayi!
You think you shall rule Zululand after my death.
No, you shall never rule. Only the swallows shall rule over it.'
15 These were the last words he uttered as he fell onto the ground.
They still stabbed him, making numerous wounds,
Still fearing he might suddenly rise
And, with the anger of the whirlwind, rush headlong at them.
He lay there, the great warrior, the son of Ndaba, the wisest of
20   men.
Emperor Shaka the Great, Ruler of Many Rulers, King of Kings!
He followed the great heroes of Zululand.
Throughout the land people wept; many ran to Dukuza in
        disbelief.
25 The poet on the verge of insanity, and to console the people,
Declaimed Shaka's heroic epic:
'You shouted from the mountain in the regions of Mandla and
        Zimema.
Summer and winter were separated.
30 The fields were left unfinished!
The grains were gobbled up by the little birds!
And the ruins of Tayi are still there!
He ate two pieces of cane, one was Gcwabe,
The other was Zihlandlo,
35 But only one bundle of chaff he discarded.
He overwhelmed Matshingele of the Khulumbeni region.
He captured Gwayi of Mazindela.
He captured Mpangalala of Nomgqobo.
He overcame Phalaza of Khanyile.
40 The breast of Mjokwane that favoured the Feasts of Return.

It favoured Jiyeza among the diviners.
The beautiful finch that adorned the Zimpohlo regiment.
They were sleeping with women in his name —
What an outrage! Short grass that pierced with fierce barbs in
5   its tender age,
The Proud One who leaned on an elephant's cave.
You brought Mangcengceza of Khali among the Mbathas.
You humbled Matiwane, the son of Masumpa of the Ngwanes.
You punished Makhedama of emaLangeni among your mother's
10   people.
Wild one, who surprised the enemy in the tall grass.
You destroyed Sigawuzana of the stubborn Mbatha clan.
You, the deep pool that is centred in the river of Mayiwane:
A man slipped while carelessly trying to bathe.
15 He sank deep and was swallowed with his head-ring.
Black staff of Mjokwane, that chastised Zwide of the
    Ndwandwes;
It castigated Nomahlanjana, the son of Zwide.
Eternal greenness, that is like the bile of a buck!
20 You destroyed Ndimndwane, the son of Msweli of the Xulu
    clan.
You annihilated Mdladlama of the Mbedus.
You captured Mphezeni of the Nxumalos.
Fierce one, who is like a vulture!
25 Thou wisest of men! Eagle that descended from the sky!
You crossed by the short route the regions of Madlungela
And seized cattle which nourished the madman of Mavela —
But those of Sihlayo simply followed him.'
In tears the poet uttered Shaka's epic.
30 Those who saw him opened their mouths and talked;
Those who were old sat quietly under the shade and spoke in
    whispers;
Their slow tears fell to the ground.
They spoke of ancient heroes; they spoke of Shaka of
35   Senzangakhona.
People came and listened. . . .
Dingane, Mhlangane and Mbopha concealed their eyes
To cover the crime and claim innocence.
The princes turned against Mbopha, the son Sithayi,
40 Finding him an easy target and a useful scapegoat.

To cleanse their hands of their brother's blood
They ordered that he be killed.
His awaited reward and praise did not come;
He suffered the fate he had planned for others.
5　The narrators of our legends tell us:
'As the team of executioners arrived
He begged them in hushed tones and he said:
"Carry out your mission before it is witnessed by my family."
In vain his wife demanded to die there with him.
10　Silently the agents of the new order fulfilled their master's
　　　　commands.'

The whole Zulu army filled the region with their mourning
　　　　songs.
They sang and played mock battles.
15　They shouted in discord the anthems of the Zulu nation.
They gestured to the skies, calling out the poems of great
　　　　battles.
It is said the heavens wept.
Many homes were left deserted as people hurried to Dukuza.
20　Large villages, small villages, vast regions sang the last songs.
At the gathering of Dukuza, as peoples and envoys stood in
　　　　anger,
Nomnxamama, the greatest of all poets, began to weep.
He cried out and howled like a child;
25　He shouted, damning those who had killed 'The great son of
　　　　Ndaba';
He threw himself on the ground near the body of his king;
He called out curses against the murderers!
He bellowed out: 'You shall never rule in peace!
30　Your rule shall swim in blood!
You shall be haunted by his shadow.
You shall die, denounced like dogs.
I am talking to you, Mhlangane of Senzangakhona.
I am talking to you, Dingane, eternal wanderer of
35　　　　Senzangakhona.
Those who kill the parent plant shall die!
They shall die an ignominious death, pursued by their enemies.
Kill me if you wish, you vile beasts!
I pay my respects to him who shall always be great.'

He spoke as if he had gone insane.
He walked slowly as though in a trance,
And began to declaim Shaka's heroic epic:
'You overwhelmed Qwabe,
5   Thou umbrage, that sheltered the Nyabase people.
Fierce calf of the daughter of Mbengi,
That overwhelmed many others:
You took the breed of cattle that was the envy of all nations.
You seized the cattle of Dlodlweni region.
10 Uncontrollable one, who cannot be restrained!
Lazy One, who seized the ripe fields of enemies.'
As he called out, the poet walked into the arena
And danced the boast-dance.
Sometimes he rushed across the open ground,
15 Declaiming Shaka's heroic poem over and over again:
'You who opened the pathway with spears,
While other kings used only their hoes!
You called an army from Menziwa saying it must reap the
     young sorghum!
20 The black Mfolozi river of Sithayi and Bhiyane,
Which allows only its favourites to cross,
It lets through those who have a calf to offer.
Those who have no calves can give their children.
If they have no children they can give a hoe.
25 Ancestral power, that is like that of Ndaba —
When he wakes he annihilates the enemies.
He makes people stop prattling.
He confiscated cattle yet he did not need them for purchase of
     weapons.
30 Only in the coming year shall he need them.
The bird that was summoned by whistling at Ngome forest.
Even today the ridge of Dladlama still trembles with shock.
Gone are the villages of Majola,
Leaving only the large settlements of Malandela.
35 He outwitted Mbiyaza, who dwelt on Machanca above,
And made him run in terror, leaving his cattle behind.
They were collected by the Ntotheleni regiment.
He made his army dance on the ridge of the children of Tayi.
The whole world turned and looked in wonderment.
40 The cattle that were not his still followed him.

Fierce descendant of Ndaba,
Who sat in anger with his shield on his knees:
They have no peace those whom he threatens,
Be they outsiders or those of his family.
5   Thou evergrowing power, like the forest of Ngome!
He crossed the river and created the Ntontela regiment.
They said he should not do it, but he did.
He tempted the ocean but did not want to cross it.
Only the swallows and the overseas people crossed it.
10 You began your journey at the peak of day, son of Ndaba,
And as the sun was turning westward!
Chaser of a man, you chased him ceaselessly,
Because you chased Mbemba of emaGozeni clan.
You chased him until he reached the regions of Siluthana.
15 You found a reed centre of the young boys-at-circumcision.
It was not of the boys, but of the Ancestral spirits.
The battle-axe of Senzangakhona,
Which was spurred on by the falling heads!
He saw a herd of cattle at the mountain top
20 And brought it down with long spears.
He washed his face with tears.
Vast enclosure that attracted bachelors;
Great One! Beautiful One! Black One!'
When the poet finished declaiming he sat down.
25 He cast his eyes at all those around him:
He took a glimmering dagger and slit his throat.
Then the mourning and the wailing were unbearable. . . .
Harassed by their crime, both Dingane and Mhlangane
Suffered hallucinations of Shaka's presence.
30 Those loyal to Shaka mobilized against them.
Prince Zihlandlo, Prince Ngwadi and all their followers died in
      these wars.
Dingane, suspecting plots against him, killed his brothers.
Of him the great poet Mshongweni says:
35 'Thou evil-hearted beast,
Who is unsparing even to your own brothers!'
Even Mhlangane was killed by drowning.
Dingane hunted all Shaka's favourites and friends.
Of all the brothers, only Mpande and Qguqgu survived.

Shaka sleeps in the land of the Ancestors.
The winds carry his voice and the Palm Race shall rise again.
It shall build its legends on his sacred ground.
He who bequeathed these things to our race shall never die.
5   For, in truth, the poet of our Forefathers has said:
'Nodumehlezi, son of Menzi,
You cannot be vanquished like water.
You, the battle-axe that towered above others.
Shaka! I fear to call him by his name,
10   Because he is the ruler adorned with many emblems!
Famed One! Of whom the women of Nomgabi gossiped,
Saying: "Shaka shall never rule. He shall never be king.
But it was then he grew to overwhelm the earth!" '

Dirge of the Palm Race

The great cloud opens: the mountain has fallen.
Silence hangs on to the shoulders of the heavens.
The thunderbolts travel making the skies tremble.
The flashes of lightning haunt our earth with destruction.
5 'The mountain has fallen, the earth's centre quivers.'
Great Protectors, Beautiful Ones, Forefathers, come!
Run into the semi-circle of the wind and carry the child.
Take him with both arms and utter these words:
'It is us who planted the sacred word
10 It is us who accompany you into the night.
We have summoned you with our songs and epics.
Our home awaits you with an eternal feast.
All the Beautiful Ones have begun to sing their anthem'
Our nation is like the wind — it will go on and on forever!

15 Great ocean throw the white wave
And let the feet of the hero be seen on the sand.
Through the mirror of the silent lake
Let us see the eyes of the Forefathers.
Let us watch the Ancestors with their children.
20 Let the generations hereafter say in their song:
'It is not I alone who was chosen by the gods
The children of the Palm Race multiply
In the eternal spring there is the song of the morning.'
Here is the mountain of Ngoye, Son of Gumede,
25 It is rising to touch the sky
And the lips of generations speak in her womb,
For whatever we do in the name of the Forefathers is eternal.

The whirlwinds shall not uproot it from the ground
Until we enter the centre of the earth . . .
30 Nandi, daughter of Bhebhe, is it you who approaches?
Touch then the wound with your fingers
Tell my child he must listen to you,
He must listen to the Ancestors as they sing the song.
Here they come! Dingiswayo, son of Jobe: 'Bayede!'
35 Mbikwane, voice of the gentle rain: 'Bayede!'

Mgobhozi, brother of the sacred mountain: 'Bayede!'
The Ancestors are bringing the emblem of the black beads.

At the grounds of Bulawayo people are frightened of the night
Shaka! They are shouting your name they are calling you,
5   Their hands are heavy like iron on their heads:
'The mountain has fallen, the earth trembles.'
The wind carries the voices of the women
The wound is tended by women, the wound is dark.
'Our child is dead, our sun breathes the final agony.'
10 Have you ever heard the wailing voices of women?
The women came first before us!
The women tell us when our calabash shall be swallowed by the
      night,
The women hear first the crying of the infant.
15 'Our child is dead, the Ancestors have come.'
They summon the rain, they speak through the opening:
'We have arrived. We have come to take the child.
Whoever was last to speak against him shall follow us,
He shall be judged among the Forefathers;
20 They shall tie him with a rope and bury him!'
They know best, they were here at the beginning of time.

They saw the procession of elephants to the mountain.
We must do their bidding and put the stone on the cairn,
We must raise the grain basket and scatter the seeds.
25 Summer will come and envelop the earth.
When all the enemies have died
And their bodies are reeked through with worms,
Those who are born from his plant shall honour him!
They shall fill the gourd with water to make the sacred mark.
30 They shall arrive at the feast at the crack of dawn,
They shall listen to the epics of the Forefathers.
Because they are older than our children
They shall ask them to tell us the truth:
'After the Mourning-of-the-Circling-Vultures
35 There shall be the Feast of Return.
Your children shall dance on the ancient grounds.
The earth itself shall yield, opening its lakes,
People shall drink and sing the song.'

Great Ancestral Forefathers because you are older than us
Accompany us into the night,
Tell us the tale while our trembling eyes follow the path;
Let us learn to speak the language of poets.
5 Beautiful Ones! Restless-feet-of-the-morning, come!
Touch our shoulders and wake the ram from sleep;
Give us the courage of the river.
He who is like an Ancestral Spirit cannot be stabbed.
He is like the stars of the milky way as they climb the heavens
10 He is like the rain that falls on the heads of the ripening plants
He is the forest that keeps secret our legends.

He is an Ancestral Spirit; he cannot be stabbed.
Even now they sing his song. They call his name.
They dance in the arena listening to the echoes of his epics
15 Till the end of time — they shall sing of him.
Till the end of time his shield shall shelter the hero from the
        winds,
And his children shall rise like locusts.
They shall scatter the dust of our enemies,
20 They shall make our earth free for the Palm Race.

Index of names

Index of names